Africa's Information Revolution

RGS-IBG Book Series

For further information about the series and a full list of published and forthcoming titles, please visit www.rgsbookseries.com

Published

Africa's Information Revolution: Technical Regimes and Production Networks in South Africa and Tanzania
James T. Murphy and Pádraig Carmody

In the Nature of Landscape: Cultural Geography on the Norfolk Broads
David Matless

Geopolitics and Expertise: Knowledge and Authority in European Diplomacy
Merje Kuus

Everyday Moral Economies: Food, Politics and Scale in Cuba
Marisa Wilson

Material Politics: Disputes Along the Pipeline
Andrew Barry

Fashioning Globalisation: New Zealand Design, Working Women and the Cultural Economy
Maureen Molloy and Wendy Larner

Working Lives – Gender, Migration and Employment in Britain, 1945–2007
Linda McDowell

Dunes: Dynamics, Morphology and Geological History
Andrew Warren

Spatial Politics: Essays for Doreen Massey
Edited by David Featherstone and Joe Painter

The Improvised State: Sovereignty, Performance and Agency in Dayton Bosnia
Alex Jeffrey

Learning the City: Knowledge and Translocal Assemblage
Colin McFarlane

Globalizing Responsibility: The Political Rationalities of Ethical Consumption
Clive Barnett, Paul Cloke, Nick Clarke and Alice Malpass

Domesticating Neo-Liberalism: Spaces of Economic Practice and Social Reproduction in Post-Socialist Cities
Alison Stenning, Adrian Smith, Alena Rochovská and Dariusz Świątek

Swept Up Lives? Re-envisioning the Homeless City
Paul Cloke, Jon May and Sarah Johnsen

Aerial Life: Spaces, Mobilities, Affects
Peter Adey

Millionaire Migrants: Trans-Pacific Life Lines
David Ley

State, Science and the Skies: Governmentalities of the British Atmosphere
Mark Whitehead

Complex Locations: Women's Geographical Work in the UK 1850–1970
Avril Maddrell

Value Chain Struggles: Institutions and Governance in the Plantation Districts of South India
Jeff Neilson and Bill Pritchard

Queer Visibilities: Space, Identity and Interaction in Cape Town
Andrew Tucker

Arsenic Pollution: A Global Synthesis
Peter Ravenscroft, Hugh Brammer and Keith Richards

Resistance, Space and Political Identities: The Making of Counter-Global Networks
David Featherstone

Mental Health and Social Space: Towards Inclusionary Geographies?
Hester Parr

Climate and Society in Colonial Mexico: A Study in Vulnerability
Georgina H. Endfield

Geochemical Sediments and Landscapes
Edited by David J. Nash and Sue J. McLaren

Driving Spaces: A Cultural-Historical Geography of England's M1 Motorway
Peter Merriman

Badlands of the Republic: Space, Politics and Urban Policy
Mustafa Dikeç

Geomorphology of Upland Peat: Erosion, Form and Landscape Change
Martin Evans and Jeff Warburton

Spaces of Colonialism: Delhi's Urban Governmentalities
Stephen Legg

People/States/Territories
Rhys Jones

Publics and the City
Kurt Iveson

After the Three Italies: Wealth, Inequality and Industrial Change
Mick Dunford and Lidia Greco

Putting Workfare in Place
Peter Sunley, Ron Martin and Corinne Nativel

Domicile and Diaspora
Alison Blunt

Geographies and Moralities
Edited by Roger Lee and David M. Smith

Military Geographies
Rachel Woodward

A New Deal for Transport?
Edited by Iain Docherty and Jon Shaw

Geographies of British Modernity
Edited by David Gilbert, David Matless and Brian Short

Lost Geographies of Power
John Allen

Globalizing South China
Carolyn L. Cartier

Geomorphological Processes and Landscape Change: Britain in the Last 1000 Years
Edited by David L. Higgitt and E. Mark Lee

Forthcoming

Smoking Geographies: Space, Place and Tobacco
Ross Barnett, Graham Moon, Jamie Pearce, Lee Thompson and Liz Twigg

Home SOS: Gender, Injustice and Rights in Cambodia
Katherine Brickell

Nothing Personal? Geographies of Governing and Activism in the British Asylum System
Nick Gill

Pathological Lives: Disease, Space and Biopolitics
Steve Hinchliffe, Nick Bingham, John Allen and Simon Carter

Work-Life Advantage: Sustaining Regional Learning and Innovation
Al James

Rehearsing the State: The Political Practices of the Tibetan Government-in-Exile
Fiona McConnell

Assembling Export Markets: The Making and Unmaking of Global Food Connections in West Africa
Stefan Ouma

Articulations of Capital: Global Production Networks and Regional Transformations
John Pickles, Adrian Smith and Robert Begg, with Milan Buček, Rudolf Pástor and Poli Roukova

Origination: The Geographies of Brands and Branding
Andy Pike

Body, Space and Affect
Steve Pile

Making Other Worlds: Agency and Interaction in Environmental Change
John Wainwright

Everyday Peace? Politics, Citizenship and Muslim Lives in India
Philippa Williams

Metropolitan Preoccupations: The Spatial Politics of Squatting in Berlin
Alexander Vasudevan

Africa's Information Revolution

Technical Regimes and Production Networks in South Africa and Tanzania

James T. Murphy
and Pádraig Carmody

WILEY Blackwell

This edition first published 2015
© 2015 John Wiley & Sons, Ltd.

Registered Office
John Wiley & Sons, Ltd, The Atrium, Southern Gate, Chichester, West Sussex,
PO19 8SQ, UK

Editorial Offices
350 Main Street, Malden, MA 02148-5020, USA
9600 Garsington Road, Oxford, OX4 2DQ, UK
The Atrium, Southern Gate, Chichester, West Sussex, PO19 8SQ, UK

For details of our global editorial offices, for customer services, and for information about
how to apply for permission to reuse the copyright material in this book please see our
website at www.wiley.com/wiley-blackwell.

Library of Congress Cataloging-in-Publication data applied for

9781118751329 C
9781118751336 P

A catalogue record for this book is available from the British Library.

Cover image: © James T. Murphy

Set in 10/12pt Plantin by SPi Publisher Services, Pondicherry, India

Printed in Singapore by C.O.S. Printers Pte Ltd

1   2015

For Africa's entrepreneurs, small businesses, and workers

Contents

Series Editors' Preface

The RGS-IBG Book Series only publishes work of the highest international standing. Its emphasis is on distinctive new developments in human and physical geography, although it is also open to contributions from cognate disciplines whose interests overlap with those of geographers. The Series places strong emphasis on theoretically informed and empirically strong texts. Reflecting the vibrant and diverse theoretical and empirical agendas that characterize the contemporary discipline, contributions are expected to inform, challenge and stimulate the reader. Overall, the RGS-IBG Book Series seeks to promote scholarly publications that leave an intellectual mark and change the way readers think about particular issues, methods or theories.

For details on how to submit a proposal please visit:
www.rgsbookseries.com

Neil Coe
National University of Singapore

Tim Allott
University of Manchester, UK

RGS-IBG Book Series Editors

Acknowledgements

A huge number of people made this book possible. In particular we would like to thank all of the interview participants for their time and insights. We are also grateful to our research assistants and post-doctoral fellows, Ralph Borland, Adrian Corcoran, Amir Mohd Anwar, David Kirima, John Lauermann, Jackson Mongi, Alex Sphar and Bjoern Surborg, for their excellent contributions in support of the project. Jim Murphy further thanks Sam Wangwe for his assistance with the Dar es Salaam portion of the research and Pamela Dunkle at Clark University for administering and managing the research grant associated with the project.

This material is based upon work supported by the US National Science Foundation (NSF) under grant no. 0925151 that was awarded to James Murphy and Pádraig Carmody. Additional support for Pádraig's work came from a Senior Research Fellowship awarded by the Irish Research Council for the Humanities and Social Sciences (IRCHSS). Any opinions, findings, and conclusions or recommendations expressed in this material are those of the authors and do not necessarily reflect the views of the NSF or IRCHSS.

We would also like to thank the publishers of the following for permission to reproduce excerpts, tables, images, and/or figures from these articles in this book:

Anwar, M.A., Carmody, P., Surborg, B. and Corcoran, A. (2013) The diffusion and impacts of information and communication technology on tourism in the Western Cape, South Africa, *Urban Forum*, October. Netherlands: Springer, DOI: 10.1007/s12132-013-9210-4

Carmody, P. (2012) The informationalization of poverty in Africa: The mobile phone revolution and economic structure, *Information Technologies and International Development* 8(3): 1–17.

Murphy, J.T., Carmody, P. and Surborg, B. (2014) Industrial transformation or business as usual? Information-communication technologies and

Africa's place in the global information economy, *Review of African Political Economy* 41(140): 264–83.

Murphy, J.T. (2013) Transforming small, medium, and microscale enterprises? Information-communication technologies (ICTs) and industrial change in Tanzania, *Environment and Planning A* 45(7): 1753–72.

Numerous other individuals provided constructive and significant insights regarding the work and our findings. We particularly thank the referees and editors for the *Review of African Political Economy, Urban Forum, Environment and Planning A and International Technologies and International Development* for their comments on papers, parts of which appear in revised form here. Additional thanks goes to Chris Benner, Richard Heeks, Dorothea Kleine and Stefano Ponte for their comments at various stages along the way.

At Wiley-Blackwell, sincere thanks and appreciation go to the series editor, Professor Neil Coe, for his detailed, constructive, and timely comments. We also thank Jacqueline Scott, Allison Kostka, and the staff at W-B for their superb handling of the submission and production process.

James T. Murphy and Pádraig Carmody
Worcester, USA and Dublin, Ireland
17 July 2014

Abbreviations

AGOA	African Growth and Opportunity Act
B&B	bed and breakfast
CAD	computer-aided design
CNC	computer numerically controlled
DMO	destination management organization
DRC	Democratic Republic of Congo
F2F	face-to-face
FDI	foreign direct investment
GCC	global commodity chain
GDP	gross domestic product
GIE	global information(alized) economy
GPN	global production network
GVC	global value chain
HIV	human immuno-virus
ICT	information and communication technology
ICT4D	information and communication technology for development
IMF	International Monetary Fund
ITU	International Telecommunication Union
MDF	medium-density fibreboard
MLIS	market linkage and information system
MLP	multilevel perspective
NBA	National Basketball Association
NEG	New Economic Geography
NGO	non-governmental organization
NTB	non-tariff barrier
OECD	Organization for Economic Cooperation and Development
PDA	personal digital assistant
RBV	resource-based view
ROCE	return on capital expended

SEO	search engine optimization
SMME	small, medium and micro-scale enterprise
SMS	short message service
SNM	strategic niche management
SSA	sub-Saharan Africa
TINA	there is no alternative
TIS	technological innovation systems
TM	transition management
TNC	transnational corporation
TRIMS	trade related investment measures
TRIPS	trade related intellectual property rights
UNIDO	United Nations Industrial Development Organization
VOIP	voice-over-internet protocol
WTO	World Trade Organization
ZATI	Zanzibar Association of Tourism Investors
ZATO	Zanzibar Association of Tourism Operators
ZATOGA	Zanzibar Association of Tour Guides

Introduction

The rapid diffusion of mobile phones in Africa is widely held to be one of the main developmental successes on the continent in the last decade. There are now more than 700 million mobile phone subscriptions on the continent, with a penetration rate of 78% (Global Systems Mobile Association [GSMA], 2011). Most people across Africa have access to mobile telephony and the rate of computer and internet penetration has increased exponentially in the past decade. Although there remain significant gaps and challenges with regard to the diffusion of mobile phones, computers, and the internet (ICTs), the pace of adoption and the innovations (e.g., mobile applications or apps) associated with them have led many to believe that these technologies will dramatically transform livelihoods, government, financial systems, and markets throughout Africa. Moreover, many see ICT-enabled improvements in the pace, scale, and intensity of the region's connectivity to the rest of the world as creating information and communication conditions that will enable Africa to engage more evenly and progressively with the world economy; one that is increasingly driven and organized by information-intensive forms of capitalism.

There have been a variety of negative Orientalist tropes around Africa propounded in the West, such as it being the "Dark" or "Hopeless" continent, but the recent ICT-diffusion success story has accompanied a discourse around "Africa Rising" (Mahajan, 2009). In this emergent discourse, Africa is the "last" or final investment frontier for international capital, which is resulting in the continent's economic transformation or "rise" (Sizemore, 2012). Mobile phones, computers, and the internet

(ICTs) are held to play a central role in this dynamic transformation, as the authors of the *eTransform Africa* report (2012, p. 6) observed:

> While the world's economy is struggling to recover from the global financial crisis, the African economy is in the midst of a long boom. Over the past decade GDP has been increasing on average at 5% a year, and over the next five years, Africa's economy will grow faster than any other continent. One contributory factor has been the take-up of information and communications technologies (ICTs) and, in particular, the spectacular growth in mobile communications. The number of mobile subscriptions in use in Africa increased from fewer than 25 million in 2001 to almost 650 million by 2012. Two-thirds of African adults now have access to ICTs. The power of ICTs is more than just putting mobile phones in the hands of poor people. By allowing people to access health information, agricultural price data or educational games, ICTs can strengthen other sectors, and possibly the whole economy.

Although the idea that Africa is in a process of rapid and structurally transformative "emergence" has been critiqued effectively (Taylor, 2014), the potential for ICTs to transform livelihoods and economies in Africa remains deeply entrenched within contemporary thinking about how to resolve pressing development challenges in the region.[1] Particularly powerful are notions about the flexibility, mobility, and reach of the information access and communications made possible through ICTs, and the subsequent contributions these can make to improvements in the material conditions of those living in poverty.

As such, new ICTs hold not only a very important place in the "Africa Rising" discourse but a particular fascination for development agencies. This fascination is most clearly apparent in the emergence of a global community of scholars, practitioners, policymakers, entrepreneurs, corporate actors, and engineers concerned with the ways in which information and communication technologies can be used for development (ICT4D). The ICT4D community is well organized (e.g., they hold a semi-annual international conference – see http://www.ictd2013.info/), has significant levels of participation from stakeholders in the Global South, and is very well funded thanks in large part to investments made by transnational corporations such as Microsoft, Nokia, Google, and IBM. Although this is a diverse group of thinkers and doers, with some taking critical positions about the limitations on ICT4D strategies, much of the community maintains an optimistic and somewhat technologically deterministic perspective on the prospects for ICTs to transform development processes in regions like Africa. ICT4D notions have also been taken up by proponents of the "New Economic Geography" (NEG) (e.g., The World Bank's *World Development Report 2009*) who suggest that African poverty is an outcome of a lack of connection to the developed world, and that new ICTs will thus help transcend this problem through their ability to facilitate socio-economic connectivity. In both cases, ICT artefacts are viewed as central to enabling development (the D) to emerge, and there is relatively limited consideration of how non-ICT-related factors and forces influence socioeconomic change, particularly in cases where they undermine the purported benefits of enhanced communications and information access.

We write this book to engage critically with both the Africa rising and ICT4D discourses through an examination of the development and economic geographies accompanying the rapid diffusion of new ICTs in sub-Saharan Africa. Our overarching argument is that studies of ICT use and impact in regions like Africa have generally lacked a sufficient geographical contextualization, theoretical grounding, and/or inter-study comparability or transferability. Instead, much of the emphasis has been placed on individual-scale or firm-scale uptake and use of new ICTs, and/or the contribution of the telecommunications industry to government revenues and employment. Where other claims are made, such as those associated with livelihoods, governance, finance, institutions, and entrepreneurship, they are often speculative, anecdotal, vague, and/or lacking a clear grounding in empirical evidence beyond a single case study community, application, and/or program initiative. As such, crucial questions often remain unanswered regarding whether, and the explicit ways in which, ICTs are transforming multi-scalar and embedded power relations, institutions, inequalities, and other structural features that have held back African economies for decades.

For example, the *eTransform Africa* report (2012) has a case study section dedicated to the role that ICTs can play in regional trade and integration in Africa. The section is largely devoted to a lengthy, somewhat abstract discussion regarding the ways in which ICTs can make cross-border trans-actions and logistics more efficient and transparent. Particular emphasis is placed on the discrete applications of new ICTs for customs and border management (e.g., tracking and tracing goods) and the kinds of capabilities, infrastructure, institutions, and incentives that can facilitate ICT uptake within exporters, importers, and relevant government agencies. Unfortunately, however, the empirical case studies – on Kenya and Senegal's customs administration – provide, at best, somewhat equivocal evidence to support the claim that ICTs can significantly facilitate cross-border trade through the implementation of a "single-window" platform for managing the flow of goods between regional trading partners. No evidence is provided to show how the (admittedly problematic) implementation of this platform is changing the volume or quality of trade relations in either country, but the logic, evident in the post-hoc analysis, holds that if it can be implemented it *must* lead to enhanced trade performance that is "good" for development within countries like Kenya and Senegal. Although the report highlights some of the ICT and non-ICT specific institutional and infrastructural chal-lenges that limited the success of these initiatives, the "gaze" remains firmly intact: if ICTs can be deployed effectively within the trade-management bureaucracy, performance will necessarily improve.

This sort of gaze, when coupled with a political-economic ideology manifest in the prioritization of markets, free trade, property rights, liberal democracy, and growth as the key drivers of development, helps to constitute a celebratory discourse regarding the power of ICTs to progressively modernize and globally integrate African economies into the world system. Individuals and individual firms are often key figures and actors in this neoliberal narrative, manifest principally as entrepreneurs, farmers, fisher folk, women, youth, and government workers who exploit the power of enhanced communications and information access in order to improve their livelihoods, innovate, profit, and/or maintain a more vibrant and healthy civil society. This individuation of ICT use and potential helps to empower the discourse among both the usual suspects (e.g., institutions such as the World Bank) and those who view ICTs as a potentially emancipatory and alternative means through which Africans might manoeuvre around the structures (e.g., weak states, exploitative value chains) that have institutionalized underdevelopment and injustice in the region. All told, new ICTs are encouraging strange bedfellows through what we describe as a meta-discourse that can be adapted to a diverse range of ideological perspectives on development.

But what has the attention to ICTs and ICT4D initiatives actually done to improve the larger-scale prospects for Africa's economies in an age of informationalized forms of capitalism? This question can be answered in many different ways but our focus is on the industrial development impacts of new ICTs in Africa. Our central hypothesis is that if ICTs are to contribute significantly to the continent's "rising" onto the global economic stage, then there should be evidence that structural changes are occurring such that African manufacturers and service providers are increasingly able to engage in or contribute to industrial and social upgrading, which they may have been hitherto unable to, thereby contributing to Africa's socioeconomic transformation.

Drawing on in-depth empirical evidence from the wood products and tourism industries in South Africa and Tanzania, this book employs concepts related to intra-firm resources and capabilities, sociotechnical systems, and global production networks to analyse the uses, impacts and transformations associated with the uptake of new ICTs by small, medium, and micro-scale enterprises (SMMEs) in these sectors and countries.[2] The findings elucidate the challenges facing African industries in an age of informational capitalism, and help to build ties between research in economic geography, development studies, and science and technology studies. In a more applied sense, the book identifies crucial, non-ICT and ICT-specific "blockages" to achieving more deeply informationalized industries in Africa, thus raising pragmatic questions about the limits to ICT4D initiatives that focus principally on the diffusion and adoption of new technologies. Our major finding is that the nature and impacts of the "information revolution" in Africa are more constrained or delimited than is often thought, especially with regard to their impacts on the development of firms and industries. This is due in large part to the structural environment that SMMEs are forced to contend with, one where import liberalization and a lack of institutional support for domestic industries is often reducing or eliminating the value creation and upgrading possibilities available to firms and regions. Even more problematically, perhaps, we demonstrate how ICTs are complicit in new forms of accumulation and concentration by firms outside Africa as the internet, in particular, enables new varieties of market intermediation.

Considered more broadly, the book provides an in-depth economic-geographic and political-economic analysis of African industries in an age of information-intensive forms of capitalist expansion and accumulation. Rather than looking "in" on Africa through the lens of global centers of power, multilateral development agencies, and/or of transnational corporations, we instead focus our analysis on SMME owners and operators and their everyday activities and experiences with new ICTs in the current age of economic globalization. Beyond providing key insights into the dynamics of industrial change, innovation, and competition within African markets, our emphasis on the agencies and practices of African SMMEs also contributes an explicitly "Southern" analysis through which we demonstrate the broader theoretical and empirical implications of doing research in places that have for too long been "off the map" of mainstream research in economic geography. As Murphy (2008, p. 867, emphasis in original) notes, a focus on Southern economic geographies has important implications for the subdiscipline as well as with regard to policy-making:

> In doing so, it may be possible to more fully understand how globalisation is articulated through livelihood strategies in 'other' places, where there are similarities and differences, and what drives variations in responses to global market opportunities and forces. This is not a question of pluralisation for the sake of pluralisation but is, instead, a case for pluralisation as a means for *explanation* and a richer epistemological and ontological foundation for the future of economic geography. Beyond this claim, this argument is also a plea for policy relevance in places where extremes of material deprivation and inequality cry out for novel insights and ideas.

This latter point regarding policy also speaks to our interest in engaging with development studies through this project, achieving what Vira and James (2011) described as a "hybrid" approach wherein economic and industrial processes are linked directly to more typical development studies interests (e.g., livelihoods, poverty). This is an important consideration given that much of the ICT4D literature largely avoids questions related to the influence of new ICTs on the structure and evolution of economies and industries.

Theoretical Approach and Methodology

Our conceptualization of the potential impacts that ICTs might have on economies and industries in Africa centers on a key distinction between what we, following Cowen and Shenton (1996) and Hickey and Mohan (2005), describe as "imminent" and "immanent" forms of development. Imminent development is that which is intended or "willed" and which is managed or instrumented by state, non-state, and private sector actors, among others. In contrast, immanent development is that which is driven by the structures and processes of capitalism and capital accumulation, which have historically reproduced poverty, inequality, and deprivation in the Global South. In deploying these terms, we assert that transformative development in Africa – long-term, widespread, structural change that leads to significant reductions in levels of chronic poverty and deprivation – can only come about through reconfigurations of the immanent conditions that determine, in large part, the prospects for most African firms, industries, and regions to benefit from the recent growth successes. If ICTs are truly having the kinds of transformative impacts that some would claim, there should be evidence that they are contributing directly to changes in the immanent conditions structuring development in the region, *and* that these changes are "progressive" in the sense that they are supportive of upgrading in SMMEs, that they facilitate more empowered engagements between African industries and global markets, and that they, ultimately, contribute to enhanced forms of value creation and capture through industrial and social upgrading.

To determine whether there are signs of immanent changes to the conditions and opportunities facing SMMEs and industries, we use a multi-scalar approach that enables us to link the everyday sociospatial and technological practices of businesspeople to larger-order industrial changes and the development of ties to global markets. At the firm level, we draw on resource-based theories to assess whether intra-firm capabilities are being enhanced, and to what benefit and/or cost, through the adoption and use of new ICTs. Through this approach we examine whether mobile phone, computer, and/or internet use can be linked to improvements in SMME performance and innovativeness. Moreover, our analysis of intra-firm capabilities more generally reveals the degree to which South African and Tanzanian firms are upgrading their positions in domestic and international markets.

At the industrial scale, we deploy sociotechnical transitions theory to examine the regimes that govern and guide the evolution of wood products and tourism industries in South Africa and Tanzania. Sociotechnical regimes not only make up the territorial/everyday contexts (i.e., the urban–regional and national settings) where the activities of firms are embedded – they are also constituted, changed, and reproduced by the routines, actions, and institutional features of states, consumers, workers, civil society, and non-local actors such as input suppliers and buyers. As such, regimes include a wide range of actors beyond the firm, and their analysis can help us to understand the broader drivers and implications of industrial–economic change. In analysing sociotechnical regimes in South Africa and Tanzania, we determine whether there is evidence that regime-specific rules, hierarchies, practices, networks, actors, and markets are changing, and whether such changes are positive as ICTs become integrated into the everyday activities of consumers and firms.

Because the development of industrial regimes is shaped significantly by translocal, distal relationships, particularly to external firms, markets, and sources of finance, information, and knowledge, our conceptual approach extends to the global scale. A central question in this regard is whether the ties of African SMMEs to international markets are developing, strengthening, or weakening in the context of dramatic improvements to transnational communication systems. In specific terms, our approach focuses on the links between firms and consumers in global production networks (GPNs), and the sociotechnical regimes and SMMEs situated in South Africa and Tanzania's wood products and tourism industries. The goal is to determine whether, how, and to what benefit or cost new ICTs are facilitating "couplings" between GPNs and regimes – linkages that can enable or prevent SMMEs and other regime actors to/from create(ing), enhance(ing), and/or capture(ing) value through ties to the global economy. As we demonstrate, couplings exist not only when firms/regimes export wood products or tourism services to foreign buyers or consumers, but are also manifest in inward flows of goods into Africa: importation linkages that can play a significant role in shaping the development of local industrial regimes. In applying the GPN approach, we examine qualitatively the nature and significance of the couplings between industrial regimes in Africa and international markets, buyers, and producers, and assess critically whether, how, and to what degree industrial regimes and urban–regional contexts are becoming more or less empowered in relation to some of the immanent structural forces and actors driving economic globalization, particularly those associated with GPN configurations.

By integrating concepts related to intra-firm resources and capabilities, sociotechnical regimes, and GPNs, we are able to assess both the general conditions and ongoing changes to the structure of these industries and the role that ICTs are playing both imminently and immanently. Moreover, our approach captures the territorial and relational dimensions of industrial change and ICT uptake in Africa. Our territorial focus is on the sociotechnical regimes situated within the four urban–regional contexts – Durban, Cape Town, Dar es Salaam, and Zanzibar – that make up our case studies. The relational characteristics of regimes and these processes are captured in two ways. First, we analyse the ways in which regimes are stabilized, changed, and reproduced through relationalities and networks linking clients, suppliers, workers, buyers, industrial promotion authorities, state actors, importers, and ICT artefacts. Second, we examine the characteristics of the relationships between non-local actors, GPNs, and our case-study regimes. The net result is a conceptual and analytical perspective that enables us to assess the on-the-ground (territorialized) dynamics of ICT use and industrial change within particular urban–regional contexts, the influence that ICTs are having on the ability of African SMMEs to reach out to the global economy, and the manner in which GPNs are "touching down" in African economies through investments in tourism and wood product ventures or through the importation of goods and services: emerging relational configurations that may be supported through ICT use.

The conceptual framework is applied to data gleaned from more than 200 interviews conducted during 2010–2012 with SMMEs in the Tanzanian and South African wood processing and tourism sectors. The goal of these interviews and analysis was to assess whether, how, and to what extent ICTs have contributed (or not) to enhanced intra-firm performance, industrial change, and the globalization of African industries. South Africa and Tanzania represent significant contrasts in terms of their national locations within the informationalized economy, and the comparison is compelling at the industrial scale given the dramatically different kinds of products, production systems, and information-communication needs of the wood products and tourism sectors. Through this comparative approach we develop findings that highlight the ways in which new ICTs are being integrated (or not integrated) into the activities of African SMMEs, and assess the extent to which ICT-enabled regime transformations and GPN integrations are, or are not, occurring at the present time.

The multi-scalar conceptual framework (at the scales of the firm, the industrial regime, and the global production network) reveals important insights into the larger-order processes of socioeconomic and technological change in Africa. Most significantly, we identify and delineate five outcomes that are visible in everyday practices and which reveal the limited role that ICTs can, and are, playing in repositioning Africa in the global economy: namely "thintegration", downgrading, differentiation, neo-intermediation, and ICT-enabled extraversion. Some of these tendencies and dynamics have already been explored in the literature (e.g., see Gibbon and Ponte, 2005, on downgrading). However, our approach differs and expands on the literature through the development and elaboration of new concepts (thintegration, ICT-enabled extraversion) in combination with extant ones and focus on the impacts of ICTs on industrial regimes. Three of the five key concepts we develop relate specifically to the impacts of new ICTs on the industries under study, whereas downgrading and differentiation are the outcomes of broader processes in combination with the impacts of these technologies. As elaborated in further detail later, the patterns we elucidate are the outcome of the interaction between firm strategies, regimes, and GPNs.

To capture the depth and significance of ICT absorption, we distinguish between "thin" and "thick" forms of ICT integration in firms, industrial regimes, and their couplings to GPNs. Thin integration can facilitate imminent forms of development as manifest in incremental improvements to efficiency and productivity of SMMEs. In contrast, thick integration involves much more transformative changes to firm and industry practices as information becomes a central organizing principle and resource: accessed, processed, and managed in ways that can stimulate upgrading and the creation and capture of knowledge rents. In making this distinction, our objective is to examine critically the extent, depth, and significance of ICT integration and whether it might lead to structural transformations of African industries and their engagements with GPNs. Through our analysis we identify key supply and demand-side limitations on achieving "thicker" forms of ICT integration and, consequently, potentially immanent forms of "informationalized" development. Our findings demonstrate that thin integration or "thintegration" is the norm in our case study industries and contexts. This outcome refers both to the overall pattern of new ICT adoption in Africa, where research, development and manufacture take place primarily overseas, reinforcing a colonial division of labour, and with reference to our specific case study industries to connote the relatively shallow and reactive forms of usage of these technologies.

The profusion of information that new ICTs can facilitate also allows increased import penetration of African economies. The liberalization of economies, when combined with improvements in transportation and information and communication infrastructures, have created hyper-competitive markets where, in effect, everywhere around the globe, depending on factor endowments, is in competition with everywhere else. This hyper-competition has generated both cost pressures, reflected in the strategy of downgrading of products to capture market share identified in the study, and the strategies of product differentiation to capture niche markets, some of which are naturally protected.

Specifically in relation to tourism, we further identify the trend of neo-intermediation. While new ICTs are meant to facilitate disintermediation, in tourism the rise of often foreign-based booking websites has resulted in new forms of intermediation and ICT-based economic extraversion. As noted earlier, in the NEG literature problems of underdevelopment are presented largely as resulting from the disconnection of the Global South from the Global North, which new ICTs will help reverse. In contrast we find that new ICTs are often being absorbed into extant economic and industrial processes and routines in ways that support, rather than challenge, the historical dynamic of economic extraversion that has helped to reproduce under- and uneven development in Africa for over a century. Extraversion is what Bayart (2000) described as a form of dependency manifest in, or realised through, ties between African elites (e.g., colonists, political leaders) and foreign actors, and economies that are primarily oriented to meet the needs of people in other places rather than the majority of the domestic citizenry. The external orientation of African political economies was instantiated under colonialism (Rodney, 1972) and is today co-produced by transnational corporations, states (e.g., the G7, China), international financial institutions and other "donors" and domestic political elites (Carmody, 2010; Peiffer and Englebert, 2012). Economic extraversion is an outcome of uneven geographies of power, specifically ownership, control, and technical capabilities, which results in social surplus or value extraction from peripheral to core regions. As Duffy (2007: 187) noted, extraversion "has resulted in the creation of a patchwork of highly globalised areas and networks which in turn produce real forms of exclusion and marginalisation." Our case-study tourism destinations and GPNs are emblematic of these processes and outcomes, with extraversion being enabled increasingly through ICT-enabled forms of intermediation such as those facilitated by booking and travel review websites (e.g., TripAdvisor). Whereas much of the literature on the impacts of new ICTs are seen to empower small producers or service providers, in fact these more powerful actors are able to successfully deploy them to reinforce their extant power advantages, to the detriment of the less powerful.

Collectively these processes are largely reinforcing extant power distributions between African localities and industrial regimes and overseas producers and companies. These processes further demonstrate the lack of depth of ICT use that has accompanied the rapid diffusion of mobile phones and the internet, the increasingly marginal positionalities and limited value-adding opportunities facing African SMMEs in the current age of economic globalization, and the rise of new (ICT enabled in some cases) forms of intermediation and extraversion that limit the prospects for value capture within African firms and city-regions through GPN couplings that promote industrial and social upgrading. In a broader sense, these processes reflect old and newly emerging challenges facing Africa in an age of informationalized global capitalism; material and institutional conditions that cannot be resolved through the diffusion of ICTs and ICT-centric development projects.

More generally, by integrating resource-based theories of the firm, sociotechnical transition theory, and coupling and governance concepts from GPN research, we are able to conduct a multi-scalar analysis of industrial and economic development processes in Africa. The analysis demonstrates how micro-scale and case study research can reveal insights into the meso- and macro-scale structures and power asymmetries driving uneven development in the world system, and in particular the ways in which ICTs are imbricated in these processes and structural configurations. Moreover, it allows us to account for the agencies, relationalities, and sociotechnical processes driving industrial change and the development of GPNs linking Africa to the world economy. Rather than starting with top-down assumptions regarding how these processes and relationships must work, our bottom-up approach enables us to reveal these structural configurations and blockages through the activities of businesspeople and consumers. Thus our framework challenges the techno-determinism and teleological belief that is built into much of the ICT4D discourse, and highlights the agencies and everyday realities that African businesspeople face in trying to compete and prosper in an age of turbulence, growth and globalization. As we demonstrate, this critical perspective shows that ICTs can help to alleviate some of the productivity challenges facing firms, but that they ultimately do relatively little to help reconfigure the power relations governing the development of African SMMEs and industries.

Finally, our study also has broader epistemological implications for urban and economic geography, given our focus on African cities, industries, and economies, and the particular role that technology plays, or does not play, in shaping their evolution. The goal in this respect is to push the boundaries of these subdisciplines further into "trading zones" (Barnes and Sheppard, 2010) with epistemic communities such as development geography and science and technology studies. Our "hybrid" analysis enables us to deploy our conceptual approach and extend the book's findings in ways that, we hope, will generate dialog and debate outside the realms of urban and economic geography, ICT4D research, and African studies. Moreover, and as some geographers have argued recently (e.g., Peck, 2012; Myers, 2013), the much needed focus on African contexts provides a basis for substantive, comparative urban and economic analyses that can lead to novel insights regarding the contemporary dynamics of globalization and its implications for pressing socioeconomic issues such as poverty and inequality.

Structure of the Book

Following this introduction, the book is organized into eight chapters. Chapter 1 traces the lineage of the meta-discourse that has been constructed around ICT4D and outlines the perspectives of the large and growing ICT4D community that works on behalf of multilateral donors, states, private companies, and non-governmental organizations (NGOs) worldwide. We then link this meta-discourse to the concept of the informationalized economy and review claims about the power of ICTs to revolutionize development processes and reposition the Global South within the world system. We characterize the ICT4D meta-discourse as a new iteration of modernization theory – one where informationalization via ICT diffusion is coupled to neoliberalization in ways that are meant to lead to new materialities of market-led growth and development. Such discourse all too often lacks a critical political–economic perspective on meanings, potential, and impacts of ICTs, and works under an implicit assumption that geography no longer matters for development or global market integration. Given the lack of empirical support for such propositions, we characterize new ICTs as "objects of ideology" and critically examine the "work" that this discourse does in promoting individuation and neoliberalization. Through this assessment we make the case for more critical and geographically sensitive approaches to the study of the informationalized economy and ICT4D strategies.

Chapter 2 moves beyond these broad ideas and into an Africa-specific discussion of the global informationalized economy and the impacts of ICTs on development in the region. We first situate Africa in the informationalized economy, and then review the grey and academic literature regarding whether, how, and when ICTs might help to empower and reposition firms and industries within that economy. Our assessment reveals that ICT4D approaches are largely complicit in market-led development strategies and that they are framed as inherently positive means for integrating or articulating African cities, economies, and consumers into the world system. We then posit that while technologies like mobile phones may be "socially articulating", by enabling easier communication between people, they can also create (new) forms of economic disarticulation, through technological dependence, for example, thereby replicating patterns of Africa's adverse inclusion in the global economy. Our study addresses the occlusion of these dynamics from the literature in order to understand more fully both Africa's positionality in the informationalized economy and the prospects for ICT-driven transformations to industries, economies, and livelihoods in the region.

Chapter 3 develops and details the book's conceptual framework, which is constituted along three axes or scales of analysis – the intra-firm, the sociotechnical regime, and the trans-local or global. At the intra-firm scale, we conceptualize the potential impact of ICTs in terms of their influence on the practices and capabilities of, and constraints facing SMMEs as they strive to survive, compete, and increase the value of their products and services. The second axis or scale of analysis is derived from science and technology studies and it focuses on the sociotechnical regimes that govern the everyday activities of firms and industries. Regimes are territorialized configurations characterized as stabilized sets of rules, norms, practices, conventions, and actor-networks that mark the organizational characteristics of particular industrial sectors and urban–regional economies; in this case the emphasis is placed on wood products and tourism in four case study locations. Our third conceptual axis builds off the intra-firm and regime-scale analyses in order to assess whether and how ICT diffusion is influencing the positionalities of African markets, firms, and industries in the global economy. Here we draw upon ideas from the GPN literature in order to evaluate whether, and to what end, African industries are becoming articulated or coupled to the global economy in part through their ability to leverage the power of new ICTs. We conceptualize two types of couplings: those enabling the inward flow of imported goods or services for African markets, and those associated with exports and the outward articulation of African manufacturers and service providers into GPNs. Through the integration of these conceptual frameworks, we are able to assess the degree to which "thicker" forms of ICT integration are occurring in firms, industries, and GPNs, and whether this is leading to positive or negative changes to the (immanent) structures governing African SMMEs and the region's engagement with the world economy.

Chapter 4 begins the empirical analysis, first describing the case-study contexts and methods used. For wood products, Tanzanian SMMEs were sampled from the large wood products market/cluster in the Keko ward and other areas of Dar es Salaam, while in South Africa firms were sampled in KwaZulu-Natal province, with an emphasis on Durban. Sampling for the tourism studies took place in two continentally significant tourism centres – Western Cape Province/Cape Town, South Africa, and Zanzibar, Tanzania – and focused on the work of travel agents, tour operators, tour guides, and hoteliers. Once the rationale for and limitations on our methodological approach are detailed, we then summarize the SMME-level findings, particularly the influence that ICTs have had on intra-firm resources, capabilities, and performance.

The findings reveal the positive impacts that ICTs have had on communications and the transaction costs associated with managing clients, supply chains, and workers, and their limitations with regard to regime transformations and GPN articulations. However, in most cases ICTs have not dramatically enhanced the information management and processing capabilities of SMMEs, nor have they enabled most firms to proactively leverage information in order to develop new domestic market niches or outward ties to GPNs. In the case of wood products, "inward" oriented GPN couplings are most prominent, manifest in the increasing importation of finished products, particularly from China, into South African and Tanzanian consumer markets. In tourism, new ICT use is much more extensive and intensive, and is necessary for SMMEs to access the GPNs linking foreign tourists to South African and Tanzanian destinations. While this is a promising development in some ways, most tourism SMMEs face increasing competition from international tour operators, foreign-owned hotels and resorts, and third-party websites (e.g., TripAdvisor). The net result is that many of the firms surveyed, especially in Zanzibar, struggle to raise their added value and improve performance in markets that have become increasingly saturated, partly as a result of new forms of intermediation. Ultimately, and perhaps despite enhanced information access and communications, most SMMEs remain non- or weakly articulated into outward-oriented GPNs, except in those cases where business owners have developed relationships to international markets through face-to-face (F2F) interactions with clients, buyers, and/or investors. ICTs can be important once these relationships are established, but trust-building depends more on non-ICT capabilities and the relational proximities that come with F2F exchanges.

Building off the empirical evidence detailed in Chapter 4, chapters 5, 6, and 7 detail five trends that emerged from the case study analyses. Chapter 5 describes in detail how new ICTs have been "thinly" integrated into intra-firm practices and sociotechnical regimes as they primarily serve as communication devices, rather than technologies that enable "thicker" forms of information management and processing that might transform industrial regimes, facilitate upgrading, and enable firms to build ties to GPNs. *Thintegration* has meant that although ICTs increase the connectivity between SMMEs and flows of information and ideas in the informationalized economy, they have had much less influence than expected on the ability of firms to improve their access to new markets, sources of finance and inputs, and/or technologies. Although there are significant exceptions to these trends, particularly among some firms in South Africa's tourist industry (which we detail), ICTs are implicated in the (immanent) reproduction of sociotechnical regimes that are struggling to compete with imports and foreign firms.

In explicating the evidence for thintegration, we focus on the supply and demand-side factors shaping ICT uptake in firms and industries, stressing the importance of GPN couplings as potential drivers of thicker forms of integration that might lead to structural changes. Given that most GPN couplings in the wood products sector facilitate the inward flow of imported goods from Asia and elsewhere, rather than substantial improvements in productive activities locally, there is little need for more advanced or sophisticated uses of ICTs by African SMMEs beyond basic communications and data processing. In tourism, the promise for thicker forms of integration is greater, but without improved coordination and cooperation amongst SMMEs in Cape Town and Zanzibar, manifest principally in the creation of effective destination management organizations, likewise there is little need for more advanced forms of information and communication handling and processing capabilities beyond those specific to individual SMMEs. All told, without markets, regime characteristics, associational networks, and GPNs "demanding" enhanced capabilities and performance standards among SMMEs, improvements that might be enabled through ICT-enabled innovations, informationally "thick" forms of value creation, enhancement (upgrading), and capture will remain elusive. Even as they are rapidly adopted, new ICTs are doing little to reverse the trend toward thintegration, as it is an outcome of the uneven competitive dynamics of the global economy and decades of market liberalization policies in South Africa and Tanzania.

A further consequence of these immanent processes is that many of our surveyed SMMEs are forced to compete in hyper-competitive, low-value markets while imports and foreign firms – thanks in part to neoliberal reforms and enhanced abilities to coordinate transnational supply chains and GPNs through ICTs – dominate higher-value niches for wood products and tourism services. The net result is the *downgrading* of the products and services of African SMMEs. Chapter 6 details the evidence for downgrading through an empirical emphasis on Dar es Salaam's wood products industry, although similar trends are also evident among SMMEs in Durban, Cape Town, and Zanzibar. In response to the threat of downgrading, the primary alternative for most firms is to differentiate their products in high-value, niche markets such as those associated with customized and/or artistic products. We document this *differentiation* trend with particular emphasis on Durban SMMEs and highlight the limitations that ICTs have in enabling access to these markets, given the importance of face-to-face interactions, personal trust, reputation, and product quality rather than arms-length forms of price-based competition.

One of the promises of ICT diffusion stems from its potential to enable African firms and industries to deal more directly with suppliers and customers beyond their local markets through ICT-enabled forms of disintermediation. In contrast to much of the prevailing rhetoric, our evidence shows that market intermediation (i.e., the phenomenon of commercial middlemen and women) is proliferating in both the wood products and tourism sectors in Africa, even as new ICTs become more commonplace. Intermediation occurs both in spite and as a result of ICTs, manifest in face-to-face (F2F) and "virtual" forms of intermediation that reduce the value of the goods and services provided by African SMMEs. Chapter 7 focuses on the tourism sector and details these different types of intermediation; arguing that ICTs are enabling new forms of intermediation – *neo-intermediation* – and highlighting the obstacles that prevent disintermediation from occurring in the tourism sector. Particularly problematic are the ways in which foreign third-party websites such as TripAdvisor, Orbitz.com, and hotels.com are facilitating a new age of what we term *ICT-enabled extraversion* through web-based forms of value capture and market concentration, creating new South–North dependencies and resource transfers. Beyond (immanently) reproducing conditions of extraversion, these corporations and websites also facilitate the fetishization and defetishization of "Africa": imaginaries that primarily serve the interests of tourists and foreign tourism interests and which shape significantly the kinds of services and products that SMMEs provide, thus limiting (from a distance) the prospects for locally determined forms of innovation in the sector.

Chapter 8 summarizes the broader findings and explores the obstacles to ICT-enabled forms of industrial development. Structural "blockages" have limited the benefits of ICT diffusion and contributed to a new age of involutionary economic growth in Africa – one where ICTs are helping to reproduce the dynamics of dependency and unequal exchange but in a context of greatly improved communications between North and South. It is this improved connectivity and communication, manifest in stronger links between Africa and the virtual space of flows (of information, ideas, and knowledge), that creates the "illusion" of development while obscuring the fact that material connections to, or articulations within, global production networks, circuits of capital, and markets remain limited, often exploitative, and ineffective as a means of providing the kinds of expansive or distributive development necessary to alleviate widespread poverty in Africa. Our findings demonstrate that building connections to these material flows depends critically upon the ability of firms and businesspeople to meet the performance standards and functional capacities demanded in global markets, overcome significant institutional and relational barriers (e.g., those based on class, gender, race), accumulate sufficient levels of capital to sustain globalized trade and investment ties, and achieve regularly the kinds of face-to-face interactions that can create and sustain trusting ties to non-local businesspeople and markets. Although some of these challenges and requirements can be better managed through ICT integration (e.g., information management and processing), these technologies alone are, at best, a partial strategy for industrial and social upgrading and one that will do little to address the structural blockages facing SMMEs, industries, and regions in Africa.

All told, our analysis details how new ICTs do not obliterate the (immanent) structural constraints or factors accompanying a political economy of neoliberalism, but are instead absorbed into this context in ways that selectively rework extant economic regimes and patterns of uneven development. The vision of development implied in much of the ICT4D discourse elides this reality and creates the illusion that modernization through informationalization will, in and of itself, transform the socioeconomic conditions that have peripheralized Africa. Missing from this discourse are critical considerations of how the informationalized economy works and why the context of neoliberal capitalism will make it extremely difficult for African firms, industries, and states to achieve "thicker" forms of informationalization that might help lead to more diverse economies, progressive couplings to GPNs, and poverty alleviation through distributive forms of growth. We provide specific points of guidance with respect to how best to achieve such contextualization – drawing primarily off the conceptual ideas developed earlier on – and also include recommendations for policy-makers and practitioners working within and beyond Africa. The final section of the conclusion also raises broader points about the value of using a sociotechnical perspective on industrial development and the need for more "hybrid" development–economic research in human geography such that we might better understand the dynamics and implications of (informationalized) capitalism's variegations and mutations in the Global South.

Notes

1 Taylor's (2014) analysis of the "Africa rising" discourse highlights the fact that the region's middle class is unlikely to grow sufficiently to drive development in the coming years and that only 4% of Africans have incomes in excess of US $10 a day. As such, it is doubtful that the region can achieve the kinds of widespread development outcomes promised in the "rising" discourse.

2 We broadly classify SMMEs as businesses having fewer than 100 full-time employees. Medium-scale firms have more than 20 employees, small-scale firms have between 5 and 20 employees, and micro-scale firms have fewer than five. In our study, the vast majority of firms are micro- or small in scale and many, particularly in Tanzania's wood products industry, operate in the informal or unregistered sector and often with a single employee-owner. While the boundaries between the small, micro-, and medium-scale are somewhat arbitrary, the sampled firms are primarily African-owned enterprises that often serve as entrepreneurial actors in the South African and Tanzanian economies. Our goal in focusing on this population was to assess whether there are indicators that ICTs are helping to empower independent businesses such as these, and in a manner that might contribute to the transformation of African industries and economies.

Notes

Chapter One
ICT4D: The Making of a Neoliberalized Meta-discourse (with Bjoern Surborg)

A little over a decade ago Africa was being written about by some commentators as a "lost" or "hopeless" continent (*The Economist*, 2000). However, recent growth success stories in the continent have made some in the popular media, investment analysts and academics "bullish" about Africa's economic prospects (e.g., Mahajan, 2009; Radelet, 2010; Robertson *et al.*, 2012; *The Economist*, 2013a). Figures are often cited from the International Monetary Fund (IMF) that Africa has recently hosted seven of the top ten fastest growing economies in the world, that poverty is now falling quickly, and that many of its countries are successfully "emerging" and integrating favorably into the world economy through increased trade and investment relationships (Radelet, 2010; Sala-i-Martin and Pinkovskiy, 2010). For these commentators, Africa is finally becoming primed to "take-off" and develop "modern" economies able to sustain growth, reduce poverty, attract investment, and support new value-adding industries in the coming decades.

Although it is clear that Africa is one of the fastest growing regions in the world, there is little evidence of positive structural transformation in the region, even in the most successful "developmental states" on the continent (Kelsall, 2013). Indeed, there is evidence of structural retrogression as the share of manufacturing in gross domestic product (GDP) falls and that of the primary and informal sectors increases (United Nations

Africa's Information Revolution: Technical Regimes and Production Networks in South Africa and Tanzania, First Edition. James T. Murphy and Pádraig Carmody.
© 2015 John Wiley & Sons, Ltd. Published 2015 by John Wiley & Sons, Ltd.

Conference on Trade and Development [UNCTAD], 2012). Moreover, state-level institutions in most countries remain poorly equipped to manage and guide economic development, provide basic social services, and/or maintain or upgrade vital infrastructures (roads, energy) needed to sustain productive industries (Rotberg, 2013). Foreign aid remains a key source of support for such investments and it accounts for a substantial proportion of the GDP of many African countries. In short, the positive news regarding Africa's recent growth renaissance needs to be tempered by a critical and careful reflection about whether and how the benefits of growth can be channeled into the kinds of structural changes needed to empower people and firms on the continent and favorably reposition the region in the world economy.

The challenges associated with deeper, structural changes to Africa's political economies are daunting, but some view the current age of growth as qualitatively distinct from prior eras (e.g., Radelet, 2010). This is due in part to the changing nature of international trade and investment relations, that is, from relatively linear value chains to more spatially dispersed and extensive production networks (Broadman, 2007), and because the contemporary global economy is now characterized by information-driven and guided forms of capitalism. In this context, mainstream analysts (e.g., Friedman, 2005) argue that firms and industries in developing regions have much greater potential to access international markets for higher-value goods and services, provided they can "plug in" to globalized flows of information and capital able to foster and sustain industrial innovation. Doing so will require both institutional changes to support global market integration, and the uptake of technologies (e.g., logistics, transport, telecommunications) that can enable African firms to reach out and productively connect to buyers and consumers in the world economy (World Bank, 2009).

For some, new information and communications technologies (ICTs such as mobile phones, computers, and the internet) are essential tools for Africa's economic transformation, having already played a significant role in the region's recent growth transition (Africa Partnership Forum, 2008). Mills and Herbst (2012) noted that African telephone connection rates were just 10% of the global average in the mid-1990s, but had risen to half of the average by 2011. While there is little doubt that the diffusion of ICTs – especially mobile phones – into and across Africa has been nothing short of remarkable, it remains unclear what their everyday availability and use has meant specifically for socioeconomic development, manifest here as improvements to livelihoods and/or social upgrading, strengthened (endogenous) industrial systems, and the more favorable positioning of African firms and industries structurally vis-à-vis GPNs. While ICTs alone cannot be expected to accomplish all of these outcomes, the literature on Africa's growth "miracle" sometimes presents them as a core aspect of the region's socioeconomic transformation. For example, Radelet (2010: 20) argues this point with regard to the more than a dozen "emerging" African economies:

> These new technologies are raising economic productivity, increasing incomes, helping to deliver basic services, and facilitating transparency and accountability, all of which strengthen the prospects for continued growth and development in these countries.

As evidenced by quotes like this, the development of the global informational(ized) economy (GIE) and society is often thought to be overwhelmingly positive for developing regions (Smith *et al.*, 2011; Rotberg and Aker, 2013). In contrast, this book argues critically that there are inherently problematic aspects to the transformations that are accompanying Africa's information revolution, and that the practices associated with the diffusion of new ICTs are often embedded in, and help to reproduce, existing (often exploitative) social relations.[1] Our analysis of the impacts of new ICTs on South African and Tanzanian industries demonstrates the limitations on ICT for development initiatives (commonly referred to as ICT4D). A central argument is that the meta-discourse and governance strategies that have accompanied ICT4D initiatives tend to focus on imminent forms of development (intentional, often individuated) whilst overlooking or oversimplifying the immanent structural drivers of socioeconomic change: realities that limit the prospects for rapid, radical, and progressive forms of information-driven and enabled development within the region. Before detailing our conceptual and methodological approach, the book's first two chapters examine broadly the nature and construction of the discourse around new ICTs globally, the political economy of the genesis and propagation of the ICT4D movement, and the literature documenting the relationships between development outcomes and the diffusion of new ICTs in Africa.

ICT4D

There are a variety of definitions of what constitutes the information and communication technologies for development (ICT4D) project (Heeks, 2007). According to Kleine (2013), the broad idea is that ICTs are considered to be the means, whereas development is the end. While few would deny that new information and communications technologies can make valuable contributions to development, the sharp or exclusive focus on information technology is interesting. There are no comparable fields of industry or agriculture for development, or infrastructure for development. This may in part be because economic sectors are thought to be development, whereas ICTs are meant to facilitate development. However, this might then be seen to call into question the means–ends relationship to which Kleine alludes.

Another perspective is that the strong focus on new information and communication technologies arises from the fact that these have long been seen as "heartland" technologies of the new global information economy (Cole, 1986; Freeman and Perez, 1988). There is an extensive literature on the nature and impacts of technological change on socioeconomic development (e.g., Rogers, 1962; Ruttan, 2001; Nye, 2006; Wilson, 2007). A core framing of the technology–development nexus draws upon and advances Schumpeter's (1939) argument that long-wave cycles of economic growth are driven by changes to the sociotechnical paradigm, which effectively shifts a country's production-possibilities frontier to higher value-added and more productive economic sectors (Freeman and Soete, 1997). However, Freeman (2001: 121) cautioned that "bubbles, euphoria and panics" are common phenomena during the early diffusion of new technologies, and ICTs are thus no different in this regard. He also argued that although ICTs were meant to make markets function more efficiently by reducing information failures, that information about prices did not necessarily lead to better investment decisions, for example, and that consequently their impacts should not be overstated.

Accompanying the often euphoric and overblown claims regarding the transformative power of new ICTs, there is a technological determinism that posits that the adoption of mobile phones, computers, and the internet will inevitably drive progressive forms of modernization in regions like Africa. As Bimber (1990) argued, techno-deterministic accounts arise from both universal logical sequences of socioeconomic development that accompany the uptake of new technologies (e.g., the steam mill follows the hand mill), and/or somewhat paradoxically, the potential for unintended social, economic, political, and/or environmental outcomes given the partial autonomy of new technologies once they are "released" into society. In the case of the ICT4D discourse, both conditions apply albeit in an essentially positive manner: universal smart phone and Wi-Fi internet access/use must follow from voice communications and texting; unintended consequences such as "Twitter revolutions" and mobile application development industries emerge and will spur democratization and innovation. All told, real, material, and social development impacts will/must result as ICTs contribute to knowledge- and communication-driven gains in productivity, innovation, employment, and the delivery of critical social, financial, and government services. However as Graham (1998: 180) noted:

> The very notion of a "technological impact", so long a central feature of mainstream technological debates in urban and regional studies... is problematic, because of its attendant implications of simple, linear, technological cause and societal effect.

For example, the US$204.8 million World Bank sponsored *infoDev* (www. infodev.org) program seeks to leverage enhanced ICT capabilities and new, largely mobile, platforms to spur entrepreneurship and innovation in developing regions. Importantly, and as is the case with many initiatives, the underlying premise is "there is no alternative" (TINA) to rapid ICT diffusion and integration, given the scale and scope of the existing socioeconomic challenges, the exigencies of global capitalism, and the perceived need to fast-track electronic (e-) and mobile (m-) based development initiatives as means to create a foundation for economic transformation.

> Innovation drives competitiveness, and maximizing competitiveness is indis- pensable to achieving sustainable job creation. Business leaders and policy- makers are wisely emphasizing the innovation imperative – a focus on continuously strengthening every economy's capacity to create new products, processes and techniques – and are putting innovation strategies at the center of their economic agenda. The Financial and Private Sector Development Network of the World Bank Group supports this priority as the only way to prosper in the relentlessly competitive global economy. *infoDev* is a key part of our effort to contribute to innovation, competitive economies and job creation. By focusing on access to knowledge, services and finance for technology- enabled start-ups and high-growth small and medium-sized enterprises in developing countries, *infoDev* is helping to shore up the cohort of businesses that creates the most jobs worldwide. (Janamitra Devan, Vice President and Head of Network, Financial and Private Sector Development, The World Bank Group: *infoDev*/World Bank, 2013: 4)

ICTs are viewed as critical for innovation, and the *infoDev* program and other World Bank initiatives broadly reflect a deep-seated belief in the (imminent, guided) growth possibilities that can accompany the diffusion of ICT artefacts and the development of related capabilities.

The ICT4D discourse also carries with it an air of inevitability to the changes that are accompanying both ICT diffusion and the evolution of the global economy, an attitude that reflects the TINA perspective and the notion that developing regions can deterministically leapfrog past the struc- tural features that have held them back from a more progressive engage- ment with the world economy. Such transformations are manifest both at the global scale, where the promise of ICTs lies in their contribution to the international competitiveness of African enterprises, and more locally with respect to their ability to improve livelihood possibilities and strategies.

> Mobile applications not only empower individuals but have important cascade effects stimulating growth, entrepreneurship, and productivity throughout the economy as a whole. Mobile communications promise to do more than just give the developing world a voice. By unlocking the genie in the phone, they empower people to make their own choices and decisions. (World Bank, 2012b)

Viewed from these perspectives, the primary challenge for African societies and economies is to effectively integrate ICTs into livelihood strategies and business practices, such that the dynamics of ICT-driven forms of socioeconomic and industrial development can gain momentum as ties to global knowledge flows are enhanced, deepened, and expanded. In other words, *material* transformations will emerge once the information-communication and knowledge management infrastructure and capabilities are put into place.

Many proponents of ICT4D acknowledge the problems associated with the hype and determinism that often accompanies new artefacts, applications, and websites, yet maintain an optimistic and often uncritical perspective on the (progressive) directionality of contributions by ICTs to development processes. Moreover, they argue that because ICTs are so pervasive and transformative, they transcend economic sectors and are thus worthy of an entire field of study and an international movement. The fact that the ICT4D "movement" has achieved such international and high-level traction, and given that it commands billions of dollars of support from the public and private sectors, speaks to a particular political economy that we now explore. This critical evaluation is not intended to deny the (socially) transformative nature of new ICTs (although it is important to specify the limits of this), but to understand their drivers and the structural context in which this takes place.

Electronic and Mobile E-/M-Business

In the most direct sense, ICTs are central contributors to the electronics industry, one that has provided a basis for the "emergence" of value-added, high-tech industries within many post-colonial countries in Asia (e.g., Malaysia, India) and other parts of the Global South. These industries co-exist with more "traditional" economic sectors in an example of what Whittaker *et al.* (2010) called "compressed development". The electronics industry has transformed the world economy, from cars to computer-aided stitching equipment and cell phones, and enabled the radical "informationalization" and globalization of sectors once confined to national boundaries and spatially concentrated value chains. As such, the products of the electronics industry (e.g., ICTs such as computers, the internet, and mobile phones) have enabled some degree of time–space compression with regard to the trade, investment, and production relations that constitute the contemporary global economy. While the electronics sector itself is worthy of detailed study (e.g., Park and Roome, 2002), our focus is instead on the impacts of new ICTs on other business and commercial activities in regions like Africa, with an emphasis on understanding their contributions to the "D" in ICT4D strategies.

While much of the academic literature focuses on ICT4D, arguably the most extensive use of these technologies has taken place outside of these parameters, in terms of their social and business uses. In recent decades, in particular, there has been a huge growth in e-business and e-commerce globally. This bifurcation of the field is worth exploring, because in a sense ICT4D may serve as a Trojan horse for certain types of e-business. Moreover, electronically enabled business activities may serve as important conduits for development in a broader sense (e.g., employment, livelihoods), rather than most ICT4D initiatives, which strive to link directly the uptake of ICTs and development objectives such as improvements to education, health, and/or government.

There are a variety of definitions of what constitutes e-business. It is often thought to be synonymous with e-commerce by internet-based stores or merchants, or business conducted online in virtual markets. Amit and Zott (2001) defined an e-business as one that derives more than 10% of its revenue online. Rather than trying to determine when the 10% benchmark is reached, this book instead adopts Molla and Licker's (2005: 90) broad definition of e-business as commercial activities that are enabled by ICTs; we would add mobile telephony networks to this definition as well:

> Conducting one or more core business functions internally with organizations or externally with suppliers, intermediaries, consumers, government, and other members of the enterprise environment through the application of solutions that run on Internet-based and other computer networks.

E- and m-business activities are referenced frequently in mainstream business culture, manifest particularly as ICT-facilitated business-to-business (B2B), business-to-customer (B2C), and business-to-government (B2G) transactions. Such transactions include wholesale input, supply, and service purchasing activities (B2B), online and phone-enabled retail sales (B2C), and electronic tax payments and bids for government purchasing contracts (B2G).

In terms of definitional clarity, the difference between ICT4D and e-business can be highlighted in two ways. First, rather than focusing on the impacts that ICTs can have on particular transactions (i.e., B2B, B2C, or B2G), the ICT4D discourse focuses on broader transformations to government (e-/m-governance), financial systems (e-/m-banking), and key economic and social sectors (e.g., e-/m-health, e-/m-agriculture). Development in this context is captured in ICT-enabled changes to the everyday practices associated with these institutions and sectors. Second, the contrast between ICT4D and e-business can be linked to the distinction between imminent and immanent development (Cowen and Shenton, 1996; Hickey and Mohan, 2005). Imminent development is intentional development, as when governments promote economic development or poverty alleviation programs. Immanent development refers to the structured patterns of socioeconomic activity and outcomes that arise from the unfolding of the capitalist mode of production on a world scale.

We characterise e-business as a form of immanent development given both its influence on the emergence of new forms of capitalist relations within the global economy, and its complicity in the reproduction of long-standing inequalities within and between nations. While some have argued that the advent of new ICTs is effectively eliminating the core–periphery distinction globally by "flattening" the world (Friedman, 2005), we argue that it is instead reconfiguring it in ways that reproduce inequality and dependency, albeit in new, informationalized ways. Global capitalism is subject to "laws of motion" or development trends, such as uneven development (de Janvry and Garramón, 1977) and extraversion (Bayart, 2000), which new ICTs are now contributing to, whilst also reshaping into new patterns and processes. For example, Dicken (1998) argued that new ICTs have enabled the creation of an integrated global economy that functions in "real time". This has, in turn, meant that shocks can be transmitted throughout (much of) the system much more quickly and forcefully than was previously the case (Freeman, 2001), as evidenced by the recent "global" financial crisis. Rather than "ending" geography (O'Brien, 1992), new ICTs are reconfiguring it. However, this does not mean that processes of over-accumulation of capital, creative destruction or economies of scale are no longer operative. Rather, the context in which these take place has been altered.

Whereas e-business represents a form of immanent development, ICT4D, arguably, is a form of imminent development where non-governmental organizations, governments and international agencies attempt to harness ICTs for intentional developmental ends. Common examples of ICT4D projects include government sponsored and supported telecenters in the developing world. In another example, more recently development agencies have experimented with projects that enable aid recipients to receive money via mobile phones (Datta et al., 2008). While ICT4D promoters tout the power of these technologies for transformative forms of socioeconomic and political development, the success rate of these initiatives has been modest at best. For example, a recent evaluation of World Bank ICT4D initiatives revealed that while the Bank had been successful 60% of the time when developing policy and regulatory frameworks in support of ICTs, it was largely unsuccessful (70% failure rate) in its attempts to provide ICT access to impoverished or marginalized groups (World Bank, 2011). Moreover, the Bank had a 75% failure rate with its efforts to develop ICT sectors in developing economies, and more demand-side interventions (e.g., e-governance, m-banking, m-health) had modest results, with most projects failing to meet their expectations or requiring significant modification from their initial designs. As the Bank's self-assessment notes, projects failed in large part due to the poor quality of their design – manifest in failures to account for context-specific capabilities, circumstances, and needs, overly complex project designs, inadequate or inappropriate forms of capacity building, and/or poor ownership of, or commitment to, the project's objectives (World Bank, 2011). More generally, ICT4D projects often fail because of lack of demand by the intended target group, and the concomitant excessive focus on the supply-side and consequent lack of financial sustainability over the longer term (Kleine, 2013).

The high failure rates of ICT4D projects is in contrast with the high level of interest in both academic and "donor" communities around the potential of information technology to reduce poverty and enable development. Thompson and Walsham (2010: 112) identified that there is a mismatch between the unprecedented level of interest in ICT4D in the African context, but very little IS [information system] literature that engages with "development" in an explicit way, with much work having focussed upon "point" implementation of these technologies. As Heeks (2002a) demonstrated, there is no direct correlation between productivity increases and ICT investments in developing regions. In spite of the evidence, however, the World Bank and others continue to promote a somewhat fantastical image of the transformative power of ICTs, even as the Bank's own evaluation unit notes that the more than 4 billion dollars it has spent on ICT projects was "largely unsuccessful" (World Bank, 2011: 4). As elaborated below, this suggests that ICT technologies and the ICT4D discourse are (sublime) objects of ideology: much more than tools or narratives aimed at enabling development (Žižek, 1989).

The focus of this book is largely on e- and m-business, as it is immanent development which is most important in shaping developmental outcomes.[2] However, e-business, to date, has not received nearly the same amount of attention in the academic literature as ICT4D has, at least in developing country contexts, for reasons explored below. Through our focus on e-business and immanent forms of development, this book seeks to move the debate over the "power" of ICTs beyond the scope of the imminent and into deeper questions regarding the long-term implications for Africa's development and its positionality in the world system. Before delving into the specific links between ICTs, business, and development in Africa, we first situate our analysis within the meta-discourse and governance strategies that have accompanied the rise of the global information economy that we describe below.

The Making and Materialization of a Meta-discourse

The origin of the dominant discourse around the transformative role of new ICTs in international development has a number of roots. It is, in part, related to the increased empirical importance of these technologies globally, but most significantly the discourse has taken on substantial global power through the work of scholars and practitioners, and the powerful imaginaries that corporations and mainstream (and even alternative) media outlets have constructed regarding the potential of new ICTs. Figure 1.1 exemplifies this imagery, as do the various entries on the World Bank's ICT4D blog (http://blogs.worldbank.org/ic4d/) that highlight the multitude of ways that ICTs can impact poverty, employment, finance,

Figure 1.1   ICT4D imagery as promoted in the World Bank's 2012 *Information and Communications for Development Report: Maximizing Mobile* (World Bank, 2012a). Reprinted with permission of The World Bank and Naylor Design.

education, health, governance, gender equality, and so on. The power of this discourse stems from its technological basis, its modernist gaze on the "development problem", its optimism, and because ICTs are framed as tools to provide individuated solutions to socioeconomic and political challenges.

Thrift (2005) questions the fundamentally transformative nature of new ICTs, but notes how their widespread diffusion across socioeconomic activities makes them both more and less important than is commonly thought. According to Sterling (2009), we live in an era of the "security-entertainment complex" which has produced, as Thrift (2011: 7) would see it, "a stance towards the world which is naturally experimental and which is able to … employ technology to make this experimental stance 'irresistible'." Whereas Latour (1987) wrote about "immutable mobiles", such as maps, which embody and convey information and meaning, new ICTs are arguably mutable mobiles which convey an almost infinite array of information and meaning through their operation, given the complexity of human and other forms of interaction that they enable. This results in an individuation of meaning around them, even as their physical features may remain relatively constant. This new cultural political economy or ontology of ICTs as enabling individuation and experimentation entrains both ICT4D practitioners (some might say governors) and subjects through a dominant discursive ideology.

The very mutability and adaptability of new ICTs has captured both "mainstream" or conservative writers, such as Thomas Friedman, and some more critical ones such as Manuel Castells. However, both perspectives continue to suffer from a technological determinism that limits their explanatory power. Friedman's claims about the world being "flat" can be easily dismissed by ongoing globally uneven development, reflected or mirrored in new digital divides such as the fact that Tokyo or Manhattan have more geo-coded content that all of Africa. Although Castells (1998) initially emphasized the importance of information technology as a tool to empower individuals, firms, and economies, his own work should have given him pause to reflect on the determinative nature of new ICTs in the version of economic development he was propounding. In *End of Millennium* (p. 122) he wrote that South Africa "is neither a low-wage dependent economy, nor a higher-skilled competitive emerging economy", albeit noting that it had the highest number of Internet hosts of any non-OECD country. The implication should have been clear – and is evident in more recent works by Castells (e.g., 2005) – that having a globally competitive economy requires a much broader suite of infrastructure and capabilities than just those associated with ICT, at least for a country the size of South Africa.[3] The possibility that marginalized or peripheral regions/peoples might tap into the potential benefits made possible by ICTs and the global network society depends upon their ability to counteract or circumvent the power relations that unevenly dictate the direction, scope, and scale of the networked flows of commodities, knowledge, and finance in the world economy (Castells, 2011). As such, the immanent power of ICTs and Africa's information revolution might be realized if they help disrupt or discontinue Africa's long history of extraverted economic relations.

Nonetheless, in the academic literature it is new ICTs (mobile phones, internet, and computers) that have generated the most interest, perhaps in part because mobile phones are relatively cheap inverse infrastructures that can travel with users, and are therefore accessible to the poor. Their potential to serve as equilibrating and poverty-reducing devices has attracted many from the mainstream ICT industry to the ICT4D community. Through organizations like the Bill and Melinda Gates Foundation and Google's foundation, ICT professionals and executives are striving increasingly to find ways of leveraging the power of information and enhanced communications toward long-standing development challenges. This is an intriguing development given that, as Richard Heeks (2008: 26) argued:

> … most informatics professionals spend their lives serving the needs of the world's wealthier corporations and individuals because … "that's where the money is". Yet seeking to squeeze a few extra ounces of productivity from firms that already perform relatively well, or to save a few minutes in the life of a busy citizen, pales in ethical importance when compared to the potential benefits of applying new technologies to our planet's megaproblems.

For Heeks and others in the ICT4D community, ICTs can be used in much more innovative and societally important ways and should be considered as critical tools to be used in the service of all kinds of environmental and socioeconomic challenges.[4]

While this recent ethical or moral shift is most welcome, the prospects for ICT-driven solutions to global mega-problems seem, at best, unlikely. This is due in part to the scale of these problems, and the vested interests that often benefit from current arrangements and resist potential solutions, given the costs of their implementation. Moreover, an alternative argument could be made that the spread of ICTs facilitates increased consumerism, which is ultimately unsustainable and a contributing factor to some of the very mega-problems that ICTs may seek to address. The "poverty-washing" of ICTs, where they are presented as the cure to global poverty, but in actuality are being primarily used to promote capital accumulation, may then serve to disguise deeper problems of the ideology of consumerism and over-consumption (Sklair, 2001). As Castells (2011) recently argued, interdependent and intertwined global finance and multimedia networks play a dominant role in promoting and enabling such consumerist ideologies, and they wield tremendous power and control over the world economy today. While it is clear that new ICTs are facilitating the rise of new forms of consumption and value chains globally (e.g., through e-commerce, B2B transactions), their implications for pressing development challenges remain far less certain.

Wade (2002) and Russill (2008) have written about the historicity of the ICT4D discourse, movement and practice. In terms of discourse, Wade (p. 443) noted:

> ICT tools can help people learn how to absorb knowledge generated elsewhere and combine it with local needs and local knowledge, and they can help raise real economic returns to investments; but they are being touted in the development community as though they can leapfrog over the more familiar development problems. This is like saying that cheap books can cure illiteracy.

This is one of the factors that explains the high ICT4D project failure rates. According to Wade, the digital divide barely exists when ICT usage is standardized against income, and may be merely a reflection of the more familiar global income divide. Despite the paradox, however, ICT4D appears to have an ineluctable momentum.

The rise of the global ICT4D movement can be related to the emergence of a North-centered global information(alized) economy in the later part of the 20th and early part of the 21st century (Heeks, 2008). As Castells (1999) argued, the collapse of the Soviet Union was partly an outcome of its missing out on the information technology revolution from the mid-1970s onwards. The rollout of the GIE can be considered not just a spontaneous economic phenomenon, as low-income consumers in the developing world access mobile phones for example, but also a planned one, with a highly developed social infrastructure behind it.

The co-founder of Microsoft Corporation, Bill Gates (2008, quoted in Roy, 2010) has argued for "creative capitalism" which could eliminate poverty through profits. Roy (2010) argues that this represents a form of "millennial development" characterized by celebratization, democratization (in the sense of Western publics being involved) and an emphasis on microfinance in particular. She asks whether (p. 23) "poverty [can] be transformed into poverty capital" through microfinance initiatives and whether the new forms of accumulation, speculation, and profit-making that accompany such programs can ever truly empower the poor within neoliberal capitalist systems. While different models and benefits of microfinance are hotly debated, microfinance is ultimately a form of global market integration of the poor: what some have labelled grassroots neoliberalism (Karim, 2011). In the context of millennial development, mobile phones are another vector of market integration and what Roy (2010: 53) considers a "new frontier of capital accumulation".

Mobile phones as vectors of market integration for the poor have a variety of axes. According to Joseph Stiglitz (1999), what separates less from more developed countries are combined knowledge and capital deficits. In the literature, mobile phones are often touted as enabling knowledge transfer and access to capital and markets – in effect market creators. We consider this assemblage (see McFarlane, 2009) of artefacts, agents, and goals to be a social movement organized and driven by corporate, celebrity, NGO, governmental and inter-governmental actors who view the creation and deepening of capitalist markets as the central challenge facing African states in an age of informational capitalism. Within this movement, ICTs are seen as critical tools to achieve these goals and are thus highlighted in much of the grey and applied literature about how to "do" development in the millennial age.

Whereas social movements are often thought to be oppositional forces, the rollout of neoliberal or corporate globalization is conducted as a social movement of its own, organized within a number of key organizational nodes such as international financial institutions or the World Economic Forum (Carmody, 2007). Elements of the ICT4D and e-business movement can be considered as forming one arm of this global social movement, which contains powerful corporations (e.g., Microsoft, Nokia, Ericsson). These business actors impact the social movement directly by serving on the committees of the European Union's Africa ICT strategy, for example (Ayonka, 2010). Corporate actors exert power through a variety of direct and indirect channels and there is much at stake for these firms with respect to their growth and shareholder value. For example, Microsoft has a 95% market share in productivity software market globally.[5] It also has a 75% share in the global operating systems market and approximately the same in the server software market (Forbes, 2013). Such market dominance by American headquartered companies such as Google, Apple, and Microsoft is facilitated both by high barriers to entry, rapid technological turnover, high rents, and complex and controversial tax avoidance structures which enable them to pay very low rates of taxation globally.[6] Simply stated, the ICT4D market is theirs for the taking, provided the consumption of software products produced by transnational corporations (TNCs) is enabled to expand through diffusion initiatives.

The mobile phone industry is dominated globally by a handful of transnational corporations (e.g., Apple, Motorola, Nokia and Samsung) based in North America, Europe, and East Asia. In recent years China has become the world's largest producer of mobile phones, accounting for over 40% of current world production (Imai and Shiu, 2007). There are approximately 50 Chinese handset makers, which account for over half of domestic market sales in that country. Some of these, such as Huawei, have expanded overseas and developed research and development centers in Scandinavia, for example, and put established companies such as Nokia under intense competitive pressure (Cooke, 2012). Nokia had, until recently, accounted for 40% of global mobile phone sales (Corbett, 2008) but the company posted a US$1.2 billion dollar loss in the first quarter of 2012, and now accounts for less than 30% of global sales (Huuhtanen, 2012).

Chinese mobile companies sometimes use independent design houses to develop their mobile handsets and produce phones for the African market.[7] Many of these companies benefit from government-provided subsidized credit and other development interventions (e.g., clusters, industrial parks) designed to make them competitive in world markets. Moving up the value chain into research and design is enabling them to capture increasing amounts of rent, which can then be reinvested for further growth (Yeung et al., 2006; Fan, 2011). Consequently the GIE is almost completely Euro-American and East-Asian dominated and it is highly profitable for the biggest market players – namely US, Japan, and Korean based brand-name handset, smart phone, chip, and notebook makers such as Nokia, Microsoft, Intel, Toshiba, PortalPlayer, Samsung, and Apple (Dedrick et al., 2010). China too has a significant stake in the industry, particularly as an assembler of these new technologies. However, despite the US$179 production cost of an iPhone, China captures only $6.50, largely from the cost of labour, whilst the major beneficiaries are transnational corporations (TNCs) based in North America and Japan, particularly Apple and retailers (Hart-Landsberg, 2013).

ICT manufacturers who successfully innovate and develop brand names in major consumer markets wield tremendous control over upstream and downstream value chains, garnering huge per-unit profit margins in some cases. For example, Apple's gross profit on each of its 30 GB video iPods (in 2005) was estimated to be $80 or 36% of the wholesale price. Despite changes in product sales and profiles, Apple's profit rates remained extraordinarily high at 22% for the first quarter of 2014 (Miller, 2014). In contrast, the Taiwan-owned, Chinese-based assembly firm Inventec Appliances could capture only $3.86 per unit or 1.7% of the wholesale price (Dedrick et al., 2009). While such disparities in value capture/profits are unsurprising, the differences in operating margins and return on assets reveal the disproportionate and increasing power that lead ICT firms based in the US, Europe, and Japan hold over East Asian component manufacturers. Specifically, even though the bulk of the production of iPods occurs in East Asia, manufacturing firms in Japan, Korea, and Taiwan (the main producers of iPod components) only capture about 16.9% of the iPod's value in contrast to US-based suppliers (namely Apple) who capture 44.6%. The remainder of the value (38.5%) goes to firms that distribute and sell iPods to consumers – markets generally controlled by large-scale retailers (including Apple) based in North America, Europe, and Japan (Linden et al., 2009). The often highly profitable nature of info-capital corporations mean they are able to fund not only extensive advertising and corporate social responsibility campaigns, but also other "outreach" efforts. For example, Microsoft funded the transition to open access by the journal *Information Technologies and International Development*, which is a key information-diffusion node for the global ICT4D community (Russill, 2008).[8]

Russill (2008) further traced the development of the ICT4D discourse through events and processes such as the United Nations ICT Task Force (2000–2005) and the World Summit of the Information Society. At their summit in Okinawa, Japan, on July 23rd, 2000, the leaders of the Group of 8 (G8) industrialized countries announced their faith in ICTs as a means to enable citizens to express themselves freely, economies to grow, and countries to better provide for the welfare of their citizens. The digital divide was to be at least narrowed, if not eliminated, and a Digital Opportunities Task Force (Dot Force) was to seek ways to provide "digital opportunities" to all (Digital Opportunities Task (DOT) Force, 2001; Alden, 2003; Molina, 2003). The potential of ICT was considered so high that the Dot Force asserted that "the basic right of access to knowledge and information is a prerequisite for modern human development" (May 2008, p. 82; see also DOT Force, 2001). The end result of these efforts was the creation of the G8 (Okinawa) Charter for the Global Information Society, which provides the basic vision for global telecommunication liberalization.

The general tenor of this discourse – that ICTs are inherently liberating, empowering, and progressive technologies – has remained largely intact since the Okinawa Charter, and there is a continued belief that information-communication driven forms of "leapfrog" development are possible in Africa.[9] Echoing controversial opinions of the former French President Sarkozy that the (Hegelian) challenge for Africans was to "enter into history" (McGreal, 2007), European Union officials have recently characterized new ICTs as "time portals" (Graham, 2011). Thus ICTs were/are seen to be fundamentally transformative, emancipatory, and deterministic technologies: a means to finally impose modernity on Africa and elsewhere in the "developing" world. This imposition of a particular (ideological) vision of modernity allows for the (material) opening up of markets for exports of hardware, software and cultural products (Ayonka, 2010). Moreover, because new ICTs can be integrated into almost every aspect of development assistance, such as health, education and agriculture, they have taken on an almost Messianic-like status within parts of the development policy and practice community. Whereas under colonialism, subject normalization was to be achieved through Christianity and commerce, now it is to be achieved through information and commerce, both for transnational corporations and local farmers and fisher folk. Entrainment in market relations is to dilute the importance of "primordialist" identities (i.e., traditions, ethnic, localized), which are seen as largely non-instrumental and self-limiting. New ICTs then become enrolled in a project of creating market subjects, normalizing (global) citizens, and facilitating a (Durkheimian) shift from mechanical to organic forms of social solidarity.

On the one hand the Okinawa Charter specifically addressed the digital divide, recognizing that there were significant inequalities in the "digital world", while on the other it expressed the belief that, if only done right, ICTs could deliver manifold benefits. ICTs could be an apolitical "magic bullet" for the problems of the developing world. However, Couldry (2004) argued that the prominence given to the "digital divide" in the 2000s arose initially from attempts by industrialized nations to open up telecommunications markets globally, rather than being primarily an effort to reduce global poverty. This is linked to "low geopolitics" (Agnew, 2012) or geo-economics, with the United States Department of Commerce claiming that "America's destiny is linked to our information infrastructure", which would help American firms "compete and win in the global economy" (quoted in Birdsall, 1996). Since the Okinawa Charter was promulgated, following advice from the World Bank, IMF, and International Telecommunication Union (ITU), most African countries, with varying degrees of enthusiasm, liberalized their telecoms markets. By way of example, this resulted in the replacement of the former public monopoly by a virtual private monopoly in Senegal where France Telecom held a 64% market share (Chéneau-Loquay, 2009). Often these companies generate substantial profits in the context of weak regulatory regimes, with Safaricom in East Africa recording almost a billion dollars of profit in 2008, for example (Chéneau-Loquay, 2009).

Safaricom's signature product is the M-Pesa mobile money platform, which is often touted as an example of how Africa has "leapfrogged" more developed regions. However, there are a number of points which should be remembered when discussing this popular service. Firstly, Safaricom is largely owned by the UK-based company Vodafone, which is the world's largest telecommunications company (Muwanguzi and Musambira, 2009), thus replicating patterns of economic extraversion. Secondly, the ability to transfer money does not result in economic transformation, but is rather an example of broader financialization in the global economy and of development.[10] In other words, it creates access to transactional forms of financial services but does not, in and of itself, enhance the ability of client individuals or firms to accumulate capital. Thirdly, the popularity of the service in Kenya results from the extent of uneven development in that country and the migrant labor system which was instituted under colonialism, with families often left behind in rural areas (International Labour Organization [ILO], 2008). M-Kesho is a new service that has been introduced to allow customers to access loans and insurance, in addition to savings. While this may encourage a broader culture of savings, it can also denude rural areas of capital which is channelled to more profitable ventures in cities more connected to the globalized economy, as has been the case in other countries such as Zambia (de Luna Martinez, 2007), exacerbating uneven development. Furthermore, according to one small to medium-sized enterprise in Tanzania, "transactive or fully integrated web-based e-commerce ... won't work here because we are already doing e-commerce using M-Pesa" (quoted in Kabanda, 2011: 7). Consequently, services like M-Pesa may impede the emergence of a more developed "digital economy".

The point here is not to be excessively pessimistic about initiatives like M-Pesa, but instead to demonstrate that the discourse of the "digital divide" has a political economy undergirding it, even if objective facts can be brought to bear in its support. The narrative of a borderless world created by ICTs, allowing for a free flow of information and opportunities around the world, implies a diffusion of economic development through market access and other channels. This could be justified on the basis that large parts of the so-called "global village" remained unconnected. Around the time of the Okinawa Summit, most of Africa was practically a blank spot on the internet map. Of the 192,544 internet host computers on the continent in July 1999, 172,179 were located in South Africa, the regional economic powerhouse (ITU, 1999). This left approximately 20,000 internet host computers, or 0.04% of the world's total, for the rest of Africa. In fact, there were more internet hosts in New York than in all of Africa at that time, including South Africa. Growth in internet use in Africa has increased significantly since this time, and this, when coupled to recent economic success stories in the region, has further empowered the underlying discourse regarding how overcoming the digital divide will enable Africa to become more fully integrated and empowered within the global economy.

Although such essentialisms are powerful ideological tropes, the true story behind the "digital divide" as development challenge/opportunity is far less promising than the ICT4D community often assumes. While information technologies are often presented as levelling artefacts, they also contribute to global class stratification through their concentrated ownership structure, research and development clusters and other effects. In terms of their usage, as Unwin (2009) noted, ICTs can make important differences to the lives of poor people but they can also be used to enable the rich to maintain their positions of privilege. Indeed, the World Bank and academic researchers have found that telecommunications rollout has historically increased inequality and only benefitted the wealthy (Forestier et al., 2002). More recent research found only a weak association between ICT usage and per capita income (Kottemann and Boyer-Wright, 2009), yet they are widely touted as technologies that will reduce poverty. That said, ICTs are "levelling" technologies in the sense that they contribute to the further development and deepening of global consciousness (Burawoy, 2000) or awareness of contemporary events, processes, and the fact that we

share one planet. Whether such a shared consciousness coincides with a levelling of material differences and economic opportunities is another
question altogether, and a key focus of the chapters to follow.

Governance and ICT4D

It is important to remember that the global ICT4D movement is not
homogenous. It meets annually at the ICT4D and other conferences and
contains both critical and "mainstream" voices, even if there is sometimes a
common tendency to fetishize the technology as enabling empowerment or
promoting domination. Moreover, and again despite the heterogeneous
array of actors in the community, there is a consistent gaze or frame
regarding how ICTs can and will be complicit in the (re)governance of
economic activities in regions like Africa. But which actors are empowered
in this ICT4D discourse, and along what axes?

Some ICT4D writers are well aware of the self-serving hype promoted by
information technology companies (Unwin, 2009). As markets are saturated in many rich countries, the Global South presents an enticing market
opportunity for ICT (info)capital. This is reflected in growing interest in
and greater focus on selling to the "bottom of the pyramid" (BOP) (Prahalad
and Hart, 2002; Hart and Christensen, 2002; Prahalad, 2004; Hart, 2005).
BOP approaches could be seen as another example of capital's spatial fix
(Harvey, 1999) to problems of over-accumulation, of which colonialism
was another iteration. According to Osumare (2012), given the (oligopolistic) nature of competition amongst telephone service providers, it is
necessary that dominant players like Vodafone compete in the whole range
of markets available to them in developing countries, from the poorest to
the wealthiest.

One example of the commercial interest of the BOP strategy is evinced
by a deal ("Facebook Zero") which allows mobile phone users in 45
African countries to access Facebook even if they do not have credit on
their smartphones (Wasserman, 2011). As Facebook is paid for in time
(advertising), this will further consumerize populations in the affected
countries. As noted earlier, this is not to deny the potential of ICTs for
poverty alleviation, enjoyment or empowerment. However, diffusion does
not equate to economic transformation or political empowerment as problems of exclusion may arise from pre-existing institutional configurations
and hierarchies (Bratton, 2013), and from "the knowledge economy where
know-how replaces land and capital as the basic building blocks of growth"
(Qureshi, 2007: 312).

According to Harvey (2013), technology is natural processes harnessed
to human ends. However, these human ends may not be just narrowly
instrumental, such as enabling communication through mobile telephony,

or making of profit, but may also serve psychological functions for the instigator of the ICT4D intervention, in addition to being forms of governance, thereby reproducing or deepening extant power relations. As Barnett (2011: 12) argues, "any act of intervention, no matter how well intended, is also an act of control... it is still a form of governance and governance always includes power".

In much of the literature on ICT4D, one of the main propounded benefits of the use of these technologies is meant to be the empowerment they generate for small-scale producers through disintermediation. Exploitative "middlemen" are meant to be bypassed and more value captured by direct producers (Jensen, 2007). ICTs are thus seen to be tools to allow for the reconfiguration of the governance and shortening of value chains. Using a Foucauldian lens, they could then be seen to facilitate forms of counter-conduct to dominant social relations, operative at the local or regional scale. However, on the supply side these technologies are provided by global corporations, so their usage strengthens these social forces, to the (some-times) detriment of local capital, however exploitative. Thus in terms of value flows there is a potential "double movement", downwards to direct producers and upwards to global corporations, arising from ICT diffusion and usage.

Furthermore, and in contrast to what is often assumed, the fact that ICTs are often absorbed into unchanged business practices in formal sector enterprises may create inefficiency (Wade, 2002), another source of the "productivity paradox" (Brynjolfsson, 1993), in addition to the well-known effects of people using social media during working hours, for example. Thus the development, production and diffusion of new ICTs and associated systems result in restructuring of different types amongst different fractions of capital, such as information and communication TNCs (ICTNCs) or fish traders, while also often being used to monitor workers (Bain and Taylor, 2000). Transnational (info)capital benefits, while other fractions may be disempowered or the benefits may not be immediately apparent. Whereas Marx (1887 [1967]) saw the concentration and central-ization of capital taking place within economic sectors, informationalization allows this process to take place transnationally and indirectly across sectors. As such, and as we detail later on, new ICTs may be implicated in other forms of uneven accumulation, economic extraversion, and market concentration.

ICTs then impact on the governance of economic processes, although not always in the way that is commonly thought. They are also increasingly thought to have impacts on political governance. For example, mobile phones are thought to be capable of reducing political corruption (Bailard, 2009), uplifting "failed states" (Rotberg and Aker, 2013), enabling democ-racy (Bratton, 2013), and contributing to progressive revolutions like the "Arab Spring", although Gregory (2013) notes the way in which the use of new ICTs interacted dialectically with particular places in this movement.

Others are more sceptical, asking whether ICT4D is "merely an extension of academic and political imperialism" rather than a tool through which more emancipatory forms of democratization might be achieved (Raiti, 2007: 4). For Bratton (2013), ICTs are at best "neutral tools" that can both enhance citizen awareness and engagement, and help to foment intolerance, violence, and distrust in society.

Given that democratizing potentialities may conflict with vested political interests, it is perhaps not surprising to note that authoritarian regimes in Africa, particularly since the start of the new century inaugurated by the Arab Spring, are paying close attention to ICTs and closing down or restricting the digital public sphere. The Ethiopian government recently sentenced a blogger to 18 years in prison, and using Skype in that country is punishable by a jail term of up to 15 years. Likewise, in Mozambique during the recent food riots, mobile phone companies seem to have allowed the government to block all text message signals (Wasserman, 2011). Thus the usage of ICTs is informed by and embedded in existing social and political relations, despite their purported multifold benefits. This again suggests the imperative of analysing them as objects of ideology that cannot be unlinked or separated from the sociopolitical processes that frame their deployment.

ICTs as objects of ideology

The diffusion of new ICTs is supported by ideology as they are represented as enabling individual empowerment and cumulative (inter)national interconnection, which when combined together constitute twin axes of neoliberalization. Some go so far as to argue that there is an international ideology of information technology that combines "free-market economies, neo-conservative politics, and technological determinism" (Birdsall, 1996). Ya'u (2004: 20–21) further claimed that ICTs have prompted a new age of imperialism in Africa:

> This new imperialism is characterised by the attempted creation of knowledge dependence in the newly re-colonised countries. It is a "soft" type that does not involve physical occupation of countries, and whose paths are mediated by the vast networks of ICTs. It is signposted by a control mechanism exerted through the WTO [World Trade Organization], which acts on behalf of western powers and their transnational corporations. It is supported by an array of means of ideological internalization that control the flow of news, entertainment and literature, as well as cultural space as a whole.

This "imperial" power is expressed through the dominance of English on the internet (55% of web pages) (W3Techs, 2013), the hegemonic standard of (Western) knowledge, and transnational capital's ability to instantaneously move capital and (profit-generating) information around the world.

As Castells (2003: 77) argued, the "networked society" has and is imposing a particular form of production that shapes social relationships globally, despite the fact that ICTs are commonly represented as tools of personal empowerment.

ICTs have also been complicit in the wider and deeper penetration of neoliberalism into the Global South, manifest principally in intensified forms of market-based competition and financialization. According to Dean (2012), the proliferation of information facilitated by new ICTs has been depoliticizing, although there are also counter-examples such as the "Facebook Revolutions" of the Arab Spring. As such, ICTs arguably have enabled the development and maturation of capitalist contradictions such as "free" initiatives like Facebook Zero. Another example relates to the financialization of the global economy and the most recent global economic crisis: an outcome of the misrepresentation of use values as many-layered exchange values in financial derivatives, whose creation and trading have been facilitated by ICTs (Knox-Hayes, 2013). This is not to say that these technologies may not be used for transgressive purposes, but they are also used by existing power holders and embedded in extant networks of power (Wasserman, 2011).

Žižek (1989) described objects of ideology as ones onto which are projected properties serving psychological functions for subjects. As Wilson (2014: 312) further notes:

> … [a] sublime object is a common material object which acquires a peculiar fascination for the subject, due not to some inherent essence, but to its symbolic location as an object that both obscures and embodies the void of the Real.

Considered in this manner, mobile phones, computers, and the internet are implicitly viewed by many in the ICT4D community as sublime objects of ideology. Whereas Western involvement in Africa, from slavery through colonialism and neoliberalism, resulted in deplorable dehumanization, ICTs can be represented as bringing development and modernity and serving the psychological function of expiating previous Western "sins". Sublime objects are then ones that have profound symbolic and overloaded meaning for the subjects who observe, and in the case of ICTs, also use them.

Roy (2010) traced the discourse around the "liberation" of Third World women through microfinance. She (2010: 72) noted that in one World Bank microfinance report, a picture of a peasant woman using both an abacus and a calculator presents her as "a fetish, a magical object" that has transcended primitivism to embrace modern, calculative technologies. Similar imagery is often used by mobile phone companies showing Maasai warriors in traditional garb using cell phones, for example, but in this instance it is arguably the mobile that is the magical object which serves as the sign of modernity (e.g., see Figure 1.1). A central argument of this book is that such fetishizations and objectifications within the ICT4D community elide many of the contradictions that have accompanied the mobile phone (and soon to be internet) revolution in Africa, particularly as they relate to their potential to transform firms, industries and economies. We identify and interrogate some of these contradictions in the chapters that follow.

Conclusion

There are different discourses surrounding ICT4D. Minority voices, such as Ya'u (2004, 2005) are highly critical of the GIE and the knowledge dependence which it has fostered in Africa. Others are much more positive and celebratory, focussing on the prospects for a new age of informational-ized, liberalized, and distributional capitalism. In part, the differences arise because the technologies themselves have different uses and consequently different ideologies associated with them by different actors; that is, they are objects of ideologies for users, development practitioners, scholars, govern-ments and others. The fact that these different ideologies about the use, exchange, symbolic and cultural values that are projected on to ICTs is a large part of what gives them their power. Their multiple meanings, uses, ends and effects – their adaptability/mutability – promote their adoption, even if their rationalities for different actors are divergent or even contradic-tory. These contradictions and ideologies become attached to and in some sense embedded in the technologies and contribute to their mystique. However, they are objects of agency for different social actors, with no necessary essential (teleological) impact, outside of the fact that they are produced in global production networks by transnational corporations, and with definite developmental impacts in particular places.

While an extensive literature has examined the ways in which new ICTs can or might contribute to poverty reduction, these works often ignore the ways in which these technologies are embedded in a broader political economy structured by power. As Castells (2011) describes, ICTs, the global information economy, and the network society are produced, embedded and diffused through powerful actor-networks, even as less powerful actors derive a variety of forms of utility from the use of these artefacts and their entrainment in the global space of flows. This book attempts to strip away the mystique and demystify these technologies, and informationalized capitalism more generally, to examine their concrete impacts on economic development in Africa. In particular, while much of the literature on ICT and its impacts has focussed on ICT4D projects, we seek to examine the informationalization of production and service provision as a (new?) round of immanent development, and to interrogate this empirically through detailed case studies of small, medium, and micro-scale enterprises (SMMEs). Before doing that, however, it is worth taking the time to theorize the channels through which ICTs influence economic structures, and consequently poverty, in more detail. We turn to that in the following chapter.

Notes

1 At a broader global scale the sometimes troubling nature of the global informationalized economy is evidenced by recent scandals concerning illicit government surveillance of social media through the US government's PRISM program, electronic waste (e-waste), or worker suicides in the factories in China that produce Apple products (Schmidt, 2006; Chan and Pun, 2010).

2 We use the term "e-business" throughout the remainder of the book to signal both electronic (e-) and mobile (m-) forms of business activities.

3 Ironically, when Castells met with the South African president in the late 1990s he told him that unless the country dramatically promoted ICT it would be "delinked" from the global economy (Alden, 2003).

4 For example, Ty et al. (2012) examined how new ICTs may be used in climate change adaptation, through participatory geographic information system mapping of soil erosion.

5 Productivity software refers to that dedicated to accomplishing a specific task, such as word processing, spreadsheets, database management, or graphing.

6 Examples of such tax structures include the so-called "double Irish" and "Dutch sandwich" ones which allow profits to be channeled to tax havens. In order to attract economic activity, the Irish government has also negotiated lower corporation taxes for Apple Corporation. Google Ireland paid an effective tax rate of 0.14% on sales of €47 billion over seven years (Burke, 2012).

7 For example, Huawei produces the best-selling phone in Kenya (Jidema, 2011).

8 Perhaps ironically, Bill Gates has argued that there are other more pressing priorities than ICTs, such as clean water, for people living in poverty (Wade, 2002) and this has been reflected in the funding priorities of the Bill and Melinda Gates Foundation.

9 Leapfrogging refers to the idea that new, modern technologies might enable developing countries to skip past the more problematic "stages" or periods of the development process (e.g., environmentally destructive or socially exploitative). It assumes a singular pathway (Rostow's stages of growth) for "development" and is often applied in highly (technologically) deterministic ways.

10 M-Pesa was started partly with seed funding from the UK's Department for International Development (DfID).

Chapter Two
ICTs and Economic Development in Africa: Theorizing Channels, Assessing Impacts

While it was once described as a "black hole" of informational capitalism (Castells, 1998), Africa now has over 700 million mobile phone subscriptions, second only to Asia (GSMA, 2011), and the fastest growing mobile phone penetration rate in the world. Africa also has the fastest growth in internet penetration, although this is reflective of a low base as only 16% of people use the internet there – half the level of Asia and the Pacific (ITU, 2013). Recently it was noted that the region had fewer broadband subscribers than Australia; a country of 21 million people (Smith, 2009). In the short run, it is clear that the use of mobile phones for voice and text communication by Africans will outweigh the impacts of other (new) ICTs such as computers and the internet. However, as prices for smartphones have fallen, some predictions suggest that almost 70% of mobile phones in Africa will be internet enabled by 2014 (Labrooy, 2013). As Figure 2.1 highlights, this rapid growth in smartphone use is partly enabled by reductions in the cost of internet access as a result of new fibre-optic cables connecting the continent to other regions.

Assuming these statistics continue their exponential rise, and that Africa's recent growth resurgence persists, many in the mainstream development and ICT4D communities believe that the region might be on the verge of a radical restructuring of its role and power in the global information(alized)

Africa's Information Revolution: Technical Regimes and Production Networks in South Africa and Tanzania, First Edition. James T. Murphy and Pádraig Carmody.
© 2015 John Wiley & Sons, Ltd. Published 2015 by John Wiley & Sons, Ltd.

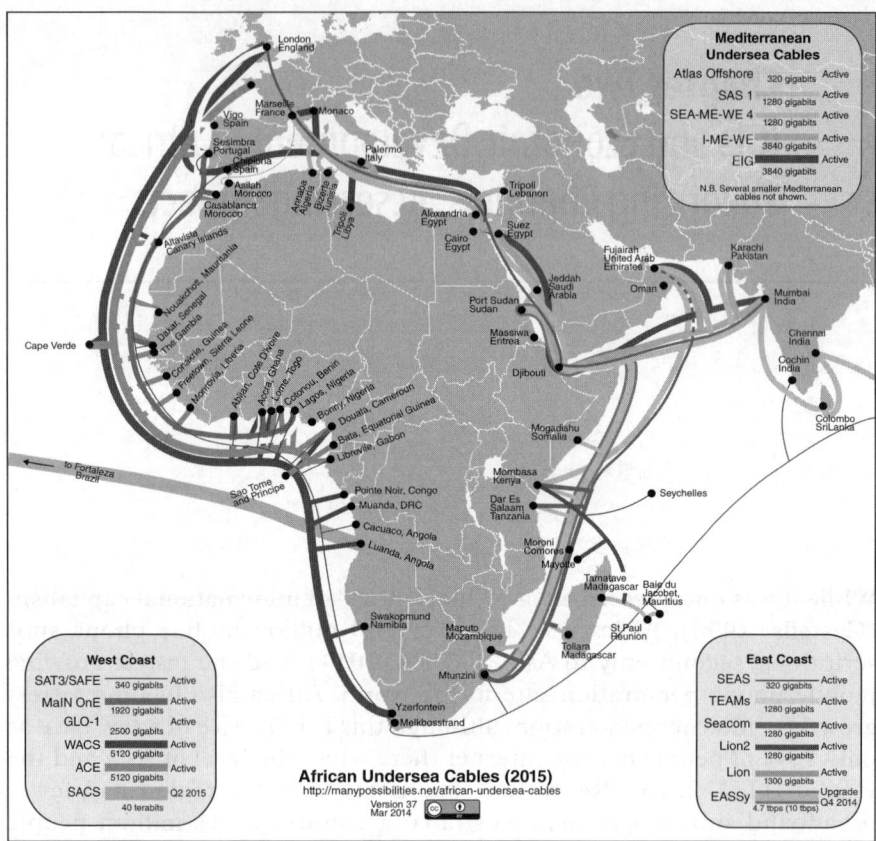

Figure 2.1   Undersea cables connecting to Africa, projected and in use by 2015. Map courtesy of Steve Song, http://manypossibilities.net/african-undersea-cables/.

economy (GIE). Okpaku (2006: 153) argues that the benefits are being observed in a wide range of institutional and socioeconomic areas:

> [ICTs have] facilitated the delivery of services such as education, health, better governance (on the part of both leadership and governed), enterprise and business development... [and have contributed] to socioeconomic well-being (especially poverty reduction), political stability and self-actualization.

From this perspective, the development challenge is to further expand and deepen ICT capabilities in Africa such that larger-order transformation becomes a reality.

While such promises of transformation and restructuring may be a welcome contrast to the often negative discourse on Africa's development prospects, the empirical evidence is rather thin to support such optimistic projections. Our project interrogates claims of transformation in a deeper and more geographically sensitive manner. The following chapters present our conceptual approach and empirics regarding the role of ICTs in Africa's economic development. This chapter examines the literature that addresses the direct and indirect causal channels between new ICTs and economic structures in Africa, in order to assess how these technologies may reduce, but also contribute to, poverty, exploitation, and underdevelopment on the continent.

ICTs and (Imminent) Economic Development

A review of the ICT4D literature as it pertains to Africa reveals generally positive assessments of both the diffusion of mobile phones and their contributions to economic development and livelihood security. Given their wide-scale diffusion, more claims are made about the impacts of mobile phones in Africa, in particular, with the well-known development economist Jeffrey Sachs arguing that "mobile phones are the single most transformative technology for development" (quoted in Etzo and Collender, 2010: 661). Mobile phones are thought to help promote democracy through delivery of voter education (Aker *et al.*, 2011) and reductions in political corruption (Bailard, 2009). Beyond their potential impacts on governance, Smith *et al.* (2011) and others argue that the benefits of mobile phones and other ICTs might be more significant in contexts where resource constraints are greater, such as in impoverished and rural communities.

The potential impacts of the internet are viewed in a similar manner, and supported by some of the same literature, despite the relatively low levels of penetration into Africa to date. As Kenny (2000) argued years ago, the promise of the internet is often seen in its ability to help isolated rural people through the provision of low-cost communications that can create access to non-local and global sources of information regarding prices and external markets. Oyelaran-Oyeyinka and Lal's (2006) cross-country study of internet diffusion in Africa sought to quantify such claims, finding that GDP per capita levels are correlated significantly and positively with the level of internet use. While such statistics are hardly definitive, there is a widespread consensus that the internet can significantly reduce the transaction and opportunity costs of sustaining livelihoods and doing business in increasingly globalized African economies. At a larger scale, some have also linked ICT uptake, particularly internet access through smart phones or computers, to changes in economic structures as they generate new kinds of employment (e.g., voice-over-internet protocol [VOIP] call-center work), support innovation systems (e.g., for the development of smartphone applications), and create new opportunities for firms to tap into global markets (Benner, 2006; Broadman, 2007; Graham and Mann, 2013).

In terms of economic and industrial development, recent studies highlight the positive implications of expanded ICT uptake and use. Within SMMEs, researchers have shown that ICTs, and mobile phones in particular, are having positive impacts through improvements in information-search processes (e.g., for market prices) (Oyelaran-Oyeyinka and Lal, 2006), expanded market reach (Chowdhury, 2006), increased market integration (Muto and Yamano, 2009), "amplified" socioeconomic relations (Donner, 2006), more productive workforces (Research ICT Africa, 2006), and reduced transaction costs (Molony, 2007). Information technologies are rapidly becoming ubiquitous tools for African firms, and many ICT4D proponents believe that these can lead to wider-scale economic transformations, provided the right kinds of ICT capabilities emerge within firms, industries, and markets. For some, such skills will help to shift African economies away from dependence on primary sector, extractive industries and into new, informationalized service-based economies.

> Building ICT skills across society (both in high-end and basic skills) will help prepare labour markets for a gradual evolution to a service-oriented, ICT-enabled *Information Society*. The development of ICT and ICT-enabled industries is an integral part of a transition to the *New Economy* through export of services over the internet, and through the growth in trade in services. (World Bank, 2010: 11)

With respect to their geographical implications, the uptake of both mobile phones and the internet can shape significantly the spatial organization and coordination of economic activities. Specifically, some production and employment activities can be relocated away from cities and create what Crang *et al.* (2006) called "more complex and geographically distanced" forms of economic organization within urban areas. Moreover, ICTs can help to spatially and temporally fragment activities/projects such that they are realised in smaller and less-concentrated blocks of time, through less continuous forms of sequencing or synchronization, and in a wider diversity of places (Couclelis, 2009; Schwanen and Kwan, 2008; Schwanen *et al.*, 2008). ICTs can also transform mobilities by enabling information access and communication activities to "inhabit" travel experiences and by facilitating the multitasking of traditionally distinct activities (e.g., when commuters use phones and computers for personal communication) (Schwanen and Kwan, 2008; Schwanen *et al.*, 2008; Line *et al.*, 2011).

Perhaps most significant in the discussions of the impact of ICTs is the issue of information asymmetry: what mainstream economists consider one of the main barriers to economic development.[1] Information asymmetry is a circumstance where buyers and sellers have different levels of information causing markets to malfunction and "fail" (Stiglitz and Weiss,

1981). In "efficient" markets, price equalization, or the "law of one price", is meant to prevail – geography is meant not to matter as information articulation between places eliminates asymmetry. Asymmetric information about prices is, of course, a critical cause of market failure, and quantitative analyses of mobile phone use in developing regions have shown how phones can significantly reduce price dispersion, or differences in prices, across subnational markets (Jensen, 2007; Abraham, 2007; Aker, 2010; Aker and Mbiti, 2010). Mobile phones and other ICTs can reduce asymmetries, particularly in commodity markets (e.g., fish, grains) characterized by many small producers and prospective buyers. For example, Aker (2010) found that the introduction of mobile phones reduced price dispersion by 10–16% for grain markets in Niger, a reflection of changing power dynamics between producers and buyers/consumers, although she did not conceptualize the outcome in these terms.[2] Reduction of price dispersion is a result of the ability of mobile phones and the internet to facilitate disintermediation, the cutting out of intermediaries ("middlemen") which can enable producers and manufacturers to gain a higher price for their products and create more efficient forms of arbitrage between different spatial markets (Subramanian and Overby, 2013).

All told, the channels through which ICTs can enhance livelihoods and economic activities are manifold, particularly with respect to their ability to help reduce transaction costs and enhance the efficiency and productivity of individuated economic and livelihood practices. Whether such outcomes are being realized beyond the somewhat inconsistent cases highlighted above is unclear, as is the significance and depth of these outcomes as measured by income changes, innovation, and industrial upgrading. Beyond these imminent contributions, it is also unclear what new ICTs mean for transformations to the structural contexts and power relations governing the development of industrial sectors, regional economies, and the interactions between Africa(ns) and the global economy. Moreover, the contributions of ICTs to poverty reductions and other forms of social upgrading remain elusive to empirical analysis and definitive cause–effect relationships. In the next section we highlight possible channels through which ICTs might contribute to immanent transformations and assess the evidence in support of, or against, such changes.

ICTs, Poverty, and Immanent Development

Beyond their implications for economic and industrial development in Africa, many argue that ICTs can contribute in significant ways to the alleviation of poverty, inequality, and to the provisioning of social services to underserved communities (i.e., to social upgrading). For some, these outcomes can be achieved through imminent changes to the capabilities of individuals and households. For others, ICTs hold the promise to fundamentally restructure the institutions, markets, and production systems that govern livelihood strategies and reproduce inequality and poverty. To understand, in particular, the possible links between the uptake and use of ICTs and such immanent transformations, it is important first to specify how we understand poverty and its possible reduction as a development outcome.

There are three main schools of thought on poverty – the palliative, the capability, and the structural conception – and each has a specific implication in the context of the ICT4D discourse. The palliative conception of poverty takes poverty as a given and asks how it can be alleviated or reduced through investment in health and education, for example (Sachs, 2005). Development interventions can have major impacts on poverty reduction (e.g., Teklehaimanot *et al.*, 2007), and there is no necessary contradiction between palliative and more structural approaches to poverty reduction (Green, 2008) – indeed, both are needed and synergize together. However, much of the literature on the poverty-reducing potential of new ICTs fits narrowly within palliation through the delivery of m/e-health or education – "m/e-development". For example, according to Aker and Mbiti (2010: 208):

> ...as telecommunication markets mature, mobile phones in Africa are evolving from simple communication tools into service delivery platforms. This has shifted the development paradigm surrounding mobile phones from one that simply reduces communication and coordination costs to one that could transform lives through innovative applications and services.

The problem here is that this perspective neglects how it is that poverty is produced and reproduced through (immanent) structural forces and embedded power relations that determine in large part the livelihood possibilities of people in regions like Africa.

A second approach to poverty seeks to understand what social structures inhibit or enhance capability development and fulfilment (e.g., Sen, 1999). If this approach is adopted, the question might be how it is that new ICTs enhance capabilities (what people are capable of doing), and how they may change social structures which influence or inhibit these (e.g., see Kleine, 2013). At first the capability approach appears to overcome the structural limitations on the palliative conception of poverty, with Sen explicitly stating that his framework draws on both Karl Marx and Adam Smith (Clark, 2006). However, the unit of analysis of the capability approach is the individual, and consequently it still suffers from an ethical, if not an ontological, individualism (Hill, 2007). This tends to obscure issues of class power, and, in particular, the class nature of the state (Jessop, 2002) that is charged with implementing policies to overcome poverty. Consequently an approach which interrogates how ICTs change socioeconomic structures enables a more accurate assessment of their poverty reduction and economic developmental potential, and impacts.

The structural conception of poverty examines explicitly and intensively how it is that poverty is produced (Lines, 2008). It seeks to interrogate the socioeconomic structures that produce inequality, marginalization and exclusion rather than assuming these as extant, and then "mopped up" through remedial public action. In this structural conceptualization, then, it is power inequality that produces poverty, as power "holders" are able to shape socioeconomic structures to their benefit, to the detriment of others (Oyen, 2004). Taking this perspective, the question in relation to ICTs is how do they reconfigure the nature of power relationships, broadly conceived, including differences in economic productivity? In this conceptualization the elimination of poverty depends upon economic transformation and thus relates directly to our interest in immanent forms of development.

Interestingly, the palliative and structural conceptualizations share some implicit similarities in their emphasis on flows (spatial articulation) between places as primary drivers of (under)development. In the palliative conception of poverty, which fits with the neoliberal project, interconnection and flow promotion will accelerate development. Market liberalization and unrestricted trade, when coupled with increased aid flows, will "end poverty". The justification for aid is that while the "free market" is beneficial, aid can accelerate growth and development beyond what would occur under a completely *laissez faire* regime, particularly when countries are caught in poverty and other "traps" (Collier, 2007; Sachs, 2008). In contrast, structuralists argue for the need to regulate international flows in order to allow for infant industry protection, endogenous technological development, and a reduction of surplus extraction through overseas debt repayments for, example (Noman *et al.*, 2012). These two approaches are characterized heuristically below:

Palliative conception of international articulation = international interconnection (trade, investment, aid, new ICTs, neoliberal ideas) enables the contagious diffusion of development, which then results in poverty reduction and its eventual elimination.

Structuralist conception of international articulation = international interconnection (trade, investment, aid, new ICTs, neoliberal ideas) creates the adverse and differential incorporation of peripheral regions into the world economy, which thus results in the (re)production of poverty.

There are extensive literatures on the impacts of trade, aid and other elements of international interconnection. In conventional economic theory, for example, all legitimate trade is meant to be developmentally beneficial under free market conditions where the theory of comparative advantage can operate. However, more recent work within the economic mainstream has cast doubt on this by incorporating economies of scale (Krugman, 1995). Others have also argued that trade will have different impacts depending on whether it is extractive, complimentary, competitive or consumptive (e.g., Carmody, 2013). An example of consumptive trade might be Zimbabwe importing luxury Mercedes cars from South Africa, which is not developmentally beneficial and results in capital leakage.

Both the palliative and structural perspectives have elements of truth to them. Some elements of the neoliberal "articulation package" (trade, foreign investment, new ICTs, and aid) can be beneficial for development. However, whether poverty reduction or reproduction results depends upon the way in which trade and the other elements of the package are structured as a result of (class and state) power relations and the path dependency of previous economic structures. Current global power relations arguably favor regressive structuralist outcomes in Africa – increasing inequality, extraversion, and the reproduction rather than reduction of poverty – where foreign investment is heavily concentrated in natural resource extraction, and the absolute number of people living in poverty continues to rise (UNCTAD, 2010). A central question for us is whether new ICTs can help to progressively reduce these power asymmetries and immanently restructure markets, industrial regimes, and GPN relations such that significant, sustained reductions in poverty and inequality levels can be achieved in the coming decades, in part through support for SMMEs.

As highlighted above, much of the ICT4D literature documents the individual development implications of mobile phone and internet use, manifest principally in the palliation of poverty, capability enhancements, and other individuated benefits such as better prices for one's products, lower-cost communications, and improvements in the ability to spatially coordinate livelihood activities. In contrast, other research demonstrates the limitations on ICTs as tools to achieve more structurally transformative or immanent development outcomes. For example, mobile phones and other ICTs may reduce price dispersion in the markets available to some fisherpeople, those whose geographic mobility enables them to strategically link mobile information access to product sales (Jensen, 2007), but this is not necessarily the case in other sectors where actors higher up the value chain have more geographic mobility and other sources of power to capture value (e.g., Graham, 2010). In the case of farmers, the circumstances are often similar – new ICTs hold out the possibility of dramatic reductions in information search costs (de Silva and Ratnadiwakara, 2009), but farmers may remain locked into forward contracts in order to access inputs, thus effectively preventing them from being able to take advantage of higher spot prices (Molony, 2008).

A lack of accounting for, or appreciation of, the market-institutional context reflects the geographic "shallowness" of many ICT4D studies which focus on spatial diffusion and connection (the "transfer and diffusion" approach), rather than on the impacts of ICTs on socioeconomic structures or vice versa (the "social embeddedness" approach) (Avergerou, 2010). In doing so, many ICT4D studies neglect or undervalue how the use of mobile phones and the internet is structured by institutions, hierarchies, histories, and other forms of spatial articulation, where one place is not just passively connected to another, but influences the development of the other through trade and other flows, creating translocalities (Appadurai, 1996).

Another limitation on many ICT4D studies is that implicit in them is an almost axiomatic belief that ICTs will enable improved socioeconomic connections or articulations and thereby reduce poverty. While there is some research (see Mascarenhas, 2010) that shows how greater mobile phone access and use in households can be associated with reductions in poverty levels, the broad-based evidence is inconsistent and/or plagued by mediating factors such as the relationship between income level and ICT affordability. Moreover, as Fuchs and Horak (2008: 101) note, ICTs may also be implicated in the production of poverty:

> … unequal patterns of material access, usage capabilities, benefits, and participation concerning ICTs are also due to the asymmetric distribution of economic (money, property), political (power, social relationships), and cultural capital (skills).

Consequently ICT accessibility and impacts cannot be analysed in isolation from pre-existing socioeconomic structures and power relations, which they may serve to reinforce but also subvert.[3] In fact, ICTs then serve as tools of domination, exploitation, cooperation and popular empowerment, given that their use is embedded in existing social relations, resource extraction and conflict, while also helping to reconfigure and reconstitute them (Carmody, 2010). Other new ICTs, such as satellite TV, are also associated with the rise of "an intolerant, and at times, aggressive, religious broadcasting culture" in Africa which may foment conflict (Hackett, 2012: 164). Power fundamentally structures how new ICTs are used, for progressive or regressive ends (Castells, 1999; Bratton, 2013).

Recent research on the sometimes negative impacts of mobile phone diffusion reveals more specifically the paradoxical nature of new ICTs. Diga's (2007a) Ugandan study quotes a respondent who states that "mobile phones bring poverty". In another study in rural Uganda, Diga (2007b) found that without a mobile phone many impoverished day laborers believed they could not find work since potential employers would be unable to contact them. The mobile phone was thus becoming a necessity for itinerant workers who often cannot afford to pay for the service and artefact. This is an example of what we might call "negative adoption", a situation where the costs of exclusion from social or employment networks would simply be too great not to pay the relatively high costs for mobile phone use, expenses that consequently impact other household expenditures (e.g., food, school fees). For example, Diga also found that most of the homes in her study had reduced their purchases of store-bought groceries to pay for mobile phone airtime. According to one woman, in reference to her husband, "he would rather not buy us food but he would rather put airtime on the phone because it is the phone that makes money" (quoted in Diga, 2007b: 66). Diga found that people, and often women in particular, were also willing to sacrifice consumption to invest in mobile phones for small-business development.[4] One can imagine a future scenario where a lack of email access might create similar kinds of negative adoption and even more intense budgetary constraints within such households.

There are other examples of the trade-offs created when ICTs are viewed as a basic necessity within impoverished households. As Figure 2.2 demonstrates, in Kenya mobile phone ownership is common even amongst the poorest households, thus raising important questions about the implications of ICT dependence for the most vulnerable Africans. There are instances in Africa, in the Millennium Villages for example, where people have chosen to spend money on mobile phone credit rather than school fees for their children (Puri et al., 2010). Consequently ICTs may, at times, be implicated directly in the production of poverty. In Ethiopia the poorest 75% of the population who use mobile phones spend 27% of their income on them, reflecting the relatively high costs of these artefacts and services (Gillwald and Stork, 2008: 14). The willingness of people to pay such high proportions of their income for ICTs reflects the social and economic utility that these devices provide. However, whether this utility reflects opportunity, or fears of exclusion and hence compulsion, varies. Such trade-offs also show that mobile phone use, or ICT adoption more generally, is often driven by a dialectic of "poverty push/opportunity pull". However, because market size is limited, ICT-enabled opportunities for some may create disadvantages for others, for whom poverty will increase as a result of this competition.

Adoption may then often represent part of a defensive livelihood strategy, given widespread poverty and the importance of extended family networks to survival (Rettie, 2008). In common with many other studies, one in Tanzania, which surveyed several thousand households, found that while the majority of respondents felt mobile phones had strengthened their social networks, more than half did not think mobile phones had increased their household income (Sife et al., 2010). In Botswana, 70% of calls were to friends and family and a proportion of these were focused on arranging financial remittances (Duncombe, 2006). James (2014), drawing on data gathered in 11 African countries by Research ICT Africa,

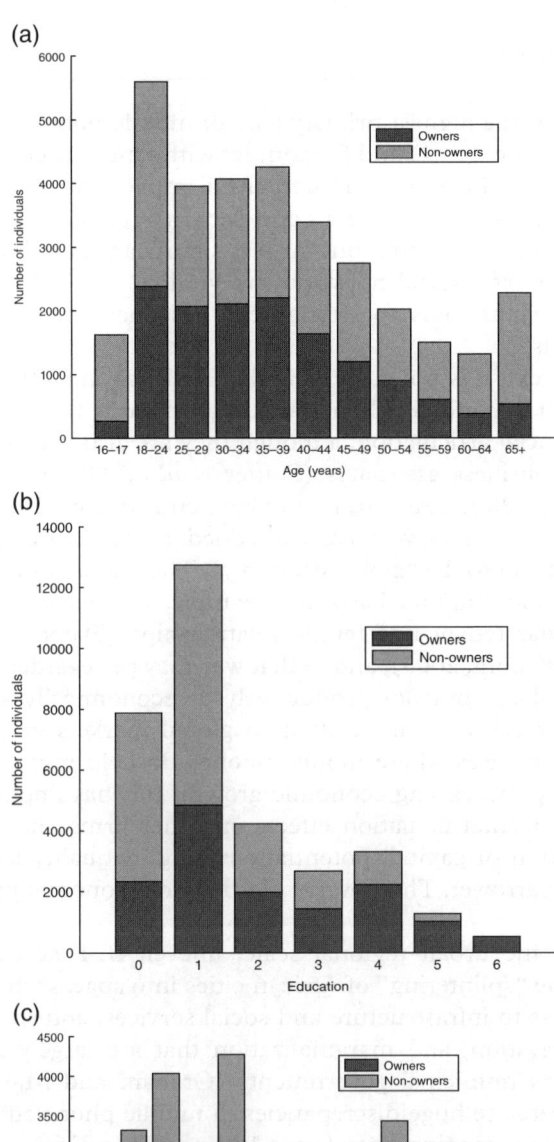

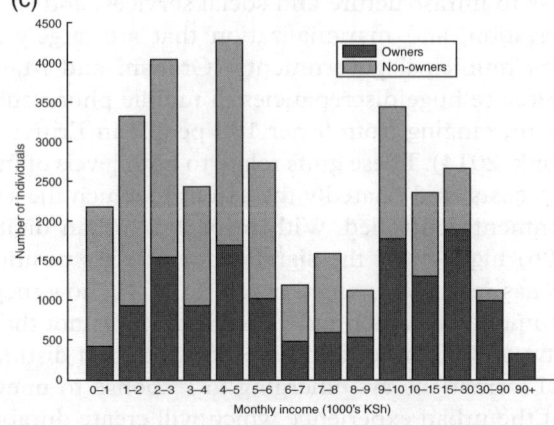

Figure 2.2 Mobile phone ownership in Kenya by age (a), education (b), and income level (c) (from Wesolowski *et al.*, 2012). Note: Education levels are as follows: 0 = none, 1 = some primary, 2 = primary completed, 3 = some secondary, 4 = secondary completed, 5 = technical training, 6 = university. Income in Kenyan Shillings at approximately 83.22 KSh to 1 USD in 2012.

reports that two of the highest priority uses of mobile phone are to check in on family (82% reporting) and for contact with family/friends (78.5%). In South Africa and Tanzania, the perceived impacts of mobile phones are overwhelmingly social, personal, and security-related, with business and employment benefits noted but far less significant in comparison. In the context of poverty, social networks are vital to survival, and mobile phones are important tools to strengthen these networks of extended family and friends.

Given this context, it is not surprising that multi-country studies across Africa have shown that mobile phones are used primarily to maintain social networks or for social articulation, although they are also used to maintain "weak links" to business associates (Souter *et al.*, 2005; Molony, 2007; Skuse and Cousins, 2007). According to Slater and Kwami (2005) mobiles are primarily used to manage local embedded reciprocities, rather than being used to connect to the "global economy". The majority of phone calls made in Ghana and Burkina Faso, for example, are related to personal issues and the maintenance of family relationships (Slater and Kwami, 2005; Hahn and Kibora, 2008), and in that way may be regarded as socially articulating or linking, but not productively or economically articulating within domestic markets or in relation to global markets or production networks.[5] Even in cases where mobile phones do help more technically efficient firms to grow, raising economic growth, this has implications for poverty through disintermediation effects on other firms and the consequent concentration of capital, potentially raising inequality and thereby making markets narrower. The poverty elasticity of economic growth may then be reduced.

Considered at the urban–regional scale, uneven ICT access and use further reflects the "splintering" of African cities into spaces where there is high-quality access to infrastructure and social services, and spaces of disconnection, deprivation, and marginalization that are largely ignored or poorly serviced by municipal governments (Graham and Marvin, 2001; Jaglin, 2008). There are huge discrepancies in mobile phone subscriptions across the continent, ranging from 5 per 100 people in Eritrea to 179 for Gabon (World Bank, 2014). These gulfs relate to both levels of income, and income inequality, costs, and relatedly the extent to which the sector is liberalized or government controlled. With respect to urban digital divides, Crang *et al.* (2006) highlighted the significance of class positionalities in determining who has regular/sustained access to ICTs, how they are used, and to what instrumental or other ends. Their point was not that there is a simple binary between ICT haves and have-nots, but that distinct cultural, social, and spatial formations are emerging in response to uneven access: fragmentations of the urban experience which will create durable inequalities as cities become increasingly "wired". Such fragmentations reflect the notion that digital inequalities may help to reproduce pre-existing social inequalities (Mwesige, 2004; Oyedemi, 2012) and that the "original" digital divide – one determined primarily by access to ICT artefacts and related infrastructure – is morphing into one based on capabilities, culture, and digitally mediated forms of socialization which will have long-term consequences for those lacking the education and income needed to plug in at an early age (van Deursen and van Dijk, 2010). Conceptualized in such terms, as James (2011) notes, the digital divide in Africa has increased in recent years, especially in the poorest countries, and this more than likely reflects the general trend toward heightened income inequalities across the continent rather than the failure of ICT4D initiatives *per se*. The wider point of this discussion is that ICTs themselves are unable to ameliorate significantly the uneven development outcomes in an age of neoliberalism, but will instead, in the absence of immanent changes to the dynamics of capitalism, be caught up in their reproduction and proliferation.

Mobile phones and other ICTs may also (re)produce poverty and negative development outcomes in other direct and indirect ways. ICTs can perpetuate technological dependence and underdevelopment, as artefacts and associated infrastructure are developed and imported from elsewhere. In a similar vein, the dependence on foreign firms for infrastructure, hardware, and financial credit can contribute to capital leakage. For example if the average cost of importing mobile phones was $15 per handset, 620 million new handsets would represent a capital loss of almost US$9 billion per handset turnover time.[6] Imports of office and telecommunication equipment for the 32 countries in Africa for which data are available was worth US$18 billion in 2009 (calculated from World Trade Organization, 2011). Shifting trade relations with Asia in particular are having mixed impacts in Africa – facilitating growth through commodity demand (Asche, 2011), while also making domestic manufacture more difficult and fostering a shift toward commercial, mainly resale and trading, activities (Gebre-Egziabher, 2007; Meagher, 2007; Lyons and Brown, 2010).

Other implications of ICTs are less direct, but no less significant when considered in relation to Africa's development and its situation in the global economy. Parts of Africa function as vital suppliers of raw materials to the ICT industry. The Democratic Republic of Congo (DRC), for example, is a primary producer of coltan, an elementary component of mobile phones (Nest, 2011; Carmody, 2012). The sourcing of coltan, necessary to make the electrical capacitors in mobile phones, is implicated in conflict in the Democratic Republic of Congo, contributing to poverty, violence, and environmental degradation (Nest and Grignon, 2006). Africa has also become an important waystation in the life cycle of ICT artefacts as a creator, recipient, and recycler of electronic waste (e-waste) generated within and outside the region (Lepawsky and McNabb, 2010). While the transformation and recycling of e-waste is creating new economic activities and supporting some livelihoods (Pejout, 2010), the significant health and environmental issues that accompany these activities are of increasing concern and they raise questions about the sustainability of ICT diffusion in the region.

The Prospects for Information(alized) Economies in Africa

Beyond their implications for poverty and (immanent) structural change, there is the question of whether the diffusion of new ICTs is enabling the emergence of information-economy industries such as those associated with ICT software, hardware, and service provisioning.[7] At present, these industries and the associated information economy, which some consider a new mode of production (Benkler, 2006), appear to be relatively weak in Africa.[8] There is very little research and development of ICT and software applications (Ya'u, 2005), with some notable exceptions such as the Otigba computer hardware cluster in Nigeria (Oyelaran-Oyeyinka, 2007) and the new i-hub in Kenya, where innovative mobile phone applications have been developed (African Brains, 2011). There have also been some very innovative applications developed such as m-Pedigree and also Simpill in South Africa, which sends a text when a patient opens their pill bottle, and reminds them if they do not (Radelet, 2010).

Outside of applications such as these, however, there is very little research and development activity in the information economy proper in Africa, such as the development of new hard- and software, where much of the value addition takes place. According to one educational institute representative in Tanzania, in reference to local companies and the government:

> They don't buy our own local software. They are just not interested – they deal with people like Oracle, Microsoft, InfoSys, SAP. So how do they expect the industry to grow? I think the reason as to why they do this is because they were used to and there is a perception that foreign is more supreme – that's the way it has always been done. (Quoted in Kabanda, 2011: 10)

The issue may be partly one of time as new technological development becomes embedded,[9] although this may also be limited by resources as Africa's most innovative economy, South Africa, has less than 20% of the number of researchers per thousand people employed as in the Organization for Economic Cooperation and Development (OECD) countries (OECD, 2009; ISO, 2009). The continent then continues to be characterized by technological "underdevelopment" (Timamy, 2007), despite substantial latent innovative potential (Muchie et al., 2003). Consequently, current modes of African incorporation into the global informational economy constitute a form of thin integration (thintegration), where Africa is imbricated in global (ICT) production networks through imports of mobile phones and other technology, with natural resources, primarily, serving as the counter-flow (Carmody, 2010).[10] We elaborate on this concept in the chapters that follow.

The telecommunications industry is arguably Africa's greatest success story with respect to the information economy, but even here we find mixed results with regard to its development implications. There are successful indigenous mobile phone companies, such as MTN (Mobile Telephone Networks) of South Africa, which employs 6000 people directly worldwide, and pays substantial tax revenue. However, according to the Nobel Prize winning economist Joseph Stiglitz (2010), companies such as this are "mining" poorer countries of their income. MTN, for example, now earns most of its profits in West Africa, rather than Southern Africa, with Nigeria being a particularly important market, despite the much lower average incomes in West Africa (MTN, 2009).

It is estimated by the World Bank that the mobile phone industry has created 3.5 million jobs in Africa, largely in low productivity and profit activities, such as selling mobile phone credit (Bhavnani et al., 2008). The marginal productivity of labor and scope for innovation and structural diversification are extremely limited in these activities. Mobile phone credit sellers represent a new hybrid (in)formal economic activity in Africa, as they work in the "unregulated" or popular economy, but are articulated to the formal economy through purchases of mobile scratch cards. Mo Ibrahim (2011) refers to people employed in this activity as "indirect employees" of his former company Celtel, although he did not have to pay payroll taxes and social insurance for them. Such circumstances effectively undermine the possibilities of a tax and accountability bargain between citizens and the state and replicate previous incentives around (poor) governance in the continent (Leonard and Strauss, 2003).[11]

The literature on the diffusion of mobile phones in Africa implicitly and sometimes explicitly characterizes these ICTs as an "inverse infrastructure": largely self-organizing and not requiring huge fixed investments, unlike roads or an electrical grid (Egyedi et al., 2009). However, the diffusion of mobile phones has been facilitated precisely by conditions of informality and state weakness in infrastructure delivery, which must be transcended for there to be more widespread development. Mobile phones, then, have contributed to the growth of the informal sector, through employment creation in selling credit, repairing phones, and so on. The informal sector is beneficial in terms of new livelihoods, but problematic in terms of its longer-term development impacts (Meagher, 1995), as it does not contribute to tax revenue, for example.

While mobile telephony may be helpful to certain small and/or microscale enterprises, the sale of airtime credit to poor populations, many of who are informally employed, could also be regarded as an example where the formal sector is extracting social surplus from the informal sector – adverse articulation, or exploitative functional dualism (Mhone, 1982), between the two "circuits" of the economy (Santos, 1979). Other potentially disadvantageous articulations are also being inscribed, as Celtel was bought out by a Kuwaiti company in 2005, replicating previous patterns of economic extraversion as rents/profits are accumulated offshore.[12] Income is then flowing up the global (social) value chain from those in the informal sector in Africa buying mobile phone credit to international stockholders, such as Sunil Mittal who now holds a majority stake in the renamed company, Bharti Airtel, and is the sixth richest person in India (Forbes, 2011).[13]

Perhaps from a developmental perspective the most important question is the indirect impacts of ICTs on other sectors of the economy, outside of the information economy proper. According to Esselaar et al. (2007: 98):

> During the hype of the dot.com bubble in 2000, there was a general perception that the provision of ICTs to SMEs…would have a transformative effect. Clearly the current view is more pragmatic. ICTs are now supported for the catalytic role that they can play within sectors of the economy.

If ICTs are to play a significant role as catalytic tools, it is imperative that they enable more productive and progressive market relationships within Africa and between Africa and the world economy. The evidence on this front is thus far unconvincing.

Plugging In, to What Ends? New ICTs and the Challenge of Global Market Integration

As was noted earlier, new ICTs are often objects of ideology, which fit into a broader repertoire of (neo)colonial imaginaries. According to Hecht (2012: 16):

> "Africa" has also been a fetish in Western imaginations…Savage and starving, inferior and infantile… "Africa" became seen as a place without "technology". Colonialism, the conquerors were convinced, would transform the continent through European science, technology and medicine.

The rapid diffusion of mobile phones, in particular, has altered this Western imaginary of Africa as a place without technology as they are thought to bring "light" (knowledge) to the "Dark Continent". However, such imaginaries do not theorize the channels through which new ICTs might impact or affect poverty through expanded global connectivity, for example.

While many of the benefits of ICTs on livelihoods and poverty reduction have been noted, the ways in which they may contribute to the reproduction of inequality have been largely ignored. According to Tim Berners-Lee, the inventor of the World Wide Web, mobile phones can be like a "drug" in the developing world (and elsewhere), as people feel they have to spend income they sometimes cannot afford to have them.[14] This is partly because they are "positional goods", showing social status, but they also make people feel included, rather than excluded, from processes of globalization (Hahn and Kibora, 2008).

The emphasis on connecting or plugging into information and communication flows as a development endpoint reveals the central, albeit often implicit assumption that the main problem is that Africa has been "bypassed" by globalization (Sachs, 2005) or that these technologies will inevitably enable economic "catch up" through technological leapfrogging (Okpaku, 2006).[15] In both cases, mobile phones and the internet are seen as potential solutions to the lack of interconnectivity, or pathways to an informationalized economy, through their ability to connect the continent to the outside world and internally.

Connection, in and of itself, in much of the mainstream literature is thought to be necessarily good, ending what former American Secretary of State Colin Powell has called "digital apartheid" (quoted in Graham, 2011: 212; see also Fuchs and Horak, 2008). The emphasis on the role that unmediated international interconnection can play in fostering market-driven (i.e., neoliberal) development outcomes has meant there is a tendency "to portray the mobile phone as an *end*, rather than a *means* to specific social improvements" (original emphases) in much of the literature (Burrell, 2010: 232). Moreover, as Park (1997: 191) noted:

> The concept of universal access carries an implicit theoretical assumption that the key to the successful realisation of [an] information society lies in the adequate provision for the widest public ... "access" to information technologies.

The form that this connection or articulation takes in relation to ICTs is meant to be through flows of information from/to internal (within Africa) and external (global) sources.

We refer to these external and internal forms of connection, heuristically, as spatial articulation (to the outside world) and social articulation (primarily within localities in Africa). However, such claims neglect how dependent, as opposed to "independent", poverty has been structurally and historically produced through colonialism and other exploitative forms of international interconnection (Carmody, 2011). As Fuchs and Horak (2008: 115) observed:

> The global digital divide is an expression of the unequal geography of global capitalism. That there is a lack of economic and technological resources in Africa is not the fault of corrupt African governments and not an effect of bad governance, market protectionism, a lack of investment conditions for Western

capital, etc., but the effect of hundreds of years of colonial and post-colonial exploitation, exclusion, and dependency of the Third World that has caused the very conditions that Africans have to face today.

In other words, it is much of Africa's type of spatial articulation with the international political economy that is implicated in its underdevelopment, rather than its lack of articulation. Such articulations have historically been characterized by extraversion and other forms of dependency between the region and core/emerging economies (Bayart, 2000; Carmody, 2010). An important question, then, is how might mobile phones and the internet, in particular, change the nature of Africa's spatial articulation with the global economy?

The ability of new ICTs to help change the nature of the relationships between African economies and the world system, and consequently the depth of poverty and exploitation on the continent, depends in part on the extent to which they result in market creation, widening and deepening. Those focusing on the personal development implications of ICT use appear to sense that there is an almost teleological inevitability to these processes, provided that technological diffusion continues at its rapid pace. However, there is no reason to think that this should be the case, and there is a need to interrogate more critically whether new ICTs might instead simply put some (overseas) firms at a competitive advantage relative to African ones, resulting in a fallacy of composition, where the growth of some companies is concomitant with the closure of others, and poverty levels remain the same or even worsen.

Partly the answer lies in the extent to which ICTs put African-based firms at a competitive advantage relative to their overseas competitors such that they become more positively and progressively integrated into global value chains and production networks. Indeed, given higher levels of development in other world regions, and consequently more conducive complementary conditions and factors of production, such as better transport infrastructure, it is likely that, if anything, new ICTs put firms elsewhere at a relative competitive advantage. Furthermore, while mobile phones, computers, and the internet can substantially reduce transaction costs (de Silva and Ratnadiwakara, 2009), "death of distance" arguments about them tend to underplay the continued importance of face-to-face communication for tacit knowledge transfers (e.g., see Bathelt and Turi, 2011). This knowledge transfer mechanism favors more developed regions, with more (business and innovation related) tacit knowledge (Amin and Cohendet, 2004). All told, much of the literature on closing the "digital divide" shares similarities with work on the "new" economic geography, which argues that Africa suffers from a "proximity gap" or "trap" as it is too far from rich countries to be able to effectively sell to them (Naude, 2009; World Bank, 2009; Wilson, 2011). However, this literature ignores the fact that it is partly the adverse (extraverted) articulation with the international system (Bush, 2007; Fuchs and Horak, 2008), rather than physical distance *per se*, that produces underdevelopment. As Heeks (2002: 7) observed, this focus on proximity belies the immanent factors that have driven Africa's marginalization in the world system:

> The notion of a digital divide has, in many ways, been unhelpful. It has given too much emphasis to the technology [and draws]... attention away from other divides and inequalities that hamper development.

Mobile phones, computers, and the internet by themselves do not have any independent causative power, as other structural factors, power relations, and capability and other constraints play a more central role.[16]

In order to understand the wider impacts of new ICTs we emphasize their potential contributions to poverty reductions, economic and industrial restructuring, and global production network (GPN) integration. An emphasis on these themes provides a means to examine whether Africa's information revolution can facilitate more progressive forms of immanent development, manifest in changes to the structures, institutions, and/or interdependencies that have traditionally locked much of the region into a particularly exploitative and regressive form of capitalism. The goal here is to think through in detail how new ICTs might impact African countries in ways that help to restructure and improve them through poverty reductions and support for informationalized economies better able to create and retain value through globalized trade and investment relationships.[17]

Conclusion

In the 1990s, the failures of neoliberal market reforms was blamed on a lack of social capital or poor governance, while the economic basis of the policies themselves were not questioned, at least by the development institutions promoting them (Carmody, 2007). More recently Africa's physical geography has been used by development institutions, such as the World Bank, to "explain" the continent's underdevelopment (Carmody, 2011). The posited solution is to reduce distance from rich parts of the world through the elimination of tariff barriers and investment in infrastructure. ICTs fit perfectly into this framing of the problem, able to speed up and enhance communications and capital flows and thus facilitate global market integration for those once "peripheral" regions. Moreover, enhancements in information access, it is argued, will reduce price distortions and enable African farmers, fisher folk, manufacturers, and service providers to modernize their production systems through the "borrowing" of best practices and ideas from elsewhere. The net result will be a "leapfrogging" scenario as African industries are transformed through productivity and efficiency gains, livelihoods are improved through individuated forms of access to markets and employment opportunities, and governments are made more accountable, responsible, and transparent through the uptake of liberal-democratic (e-government) initiatives.

This chapter reviewed the evidence in support of these optimistic claims through a focus on the various channels that might link ICT uptake to socioeconomic transformations in the region. While there is little doubt that ICT, particularly mobile phone, diffusion has been a success story, there remain highly significant limitations on these technologies as tools to help reduce poverty and reverse decades of regressively immanent articulations of Africa into the world system. With respect to livelihoods and poverty, the findings are somewhat paradoxical in that ICTs have had some palliative and capability impacts, namely through the enhancement of communications and information flows for individuals, especially within family and friend networks that are often critical for livelihoods, but they remain largely unable to alter unfavorable structural conditions, including weak political institutions, dualistic economic structures (i.e., informal/formal), and extractive international trade relationships. Moreover, mobile phone and other ICT services are increasingly viewed as "necessary" consumer goods among the poor, thus creating further strains on incomes that often lie below the poverty line. Information-economy industries – such as mobile phone providers and call centers – have emerged over the past decade, but these too are caught up in the reproduction of extraversion as control over these often lucrative enterprises remains outside the region. With respect to global integration, these channels too remain largely unexploited on a large scale by African firms, and ICTs have done little to reduce the power of foreign capital to dictate the terms and possibilities of the spatial articulations, namely GPN integrations, linking Africa to the international political economy.

With the intellectual landscape for ICT4D debates detailed, we now shift into our specific analysis of the impacts that new ICTs are, and are not, having on economic and industrial change in Africa. The goal in the chapters that follow is to take these broad perspectives, on poverty, livelihoods, informationalization, connectivity, and globalization, and translate them into a coherent and specific framework that links ICT uptake and use to industrial and economic development. We start by elaborating on our conceptual framework and then proceed to our case studies in South Africa and Tanzania.

Notes

1   Development is a notoriously contested term. We adopt Seers' (1963) classic definition. He argued that when unemployment, poverty and inequality are decreasing, development is taking place. There are also many definitions of poverty, but for our purposes it is broadly defined as living below a minimal socially acceptable standard of living.

2   However, Aker (2010) notes that reductions in information asymmetries are a necessary, but not sufficient condition for welfare improvements in the context of other market failures, such as poor transportation infrastructure.

3   According to Fuchs (2010: 194), "informational capitalism is an antagonistic system that by transnationalisation and informatisation produces at the same time new potentials of class domination and class struggle." According to him it may create a cybertariate, such as those engaged in microwork in Kenya, for example.

4   In Niger, the 12th most expensive African country wherein to purchase airtime, a one-minute call off-network to the US is $0.38 per minute, representing approximately 40% of an average household's daily income (Aker and Mbiti, 2010: 227). Research amongst university students in Tanzania found they were spending five times more on mobile phone connectivity than they were on food (Kleine and Unwin, 2009).

5   Another way to conceptualize this would be as strengthening "bonding" social capital (Putnam, 2000).

6   Some handsets are of course more expensive and others cheaper than this, and a small number of mobile phones are also assembled in Africa.

7   There are many examples of the informationalized economy in Africa: for example, the Song-Taaba Yalgré women's organization in Burkina Faso exports shea butter and sells over 90% of its output over the internet. Its members use mobile phones and global positioning systems to "track locations, surface area, numbers of trees, and other field data to harvest shea butter [sic] more effectively" (Radelet, 2010: 109).

8   For example, Benkler (2006: 4) argues that "as the material barriers that ultimately drove much of our information environment to be funneled through the proprietary, market-based strategies is removed these basic nonmarket, non-proprietary, motivations and organizational forms should in principle become even more important to the information production system."

9   We are grateful to Chris Benner for this point.

10 One academic estimates that up to 20% of sub-Saharan Africa's phones pass through one housing complex in Hong Kong called Chungking Mansions (Shadbolt, 2009), many of which are retrofitted (fakes).

11 This is somewhat ironic given the Mo Ibrahim Foundation's focus on governance.

12 Although Ibrahim was living in London at the time and had sourced capital for Celtel from international private equity groups such as Emerging Capital Partners. The renamed company was later bought by an Indian company.

13 In a sense the change in ownership may make little developmental difference as both Ibrahim and Mittal are members of the transnational capitalist class, who are based, for the most part, outside of Africa (Sklair, 2001).

14 Keynote address at ICTD Conference, Royal Holloway, University of London, December 14, 2010.

15 Leapfrogging is "bypassing stages in capacity building or investment through which countries were previously required to pass during the process of economic development" (Steinmueller, 2001: 194). A good example of this kind of perspective is evident in the views of the Rwandan President Paul Kagame. Kagame recently argued that because his country missed the

agricultural and industrial revolutions it must take advantage of the information one by effectively leapfrogging over these prior development eras (Asche and Fleischer, 2011).

16 As Richard Heeks (2002b: 2) has observed: "What do ICTs do? They handle information in digital format. That's all."

17 By value we signal the profit-making capabilities of SMMEs as determined by the price of their goods and services in global markets.

Chapter Three
ICTs, Industrial Change, and Globalization in Africa: A Conceptual Framework

As Peter Dicken (2004: 6, italics in original) observed, globalization is not a causal force but rather an uneven and indeterminate "syndrome of *material processes and outcomes*" in need of more substantive and grounded theoretical and empirical investigations. For most scholars, globalization implies increased, extended, accelerated, and/or intensified sociospatial relations, flows of resources, information, and people, and interconnections between places at a worldwide scale that have significant economic, political, social, and cultural consequences (Held *et al.*, 1999; Friedman, 2000; Taylor and Flint, 2000; Bhagwati, 2004; Stiglitz, 2006; Sparke 2013). Beyond this there is much debate about the contemporary drivers of globalization and its implications for the welfare of developing regions, such as sub-Saharan Africa. For some (e.g., Friedman, 2000; Bhagwati, 2004; World Bank, 2009), globalization is a "natural" and rational outcome of new information, communications, and logistics technologies, deeper geopolitical ties between countries, and market-oriented institutions and policies that open up economies to trade and foreign direct investment (FDI). Viewed in this manner, globalization is creating the conditions for poor countries to converge developmentally with wealthier ones, provided they exploit their comparative trade advantages, reduce barriers to transnational flows of resources, and facilitate the creation of urbanization and localization (specialization) economies (World Bank, 2009).

Africa's Information Revolution: Technical Regimes and Production Networks in South Africa and Tanzania, First Edition. James T. Murphy and Pádraig Carmody.
© 2015 John Wiley & Sons, Ltd. Published 2015 by John Wiley & Sons, Ltd.

Others are much more sceptical, viewing this process as one aimed at furthering accumulation in core economies through a wider and deeper penetration of exploitative forms of capitalist social relations into the Global South (Hardt and Negri, 2000; Peet, 2007; Cox, 2008). Such critiques highlight the ways in which core economies and multilateral institutions (e.g., the US Department of Treasury, IMF, and World Trade Organization) have constructed market-friendly institutions and rules, such as patent protection laws, that largely benefit transnational corporations based primarily in core economies. This, in turn, will reproduce dynamics of extraversion and sustain a disempowered and impoverished periphery for many years to come.[1]

These meta-theories raise important questions about globalization's meanings, contradictions, and implications, but the empirical evidence in support of them is sometimes lacking, particularly with regard to the role that geography and context-specific factors play in shaping the globalization–development nexus (Dicken, 2004). This is because grand theories tend to be totalizing, while globalization is a highly complex, multifaceted entanglement of processes, materials, people, technologies, and places, producing spatially differentiated outcomes. While broad theoretical approaches can help to spur debates and discussions about globalization as an idea or meta-phenomenon, there is also a need for multiscalar and multidimensional frameworks that can enable us to link both "global" processes to locally contingent development outcomes, and localized socioeconomic and political processes to changes at a global scale (Bridge, 2002; Dicken, 2004). The grounding and scaling-out of globalization as a concept is essential if we are to understand more critically and deeply the nature of the contemporary world system and how it shapes the dynamics and distribution of development within and between places.

Such considerations are central to our conceptualization of what sub-Saharan Africa's "Information Revolution" might mean for the region's economies and industries. As highlighted earlier, many view ICT diffusion as an unambiguously positive and transformational success story in terms of development, particularly when coupled with the region's recent "growth renaissance" (e.g., Radelet, 2010). But beyond the often superficial assertions about Africa's rising power, prestige and position in the global economy, there is little concrete, systematic evidence regarding what this "revolution" means for issues such as inequality, industrial development, economic restructuring, poverty, and political reform in the region. We aim to address some of these concerns through an analysis that determines whether ICTs are complicit in a significant repositioning of Africa within the world economy in ways that can more evenly distribute development, spur innovation, and enable the region's firms and industries to become more profitably and progressively integrated into international markets through scale-expansion, economies of scope, and industrial and social upgrading.

The Limitations on Existing ICT4D Conceptual Frameworks

As chapters 1 and 2 demonstrate, there is no shortage of studies examining or conceptualizing the role that new ICTs can play in support of development and/or economic globalization. However, there are significant conceptual limitations to existing frameworks, particularly when one considers the immanent (i.e., structural, potentially transformational) development implications that may accompany ICT diffusion and uptake. Alternative perspectives are badly needed, given that much of the ICT4D literature focuses almost exclusively on the imminent development (intentional, individuated, short-term) implications of ICTs for economic agents (i.e., firms, entrepreneurs), manifest principally in ICT-enabled capability changes, performance enhancements, commercial activities, transaction-cost reductions, labor-saving practices, and/or information-driven innovations within firms. Such considerations are, of course, important but a focus exclusively on these ignores or underrepresents the structural context that shapes the agencies of economic actors and determines significantly the degree to which industrial transformation might be possible in an age of information-driven and facilitated forms of capitalism.

In broadly considering the ICT4D literature, two conceptual limitations are worth highlighting here. The first relates to the apparent teleological implications of ICT diffusion: what some see as an inevitable outcome of agency-intensive perspectives regarding what ICTs can "do" with respect to economic and industrial development challenges. Through the extensive and intensive adoption of ICTs it is assumed that information- and communication-driven forms of (progressive) development will ensue across a wide range of societal actors as economies and countries experience a (Rostowian) "take-off" en route to a new age of information-driven capitalism. In short, there is an assumed informational–developmental ladder that Africans must climb, and as they do so socioeconomic convergence with the North can become a possibility as opportunities emerge from within the global economy. The challenge for development practitioners and policy-makers, thus posed, lies in creating enabling and supportive environments for the *adoption* of new ICTs by firms and individuals. All told, conceptual emphasis is placed on the supply of ICTs and infrastructure, and their diffusion through individuated income, access, and behavioral changes, rather than on the wider structural concerns (e.g., non-ICT infrastructure, political and socioeconomic institutions) that will inevitably shape the extent, quality, and implications of ICT use.

The second, and related, limitation on most ICT4D conceptualizations is that they tend to conflate access to (often globalized) information and knowledge flows as being akin to, or on a par with, improved access to flows of material resources and capital. While ICTs can surely improve business peoples' access to codified forms of information that are available through voice and text communication and web-page browsing, this, in and of itself, does not translate inevitably into better access to markets, input supply chains, GPNs, and/or financial capital. In fact, it is clear to most that conventional forms of structural power – such as market or firm size, wealth, class, gender, ethnicity, geopolitical influence, and other political positionalities – continue to play a critical role in governing access to capital flows despite the purported flattening of the global economy. Furthermore, while some forms of knowledge may be increasingly public goods under informationalized capitalism, the ability to deploy them for productive purposes is heavily circumscribed by a restrictive international intellectual property regime, in contrast to that when Europe underwent industrialization, for example (Chang, 2008). By ignoring or underestimating the role that these structural considerations play in spatially splintering the impacts of ICT diffusion and shaping the ability of African firms to exploit ICTs for developmental ends, most ICT4D conceptualizations tell us far too little about the role that socioeconomic, political, and structural context plays in influencing the transformative potential of new forms of communication and information management.

In short, and despite the often region-specific empirics associated with ICT4D studies (e.g., in Africa), the conceptual frameworks that link ICT adoption with development outcomes such as growth, distribution, poverty reduction, and global market integration generally lack a geographic sensitivity. In doing so there is a failure to adequately acknowledge or account for the power of place or context-specific contingencies, institutions and power relations in structuring the agencies that are at the center of most ICT4D studies. Moreover, there is a near absence of considerations regarding the role that multiscalar and translocal relationships play in shaping the implications of ICT uptake for development: particularly whether ICTs are contributing to the progressive development and globalization of firms and industries in (parts of) the Global South.

Through an integrated perspective on this question – one that accounts for both agencies and capabilities within firms, and the structural and relational contexts in which they operate or compete against (sociotechnical regimes and global production networks) – we are able to provide a more comprehensive perspective on ICTs and their link to development processes in Africa. Our conceptual approach emphasizes the geographies of ICT adoption and is explicitly multiscalar such that we can evaluate whether, and how meaningfully, new ICTs are influencing performance in SMMEs, enabling structural changes in industries and markets, and enhancing the quality and significance of the Africa's ties to the world economy. Following Graham (1998, 176), we adopt a political economic perspective which:

> ...underlines that the development of the new telecommunications infrastructures is not some value-neutral, technologically pure process, but an

asymmetric social struggle to gain and maintain social power, the power to control space and social processes over distance.

The result is a multiscalar conceptual approach that contrasts significantly with (most) ICT4D studies that focus primarily on the contributions of ICTs to intra-firm development through changes in market access and transaction-cost reductions (e.g., Overa, 2006; Donner, 2006; Muto and Yamano, 2009). As detailed below, our framework is derived from the integration of a range of concepts that allow us to capture both imminent and immanent forms of development and their relationships to the diffusion of new ICTs in Africa. In our analysis, imminent forms of development are addressed through a focus on the contributions of ICTs to firm- or SMME-specific capabilities and performance. The immanent development implications of ICTs are analysed in two ways. We first draw on sociotechnical transition theory to assess the implications of ICT diffusion for the regimes governing or guiding the evolution of industries in our African case studies. We then apply concepts from global production network (GPN) research to examine whether or not ICTs are influencing the ways in which African firms and industries engage with, or become integrated into, global markets for goods and services.

Conceptualizing the Contribution of ICTs to Imminent Development

As highlighted earlier, imminent forms of development are manifest in the intentional and direct actions and impacts that can accompany initiatives or programs aimed at socioeconomic change, innovation, poverty alleviation, and in our conceptualization, firm strategies aimed at growth and development. With respect to ICT4D projects, such outcomes are understood generally to be evident in improvements to, or enhancements of, the information management and communication capabilities of firms, households, and individuals. This being the case, a key question for our study is whether such transformations are visible as ICTs become widely distributed within African economies and ICT-related capabilities improve through intensified experiences with these technologies. Simply stated, is improved access to information and communications linked directly to purposive changes in the capabilities, performance, and productivity of African SMMEs?

To examine these imminent development implications, we conceptualize ICTs as tools that can enhance intra-firm capabilities such that firms are able to obtain better prices, access and expand markets, improve business networks, and create efficiencies with regard to logistics, labor management, banking, and transaction costs. Capabilities are conceptualized as firm-specific resources, and here we draw on resource-based views (RBV) of enterprise development from organization and management studies. RBV scholars strive to understand how enterprises gain sustained competitive advantages through the development of strategic resources that enable them to exploit new market opportunities and neutralize threats from the competition (Barney, 1991; Barney et al., 2001; Carmeli and Tishler, 2004). Resources are manifest in human capital (technical and managerial skills), physical capital (infrastructure), and the organizational capital or less tangible assets associated with such activities as knowledge management, customer relations, planning, and production coordination (Barney, 1991; Bharadwaj, 2000; Galbreath, 2005; Acedo et al., 2006). ICTs are often thought to play a key role in transforming a firm's resources, and much of the RBV literature has focused on whether and how these technologies contribute to performance and competitiveness (Mata et al., 1995; Santhanam and Hartono, 2003; Tippins and Sohi, 2003; Barua et al., 2004). ICTs can help to generate value for firms through productivity increases, cost savings, and improved supplier relationships (Melville et al., 2004). For this to occur, firms need to create or obtain ICT-specific technological and human resources and to develop complementary organizational resources (e.g., workplace practices, structures) that can translate into improved business processes.

While some studies indicate that there is a positive and significant correlation between a firm's performance and its investments in ICT infrastructure and managerial and technical skills (e.g., Bharadwaj, 2000; Rai et al., 2006), important caveats remain. The impact of ICT-related resources is context-dependent (i.e., industry, region, country-specific) and ICT investments alone are insufficient to improve firm performance substantially, as it is critical to develop the managerial skills necessary to integrate these strategically into the practices of supply-chain management, information management, and customer relations (Mata et al., 1995; Brynjolfsson and Hitt, 2000; Subramani, 2004; Melville et al., 2004; Krishnan et al., 2007). In other words, if ICT-related capabilities are to improve performance and productivity, they will do so primarily by helping to enhance the value of other resources in the firm (Tippins and Sohi, 2003). For example, customer-relation capabilities can be improved by developing databases that monitor consumer preferences or which provide real-time tracking of product shipments (Brynjolfsson and Hitt, 2000).

Following Gregor et al. (2006), we categorize ICT-related resources and benefits in four ways. Informational resources contribute to decision-making processes in the firm by improving access to information, supporting strategic planning processes, and/or enhancing information formats (e.g., through the creation of commensurable or comparable forms of data) in ways that can improve the ease of communication within the firm. Transactional resources are those that relate directly to the costs and benefits accrued from accounting and operational processes such as those associated with supply-chain management, worker productivity, and finance. Strategic resources contribute to the longer-term competiveness of the firm and include: product and service improvements; increased responsiveness to market changes; and/or a closer/deeper alignment between the firm's ICT development priorities and its business strategy (e.g., ICT use and adoption is consciously and explicitly linked to the strategic priorities in the firm). Finally, and perhaps most significantly, ICTs can provide transformational benefits through the upgrading of employee skills, by contributing to the development of new business plans, models, and/or organizational structures, and by expanding organizational capabilities through new processes and functionalities.

In order to assess whether these benefits are being realised in African SMMEs, we focus on four broad indicators of ICT capabilities, uses, and resources: (a) the extent and intensity of ICT infrastructure and use; (b) ICT-related levels of human capital or technical expertise; (c) how, and with what intensity, ICTs are used for communication and networking activities (e.g., for customer relations, labor management, and inter-firm communications); and (d) if, how, and to what effect ICTs are used to codify, store, track, and disseminate information that is consequently used for strategic purposes such as marketing, product development, and process improvements. With these dimensions assessed, we then determine whether, and to what degree, there is an association between lower or higher levels of SMME performance and the extent and depth of ICT capabilities. Our goal is to determine qualitatively whether ICTs are playing a key role in innovation, upgrading, and business development, and to assess the degree to which the wider contexts of industrial change in Africa are rewarding of or synergize with ICT-driven forms of upgrading. More broadly, we seek to provide the basis for a comparison between the imminent and immanent development implications of ICT diffusion.

Conceptualizing ICTs and Immanent Development: Sociotechnical Regimes and GPNs

Beyond assessing their imminent development implications, our analysis addresses whether and to what degree ICTs are contributing to larger-order transformations of African industries and economies. We view such (potentially positive or negative) transformations as forms of immanent development manifest in the evolution of socioeconomic and industrial systems in Africa, as the region becomes more extensively and intensively integrated into the world economy through ties to global production networks. To conceptualize these systemic changes, and the implications of ICTs in relation to them, we draw on concepts from two sets of literature.

The first, sociotechnical transitions theory, is applied to understand whether and how ICTs are complicit in significant transformations to the industrial regimes governing production, marketing, innovation, and service provisioning activities in Africa. The second literature, on global production networks (GPNs) and their relationships to regional development processes, is used to assess whether ICTs are enabling new couplings to emerge between African firms, industries and the global economy, and/or whether the region's ties to the world system remain largely unchanged in structural terms. Taken together, these conceptual approaches enable us to develop a critical understanding of how ICTs are becoming integrated into the institutions, GPNs, and markets governing the evolution of African industries.

Industries as Sociotechnical Regimes

A central question framing our analysis is whether or not ICTs are contributing to changes in the structural and relational contexts wherein firms and industries operate, compete, and innovate. By context we mean the sociospatial relations (e.g., for inputs, distribution, information, sales, etc.) and place-specific institutions, conventions, norms, rules, hierarchies, and everyday practices that constitute markets and production systems. These contextual features make up what evolutionary economists call a selection environment that shapes the cognitive, innovative, and organizational capabilities that are embedded in industries and technological regimes (Nelson and Winter, 1982; Lambooy, 2002). To operationalize the selection environment concept, we draw on sociotechnical transition theory, a diverse field that has emerged out of evolutionary economics (e.g., Nelson and Winter, 1982; Freeman, 1991), science and technology studies (e.g., Dosi, 1982; Bijker et al., 1987), system-innovation research (e.g., Nelson, 1993; Freeman, 1995) and institutionalist approaches to industrial and technological change (e.g., Florida and Kenney, 1994; Juma, 2001). The sociotechnical approach provides a highly useful framework through which one can understand and account for the interrelationships between technologies and socioeconomic systems and structures.

Sociotechnical systems thinking emerged in large part as a response to concerns over the productivist bias of innovation systems research: works that primarily emphasize how innovations are developed within sectors or industries (Geels, 2004a). Missing from such accounts was a more substantive and inclusive understanding of heterogeneous and multiscalar factors or elements (e.g., technology, culture, global markets, state policies) that guide and govern the evolution of sociotechnical systems, such as those associated with energy, water, food, transportation, and factory production. Sociotechnical transitions theory takes a functionalist approach wherein systems are constituted by networks of interdependent actors (firms, individuals, states, consumers, households, workers) who serve particular intended and unintended roles in reproducing, transforming, or destabilizing them (Geels and Schot, 2007). Sociotechnical systems are viewed as fulfilling essential societal functions (e.g., housing, food, energy, and manufacturing) and they themselves are constituted by three central "subfunctions" – the production of goods or services, the diffusion or distribution of goods or services, and the actual use of technologies and/or the artefacts produced by the system (Geels, 2004a). These subfunctions provide a means to account for the processes through which innovations or technical variations emerge, user or consumer environments that "select" for particular innovations, and the role that societal groups and other actors play in shaping both innovation and consumption processes.

Beyond describing the actors, artefacts, innovations, and institutional features associated with particular sociotechnical systems, this approach seeks to understand how and why systems change through transformations to the linkages between or configurations of the heterogeneous elements constituting them (Geels, 2004b). Rather than assume that there is a singular/primary actor or element driving such changes (e.g., the state, the market), sociotechnical transitions scholars strive to account for the distributed factors – culture, values, ideological shifts, technologies, firms, entrepreneurs, state agents, politicians, finance capital, regulation, policy – influencing the direction, pace, and scale of continuously evolving systems. The challenge in this regard is to provide evidence and explanations that do not *a priori* favor the "usual suspects" (e.g., corporations, finance capital, consumerism, neoliberal ideologies) commonly identified as key drivers of the development of sociotechnical systems (Smith *et al.*, 2009). This is not to suggest that such actors or factors are less relevant, but that transition scholars strive to understand the interconnections, interdependencies, and contingencies between the diverse range of social, economic, and political actors complicit in the shift from one (temporarily) stabilized sociotechnical system to another.

As Markard *et al.* (2012) demonstrate, there is no single or unified approach to the study of sociotechnical transitions, and the field can be divided into four distinct but overlapping realms: transition management (TM), strategic niche management (SNM), the multilevel perspective (MLP), and technological innovation systems (TIS). While each has strengths, weaknesses, and particular applications, our interests lie in the intersections between individual firms, industrial organization, market structure and dynamics, non-market factors (e.g., culture, politics), and non-local or global issues and forces. Given our needs, the multilevel perspective (MLP) provides the most powerful and inherently geographic/ spatial heuristic for imagining the interplay between these factors in the context of ICT diffusion in Africa. In more specific terms, the MLP approach offers a conceptual framework wherein to situate ICT diffusion such that we can assess the role that they play in a (possible) structural reordering of African industries: one that (ideally) empowers SMMEs and enables manufacturing and service sectors in the region to upgrade their activities and create and capture greater value locally.

As Figure 3.1 shows, the MLP is an attempt to understand the interrelationships that enable sociotechnical regimes to evolve or shift from one form of governance to another. The framework's multiple levels are conceptualized as niches (the smallest, bottom-up level of experimentation and innovation), regimes (the meso-governance level of established rules, norms, hierarchies, and practices), and landscapes (the "external" environment, macro-level). These are not scales *per se* but heuristic levels through which one can analyse the distributed elements that shape the evolution of sociotechnical systems, many of which are simultaneously situated in

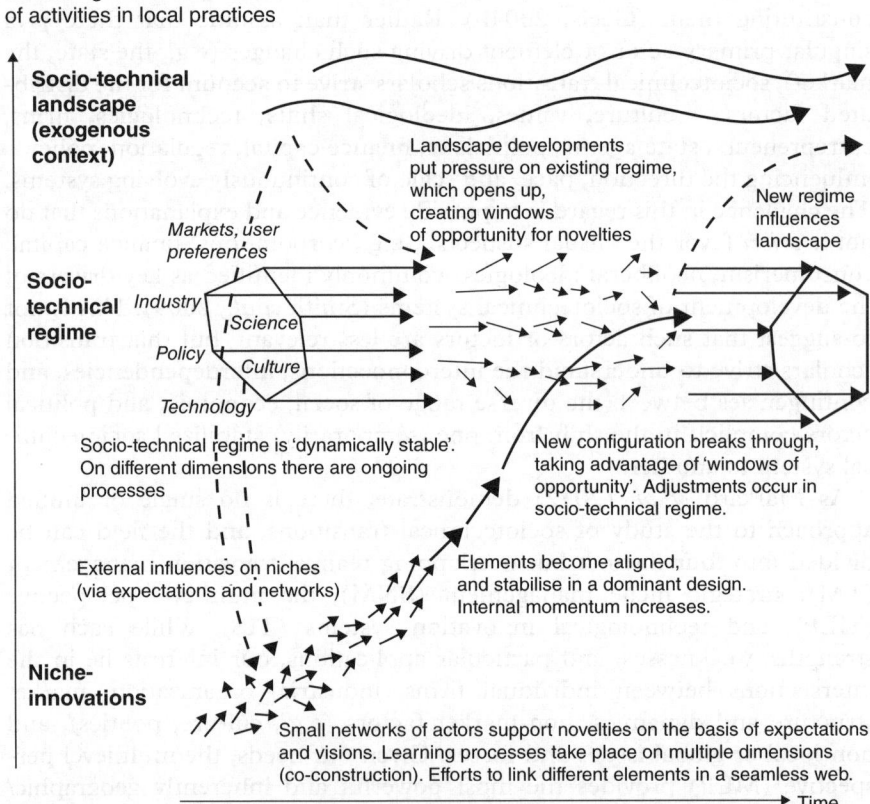

Figure 3.1   The multilevel perspective on sociotechnical regime transitions (from Geels, 2002). Reprinted with permission from Elsevier.

different places, scales, and/or sociotechnical systems. Moreover, each level is constituted by particular relational–territorial configurations: networks of linked elements that are grounded and bounded within nation-states, cities, regions, and other locations. For example, transition researchers might focus on the transportation system associated with a particular city- region – a sociotechnical system shaped significantly by urban-scale policies, cultural factors, markets, and histories, in addition to those emanating from the national or global scale. In contrast, many MLP studies focus on the nation-state scale, with niches often situated within particular city-regions and landscape factors manifest in global and national influences.

Technological niches emerge in response to firm or cluster-specific innovations that can help to transform industry-wide practices, if the sociotechnical regime and landscape conditions are able to absorb and integrate them into standard practice (Kemp *et al.*, 1998; Geels and Schot, 2007). Alternatively, niches may destabilize extant regimes and/or land-scapes, thus enabling more discontinuous or radical transformations to occur. Sociotechnical landscapes are the external contexts for niches and regimes and are constituted by "a set of heterogeneous, slow-changing factors such as cultural and normative values, broad political coalitions [and] long-term economic developments" (Geels, 2004b: 34). Following on from seminal ideas in evolutionary economics (Nelson and Winter, 1982; Freeman, 1991, 1994; Boschma and Lambooy, 1999; Lambooy, 2002), sociotechnical landscapes and regimes constitute the "selection environments" that dictate or guide the ways in which ICTs are absorbed into industries and economies. These selection environments are made up of market, institutional, and spatial elements that shape the supply and demand for ICTs, the society-wide norms, rules, and values influencing ICT use, and the geographic distribution of the capabilities, markets, institutions, and infrastructure that determine the "wheres" and "why theres" of ICT use (Freeman, 1994; Lambooy, 2002). As Freeman (1994) observed, selection environments play a key role in transforming the heterogeneity and uncertainty of innovation into a seemingly orderly process of technological change.

While niches and landscapes are important influences on sociotechnical transitions, regimes are the central drivers of system-wide changes. Regimes can be associated with large-scale sociotechnical systems (e.g., energy, water, transportation) or, in our case, in relation to particular industrial sectors. Regimes are dynamically stable arrangements that govern sociotechnical systems and create path-dependencies and momentum with regard to their evolution (Kemp *et al.*, 1998; Geels, 2004b; Kemp and Rotmans, 2005; Geels and Schot, 2007; Smith *et al.*, 2010). The regime "imposes a logic" for sociotechnical change and its reconfiguration is concomitant with system-wide sociotechnical transitions (Markard *et al.*, 2012: 957). In operationalizing the regime concept, some (e.g., Geels, 2004b; Geels and Schot, 2007) view them as primarily *rule structures* (cognitive, normative, and regulative) that are stabilized through Giddensian-like structuration processes (Giddens, 1984). For others (e.g., Shove, 2004), emphasis is placed upon examining the everyday *practices* – of consumption, production, innovation, regulation, and so on – that reproduce and stabilize regimes in more or less sustainable ways. Still others view regimes as complex, heterogeneous, and multiscalar *assemblages* of structures, technologies, knowledges, identities, logics, meanings, consumer preferences, policies, power relations, formal regulations, and cultural traits (Smith *et al.*, 2009; Smith and Raven, 2012).

While we recognize the importance of assemblage-oriented perspectives on socio technical regimes, our operationalization of the regime concept focuses on the evolution of industry-specific governance structures (e.g., production networks, markets) and the everyday practices of firms, consumers, and other relevant actors.[2] This approach provides coherent analytical objects – "rules", hierarchies, institutional features, and practices as constitutive elements of regimes – that we can then link to ICT uptake within SMMEs and influences from niches and landscape-level factors. Our focus is on industrial regimes that are territorialized within city-regions in Africa – namely Dar es Salaam, Zanzibar, Durban, and Cape Town – albeit with significant (relational) influences coming from landscape features such as global production networks and national regulations, and from niches within local markets such as those associated with product and service differentiation strategies.

Through the analysis of the governance structures and practices constituting our case-study industrial regimes, the goal is to determine both the direction and meaning of ongoing transitions and the role that ICTs are playing in these processes. Sociotechnical regime transitions occur when the networks, rules, and institutions governing an industrial regime are restructured and restabilized in a manner that (ideally) increases the competitiveness and sustainability of the industry (Berkhout *et al.*, 2004; Geels and Kemp, 2006; Geels and Schot, 2007). Transitions are influenced from "below", by niches, and from "above" by the sociotechnical landscape associated with a particular system (Kemp *et al.*, 1998; Kemp and Rotmans, 2005; Geels and Schot, 2007). Not all transitions are good from a development perspective, as in some cases (e.g., the centralization of industrial control through oligopoly or monopoly) a new regime may be less sustainable, unsupportive of innovation, and unable to reduce economic inequality through better jobs, income redistribution, and/or support of SMMEs. The direction of transitions is determined in large part by power struggles and inequalities between actors in the sociotechnical system (e.g., government officials, lead firms, labor unions, civil society organizations, etc.) that give some voices much greater say in enabling and/or legitimating the introduction of (new) rules, practices, and/or logics (Meadowcroft, 2005; Smith *et al.*, 2005; Lawhon and Murphy, 2012).

In applying this approach, we contextualize ICT diffusion within industrial regimes and in relation to the market niches and sociotechnical landscapes (i.e., selection environments) that guide their evolution. Through this analysis we are able to assess the contribution of ICTs to structural change (i.e., industrial regime transition) and to determine whether ongoing transformations are supportive of African SMMEs and the livelihood strategies of those individuals owning or working within these enterprises. Moreover, applying the MLP with a focus on regime dynamics provides a means to link city-region specific transitions to global processes such as those associated with "couplings" between GPN and regional development processes, as we describe below. In a broader sense, sociotechnical transition theory provides a grounded conceptual framework for determining whether changes to information and communication practices can, at present, be considered part of a significant and progressive transformation to the immanent structural forces governing African industries.

Global Production Networks (GPNs) and Couplings to Industrial Regimes

The analysis of the contribution of ICTs to SMME capabilities and constraints and industry-specific sociotechnical regimes enables us to understand the localized and national-scale economic implications of sub-Saharan Africa's ICT revolution. Missing from these perspectives, however, is a clearer sense of what ICTs actually mean for the region's ties to the world economy. To assess these circumstances, we draw on ideas from the rich literature on global commodity chains (GCCs), global value chains (GVCs), and global production networks (GPNs) to conceptualize the factors driving the development of linkages to international markets, the possible implications of these ties for enterprise and industrial development, and the role that new ICTs are (or might be) playing in shaping the region's ties to the broader world system. While recognizing the importance of GCC and GVC contributions, we focus particularly on the GPN framework, given that our goal is to link global market integration to local development outcomes. GVC and GCC approaches are able to inform our understandings of these relationships, but they remain focused primarily on industrial organization and imminent development within firms (e.g., upgrading), rather than linking changes in the structure and functioning of value chains to local and region-specific development processes.

The GPN framework was developed in part to respond to the GCC and GVC literature's (e.g., Gereffi, 1999; Humphrey and Schmitz, 2000; Kaplinsky *et al.*, 2003; Gereffi *et al.*, 2005) emphasis on the largely linear structure of supply chains linking consumers in the core to producers in the Global South, and to provide a means to more effectively ground these relationships analytically within particular places. In doing so, the GPN approach shifts the focus from the global structure of industry value chains to the ways in which GPNs are articulated within particular regions and territories (Henderson *et al.*, 2002; Coe *et al.*, 2004; Murphy, 2012). Moreover, GPN scholars are keen on understanding how non-firm actors (e.g., state agencies, social movements, and civil society) influence the nature and implications of these articulations, with an emphasis the kinds of "globalized" regional development that are made possible or impossible through them (Murphy and Schindler, 2011). As Coe *et al.* (2008: 272) noted:

> The GPN approach is a broad relational framework, which attempts to go beyond the very valuable but, in practice, more restricted, global commodity chain (GCC) and global value chain (GVC) formulations. Although the core of all three conceptualizations is similar – the nexus of interconnected functions, operations and transactions through which a specific product or service is produced, distributed and consumed – there are two crucial differences, in practice, between GCCs/GVCs on the one hand and GPNs on the other. First, GCCs/GVCs are essentially linear structures, whereas GPNs strive to go beyond such linearity to incorporate all kinds of network configuration. Second, GCCs/GVCs focus narrowly on the governance of inter-firm transactions while GPNs attempt to encompass all relevant sets of actors and relationships.

Under globalization, and with the advent of "network trade" where components for final products come from many countries (Broadman, 2007), the links between firms, regions, and GPNs play an increasingly central role, for better or worse, in economic development (Coe *et al.*, 2004). Whilst most GPN studies focus on the "outward" or upstream links between firms/regions – manifest principally in the ability of "local" firms to supply components or products to foreign buyers or lead firms – links can also be understood in relation to inward flows of commodities such as consumer products. GPN studies are generally/overwhelmingly "productionist" in orientation and there is a need for more studies that address the contexts, practices, and impacts of final consumption of the GPN products and services (Coe *et al.*, 2008; Coe and Hess, 2013). Our approach takes such concerns into account, as we address both SMME production of goods and services for domestic markets and GPNs, and the ways in which imported products and services link GPNs to consumer markets in Africa.

Another concern of recent GPN scholarship is the need to better understand the influences of new technologies such as ICTs on the governance and organization of GPNs. ICTs are an important aspect of global innovation and are also vital in the creation of the "economies of time" (Best, 1990) and to the coordination of GPNs. Productive insertion of firms into GPNs and GVCs are considered by many to be central to Africa's long-term economic transformation (Gibbon and Ponte, 2005; Broadman, 2007), and ICTs do offer important opportunities in this regard, both with respect to "inward" flows of imports and exported goods and services. Importing consumer goods and services is a relatively straightforward process and one that can be greatly facilitated through improved communications. On the export side, the situation is more complicated and requires that African firms achieve "critical success factors" relating to quality, price, delivery, and product standards – improvements that typically require more formalization of information systems than is needed for domestic markets (Kaplinsky *et al.*, 2003; UNCTAD, 2010). Without substantial foreign direct investment in manufacturing, it is the impacts on locally-based firms, or the ways in which they use new ICTs, which are most important, and in particular whether or not these allow SMMEs to connect to international markets and GPNs.

In addition to firms, consumers and the role of new technologies, recent scholarship has also sought to assess the implications of GPN integration for workers and labor movements, particularly in the Global South (Coe and Hess, 2013; McGrath, 2013; Smith *et al.*, 2014). A key concern is whether ties to GPNs can facilitate "social upgrading" – manifest in improved wages, working conditions, and prospects for workers to advance themselves through the development of skills and capabilities (Barrientos *et al.*, 2011; Selwyn, 2013). The benefits of social upgrading can impact communities as the externalities associated with healthier, wealthier, and more skilled workers spill over into regional economies, and labor movements and civil society organizations help to institutionalize and monitor/ maintain improved working conditions. In many cases, however, GPN relationships may not foster social upgrading as they instead promote low wages and sometimes dangerous/unhealthy working conditions (McGrath, 2013). In examining the links between African city-regions and (inward/ outward) GPNs, a key question is whether the social upgrading of labor and communities is occurring in our case-study contexts.

Beyond assessing the potential for social upgrading and new forms of ICT-enabled integration within global markets, our use of GPN concepts seeks to overcome what Bair and Werner (2011) label the "inclusionary bias" in GPN research: the tendency to focus on places and firms that have been connected into global networks. In response to this concern, they develop a "disarticulation" framework to explore why places might become disconnected from GPNs and the impacts of this. However, Bair and Werner do not explore, given their focus, why places may not become connected to GPNs (through production) in the first instance, despite often having access to new ICTs. The impacts of new ICTs may be incremental in much of Africa as they are absorbed into existing routines (Murphy, 2013), rather than transformational by enabling processes of production-based upgrading, which could facilitate exports.

In other words, ICT uptake may be coincidental with a continued non-articulation or non-integration of African firms into GPNs, or a unidirectional integration whereby the primary linkages to GPNs are for imported goods and domestic consumption. If either of these circumstances is evident, significant questions arise about the immanent development implications of ICT diffusion, particularly given the region's increasing and deepening integration into agricultural and mineral-based GPNs, which are governed primarily by non-African TNCs. Rather than marking a new age of African development, the ICT revolution may instead simply be associated with a continued reliance on natural resource-based extraction and exploitation for growth, and a marked increase in penetration of foreign consumer goods whose importation into the region is enabled through GPN linking of local retail distributors to manufacturers based in regions such as East and South Asia. An outcome such as this would arguably mark a further iteration of the historical pattern of Africa's largely "adverse incorporation" into the world system (Bush, 2007).

The depth, extent, and significance of ties between firms, industrial regimes, and GPNs are conceptualized as "couplings" (Coe et al., 2004). The constitution and significance of couplings for development depends on the multiscalar power relations associated with a production network's governance (e.g., the demands and expectations of foreign buyers or producers), a firm's internal capabilities, and the manner in which local firms are embedded within a particular industrial and regional context (Coe et al., 2004; Hess, 2004; Yeung, 2005). By multiscalar, we mean that the key power relations shaping the impacts of GPN couplings are found both within the global-to-local relationships linking Southern producers to international buyers, and within the regimes (territories) where these firms are based. These intra-territorial relationships or networks include actors who are involved directly in the GPN (e.g., workers, business owners, intermediaries) as well as others (e.g., non-governmental organizations, state agencies, and civil society organizations) who can influence the quality of the region's ties to the global economy. The net result of all these linkages is a "relational geometry" constituted by linked nodes of direct value creation (e.g., production or service provision by firms, corporations) and place-specific relationships that influence the possibility for value enhancement by firms and value capture within regions (Yeung, 2005).

Value enhancement is, at its core, about upgrading in firms, industries, and regions, and with respect to the links between these entities and the global economy. Upgrading is a process through which suppliers or distributors in a GPN increase their power, profit, and control through innovation, clustering, and/or the integration of additional value-adding activities (Gereffi, 1999; Humphrey and Schmitz, 2000, 2002; Kaplinsky et al., 2003; Sáinz, 2003; Gibbon and Ponte, 2005; Giuliani et al., 2005; Scott, 2006; Murphy, 2007). Upgrading can occur through product development, process improvements, functional changes, and/or the development of novel inter-sectoral linkages, and thus serves as an important mechanism for suppliers to "trade up" in international markets (Gereffi, 1999; Gibbon and Ponte, 2005). ICTs are thought to play an important role in upgrading processes by improving inter-firm relationships, creating new market opportunities, and increasing a supplier's access to information (Dunn *et al.*, 2006). In operationalizing these ideas, we examine whether and how ICT adoption influences the functional capacities (i.e., what firms are expected to be able to do) and performance standards (i.e., how well they can actually do it) of African SMMEs such that they can improve the quality of their couplings to GPN and international markets (Gibbon and Ponte, 2005). Our analysis identifies these influences both positively, manifest in real changes to firm-specific capabilities and forms of market access (see above), and less positively in the form of the limitations on new ICTs as means for global market integration.

A final component of this analysis is to determine whether Africa's information revolution is helping to reposition SMMEs and industries within, and in relation to, GPNs such that industries and communities can capture greater value through economic globalization. Value capture is conceptualized here in broad terms, manifest as non-firm specific capital investments (e.g., transportation infrastructure) and forms of social upgrad-ing such as human capital improvements, environmental sustainability, poverty reductions, and institutional reforms that are encouraged or driven in part by a region or industry's ties to a GPN. The degree to which value capture is possible depends upon the quality of the ties linking local firms to GPNs, and upon whether local institutions and non-firm actors can gain access to and channel some of the profits and benefits into investments vital for long-run regional development (e.g., infrastructure, public health, human capital) (Murphy and Schindler, 2011; Murphy, 2012). Stated another way, the amount of value captured within a region is determined by the structure, strength, and relational basis of the couplings between GPNs and the sociotechnical regimes constituting industries.

Beyond these positive potential outcomes, not all GPN couplings are conducive to upgrading and regional development, as some can prevent or limit local value creation, enhancement, and capture, particularly in cases where ICTs enable foreign firms to "reach in" more effectively to local markets through FDI or imports. As MacKinnon (2012) and Horner (2014) highlight, there are dark sides to GPN–region couplings, particularly in cases where transnational corporations are able to exercise significant power over local workers, states, consumers, and civil society actors. This can result when TNCs co-opt local officials such that labor regulations are ignored, when TNCs actively discourage social or industrial upgrading amongst local suppliers, and/or when GPN-generated imports effectively crowd out local manufacturers and service providers, as we demonstrate below.

The quality of couplings is determined in large part by the value of regionally embedded assets (e.g., skills, markets, and other resources) to leading firms in GPNs, the efficacy of regional authorities and GPN actors in strategically "selecting" for particular sectors or regions, and the structural-historical relationships between a region and a GPN (MacKinnon, 2012). Ideally, regions benefit the most from GPN integration when couplings are "organic" – based on high-value, complementary regional assets that are sought after by lead firms in GPNs. While regional actors such as firms, industrial promotion agencies, and policy-makers can "strategically" seek out GPN ties through trade junkets, fairs, and other forms of outreach, the likelihood of achieving such couplings, and having them contribute to social and industrial upgrading, may be limited in the absence of high-value regional assets. Instead, many city-regions – such as those in Africa – are subject to what MacKinnon (2012) calls "structural couplings", determined in large part by longstanding dependencies, extraversion relationships, and a desire for GPN actors to exploit "assets" such as low wages, poor regulation, consumer markets, and/or natural resource abundance. In such cases, regions may be better off strategically "decoupling" from GPNs in order to develop industrial sectors independently, as was the case with India's pharmaceutical industry: an option that is perhaps not a realistic alternative for most countries in the Global South (Horner, 2014).

Non-couplings to GPNs are also a distinct possibility, manifest in circumstances where African SMMEs remain disconnected from transnational flows of capital, goods, knowledge, and services, able only to access local or domestic markets where value-adding opportunities may be greatly limited as competition is primarily price-based. The net result of this process is that marketplaces may be characterized by discontinuous or fragmented production networks serving consumers – some of which are "globalized" yet organized largely by African-based importers, traders, intermediaries, and retailers. In other cases, production networks are largely local in nature and support manufacturing and service-providing firms that produce and sell goods and services for mainstream domestic markets. If either of these circumstances are evident, it is critical to determine whether and how ICTs support different types of GPN–region relationships and to assess their development implications as manifest in value creation, enhancement, and capture processes (especially industrial and social upgrading).

In applying concepts from GPN studies, we examine whether/how new ICTs are influencing the quality of the couplings or non-couplings between African SMMEs, industrial regimes, city-regions, and GPNs. In theory, ICTs can influence these relationships in positive ways by speeding up communications between African SMMEs and international buyers or suppliers, by facilitating access to market information and process or product innovations, and by enabling SMMEs to market their goods and services to consumers globally and in more direct (i.e., disintermediated) ways. By doing so, ICTs can help SMMEs to "reach out" and create value for the global economy, to gain access to communication and information flows that can support upgrading (i.e., value enhancement), and, following Gibbon and Ponte (2005), to reorganize or restructure industrial (sociotechnical) regimes such that they are more in line with the performance standards and functional capacities demanded in international markets. ICT-facilitated GPN couplings can thus ideally help to empower African SMMEs and industries in ways that lead to greater value capture and social upgrading in the region.

Integrating the Conceptual Approaches: A Multi-scalar Framework

To integrate the three approaches detailed above – resource-based views of intra-firm development, sociotechnical transitions theory, and the global production network framework – we develop a multi-scalar framework that situates SMME activities and practices in the context of, and in relation to, industrial regimes and global production networks. Figure 3.2 outlines the framework, which is based on three underlying notions derived from the integration of concepts from these literatures. First we argue that industrial (sociotechnical) regimes and urban–regional contexts are constituted by multi-scalar webs or networks linking heterogeneous firm and non-firm actors through power relations, interdependencies, and flows of commodities and capital. These actors include consumers, industrial promotion agencies,

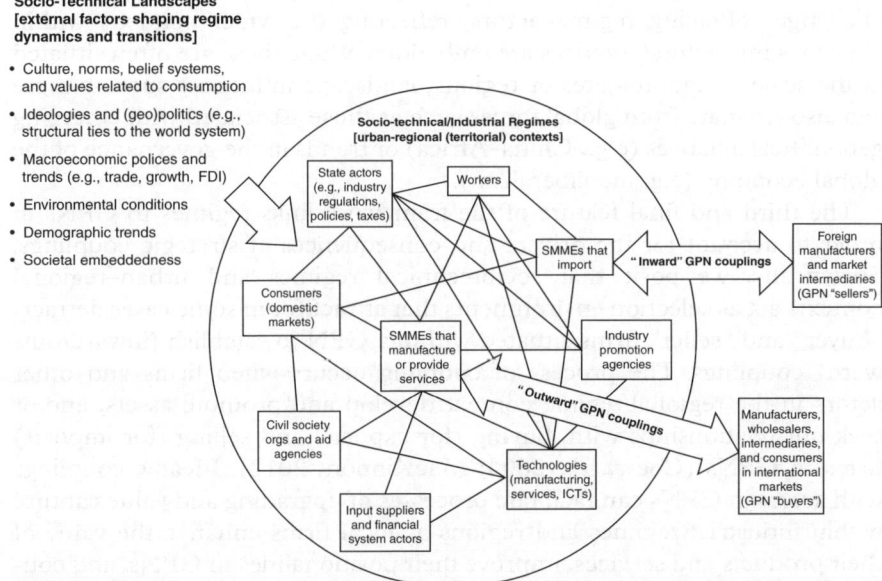

Figure 3.2   Integrating the conceptual components – SMMEs, industrial regimes, and GPNs.

firms, workers, technologies, and civil society organizations connected or related to one another through business transactions, regulatory/taxation agencies, industry associations, intra-firm management, institutions (e.g., custom authorities, labor unions), and everyday production and consumption activities. The multi-scalar relationalities binding these actors together are stabilized and reproduced through rules, power asymmetries, and practices (formal and informal) that create path dependencies in urban–regional economies and guide innovation processes in industrial regimes. Moreover, intra-firm capabilities and resources are manifest in, revealing of, and influenced by these rules, power relations, and practices, thus providing a means to interrogate the links between the regime's characteristics, its evolutionary trajectories, and the actions of individual SMMEs.

The second feature of this framework is recognition that the relational configurations described above are territorially situated within particular places which are in turn embedded within and related to wider societal values, cultural contexts, institutional arrangements, environmental and demographic conditions, and political-economic processes (i.e., sociotechnical landscapes). The point here is to recognize what Coe et al. (2008: 280) call the "place-related situatedness" of firms and industries within regions and particular societies (see also Hughes et al., 2008). Regimes are thus shaped significantly by spatially proximate interactions, place-specific histories and path dependencies, and by the territorial strategies of firm and non-firm actors. Moreover, societal, (geo)political, economic, and cultural factors also influence the attitudes, values, desires, prospects, and structural challenges of/facing regime actors, reflecting the wider contexts within which regime actors/practices are embedded. While these are often situated at the scale of nation-states or regions, landscape influences such as these can also emanate from global forces such as those associated with emerging geopolitical alliances (e.g., China–Africa) or trends in the governance of the global economy (e.g., neoliberalism).

The third and final feature of the framework links regimes to GPNs in order to account for the drivers and consequences of strategic couplings. Specifically, we posit that sociotechnical regimes and urban–regional contexts act as selection environments that attract (or in some cases detract) "buyer" and "seller" firms situated within a GPN to establish (inward/outward) couplings. The process of coupling occurs when firms and other actors in the regional/regime context develop and promote assets, and/or seek out relationships with, buying (for exports) and selling (for imports) firms in GPNs (Coe et al., 2004; MacKinnon, 2012). Ideally, couplings with actors in GPNs can facilitate processes of upgrading and value capture within industrial regimes and regions as local firms enhance the value of their products and services, improve their positionalities in GPNs, and contribute to the social upgrading of workers, communities, and civil society. Following MacKinnon (2012), our goal is to understand whether these couplings are structural, organic, or strategically driven – or if decoupling or non-coupling with GPNs is observed.

Conceptualizing the Development Implications of ICTs: Thin and Thick Integration

While the framework described in Figure 3.2 outlines our approach to analysing the interrelationships between firms, industries, and global actors within and in relation to Africa, it is less clear on the links between ICTs and development. To interrogate critically the degree to which ICTs are implicated in imminent and/or immanent forms of development, our analysis focusses on whether ICT absorption is associated with a restructuring of the communication, innovation, and knowledge creation, management, and processing activities within firms, and whether there are signs that an information-driven transformation might be under way in some firms, industrial regimes, and with respect to the couplings between these and GPNs. We make this assessment by drawing a distinction between "thin" and "thick" forms of ICT integration, arguing that while imminent forms of development may be possible through thin integration, more structurally transformative immanent development is only possible if, among other structural changes, thick ICT integration is achieved. Through thick integration, industrial regimes, markets, production networks, and socioeconomic relations might be reorganized so as to enable African enterprises and communities to generate and capture greater value through information-driven and facilitated forms of capitalist production.

The distinction draws initially on earlier work (Carmody, 2010) where it was observed that thin-integration or *thintegration* of ICTs was the norm in sub-Saharan Africa, a situation marked by the widespread use of, in particular, mobile phones, but in ways that did relatively little to enhance the value of the products and services produced by small enterprises and farmers:

> Africa's integration into the global information economy is characterised by a missing top and a missing middle. The continent provides raw materials, associated with conflict, and consumes mobile phones and engages in some limited low-tech assembly operations. The high value-added activities in the chain take place elsewhere. These activities and the use of mobile phones then represent a form of thintegration into the global economy. It is not that Africa is excluded from the process of globalization, indeed it is integral to it as a supplier of raw materials. Use of mobile phones, by itself, does not change this context.(Carmody 2010: 127)

Working off this broad notion, we link the capability, sociotechnical regime, and GPN framework to a multidimensional conceptualization of thin versus thick forms of ICT integration. Table 3.1 summarizes these distinctions.

Table 3.1 Conceptualizing thin and thick forms of ICT integration in firms (adapted from Murphy *et al.*, 2014). Reprinted by permission of Taylor & Francis Ltd, http://www.tandf.co.uk/journals

	Thin forms of ICT integration (thintegration)	Thick forms of ICT integration
Characteristics of ICT-enabled communication and information access	Discrete and codified (e.g., numbers, sizes, prices, dates, locations) information that can be communicated easily via voice or text. Information must be manually transferred into processing and management programs (e.g., accounting software). **Minimal or superficial enhancement of intra-firm resources, particularly to transactional and (basic) informational resources. Capability and coupling constraints relieved but structural constraints remain significant.**	More complex and diverse forms of information accessed, controlled, processed, and used (e.g., through internet cookies, shop-floor management systems) that go beyond basic one-on-one communication exchanges. This information is processed (e.g., through algorithms or software packages) and the resulting knowledge fed back into the development of product and process innovations. Real-time tracking of trends and automated transfer of information into processing and management systems. **Significant enhancements of intra-firm resources (transformational). ICTs can enable SMMEs to overcome structural constraints related to market access, expansion, and quality.**
Value of ICT-enabled communications and information access	ICT-enabled communication and information access used in largely responsive or reactive ways, to meet customer needs, resolve immediate problems, or keep apace with the competition through imitation. Deeper forms of ICT-enabled information processing are absent.	Information is a proactive and strategic resource that is managed through ICTs in ways that create knowledge rents through new products, production efficiencies, and marketing strategies. ICT capabilities deeply integrated into innovation processes and production/service provisioning systems.
Life-span of information accessed or exchanged	Mainly of short-term utility in the context of daily needs or a particular project or customer.	A continuous, long-term process of accumulating and processing information to facilitate product, process, and marketing innovations.
Implications for innovation and industrial development	ICTs can increase productivity, visibility (e.g., through web pages, social media), and market responsiveness through improved communications and greater access to non-local sources of information. ICTs help firms keep pace with or adjust to shifting market conditions but do not enable them to profitably exploit these dynamics through information-driven forms of innovation.	Upgrading possibilities and new value-creating activities identified through intensive forms of information management. ICT provides a crucial means to stay ahead of the competition through quality, price, and productivity improvements and to identify emerging market trends in both domestic and international markets.
Implications for the firm, industry, or region's positionality in global production networks (GPNs)	ICTs are necessary, ubiquitous technology for the everyday performance and survival of firms but their thin use precludes dramatic changes to industries or a region's positionality in GPNs.	Firms and industries are able to develop the needed capabilities to capture greater value from international markets through knowledge rents generated in GPNs. Innovation, inward investment, and long-run growth can be sustained through ICT-empowered clusters of innovative firms and regional innovation systems.
Key limitations on this form of ICT integration	Thintegration does not significantly challenge or transform the power relations and structures that sustain extraversion and underdevelopment.	The quality of products, services, infrastructures, labour, socioeconomic institutions, and political systems remain critical factors in determining whether the benefits of thick informationalism can be translated into wider development outcomes. The "basics" still matter.

The goal is not to provide a precise boundary between thin and thick, but to apply these ideas heuristically such that we can better and more consistently assess the impacts of ICT integration within our case study firms, industries, and contexts.

The depth of ICT integration can be understood along three key dimensions – the type, value, and lifespan of the information that is accessed, processed, and used, and the kinds of everyday communications that are relied upon by firms. At its most basic or "thin" level, ICT integration enables discrete and codified bits of information to be communicated and compiled (e.g., prices, specifications, itineraries) via voice, email or text. This information might then be used in other ICT applications (e.g., accounting software), but in the case of thintegration, the transfer of this information is done manually and discretely rather than automatically and continuously. Viewed in relation to the capability and resource frameworks described above, thin use of ICTs can relieve constraints on production and service provision and complement some intra-firm resources, particularly those associated with commercial transactions and basic information access, but it does relatively little to enhance strategic and transformational resources.

In terms of its value, thinly communicated forms of information are important but primarily in reactive or responsive ways – to solve real-time problems, to modify ongoing work schedules or designs, and/or to monitor and keep pace with the activities or products of competitors (e.g., web-based browsing of furniture designs). As such, these kinds of communications, and the information they enable access to, have a real-time or relatively short lifespan (e.g., in the context of a particular customer order, market season). This is due in part to the type of communication or information exchange, and because the information is not processed in ways that feed back into longer-term innovation and/or productivity-enhancing processes. As a result, thin integration means that ICTs are of relatively limited significance to the development of most firms, industries, and national economies, except in as much as they may facilitate greater import penetration. Enhanced communications and information access can help to increase a firm's productivity, visibility (e.g., through web pages), and market responsiveness, but such gains do not lead to its significant repositioning within an industry or in relation to international markets. Instead, the improvements concomitant with thin forms of integration are essentially about keeping pace with the competition as technologies like mobile phones become ubiquitous parts of everyday business activities.

Thick integration, in contrast, entails information-communication practices that are qualitatively different in terms of the type of communications and information that is processed, and their subsequent value and lifespan in relation to a firm and industry's development. In this case, ICTs are used to access, create, and communicate more complex and diverse forms of information (e.g., through internet cookies, production management systems) that are not necessarily in voice or text form. Communications may transcend basic one-to-one exchanges and information is processed (through applications, software packages) and fed back into the decision-making structures and dynamics of the firm. Moreover, automated and/or real-time tracking of market and production activities may occur such that the firm can adjust more rapidly to shifting demand, changing input prices, and/or other external factors. All told, thickly integrated ICTs enable significant enhancements to intra-firm resources (transactional, informational, strategic, and transformational) and can help SMMEs to overcome structural or authority constraints related to market access, expansion, and quality. These resources are, in turn, mobilized proactively to help firms create competitive advantages and knowledge "rents" through new products, enhanced efficiencies, and novel approaches to marketing. Information thus shifts from being a short-term resource to a key ingredient in the long-term development of the firm, industry, and GPNs.

The thick integration of ICTs can enable SMMEs to upgrade their products, processes, and services more effectively such that they can outpace the competition by identifying emerging trends in domestic and international markets. ICTs can be deployed strategically if the firm develops the right kinds of capabilities and applications to create knowledge rents: understandings, capabilities, and information management systems that enable the firm to capture greater economic value. Through these value creating and enhancing processes, thick integration can enable domestically oriented industries to evolve into internationalized sectors able to develop and sustain linkages to higher value-added GPNs. In short, thick integration enables transformations to firms and industries that can potentially facilitate more productive, progressive, and innovative forms of engagement with domestic markets and the global information economy (GIE).

Importantly, thick integration can only occur if the structural context – the sociotechnical regimes, landscapes, and GPN-specific institutions and governance arrangements – provide sufficient support or demand its emergence. In other words, and in contrast to the agency-intensive approaches (where the power resides with individual capabilities) of much of the ICT4D literature, we conceptualize that the quality, extent, and "thickness" of ICT integration is dependent in large part on the demand generated by the structural contexts in which firms are embedded. If the context is supportive or positively demanding, than informationalized forms of immanent development – manifest in structural changes to production networks, markets, industrial regimes, and socioeconomic relations – are more likely to result and in a manner that can (recursively) transform institutions, interdependencies, and structural features such that African firms are better able to exploit opportunities from the GIE. Crucially, however, progressively immanent changes to the nature of capitalist dynamics in Africa will also require other non-ICT specific structural transformations: issues we high-light in the analyses and discussions that follow.

Conclusion

Figure 3.3 outlines the framework for evaluating the contribution of ICTs to economic and industrial development in Africa. In the chapters that follow, this framework is applied to the study of SMMEs in South Africa and Tanzania's wood product and tourism industries. The goal is to deter-mine whether there are signs that ICTs are contributing to transformations supportive of African manufacturing and service-provisioning firms, and are able to empower domestic industries in the context of two rapidly glob-alizing economies. The conceptual components are integrated through a step-by-step process beginning at the firm-specific scale, where we examine the links between ICT uptake and the development of intra-firm resources and capabilities that can improve product and service-delivery quality, enhance productivity, foster innovation, support ties to global markets, and/ or increase the competitiveness of African enterprises in relation to imports or foreign firms. Through the analysis of these capabilities we determine whether there are indications that "thick" integration of ICTs is underway in these firms and sectors, such that they can become better equipped to com-pete in, and in relation to, GPNs.

We also address the question of whether thin or thick integration extends beyond the scale of individual enterprises and toward that of the sociotech-nical regimes, markets, and production networks governing industries. Here

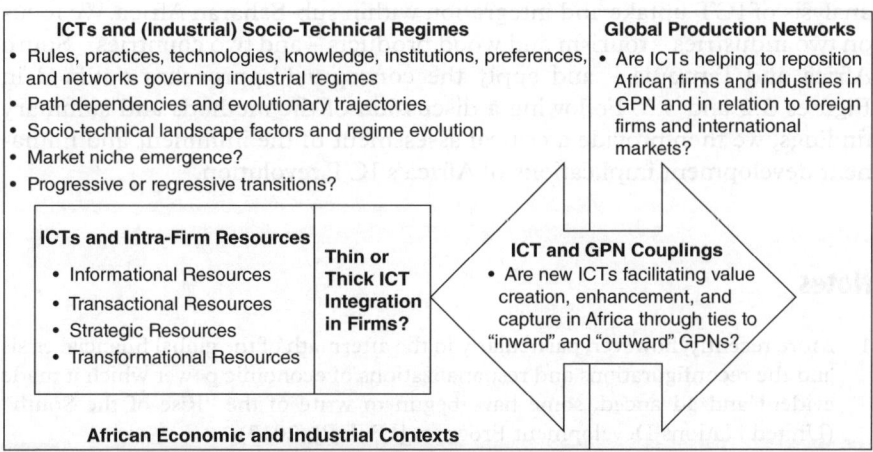

Figure 3.3   A multi-scalar and integrated approach to the study of ICTs and industrial change in Africa.

our emphasis is on whether and how ICTs are contributing to the evolution of industrial regimes, and what these trajectories mean for SMMEs and urban–regional development processes. Simply stated, the goal is to assess whether Africa's so-called information revolution is coinciding with a progressive industrial transition – one that is supportive of upgrading in SMMEs such that they are empowered by becoming more competitive in relation to foreign capital and imported goods and services. Moreover, we evaluate whether new, innovative, and profitable market niches are emerging, and whether/how ICTs are contributing to their development. This analysis of sociotechnical regime evolution also explicitly accounts for the role that landscape features and factors (e.g., societal values, political institutions, geo-economic relations) play in guiding the evolution of sociotechnical regimes through incentives for innovation or through the imposition of structural blockages that constrain progressive transition possibilities.

At the trans-local or global scale, our study asks three questions regarding the prospects for immanent transformations to structural relationships between African firms and the world economy. First, are there indicators that ICTs are helping SMMEs and African industries (i.e., sociotechnical regimes) to become integrated into inward or outward GPNs for their goods and services? Second, what is the significance of these GPN couplings for industrial and social upgrading within SMMEs and the city-regions in Africa where they are located? Third, and most broadly, are ICT-enabled firms and industries able to reposition themselves progressively within GPNs? In other words, are there promising signs that sub-Saharan Africa's recent "growth renaissance" and ICT diffusion success story are restructuring the region's relationship to the world system such that it becomes less extractive, exploitative, and uneven?

With our conceptual approach now specified, we shift to an empirical analysis of ICT uptake and integration within sub-Saharan Africa. We focus on two industries – tourism and wood products – and two countries – South Africa and Tanzania – and apply the conceptual approaches outlined in Figures 3.2 and 3.3. Following a discussion of the methods and summary findings, we then provide a critical assessment of the imminent and immanent development implications of Africa's ICT revolution.

Notes

1 More recently, however, particularly in the aftermath of the global financial crisis and the reconfigurations and respatializations of economic power which it made evident and advanced, some have begun to write of the "Rise of the South" (United Nations Development Program [UNDP], 2013).

2 Our understanding and use of practice as an analytical or epistemological object draws directly on the work of Jones and Murphy (2011).

Chapter Four
ICTs in Action: SMMEs and Industrial Change in South Africa and Tanzania

With the conceptual and literature foundations developed, we turn to our empirical investigation of the impacts of new ICTs (mobile phones, computers, and the internet) on the activities of firms and industries in Africa. Our study focussed on the links between ICT uptake and use, and the development of SMMEs and the wood products and tourism industries in South Africa and Tanzania.[1] Through a mixed-method analysis of the production, marketing, management, and innovation development activities of SMMEs, and the changing role that ICTs play in these, we seek to characterize both the imminent and immanent development implications of information and communication technologies. By imminent development we mean changes in firm-specific capabilities that have been promoted by or accompanied the adoption of new ICTs and the degree to which these are responsible for improved performance indicators. Immanent development impacts are then assessed through an examination of the sociotechnical regimes and global production networks guiding and governing industrial change in these sectors and urban–regional contexts. The net result is an extensive and intensive comparative analysis that demonstrates the paradoxical, sometimes problematic, complex, and contingent nature of the relationships between new forms of communication and information access/exchange, and socioeconomic and industrial change in Africa.

Africa's Information Revolution: Technical Regimes and Production Networks in South Africa and Tanzania, First Edition. James T. Murphy and Pádraig Carmody.
© 2015 John Wiley & Sons, Ltd. Published 2015 by John Wiley & Sons, Ltd.

In more specific terms, the findings presented in this chapter highlight the varying extent, and sometimes somewhat surprising similarities, of ICT uptake in South Africa and Tanzania and the differences in use and significance that are evident in the wood products and tourism industries. Some of the distinctions (e.g., the highly limited use of computers and the internet in Tanzania's wood products industry) are not surprising given the differences in the levels of industrial and economic development between the country case contexts. Other distinctions are more subtle and reflect the contingent factors that determine the degree to which an SMME is more or less successful, such as experience, training, location, and social capital. One of the primary analytical goals of our study was to determine whether or not it was possible to associate a greater level of ICT use and capabilities with a consistently improved performance in the firms studied. At a broad level our findings reveal that there is no clear, significant relationship in this regard. There are two possible explanations for this. The first might relate to the difficulty of discretely and definitively isolating the impacts of new ICTs on performance. The second possible explanation is that ICTs are simply not having the kinds of imminent development impacts widely proclaimed in much of the ICT4D literature, and that they comprise only one set of technologies, in combination with multifold other capabilities, which are necessary for competitive success. As elaborated below, we find support for the second explanation in our analysis.

This chapter first briefly describes the contexts of, and methods used in, our case-study locations in South Africa and Tanzania, with some discussion of our justification for these locations. The second part of the chapter shifts to a presentation of the empirics as they relate to the development of ICT-specific capabilities that can enhance productivity or facilitate innovation. Our analysis summarizes the extent and depth of ICT use in our case studies, and then examines whether or not there are significant links between ICT-related capabilities, qualitative performance indicators, and/or the ability of SMMEs to compete effectively in South Africa and Tanzania's tourism and wood products sectors. The focus here is on more discrete indicators of use and perception, with the chapters that follow expanding on these findings in order to explicate the significance of ICTs for structural transformation or immanent development.

Situating the Analysis: South Africa and Tanzania's Tourism and Wood Products Sectors

Our fieldwork, undertaken between 2010 and 2012, focussed on the impacts of ICTs on SMMEs and industrial change in South Africa and Tanzania in the tourism and wood products subsectors.[2] South Africa and Tanzania represent significant contrasts in terms of their national locations within the global information economy and society. South Africa is a middle-income country that accounts for a third of sub-Saharan Africa's gross domestic product, has a highly developed telecommunications infrastructure, and also ranks highly on the ICT Development Index compared with other African countries. In contrast, Tanzania is a low-income country which, in the mid-2000s, had a Digital Opportunity Index (DOI) score of only about one-third of South Africa's (ITU, 2006).[3] Table 4.1 summarizes basic development indicators, recent measures of ICT adoption, and statistics about the selected industries in both countries. South Africa and Tanzania's significantly different levels of development and ICT use/access, and their relatively stable political and economic conditions, enabled us to compare and assess differences in usage and significance. Moreover, and in (Rostowian) developmentalist terms, our analysis enabled us to assess whether there is an ICT4D "ladder" that countries might be expected to climb as they advance from low to high levels of industrial "informational-ization" and integration into the global information economy. If this is the case, the expectation was that South Africa would be much further

Table 4.1   Development, ICT, and industrial indicators for South Africa and Tanzania

	South Africa	Tanzania	Sub-Saharan Africa
Population (million, 2011)	50.6	46.2	865.2
Economic density ($1000 per sq km)	$336	$27	$54
GDP growth rate (2011, per capita at PPP)	1.9%	3.3%	2.10%
ICT Development Index (2011, rank out of 155 countries)	91	139	Not available
Mobile phone subscribers per 100 inhabitants (2011)	126.5	55.5	53.9
Internet users % of population over 15 years age (2011/2012)	33.7%	3.5%	12.8%
Value of wood product exports ($ million, 2011)	$1972	$59	Not available
Mean growth in value of wood product exports (%, 2008–2011)	4%	37%	Not available
Trade performance index rank – wood products (2011, out of 145)	70	44	Not available
International tourism receipts ($ million, 2011)	$9170	$1487	$23,100
% Growth in international tourist receipts (2010–2011)	0.7%	13.1%	6.3%
Rank by tourism market share in sub-Saharan Africa (out of 46)	1	3	Not available

Compiled from World Bank (2013b), ITC (2013), ITU (2012), South Africa Tourism (2012), Stork *et al.* (2013), United Republic of Tanzania (2007), World Tourism Organization (2013a,b)

along than Tanzania with regard to both ICT uptake and potentially immanent forms of ICT-enabled industrial development.

With respect to the diffusion and uptake of new ICTs, there are significant
contrasts between South Africa and Tanzania. In South Africa, mobile
phone subscriptions were at 59.5 million in 2011, a number higher than the
country's population and one constituting 10% of all subscriptions in Africa
(GSMA, 2011). Of these subscriptions, 81% are pre-paid or pay-as-you-go,
with the remainder as post-paid accounts. South Africa, and particularly its
major cities (Johannesburg, Durban, and Cape Town), is well, if differentially, serviced by ICT and connected through fibre-optic cables. New sub-
marine cables, depicted in Figure 2.1, are dramatically increasing the
band-width capacity available to African countries.

In 2011–12, a third of South Africans used the internet ,with 65% having
first done so through a computer and 35% through a mobile phone (Stork
et al., 2013). When asked about the last time the internet was accessed, the
majority of Research ICT Africa's (see Stork et al., 2013) survey respondents stated that it was done through a mobile phone, at work, or in an
internet cafe. In terms of costs, the cheapest monthly rate for fixed broadband access (unlimited data access) was $64.87 per month in 2011–12,
while mobile broadband rates were significantly lower, albeit with greater
constraints on data transfer speed. When considered with respect to South
Africa's GDP per capita ($7508 in 2012: World Bank, 2013a), fixed broad-
band access would take 10% of the average individual's income per year,
accounting for relatively low levels of penetration.

In Tanzania, the number of mobile telephone subscriptions increased
from 110,000 to over 19 million between 2000–2012 (Tanzania's population
is about 44 million), spurred in part by the privatization of the telecommunications industry and by declining tariff rates and mobile phone purchase
costs (Tanzanian Communications Regulatory Authority [TCRA],
2010a,b). In 2011, the mobile phone penetration rate reached 50%, with
nearly 100% of all mobile phone subscriptions as pre-paid or pay-as-you-go
accounts (GSMA, 2011). Mobile phones are accessible to most urbanites
and are used primarily for domestic/local voice communication and texting
or short message services (SMS). In 2010, international calls accounted for
2.8% of all voice communication, international messages about 12% of all
SMS, and multimedia messages (MMS) for only 0.01% of all non-voice
communication (Tanzanian Communications Regulatory Authority
(TCRA), 2010a,b). Smartphone usage, while on the rise, remains low,
although a majority of Tanzanian internet users (54.2%) rely on mobile
broadband to access the internet (Stork et al., 2012).

With respect to computers and the internet, the data are more difficult to
track, but there is little doubt that the diffusion of these technologies has
been limited in Tanzania. In 2011–12, Research ICT Africa (Stork et al.,
2013) estimated that the overall internet penetration rate was 3.5%, with a

growth rate of only 1.3% between 2007 and 2011. The same survey high-lighted the fact that the internet is most commonly accessed through mobile phones, internet cafes, and places of employment rather than within homes. Not surprisingly, mobile and fixed broadband penetration rates are extremely low (0.1%) and the revenues generated by the mobile phone industry are far below South Africa's US$12.7 billion, at $0.9 billion (GSMA, 2011). Moreover, the cost of unlimited broadband internet access in Tanzania, even at its lowest rate ($19.20 per month: Stork *et al.*, 2013) is equivalent to about 38% of the average individual's annual income. As such, internet afford-ability remains a crucial constraint on its widespread diffusion in Tanzania.

These issues notwithstanding, the Tanzanian government and the United Nations Industrial Development Organization (UNIDO) view new ICTs as a critical "soft" infrastructure that will help to transform the country into a "knowledge-based society" and enable its industries to exploit international markets (Mbelle, 2005; United Republic of Tanzania, 2003).

> Rapid advances in ICT have eroded the strength of long standing "compara-tive advantage" theory in international trade as far as the availability of factor inputs is concerned, at the same time lowering transaction costs considerably. Space, time, and endowments no longer dictate production, since ICT advancement allows easier production of customised goods and services. (Mbelle, 2005: xii [UNIDO report])

Achieving such a transformation would require the state and the private sector to leverage ICTs in ways that could help the country's industries overcome several major constraints, including low levels of productivity, an inward/domestic market orientation, poor infrastructure systems, limited technological capabilities, weak business promotion institutions, a lack of state support, inadequate access to finance, and consumers who often prefer foreign-made products (Mbelle, 2005; Nelson and de Bruijn, 2005; Goedhuys, 2007).

Our project compared the influence of ICTs on a manufacturing industry (wood products) and a service industry (tourism). The comparison was compelling for three reasons. First, it enabled us to understand whether and how ICTs differentially influence the development of "network economies" for small firms and intra-national and transnational value chains in industries having dramatically different kinds of governance and production systems (Perry, 1999). Wood product firms – like many manufacturing enterprises – generally operate as nodes in linear value chains that rely on relatively few points of contact (e.g., to suppliers, customers, or subcontractors) for production and sales (Allen and Chandrashekar, 2000; Kaplinsky *et al.*, 2003; Ellram *et al.*, 2004). Tourist firms, in contrast, deal with a large number of diverse clients and suppliers, based locally and internationally, and the industry more closely approximates a dynamic aggregation or "value web" of goods, services, spaces, and experiences (Debbage and Daniels, 1998; South African Information Technology Industry Strategy Project (SAITIS), 2002; Judd, 2006). As such, our expectation was (correctly) that the frequency, intensity, and quality of ICT use for information transfer and communication should vary significantly between wood products and tourism, thus enabling us to better understand how an industry's organization influences the impact that ICTs have on its development.

Second, wood products and tourism require different kinds of technological and organizational capabilities and the comparison helped us understand whether and how ICTs differentially influence learning and knowledge development processes in manufacturing and service industries. In wood products, like many manufacturing sectors, a firm's key capabilities primarily relate to the design, production and sale of goods that have measurable, consistent, and durable characteristics or indicators of quality (Dean and Evans, 1994; Yilmaz and Bititci, 2006). These "production" capabilities depend on industry-specific knowledge that is tangibly reflected in the quality of the firm's goods, the timeliness of deliveries, and the profits achieved through productivity improvements. In some market segments, such as custom furniture production, creativity and design skills may also contribute significantly to a firm's ability to establish and sustain ties to higher-value markets both domestically and internationally (Murphy, 2012). In these cases, manufacturers need to develop both an intuitive sense of style and to keep abreast of local and global trends in fashion and design through attendance at trade fairs, the maintenance of close working relationships with interior designers or architects, and ties to a network of demanding clients.

In contrast, tourism "products" are often intangible, heterogeneous, more place-specific, and perishable; quality is subjective and largely dependent upon how firms and customers co-produce a tourism experience (Debbage and Daniels, 1998; Crouch and Ritchie, 1999). Coordination capabilities are essential for this co-production process, and these are evident in a firm's ability to flexibly meet the diverse and often intense demands of clients through service provision, logistics, and labor management strategies that lead to high quality experiences (e.g., relaxation, memories, education) that remain with them long after returning home. While industry-specific knowledge is undoubtedly important, place or destination-specific knowledge also plays a key role in enabling firms to provide unique "post-Fordist" tourism experiences (Judd, 2006). For SMMEs in popular tourism destinations (e.g., Cape Town, Zanzibar) such local knowledge can provide a critical competitive advantage that establishes and sustains a steady flow of clients from year-to-year.

Given the diversity of land rents and tourist attractions, the industry tends to have a relatively spatially dispersed structure rather than being characterized by dominant and clearly defined industrial districts or clusters as one might expect in wood products (although beach fronts or other attractions may concentrate touristic activities and accommodation). Also given the experiential nature of tourism, imagery is particularly important. As Büscher (2010: 261) observed:

> Nature and rural communities… are increasingly becoming "underlying assets" for what has become the primary source of value of neoliberal conservation, namely idealised images within the realms of branding, public relations and marketing.

According to one industry insider in Lesotho, "in tourism you don't cater for reality, you cater for perceptions" (quoted in Büscher, 2010: 268). This fetishization also works in the other direction, however, as was observed when the compere (emcee) at a tourism conference in South Africa referred to "that very important commodity – the tourist" (Tourism Destination Conference, Cape Town, April 2012).

Innovation in tourism is also different from that in manufacturing. Tourism firms are commonly less innovative than manufacturers, given that many facets of their service delivery, such as cooking, touring, and serving breakfasts, are not open to substantial innovation and because the technologies and techniques are low-tech and relatively settled (Sundbo, 2001; Mattsson *et al.*, 2005). Where innovation does occur, much of it is social – place branding and marketing, for example – and focussed on generating and increasing the "place rents" from which tourism derives its value (Mattsson *et al.*, 2005). However, how these rents are spatially distributed between overseas firms and firms in the tourist region are matters of contention. For example, the TripAdvisor website, which has become of central importance globally in rating tours and hotels, can help to create a "global gaze" on a particular destination with sometimes critical implications for particular firms such as hotels and restaurants, for example. Negative reviews may result in a loss of business and ultimately firm closure, potentially increasing the centralization of capital. We detail these dynamics in Chapter 7.

Wood products and tourism are both important industries for South Africa and Tanzania's economies, thus giving the study added policy relevance. Wood products – especially furniture and furniture components, flooring, and construction materials (e.g., doors, window frames) – are significant value-added industries, and in 2005 nine out of 20 of the world's leading exporters of wood manufactures were developing or emerging economies (International Trade Center (ITC), 2008). Wood products are especially significant for developing economies because they are traditionally resource- and labor-intensive activities undertaken by a diverse group of enterprises: from craft-based micro-enterprises to larger-scale and high-volume producers (Kaplinsky and Readman, 2000).

The South African and Tanzanian wood products sectors are characterized by different structures. South Africa ran a trade surplus of US$103 million in "wood, articles of wood and charcoal" in 2010, in addition to having exports of almost US$250m in "fuel wood, wood in chips or particles and wood waste" (calculated from United Nations Comtrade database, 2011). In 2011, South Africa's wood products sector was ranked 70th out of 145 countries with regard to its trade performance. Although there is increasing market concentration, SMMEs remain predominant in production for the large domestic economy, particularly in the furniture sector (Kaplinsky and Manning, 1998; Kaplinsky *et al.*, 2002, 2003; Moodley, 2003). While the value of South African wood products was nearly $2 billion in 2011, growth in the sector was moderate (4%) between 2008 and 2011 (ITC, 2013; World Bank, 2013a). Intense international price competition has put pressure on returns in some market segments. Production for export is concentrated amongst a number of large-scale firms, and the situation facing high-volume exporters was considered dire a decade ago, as Kaplinsky *et al.* (2003: 20) observed:

> South African [furniture] producers are only staying in the [international market] by virtue of price competitiveness, since their quality and delivery reliability were poor, they were distant from final markets and showed little capacity to develop related capabilities in other sectors.

As such, South African manufacturers are increasingly marginal to "outward" (exporting) GPNs, while there are increasing inward flows from wood product furniture producers in Asia and elsewhere (i.e., from "inward" GPNs). In Durban, KwaZulu-Natal, our case study location, there is also substantial local/domestic competition, evident in the approximately 350 furniture companies in the metropolitan area (Robbins, 2010).

With respect to wood products, Tanzania is currently a net importer in value terms (with a $5 million deficit in 2011) after achieving significant trade surpluses (as high as $29 million) between 2005 and 2010. Although its exports have been traditionally strong in basic wood product products (e.g., sawn wood, rough wood), these have been weakened in recent years due in large part to an increase in imports of plywood, fibreboard, joinery, particle board, and other articles of wood (ITC, 2012). That said, Tanzania's wood products sector grew 37% between 2008 and 2011. As for furniture, Tanzania is a net importer and, despite significant gains in the exportation of mattresses and mattress supports, the country's furniture trade deficit with China alone increased dramatically from $490,000 in 2002 to nearly $13 million in 2011 (ITC, 2012). This increase reflects the failure of Tanzanian manufacturers to develop the capabilities necessary to compete in domestic/export markets and the rising importance of "inward" directed GPNs for wood products across a wide range of markets, including imports in the low-quality and low-price market segments traditionally served by local manufacturers. Tanzania's wood products and furniture sector is arguably emblematic of wider conditions in low-income sub-Saharan Africa and thus serves as an excellent case study to assess the significance of ICT diffusion for industrial change. While the industry is tiny in international terms, its contribution to domestic consumption and employment generation is quite significant given the dominance of SMMEs in the sector (Murphy, 2002, 2006a, 2007). Dar es Salaam, particularly the wood products cluster in Keko ward, is the major market and production center for the country and a site of intense competition.

Tourism is a particularly labor-intensive industry and is thus important in South Africa and Tanzania where unemployment levels are high. Moreover, given its intrinsic emphasis on foreign travellers, the sector is also clearly implicated in "outward" GPNs through which tours and tourists are produced/served through networks of tour operators, travel agents, hoteliers, transporters, restaurateurs, and so on (Christian, 2012). As is typical globally, SMMEs play a key role in meeting the demands of foreign visitors and domestic travellers through retail operations (South Africa Tourism, 2012). Unlike manufactured goods, African tourism is complementary to China's growth, and China has granted both countries "approved destination status": a recognition that allows South African and Tanzanian firms to conduct direct destination marketing in China (Goldstein *et al.*, 2006). Both countries have unparalleled touristic resources (e.g., Serengeti National Park in Tanzania, the Cape Floral Kingdom in South Africa), tremendous potential for tourism growth, and have experienced tourist-led local development (World Bank, 1998; Binns and Nel, 2002).

South Africa is one of the continent's premiere tourist destinations and it is the only sub-Saharan African country to rank in the top 50 tourist destinations worldwide. South Africa's tourism trade is responsible for nearly 40% of all international tourism receipts in sub-Saharan Africa, and in 2006 was estimated to account for 8.2% of the country's total GDP, 7.5% of employment, and 13.9% of "exports" (World Travel and Tourism Council [WTTC], 2006; World Tourism Organization, 2007; South Africa Tourism, 2012). Growth in 2010–11 was low, at 0.7%, but this is still creditable as it came in the wake of the World Cup "mega-event" held in South Africa in 2010. The country has a wide variety of attractions and climates, and since the end of apartheid in the early 1990s tourist numbers have increased dramatically (Rogerson, 2013). South Africa also has a substantial advantage over its neighbors because of its much more highly developed infrastructure, and this is reflected in marketing campaigns advertising tourism as South Africa's new "gold" (Büscher, 2013).

Although the largest share of visitors to South Africa originates from within the southern African region, the most valuable tourist market segment is the long haul one that brings Europeans, Asians, and North Americans to the country. In terms of business ownership and management, firms in the industry are mostly "white"-owned, with foreign companies also having a significant presence in prime tourist locations (Van Amerom and Büscher, 2005). Cape Town and the surrounding Western Cape region are amongst South Africa's foremost tourist destinations, and the industry has expanded dramatically in the city, with the number of hotel rooms rising from 4000 to 13,000 from 1990 to 2010 (Rogerson, 2013).

In Tanzania, tourism – particularly in the country's vast game reserves, national parks, and the Zanzibar archipelago – is a crucial source of foreign exchange and investment and was responsible for 47% of Tanzanian "exports" in 2002 (World Bank, 2004; United Republic of Tanzania, 2007; Emerging Market-Org, 2007). Growth in the sector has been strong in recent years (13.1% in 2010–11) and international tourism receipts topped $1 billion in 2011, placing the country third within sub-Saharan Africa (World Tourism Organization, 2013a,b). Zanzibar is also a major international tourist destination. The island has a unique history, having previously been the seat of the Sultan of Oman and infamously remembered as the site of the shortest recorded war in world history, lasting roughly 40 minutes between the Sultanate of Oman and the British Empire. Growth in Zanzibar's tourism industry has been impressive since 2000, as international arrivals increased from just under 100,000 to nearly 170,000 in 2012, keeping in mind that these figures represent only those visitors who arrived by air and the fact that most travel to the islands by ferry from Dar es Salaam (Zanzibar Association of Tourism Investors [ZATI], 2013).

In sum, South Africa and Tanzania's wood products and tourism industries offered an excellent means through which we could assess how ICTs influence the development of different kinds of skills and knowledge within SMMEs (their imminent impacts), and whether they are complicit in transforming these industries such that they are better positioned vis-à-vis global markets, imports, and foreign investors or large-scale enterprises (their immanent impacts). Our comparative approach was designed to capture a wide range of potential impacts that ICTs might have within firms (SMMEs) and allowed us to determine whether the sociotechnical regimes and (inward/outward) global production networks (GPNs) in which they are imbricated were in the midst of a significant transformation in response to new and improved forms of communication and information management and access. The remainder of this chapter describes briefly our methods and then presents the findings as they relate to the imminent development implications of new ICTs, with a particular emphasis on whether changes in information and communication capabilities are translating into improvements in the performance, productivity, and/or innovativeness of SMMEs in South Africa and Tanzania.

Methodological Approach

To capture the imminent and immanent implications of ICTs, we employed in-depth interviews, direct observation, and a structured survey to determine whether/how ICTs contribute to SMME development, industrial change, and the global integration of South African and Tanzanian SMMEs, and if so, along what dimensions (exports, raw material imports). Our focus was on mobile phone, computer, and internet use, and we examined the influence of ICTs on enterprise and industrial development. After collecting basic data from firms on ICT access, use, and significance, our primary data-gathering was done through in-depth interviews with SMME owners and managers, and key informants familiar with the industries and/or ICT use in South Africa and Tanzania. These interviews were undertaken to determine whether and what specific contributions ICTs make to SMME performance, technological capabilities, and to the everyday management of supply chains, production activities, and customer relations. Interview questions focussed on the marketing, service provision, and management practices of firms and the role that ICTs play in these activities. In addition, respondents were asked about trends in the industry and the key market, and material and institutional challenges that they are facing at present.

The goal of the interviews was first to develop a detailed understanding of the everyday business practices associated with critical SMME functions (e.g., marketing, production, service provision, and product development) and then identify the specific roles that new ICTs play in these activities. In doing so, our goal was to gather data regarding the specific ways in which new ICTs are embedded in the operations of firms, rather than simply, for example, determining whether a business owner used a computer or the internet. These data were integrated and analysed qualitatively, and they provide multiple and overlapping vantage points from which to assess if, how, to what degree, and under what contextual conditions ICTs contribute to SMME performance, industrial development, and to changes in our industry case-study relationships with global markets.

For wood products, Tanzanian SMMEs were sampled from the large wood products market/cluster in the Keko ward and other areas of Dar es Salaam (see Figure 4.1), while in South Africa, firms were sampled in KwaZulu-Natal province, with an emphasis on Durban. Sampling for the tourism studies took place in two continentally significant tourism centers – Western Cape Province/Cape Town, South Africa, and Zanzibar, Tanzania – and focussed on the work of travel agents, tour operators, tour guides, and hoteliers. In each site, 47–53 business owners were interviewed and additional interviews were conducted with key informants in industry-promotion agencies, government ministries, universities, and relevant non-governmental and aid organizations. Given the sample size, the geographic locations of firms, and our focus on SMMEs participating in similar market segments – mainly furniture-makers, tour operators, and hoteliers – we are confident of the sample's coverage and representativeness vis-à-vis the populations constituting the industries in these locations.

Our sampling strategy was aimed at ensuring that the diversity – in terms of products, scale, gender, and location – of the SMMEs in both industries

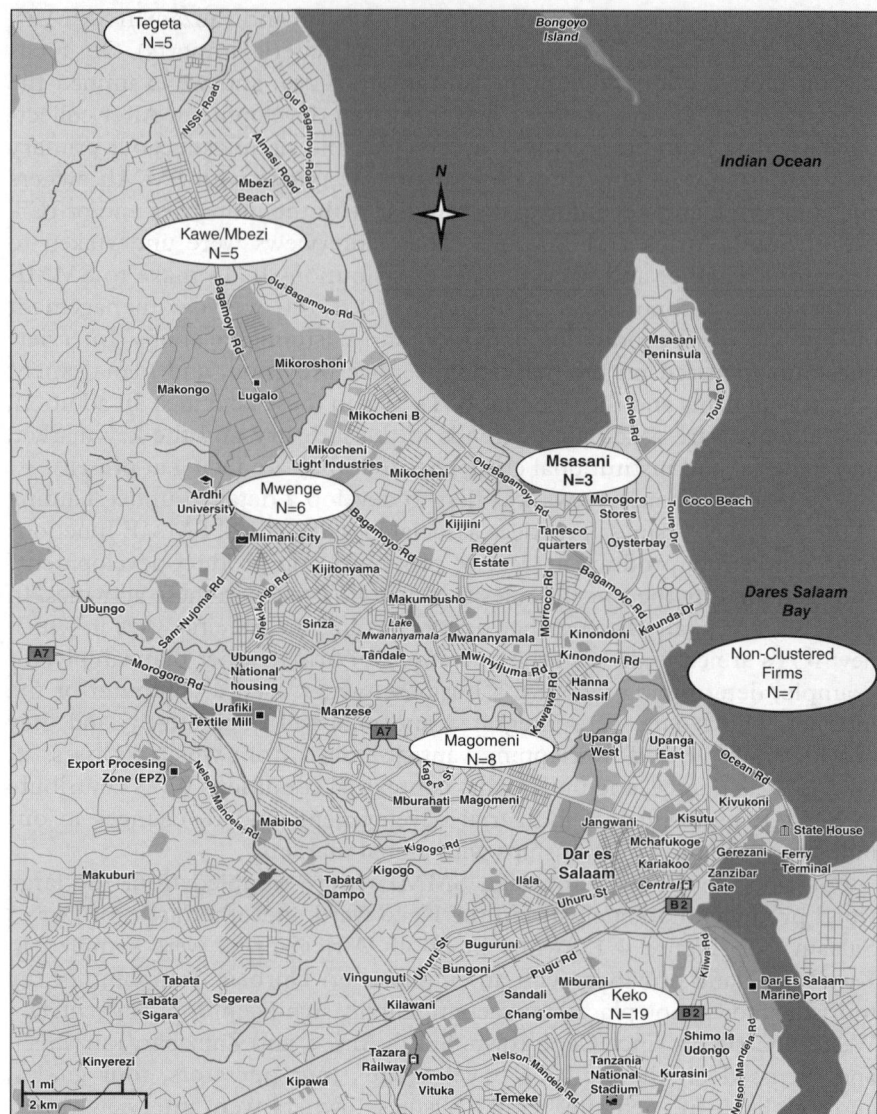

Figure 4.1   Map of the location of wood product SMMEs sampled in Dar es Salaam in 2010 (from Murphy, 2013). Reprinted with permission from Pion Ltd, London, www.pion.co.uk and www.envplan.com.

and countries was represented to the fullest extent possible. We achieved this through the up-front identification of, and email communication with, relevant firms wherever possible – but especially in the tourism sector and Durban's wood products sector – and through a snowball sampling strategy based on inquiries with business owners who had already been interviewed.

Firms were also enrolled in the study through a convenience sampling strategy based on face-to-face introductions made while working/walking in the industrial areas and tourism destinations of our case study locations. Through these methods we were able to achieve our goal of around 50 in-depth interviews in each case study location, and a representative sampling of tourism and wood products SMMEs.

The interview data from both field sites were compiled using qualitative data analysis software (QSR NVIVO 9.0) and analysed through a thematic coding process. Interview data were coded in relation to the following themes:

(a)   communication uses of new ICTs;
(b)   information uses of new ICTs;
(c)   the intensity of new ICT use;
(d)   computer and internet capabilities;
(e)   performance and innovation constraints;
(f)   sociotechnical regime and landscape characteristics and changes; and
(g)   emerging sociotechnical niches and other forms of innovation.

ICT-specific data (codes a–d above) were converted into frequency counts and combined in order to create an ICT use and capability score. This score is a discrete indicator of the extent and depth of ICT use within the SMME and was used to create three categories of firms: high usage firms, average usage firms, and low usage firms. Similarly, a set of performance indicators were coded and counted in order to create a qualitative performance "score" that distinguishes between low, average, and high performing SMMEs.

Beyond developing these scores, our thematic analysis enabled us to construct detailed narratives describing how the study's firms and industries operate on a day-to-day basis, how the regimes governing everyday activities are changing or evolving, and what challenges and opportunities exist in domestic markets and GPNs. In developing these narratives, emphasis was placed on situating new ICTs within the context of these activities, regimes, and issues, and determining how important a role they might play in immanent forms of development. The goal here was to assess whether there is evidence that "thicker" forms of ICT integration are empowering SMMEs with regard to the structural and material challenges that have generally limited their abilities to create and capture more value from the wood product and tourism markets.

While there are clearly limitations with regard to the specificity of some of the data, they do support our general arguments regarding the depth of ICT integration and enable us broadly to assess whether ICTs might facilitate a progressive transformation of African industries in an age of information-driven forms of capitalism. Our discussion in this chapter focuses on the imminent development implications of ICT use, manifest principally in the development of intra-firm capabilities and resources, the ability of SMMEs to overcome constraints on their ability to do business, and the links between ICT uptake and performance. The chapters that follow examine the immanent implications of ICTs, highlighting their limitations and possibilities given the economic contexts, institutional environments, and global markets facing firms and industries in South Africa and Tanzania.

ICTs and Imminent Development in South Africa and Tanzania's Wood Products Sectors

The discussion that follows draws upon interviews conducted in Dar es Salaam, Tanzania (hereafter Dar), and Durban, South Africa, in 2010–11. Table 4.2 summarizes the basic characteristics of the sampled firms. In Dar es Salaam, interviews were conducted with 53 SMMEs: 46 informal and small- to micro-scale enterprises, and 7 medium-scale, more formal producers or importers of wood products or furniture. The interviews were carried out throughout the city with an emphasis on six clusters of SMMEs (see Figure 4.1 for a map of Dar es Salaam with the SMME

Table 4.2   General information on the wood products SMMEs sampled

	Dar es Salaam (*n* = 53)	Durban (*n* = 52)
No. of employees		
Cooperative/owner-operator	16	3
1–5	9	14
5–10	13	7
10–20	3	12
20–50	5	9
>100	2	3
Years in business		
<1	1	2
1–5	7	9
5–10	9	6
10–20	20	17
>20	10	12
Type of business		
Manufacturer/retailers	48	50
Importer/retailer	3	2
Importer/manufacturer/ retailer	2	0
Regular exporters	0%	28%

locations specified). In Durban and the surrounding KwaZulu-Natal region (hereafter Durban), 52 SMMEs were surveyed, all of which were formal enterprises.

In terms of their size, as measured by numbers of employees, Tanzanian firms were typically much smaller operations: 47% were micro-enterprises (fewer than five employees) that operated either independently or as loose collectives of individual craftsmen (*mafundi*) who shared tools and rent showroom areas where their works are displayed. Figure 4.2 shows a typical group as was sampled in Dar. Such collectives are governed largely through informal rules and norms and each *fundi* views himself as an individual businessperson as much as he sees himself as a member of a cooperative. That said, loyalty and trustworthiness from one's partners in a collective is crucial for success, particularly when a *fundi* is unable to be at the workshop when customers may choose to purchase his furniture. As is customary, most of these manufacturers learned the trade as apprentices, working their way up from basic sanding and sawing work to making stools, bed frames, cabinets, tables, and chairs.[4] Several had received some formal training from technical schools, but none of those interviewed had received any tertiary education. In contrast, the Durban SMMEs were

Figure 4.2   Members of a typical furniture-making cooperative in Dar es Salaam. Photo by James T. Murphy.

formally incorporated, with 33% operated as micro-enterprises and 46% having ten or more permanent employees. Figure 4.3 shows a typical manufacturing operation for one of the Durban SMMEs that was sampled.

With regard to years in business, the samples are remarkably similar and cover a wide range of durations from brand-new businesses to long-standing operations. Most SMMEs were more than ten years old and had thus experienced a significant transformation with regard to their access to and dependence on new ICTs such as mobile phones, computers, and the internet. In terms of their manufacturing specializations, most of the firms surveyed produced, imported, or sold wood products or furnishings as retailers or, in fewer cases, wholesalers. In Durban, many companies produced customized furniture for domestic middle and higher income customers as they could not compete on price with standardized, often "flat pack", furniture being imported from China and elsewhere. There is a certain amount of "natural protection" for customized furniture provided by lead times and the fact that customers sometimes want to see the furniture as it is being made. In the Durban case, all of the firms were South African owned and operated, while in Dar several of the larger and

Figure 4.3   A typical manufacturing operation for the SMMEs sampled in Durban. Photo by Ralph Borland.

more formal firms were owned by foreigners, expatriates, or Tanzanians of non-indigenous extraction. Two of the businesses surveyed in Dar were major importers and retailers, one owned by a Turkish parent company, the other by a Chinese transnational business dependent on inward ties to GPNs.

As for exporting, very little was evident in the SMMEs sampled, with only 28% of the Durban firms being regular exporters, while the remainder catered exclusively to the domestic market. In Dar, a few sampled firms reported that they used to export but that it was no longer viable due to the costs and complications involved. That said, numerous micro-scale enterprises reported that some of their products have made their way to regional destinations such as the Comoros, Congo, Rwanda, and Kenya. Importantly, however, these sales occurred sporadically, at best, and were coordinated through face-to-face and cash transactions within Dar, with the buyer taking responsibility for the shipping arrangements and costs. While the links to outward GPNs were generally weak, several of the African-owned SMMEs sampled – but especially in Dar – were connected to inward GPNs through the importation of furnishings manufactured in Asia or the Middle East.

As Table 4.3 demonstrates, mobile phones are ubiquitous in both locations and they serve as critical, everyday technologies used in a wide range of business activities. As such, it is very difficult to break down systematically mobile phone use with respect to particular actions within wood products (or tourism) firms, and to determine which SMMEs are more or less reliant on mobiles for marketing, innovation, production, and so on. What is clear is that they are considered to be vital technologies even among the smallest, informal enterprises in Dar. Beyond this general observation, there are interesting contrasts in phone use, particularly with regard to landlines and smartphones or personal digital assistants (PDAs). Landline use is nearly absent in Dar, but it remains highly significant for most Durban firms as reflected in the lower rates of dependence on mobiles for communications with customers and suppliers. The mobile-phone use/dependence percentages are higher in Dar in large part due to the absence of landlines for use in business, with the exception of a minority of formal-sector enterprises. The nearly sole reliance on mobile phones in Dar is further reflected in the more frequent use of SMS or text messages as a form of business communication. Perhaps not surprising is the fact that smartphone or mobile PDA (e.g., iPhones, Blackberries) use is significantly higher in Durban, a reflection both of the relative affordability of ICTs and general differences in levels of ICT infrastructure and internet use and incomes in South Africa and Tanzania. But even in Durban it is clear that smartphones are not yet widely relied upon for everyday business, a reflection of their limited integration into manufacturing activities.

Table 4.3   New ICT use among the wood products SMMEs sampled

	Dar es Salaam ($n = 53$)	Durban ($n = 52$)
Mobile phones		
General business use	88.7%	94.2%
Customer communications	86.8%	59.6%
Supplier communications	41.5%	38.5%
SMS or MMS business use	43.4%	26.9%
Smartphone or mobile PDA	0.0%	11.5%
Email and internet use		
General email use	24.5%	92.3%
Customer communications	5.7%	75.0%
Supplier communications	7.5%	48.1%
Skype use	1.9%	13.5%
General internet use	9.4%	61.5%
Market information	1.9%	40.4%
Business ideas	9.4%	59.6%
Seeking clients or investors	0.0%	21.2%
Business website development	3.8%	69.2%
Use of third-party websites (marketing)	1.9%	13.5%
Electronic (e) banking	0.0%	36.5%
Computer use		
Bookkeeping software	9.4%	32.7%
Product design	1.9%	21.2%
Process and/or labor management	0.0%	23.1%
Customer or product database	5.7%	9.6%

As Table 4.3 shows, perhaps the most striking comparison between Durban and Dar with respect to new ICT use is the vast difference in the levels of internet and computer use. In Durban, email use is ubiquitous, and many find the internet to be an important tool for gathering information about markets and business ideas. Many customers expect firms to communicate via email, and use of email for supplier communications is viewed as significant by nearly 50% of the firms surveyed. In terms of marketing, nearly 70% of Durban SMMEs have websites, and increasingly there is a move by some firms to market their products on third-party websites. In terms of the internal management of firms, namely product design, payroll, accounting, and logistics, computers and the internet are significant for a number of Durban SMMEs who use e-banking, bookkeeping software (e.g., Quick Books), design software (e.g., AUTOCAD), and/or who maintain product or customer databases.

In stark contrast, only about 20–25% of the Dar SMMEs were using computers or the internet regularly. This was true even in the case of some importers who generally prefer voice or face-to-face communication when organizing shipments of new products from overseas. In one case, an importer had let his email account expire due to a computer malfunction, having little concern about needing it again anytime soon. Perhaps most significantly, there were few indicators that this situation is likely to change in the short term, given both the low penetration rate of smartphones and the relatively high cost of internet access relative to mobile phone use.

In terms of the association between the performance of SMMEs, and the breadth, depth, and intensity of ICT use, there is little or none in both cases. Table 4.4 summarizes the relationship between performance and ICT use and capabilities. High-performing SMMEs were less likely to have a high ICT use and capability score than average-performing firms, and average-performing firms are more likely to have a low ICT use score than a high score. As for low performers, only one such Durban SMME scored highly in ICT use and capability and most were in the average use category. Moreover, it appears that in only one case in each location is high performance associated with a high-level of ICT use and capabilities. In the Dar case, this high performer was a large-scale Chinese importer/manufacturer that distributes

Table 4.4 Summary statistics on ICT use and performance for the wood products SMMEs sampled. After Murphy, 2013, used with permission from Pion Ltd, London, www.pion.co.uk and www.envplan.com

	Dar es Salaam ($n = 53$)	Durban ($n = 52$)
High-performing SMMEs[a]	8	8
New ICT use and capability score[b]	1 high score (12.5%)	1 high score (12.5%)
for high performers	7 average score (87.5%)	5 average score (62.5%)
	0 low scores (0%)	2 low score (25%)
Average-performing SMMEs	35	37
New ICT use and capability score	8 high score (22.9%)	3 high score (8.1%)
for average performers	17 average score (48.6%)	19 average score (51.4%)
	10 low score (28.6%)	15 low score (40.5%)
Low-performing SMMEs	10	7
New ICT use and capability score	0 high scores (0%)	1 high score (14.3%)
for low performers	9 average score (90%)	4 average score (57.1%)
	1 low score (10%)	2 low score (28.6%)

[a]Performance scores were generated by tabulating positive and negative indicators coded for in the qualitative analysis of the interviews. These scores were then clustered into low-, average-, and high-performing groups.
[b]New ICT use and capability scores were tabulated as the sum of a communication use score, an information use score, an intensity of use score, and a capability score based on the respondent's self-reported ICT skills. The scores were then clustered into low, average, and high use and capability groups.

furniture to a wide range of resellers and who coordinates personal business trips to China for some of the larger, more formal importers in the city. We discuss these particular GPN relationships, and the role that ICTs play in them, in Chapter 6. Otherwise, average ICT users dominate the high and low performance groupings, and above average or high rates of ICT use are more likely to be associated with average performance. All told, there is no indication that there is a significant added benefit to Tanzanian and Durban SMMEs who are early or advanced adopters of new ICTs.

While the statistical evidence provides a basic overview of the use and significance of mobile phones, computers, and the internet for wood product SMMEs, it fails to tell us what, if any, imminent impacts that new ICTs are having on firms. We find some of these to be significant, particularly with respect to the influence of ICTs on the productivity of firms and their ability to overcome some activity constraints associated with production, marketing, and customer relations. More specifically, the benefits of new ICTs are manifest in improvements to the temporal and spatial management of firms, their ability to source raw materials, design-development enhancements, customer relations, and in labor management. In these respects ICTs are contributing in real ways to the capabilities and resources that SMMEs draw upon in their everyday activities.

Based on a close analysis of the interview transcripts, the main impact, at a broad level, of new ICTs seemed to be time-saving. For example, firm managers in Durban said things like "with the cellphone you get the message quicker" in communicating with customers and suppliers. Another noted that you could "ask ten people for quotations, just sitting on your computer". For some the internet was "mind-blowing" or a "window to the world". A micro-entrepreneur noted that "if there were no mobile phones we would be starving" (Durban), as he used his mobile phone to get in contact with customers, keep appointments, and so on. Others expressed opinions such as "you cannot do business without the phone" (Dar), the "mobile phone is my life" (Durban), "my phone is my business" (Durban), ICTs "make the world smaller" (Durban), and "the phone is important in that it saves time talking to different places and it reduces the time for communication" (Dar).

In Dar es Salaam, enhanced voice communication has meant that SMMEs are less tied down to specific market clusters and that it is easier to separate production facilities from sales locations. In particular, there has been a significant shift away from the traditional wood products center in the Keko area as many SMMEs now produce, sell, and/or finish furniture or other wood products (e.g., doors, window frames) in close proximity to new or expanding markets (e.g., Mwenge, Kawe, and Tegeta: see Figure 4.1). Wood supplies and, in some cases, furniture or door production may still occur in, or be sourced from, traditional clusters (especially Keko), and mobile phones make it much easier for manufacturers in outlying markets to place orders and coordinate deliveries from these areas.

> The doors are produced in Keko and if we need this or that we call there and they bring the shipment. We watch where the construction is going on and follow the market there. (Tegeta furniture manufacturer)

> Keko is for manufacturing only… In Magomeni, we are only selling. The customer tells us what they like and we use the mobile phone to tell people in Keko to make it. (Magomeni furniture manufacturer)

The ability to do so has been especially beneficial for those manufacturers able to meet the quality expectations of higher-end clientele (e.g., wealthy individuals buying new homes) and those SMME owners who have their own machinery. Mobile phones have enhanced the location-selection capabilities of producers and have helped several SMMEs to overcome communication constraints that have traditionally forced them to locate in or near the industry's traditional cluster in the Keko ward. As such, Durban and Dar SMMEs have experienced the well-known "space-time compression" effects of new ICTs.

ICTs have also played a significant role in improving marketing practices and communications with clients and customers. In Dar, mobile phones are an essential tool for maintaining ties to existing customers and for getting third-party referrals from old ones. As several business owners asserted, the phone is a critical tool for making sure that one can obtain repeat business, and it is especially valuable in that one can make specific arrangements to meet with a client rather than having to be present at the workshop or retail space all of the time. In Durban, the internet and email have added a layer of sophistication to marketing practices. Several Durban firms had a website through which to market their products, although most did not, and one noted that it would not be worthwhile to have one as they did not deal directly with the public. One company was going to start using a package from Mweb, a South African service provider that sends out bulk emails and text messages. It was felt that this was more effective than email, for example, because of the firm's market segment, as many of their elderly customers had mobile phones, but not computers.

Durban firms have also been able to access new customers through placing ads on the South African instant messaging service and social networking site MXit, which has about 20 million subscribers, and 350 million posts per day, more than seven times the number posted on Twitter globally (Cape Town Partnership, 2011). Other firms touted the significance of email direct marketing as a business-building tool. One manager recounted how they had sent an email to 25 clients. One of these clients sent it 40 people, who in turn sent it out to hundreds. Consequently "the phone did not stop ringing" and the company was kept busy for 18 months.[5] Another Durban business owner noted that business was "more busy" because they used the internet and email.

As Table 4.3 indicates, 60% of Durban SMMEs used the internet to look for ways to improve performance, with new business ideas (especially product designs) being a particularly significant search activity. Consequently, many South African firms, who have more developed capabilities and greater access to capital and new ICTs, were able to use the internet to create (thin) global knowledge "pipelines" (Bathelt et al., 2004). Firms reported finding new chemicals to achieve better finishes or glue components together better. One company found "Coosa" (high-density polyurethane) and used it as a replacement for plywood in its production process. Others reported sourcing new financial and management software or new machinery online.

Companies with more highly developed capabilities were able to use new ICTs most effectively. For example, there were a range of ICT facilitated services also being offered by companies. One company in Durban allowed potential customers, such as architects, to download computer-aided design (CAD) drawings from their website, while another used electronic funds transfer from customers facilitated by the internet. There were also instances where there was an intersection of ICT with high engineering technology. One company had outsourced its cutting to a computer numerically controlled (CNC) company and would email the drawings to them. They would also order the materials, which would be delivered to the CNC company for cutting. Another manager in Durban noted that they had a greater diversity of suppliers now because of new ICTs, while others noted that the spatial extent of suppliers within South Africa had increased. As a result, they were able to find out about suppliers in Johannesburg and Cape Town, whereas previously all of their supplies came from Durban. Cheaper inputs could be sourced, such as handles for furniture, which might have cost 7 South African rand (R7) each previously, but might only be R2 now. In Durban others noted that ICTs, especially computers and the internet, had helped them improve quality and better plan production, while one was able to track the location of its container-ized inputs from Asia in real time.

Finally, one of the most striking themes to emerge from the survey in Durban was the way in which new ICTs are used to manage/control labor, with 72% of firms using them (primarily mobile phones) in this way. This was different in Dar es Salaam; given that many of the "firms" were essentially self-employed producers, only one firm used them to manage labor and none used it to source employees. In contrast, several Durban managers noted how ICTs helped them manage and control workers through such tactics as internet-linked video surveillance and, much more commonly, phoning absent workers on their mobiles to see why they had not reported for work.[6] One company had given their employees mobile phones and the manager noted that even though these had sometimes been stolen or were switched off, it nonetheless made management easier. Another felt mobile phones had "instilled a sense of discipline" in their workforce, and the fact that so many companies in the survey used mobile phones to manage labor suggests their utility.

In sum, the evidence makes clear that new ICTs – but particularly mobile phones – have had a significant and positive impact on the transaction costs and constraints associated with supply-chain management, design development, customer relations, production activities, and labor management in Dar and Durban's wood products sectors. These capability and resource changes reflect the imminent development implications associated with ICT uptake and use, and the SMMEs we interviewed cannot, by and large, imagine doing business without a mobile phone and, in some cases, a computer with internet access. But are these technologies enabling the immanent forms of innovation, restructuring, and industrial upgrading needed to more progressively position and empower African manufacturers vis-à-vis imports and larger-scale (often foreign-owned) manufacturers (a few of which were included in our sample)? While the utility of new ICTs is clear, manifest in their amelioration of certain kinds of information and communication-coordination constraints and their contribution to everyday management activities, their implications for the performance of SMMEs is much less so, for the reasons we detail in the chapters that follow.

ICTs and Imminent Development in South Africa and Tanzania's Tourism Sectors

To assess the impacts of new ICTs on the tourism industry, we conducted in-depth interviews with 98 SMMEs based in Cape Town and the Western Cape region (hereafter referred to as Cape Town), South Africa, and Stone Town, Zanzibar in the United Republic of Tanzania (hereafter referred to as Zanzibar). Key informant interviews were also conducted with industry representatives (e.g., Cape Town Routes, Zanzibar Association of Tourism Investors) and, where possible, government officials (e.g., Zanzibar Commission for Tourism). These interviews were used primarily in the discussion that follows to support the empirics we present and arguments we develop. Table 4.5 provides summary statistics for the sampled firms, and Figures 4.4 and 4.5 show typical street scenes in the locations where interviews were conducted. Sampled firms in Zanzibar were mostly tour operators, travel agents, and small-scale hoteliers, but we also interviewed a registered tour guide. These SMMEs included both low-end as well as high-end and boutique operations owned and operated by Zanzibaris or expatriates living in Zanzibar.

Table 4.5   General information on the tourism SMMEs sampled

	Zanzibar (*n* = 47)	Cape Town (*n* = 51)
No. of employees		
1–5	Difficult to determine beyond core	16
5–10	staff due to temporary labor and	5
10–20	subcontracting practices. Typically	1
20–50	between 1 and 5 employees for	2
50–100	tour operators and small hotels.	2
	Only a few larger operations were	
	surveyed with a maximum of 20 to	
	25 employees in a few firms.	
Years in business		
<1	3	1
1–5	14	9
5–10	6	10
10–20	6	9
>20	8	2
Principal business		
Tour operator	27	13
Hotel or bed & breakfast	15	27
Retail or restaurant	0	6
Mixed tour operator and retail	0	2
Travel agent	4	0
Tour guide	1	0

In Cape Town, the sample was more biased toward hoteliers and guest-house owners, but there were a significant number of tour operators and other retail-business operators included as well. With respect to size, both samples are quite similar, with the majority of businesses having fewer than five permanent employees and a very few with more than 20. In the Zanzibar case, employment numbers were particularly challenging to obtain given the temporary nature of most hiring practices and the use of subcontracting arrangements by most firms. In terms of experience, firms in both study locations showed similar trends, with the majority between one and ten years old, an indication of the general trend toward a somewhat high business turnover rate in both contexts. This is perhaps not surprising given the nature of tourist-oriented economies where seasonality concerns and other contingencies (e.g., weather, geopolitical issues) can make markets highly volatile, thus contributing to SMME failure.

In terms of their use of ICTs, the tourism sample is generally much more sophisticated with respect to types and uses of mobile phones,

Figure 4.4 Stone Town, Zanzibar, street scene and typical tour operator. Photos by James T. Murphy.

Figure 4.5   Hout Bay Harbour (Western Cape) and Cape Town, South Africa, tourism centers. Photos by Bjoern Surborg.

computers, and the internet. Table 4.6 summarizes the results with regard to mobile phone, computer, and internet use in both locations. As in the wood products sector, mobile phone use is ubiquitous and vital for the everyday operations of firms. Given that email communications are also ubiquitous in both locations, smartphone use is significantly higher in both Cape Town and Zanzibar, a reflection of the need for many business owners to be available as often as possible in order to respond to email queries from international customers. As Table 4.6 indicates, email is an important means of everyday communication, particularly for communications with clients and customers regarding pricing, logistics, accommodations, and the scope of tours. Email helps SMMEs move past initial inquiries in order to land customers, and many business owners thus spend a large amount of time at their computers or smartphones sending and responding to emails. For some, particularly tour operators in Zanzibar, solicitation emails are also used as a marketing strategy. Tour operators will first typically use the internet to obtain the email addresses of travel agents and other tour operators based in desired markets (e.g., Russia, Europe) and will then send them electronic solicitations for

Table 4.6   New ICT use among the tourism SMMEs sampled

	Zanzibar ($n = 47$)	Cape Town ($n = 51$)
Mobile phones		
General business use	100%	100%
Smartphone or mobile PDA	25.5%	37.3%
Email and internet use		
General email use	97.9%	100%
Customer or marketing communications	93.6%	94.1%
Skype use	19.1%	15.7%
General internet use	97.9%	61.5%
Market and/or business ideas	29.8%	40.4%
General information search	46.8%	59.6%
Seeking clients or investors	14.9%	21.2%
Business website development	87.2%	69.2%
Use of third-party websites	54.2%	13.5%
TripAdvisor or rating website	27.7%	78.4%
Booking website	17.0%	41.2%
Social media or networking sites	36.2%	58.8%
Other computer use		
Computerised booking system	23.4%	Some form of computerized booking in nearly all firms

business. While this appears, superficially at least, to be a significant use of ICTs for business development, the truth is that these kinds of "fishing expeditions" rarely lead to new realized business dealings as one respondent noted:

> If I send 100 emails [to foreign tour operators or travel agents], I will get approximately 30–40 responses but many of these will be impersonal or they will make clear that it will be impossible for them to do business due to some complication or situation. Some respond that they don't work in Africa, and others simply sell their tour packages through other tour operators based outside Africa... very few of these emails seem to work out... (Tour Operator, Zanzibar)

In addition to a heavy reliance on email, SMMEs in both locations used or relied upon the internet extensively and similarly as part of their daily business activities. Internet use involved basic information search activities related to tourism market trends, the activities of the local competition, and, particularly among tour operators in Zanzibar, the identification of potential intermediaries (tour operators and travel agents) based in key tourism markets in Europe and Asia. Internet reliance is associated primarily with website development and use, with nearly all the sampled firms having web sites of their own. Figure 4.6 shows a typical webpage managed by a tour operator in Cape Town, giving an overview of the services provided, contact information, and promotional materials regarding the sights and activities available to visitors. In addition there are often links to social media websites such as Facebook or Twitter, and/or a news feed or blog where the SMME owner/operator can post updates about services or highlight events or activities going on in the destination. In most cases there is a contact page, typically manifest as a SPAM-preventing email-based query form where prospective clients can generate an inquiry email which will be sent directly to the business owner or manager.

In some cases, more commonly in South Africa, booking may be done directly through the website with payment made with credit cards. In Zanzibar this is less common given the lack of trust and supporting financial institutions needed to enable the widespread use of credit cards. In this context, the vast majority of SMME owners are more comfortable with cash payments and/or wire transfers through banks. Those that do allow credit card payments, typically hoteliers, often levy surcharges and additional fees to the tune of 5%, in addition to foreign transaction fees facing many credit card users.

> Balance should be received at least one month prior to arrival. All payments via bank should be made without any bank transfer charges for us. Payments via credit card are subjected to 5% surcharge for administration costs. (Hotel website, Zanzibar)

Figure 4.6   A typical home page for a tour operator in Cape Town. Reprinted with permission of AWOL Tours. Main photo credit: Bronwyn Lloyd.[7]

Even in the case of the domestic airlines servicing Zanzibar and its sur-rounding islands, credit card use is relatively uncommon and somewhat of a bureaucratic hassle.[8]

In addition to marketing their businesses on firm-specific websites, many tourism SMMEs rely on third-party websites as a means of attracting pro-spective clients. This phenomenon, while more common in Cape Town (84.3%, versus 54.2% in Zanzibar), nonetheless reflects the importance of centralized websites as conduits through which tourists obtain information on lodging, activities, and possible travel itineraries. Such websites are organised at the local level, such as those associated with tourism promotion organizations and/or chambers of commerce (e.g., see http://www.capetown.travel/ or http://www.zanzibartourism.net/), the regional or national level (e.g., Western Cape tourism [http://www.thewesterncape.co.za/], Tanzanian hotels [http://www.hotels.co.tz/], or the Africa Travel Resource website [http://www.africatravelresource.com/]), or as globally centralized websites which may or may not enable booking through them (e.g., Expedia.com, TripAdvisor.com, or Lonelyplanet.com). TripAdvisor (tripadvisor.com) is a particularly powerful search engine and review website, and nearly 80% of the Cape Town SMMEs surveyed have a presence on its web pages. The numbers are much smaller in Zanzibar, but this is primarily a reflection of the smaller number of hoteliers who were interviewed, given that local tour operators are less likely to be reviewed or listed on TripAdvisor's pages. Getting listed on these sites is viewed by many as an important marketing strategy, and in some cases, especially with hotels, it can provide a key channel for an SMME's business to connect with tourists and other GPN actors. As we detail in Chapter 7, there are significant "catches" associated with third-party sites related to the costs of being listed, commission fees, the quality of communication with clients, mandates regarding the number of rooms or reservations that must be held for the website owner, and the challenge of maintaining a necessarily overwhelmingly positive online reputation, given the inevitable dissatisfaction that some tourists will experience.

In the case of bed and breakfast establishments (B&Bs), lodges, and hotels, several third-party websites (e.g., SAVenues.com, Expedia.com, and Bookings.com) offer direct bookings of a portion of their rooms. Two-thirds (67%) of the Cape Town hotels/lodges surveyed use this service, while only a third of hotels surveyed in Zanzibar garner business through such websites. Further evidence for the disparity can be seen at the Bookings.com website where only eight hotels are listed for booking in Stone Town, Zanzibar, a small fraction of the overall number of these businesses. For those using third-party booking sites, the typical arrangement is that a hotel must set aside a minimum number of rooms to be sold exclusively through the third party, but with a pre-set release date after which the proprietor can sell the rooms through other means. For example, one hotelier in Zanzibar sets aside four rooms on Expedia with a seven-day release date. When rooms are booked through such services, the hotelier receives a notification of the booking but is unable to communicate directly with the client prior to their arrival. Payments are transferred to the hotel on a periodic basis (variable) either through direct transfers or "ground handlers" (in the case of Tanzania) with a percentage commission deducted by the owner of the third-party website. A typical commission was reported as somewhere between 13–15% in the case of South Africa, although Bookings.com was reported to charge only 12%, making it particularly popular among SMMEs.

Within many SMMEs, computers and the internet play a central role in the organization and administration of bookings and reservations. While email communication is used to make, modify, or confirm some or all reservations in the enterprises studied here, the actual organization of bookings, room reservations, and/or tour operations varies in terms of the role that computers and the internet play. In Zanzibar, relatively few of the sampled firms (23.4%) have computerized booking systems, although most use email and word processing or other MSOffice software (e.g., Excel) in the day-to-day management of the business. Much of the reluctance to computerize bookings stems from the island's power supply problems, which were manifest most severely from December 2009 until March 2010 when a transformer failed, leaving Zanzibar without grid-based electricity for three months. In this context, many tourism SMMEs became very reluctant to move beyond traditional, paper-based reservation and operations-planning systems (usually relying on ledgers), and this trepidation was quite evident during the field research.

Firms in Cape Town differ dramatically in this regard as nearly all of surveyed SMMEs organize their bookings and reservations using a computer. A website was usually a primary component in organizing bookings and reservations, but the degree to which it was directly integrated into the back-end administrative system varied considerably between companies. A website is usually a primary marketing tool, providing general information about a tour operator, guest house or other tourism business, but the technological strategies to generate reservations from this vary considerably depending on the business size, administrative setup and technological capacity. There are two main strategies: first, as noted above, the website provides an email link or an online form that automatically generates an email for inquiries, which then have to be replied to individually and handled by a person. Second, the website is directly linked to the reservation system through in-house software, or it is linked to an external web service that synchronizes with the in-house reservation system. Both approaches allow for instant inquiries, confirmation and online payment.

In Cape Town, 41% of firms interviewed outsourced their online booking to third parties. This was predominately the case for accommodation providers (67%) rather than tour operators (14%). The main sites mentioned were Bookings.com and Expedia.com, both of which are foreign-owned. Of the 27 accommodation firms in the survey, ten (37%) use the South African company Nightsbridge (http://www.nightsbridge.co.za/) to manage bookings directly from their website. This service offers inventory management and online payment processing. It also integrates with booking websites (such as Expedia and Bookings.com) to block off rooms automatically when booked via those services. Figure 4.7, taken from the Nightsbridge website, provides an example of what this interface typically looks like to the

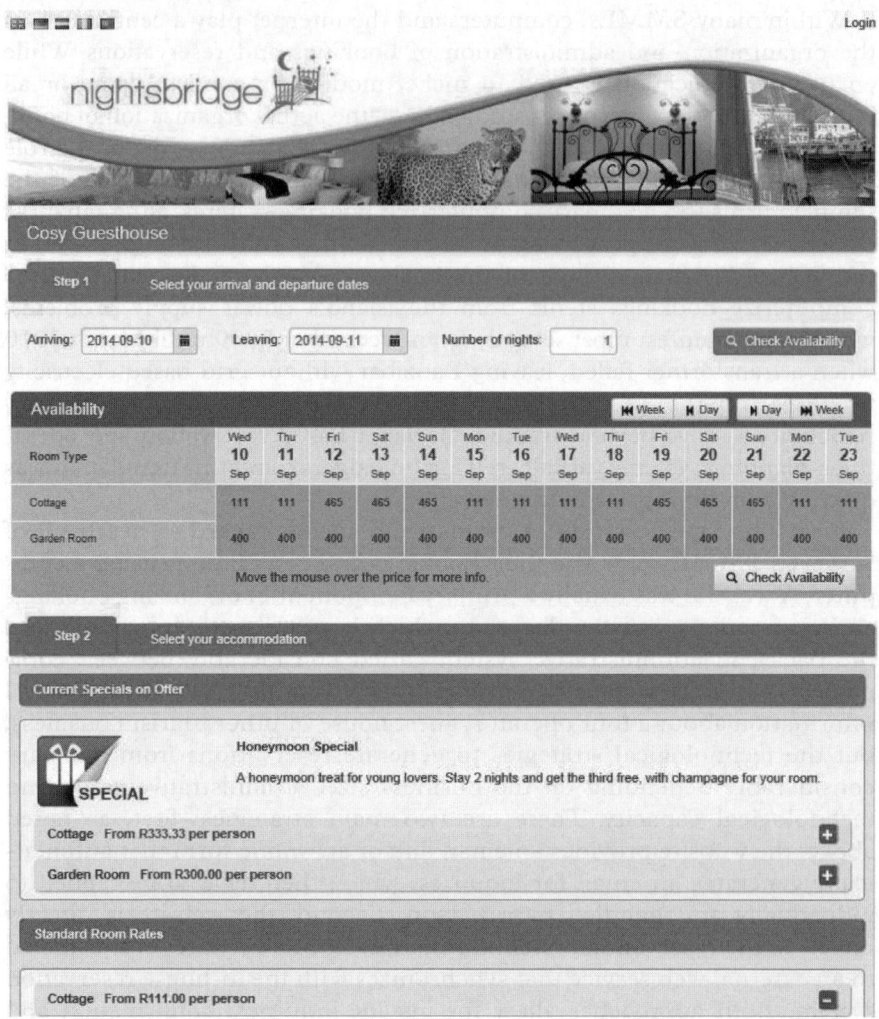

Figure 4.7   A Nightsbridge booking interface. Source: http://www.nightsbridge.co.za/. Reprinted with permission.

customer. Only two accommodation firms had their own direct online payment options (PayPal or credit cards), whereas three tour operators offered direct online payments. Nightsbridge appears to have something of a monopoly in this area, and the cost of using the company's services depends on the number of rooms you have. For example, a 10-room guest house will be charged R350 per month (about €30 or $34 per month). Firms seem happy with the service, as there were no negative comments about Nightsbridge.

To summarize, our interviews revealed that mobile phones, computers, and the internet are integral and ubiquitous technologies used by tourist SMMEs in Cape Town and Zanzibar. New ICTs are crucial technologies for SMMEs, used for online and direct marketing activities, arranging bookings and other services, general communication with customers, and, particularly in the case of mobile phones, essential for the day-to-day management of activities within the firm (e.g., coordinating transport, managing workers). As Table 4.6 indicates, when comparing SMMEs within and between Zanzibar and Cape Town there is variability in terms of ICT investments and capabilities – especially with respect to the use of third-party websites, computerized reservation systems, social media, and the internet as a source of business-relevant information. But can these differences be associated with variations in imminent development outcomes, measured here in terms of the firm's performance? Table 4.7 provides some perspective on this question as it compares the extent and depth of ICT usage and capabilities with context-specific indicators of performance.

The results, as they were in the case of wood products, are ambiguous albeit slightly more positive overall, particularly in the case of South Africa. In Zanzibar, high-performing SMMEs ($n = 8$) were equally likely to have high-end (37.5%) or average ICT capabilities, and a quarter of the high performers were in the low end of the capability range. The majority of

Table 4.7 Summary statistics on ICT use and performance for the tourism SMMEs sampled

	Zanzibar ($n = 47$)	Cape Town ($n = 51$)
High-performing SMMEs[a]	8	9
New ICT use and capability score[b]	3 high score (37.5%)	3 high score (33.3%)
for high performers	3 average score (37.5%)	6 average score (66.7%)
	2 low score (25%)	0 low score (0%)
Average-performing SMMEs	34	37
New ICT use and capability score	3 high score (8.8%)	7 high score (18.9%)
for average performers	26 average score (76.5%)	24 average score (64.9%)
	5 low score (14.7%)	6 low score (16.2%)
Low-performing SMMEs	5	5
New ICT use and capability score	1 high scores (20%)	1 high score (20%)
for low performers	3 average score (60%)	2 average score (40%)
	1 low score (20%)	2 low score (40%)

[a]Performance scores were generated by tabulating positive and negative indicators coded for in the qualitative analysis of the interviews. These scores were then clustered into low-, average-, and high-performing groups.
[b]New ICT use and capability scores were tabulated as the sum of a communication use score, an information use score, an intensity of use score, and a capability score based on the respondent's self-reported ICT skills. The scores were then clustered into low, average, and high use and capability groups.

average-performing SMMEs had capabilities within the mid-range as well (76.5%), with a few "outliers" with high capability (8.8%) and low capability scores (14.7%). As for the low-performing Zanzibar SMMEs, most of these had average or typical ICT capabilities with the exception of one highly capable firm and one firm on the low end of the spectrum. In Cape Town the results were a bit more definitive with respect to the associations between ICT capabilities and high-performing SMMEs. Specifically, high performers had only average (67%) or high (33%) capability scores, whilst no low-ICT-capability SMMEs were high performers. Otherwise, the results were similarly mixed for the average- and low-performing tourism firms in Cape Town as these firms had a wide range of ICT capabilities.

Beyond these somewhat ambiguous associations, the imminent development implications of new ICT adoption are significant in both cases and are manifest in improved communications and accessibility, enhanced efficiencies related to reservation management and other logistics, and globalized marketing capabilities through the internet. As in the case of wood products, new ICTs have enhanced SMME communication capabilities and made them more accessible and responsive to clients, thus proving to be extremely important from a customer service perspective. For example, a tour operator in Zanzibar conveyed the following stories:

> Today I was helping 10 Norwegian students who were stuck in Lusaka for 3 days due to some airline troubles and who had to keep booking and rebooking their ferry tickets. I renegotiated their ferry bookings several times, and when they arrived at the Dar airport unexpectedly at 4:00 am they called me on the [mobile] phone because they had no idea what to do. I kept talking to them and relaxing them and I promised to take care of the problems with the ferry tickets and to help them arrange transport to the ferry terminal in Dar es Salaam. I called the reservation manager at the ferry and took care of the whole issue as best I could. In another case, I arranged a tour for two Danish tourists and managed to respond to all of their emails within 15–30 minutes of receipt. In the end, the clients are very happy about how it all turned out and relaxed to be in Zanzibar. (Tour operator, Zanzibar)

These sorts of sentiments were commonplace and reflect a crucial contribution that new ICTs have made to tourism activities in South Africa and Tanzania: they have made it possible to have more direct and personal communication with tourism clients prior to their arrival at the destination. Such communications are vital for creating trust and a sense of security, particularly for those tourists who may be travelling to Africa for the first time and/or who have some trepidation regarding their security and the trustworthiness of African businesspeople. ICTs have thus helped to reduce these challenges and to demystify some of the upfront uncertainties that travellers often have by providing an easier, efficient, and more direct means for achieving transnational communications.

The second major imminent development implication of new ICTs in the tourism sector relates to efficiency improvements in the day-to-day management of firms, particularly those who have adopted computerized and internet-based reservation systems. This is mainly the case in South Africa and among larger-scale hoteliers in Zanzibar, and the reported benefits are quite significant. In terms of formal systems, Expedia, TripAdvisor, Bookings.com, and other country- or region-specific websites have become essential commercial sites for many SMMEs, and the most sophisticated firms have their links to these websites integrated into their internal booking systems that are run through programs/services such as Nightsbridge (see above), Opera (www.micros.com/Solutions/), and ResRequest (www.resrequest.com). Real-time integration is reaping significant benefits for some SMMEs as they are able to manage their "inventories" more efficiently and strategically. As a lodge owner in South Africa noted:

> IT has dramatically changed the business. Most people in the business are not oriented to tech systems, but I was from the beginning and very quickly moved from charts to an online system – it was simple at first and provided what was needed. The system has developed itself and become quite sophisticated – it is linked in to Nightsbridge and that ties in all systems. For example if they close out a room in Nightsbridge, that closes out rooms in the other systems that it is linked into such as Expedia, Lastminute.com and numerous others. (Lodge owner, Cape Town)

The benefits extend beyond hotel and lodging reservations and are becoming evident to some of South Africa's tour operators, who are turning increasingly to third-party websites in order to capture a greater volume of business. As one tour operator noted:

> We are setting up a system to be on Webtickets [http://webtickets.co.za/] and are the first smaller tour operator to do so. People can book [tours] on the web and come with their print-out ticket. The ticket will have a bar code to scan. Concierge services in hotels, agents and so on will be linked into that system as well, but they all need log-ins. Our Table Mountain and the Robben Island tours already use webtickets… Sales are all moving online. If people call in we direct them to the website. The online booking system will be up and running from next month. (Tour operator, Cape Town)

Such developments are indicative of the increasing power and significance of third-party websites for the tourism industry, a development that has positive imminent development implications, as highlighted above in relation to intra-firm capabilities, but which raises important concerns regarding the evolving structure of Africa's tourism trade. We address these issues in detail in the coming chapters.

A third imminent outcome of the penetration of new ICTs into Africa's tourism industry relates to the ability of SMMEs to market their services and products more directly to foreign-based tourists and intermediaries. In this regard, the internet has become a crucial tool or platform for doing so. While a website is usually the centerpiece of a tourism enterprise's internet presence, the sector utilizes a variety ways of engaging with the internet, and more broadly ICT, for marketing, public relations and sales activities.[9] Table 4.8 lists a number of themes that emerged from the interviews and describes their opportunities, challenges, and importance for SMMEs in the tourism sector. Particularly significant, as highlighted above, is the use of social media (e.g., Facebook, Twitter) and third-party ratings and business platform websites (e.g., TripAdvisor, LonelyPlanet.com, and Bookings.com), while some SMMEs also generated content for their webpages through blogs that allow for feedback from viewers and clients.

In the most sophisticated cases, SMME owners are closely monitoring their web presence through tools like Google Analytics, or optimizing web searches and increasing ALEXA hit rates (see http://www.alexa.com/) through techniques such as "ant-colony optimization", which mimics the behavior of foraging ants (and their pheromones) in order to draw visitors and potential clients to its website. Still others use simpler and lower-cost techniques such as SMS marketing through text messages sent directly to regular clients, although such strategies are typically constrained to the domestic market. Beyond ICT-enabled strategies, most businesses still rely on non-digital media and strategies, such as printed materials and physical sales offices. Nonetheless, ICT clearly dominates communication in the sector, and almost all the firms surveyed view ICTs as essential tools for the future development of their businesses. As such, most SMMEs are by and large committed to expanding their internet presence and ICT marketing capabilities in the coming years.

To summarize, it is clear that new ICTs are playing a significant role in the tourism industry in South Africa and Tanzania, and that SMMEs rely heavily on these technologies for customer relations, marketing, bookings, and, particularly in South Africa, inventory (e.g., guest room) and other forms of logistics management. As such, the imminent development implications are clear: SMMEs must have an adequate level of ICT capability and web presence if they hope to tap consistently into the growing global market for travel and tourism. While the quality of service provision still matters immensely, the internet in particular has offered new and diverse ways through which tourism SMMEs can position themselves in the marketplace, manage their reputational capital, differentiate themselves through online personalities, link in to new market segments, and identify and track market trends through search engine optimization (SEO) and web-based analytical tools. But given the costs associated with the time and capabilities needed to exploit web-based opportunities, and the high levels of competition, SMMEs

Table 4.8 Tourism SMMES' use of the internet in the Western Cape/Cape Town and Zanzibar

Theme	Short description	Opportunities	Challenges	Strategic importance
Business website	Website of great importance as it is often the primary tool to market services on offer.	Relatively cost effective tool to market to a global audience while maintaining control over content.	Regular updates are challenges.	Most businesses identified their website as an important tool, often the single most important one.
Social networking websites (e.g., Facebook)	Have received considerable attention from businesses, but limited new business.	Provide the possibility to reach large numbers of people with up-to-date information.	Updating these sites is time-consuming and labor-intensive.	Limited resources invested, but many feel it necessary to maintain a presence.
Blogs and content-sharing sites	Blogs of little significance. Small number of adventure-oriented businesses utilized YouTube.com to post videos.	Cost-effective way to provide information on a business.	Professional content generation (i.e., videos or blog entries) may be difficult and costly to produce.	Generally low.
Third-party rating and review websites (e.g., TripAdvisor)	Websites that allow travellers to review and rate tourism businesses and, in some cases, upload pictures.	Positive reviews are very beneficial for a business as many travellers consult TripAdvisor before making a reservation.	Concern that TripAdvisor is open to fraudulent reviews, e.g., by business owners posing as travellers.	TripAdvisor central for guest houses. For tour operators and other businesses seems to be considerably less important.
Third-party booking websites (e.g., Bookings.com, Expedia.com)	Allow travellers to book accommodation or tours.	These sites allow guest houses especially to gain web visibility.	Some portals charge very high commissions.	Important for the administration of bookings and reservations.
Search engine optimization (SEO)	SEO builds a website with specific terms and links that will be found more easily by search engines.	Links created through specific keywords in search engines can also increase visibility of a business online.	SEO advertising and/or consulting fees can be costly.	A small number of businesses reported that SEO is of great importance.
SMS marketing through mobile phones	Brief message to potential clients regarding a service or sale.	Cost-effective way to reach a targeted audience.	Little information can be transmitted and clients may easily disregard message.	SMS marketing of little strategic importance beyond domestic or local market and return clients.

face in the Cape Town and Zanzibar markets, we again need to ask whether new ICTs are enabling immanent changes in the positionalities and profitability of these firms vis-à-vis new forms of value creation and intermediation that have accompanied the rise of ICT-enabled tourism markets.

Conclusion

As this chapter has detailed, new ICTs are making significant contributions to the everyday practices of SMMEs in South Africa and Tanzania's wood products and tourism industries. Communication, service provisioning, and production/distribution coordination capabilities have been most significantly influenced, and most business owners cannot envisage doing their work without mobile phones and, in many cases, computer and internet access. Wood products firms rely on ICTs – especially mobile phones – for basic voice communications, and some, especially in South Africa, use computers and the internet regularly to manage supply chains, do design work, manage accounts, conduct payroll and other banking transactions, and monitor/manage workers. Not surprisingly, tourism enterprises are much more heavily dependent on ICTs for their marketing activities, service provisioning, and business transactions, due in large part to their need to act at a distance with foreign clients and intermediaries. In this context, ICTs have proven to be essential tools for enabling/strengthening couplings to GPNs in the tourism industry, although many SMMEs are struggling to enhance the value (i.e., upgrade) of their activities through them, as we detail below.

When considered in relation to Gregor *et al.*'s (2006) intra-firm resources, the findings are largely mixed and reflected in the weak associations between performance and ICT capabilities in SMMEs. The transactional resources of SMMEs – particularly those associated with the costs and benefits derived from everyday operations, worker productivity, and supply-chain management – have been marginally, and in some cases significantly, enhanced within most firms, thus making ICTs indispensable and fully absorbed into the routines and practices of firms. Informational resources – especially those associated with basic access to information about markets, competitors, and prospective clients – have too been improved, particularly for those firms having regular internet access and the ability to conduct online searches. Mobile phones also contribute to informational resources, albeit primarily in relation to local markets and industrial areas, as they facilitate the creation of "buzz" within industrial clusters and tourism destinations through more efficient, real-time communications between business owners, workers, and customers.

While these benefits are noteworthy, far less significant and evident throughout our case studies are the contributions of ICTs to strategic and transformational resources in SMMEs. Firms are experiencing efficiency gains and improved access to basic information, but most business owners surveyed do not deploy ICTs in ways that might (clearly) contribute to product innovations or enhance their long-term competitiveness in domestic markets and in relation to inward/outward GPNs. With respect to transformational resources, the evidence is similarly limited, as most SMMEs are not experiencing social or industrial upgrading in relation to employee skills, organizational capabilities, and/or the capacity to develop new business models or plans. In fact, as is evident in Durban's wood products sector, workers in SMMEs are experiencing greater monitoring and supervision through ICTs in order to increase their productivity. What this means for working conditions, labor movements, and the prospects for social upgrading is uncertain and worthy of further research.

Having detailed and summarized the imminent implications of new ICTs for African SMMEs, we turn to an analysis of their implications for the development of the sociotechnical regimes and GPN couplings associated with the wood products and tourism trades. At the heart of our analysis is the question of whether, how, and why these territorialized structures and relational configurations are being transformed in ways that enhance and/or limit African industries and urban–regional contexts from being able to create, enhance, and capture more value through improvements in communications, information access, and connectivity to non-local actors in GPNs. We now address these immanent development implications, highlighting five trends – thintegration, downgrading, differentiation, neointermediation, and ICT-enabled extraversion – that raise critical questions about the long-term impacts of and promise of new information and communication technologies and ICT4D initiatives in Africa.

Notes

1 We defined SMMEs as firms with fewer than 200 employees. That said, the vast majority of the firms included in our study have fewer than 50 employees and many, particularly in the Tanzanian and tourism case studies, have fewer than five.
2 This research project was supported primarily through a grant from the US National Science Foundation (#0925151), which supported the work from 2010–2013.
3 The digital opportunity index (DOI) is a composite score reflecting a country's extent and depth of ICT uptake and use. The DOI uses 11 different ICT indicators, grouped into three dimensional categories – ICT opportunity, infrastructure, and utilization. See https://www.itu.int/ITU-D/ict/doi/index.html for details.
4 The analysis of Dar es Salaam's wood products industry was informed significantly by prior research conducted by Murphy in 1999–2000 on the wood products and furniture manufacturing sector of Mwanza, Tanzania (see Murphy, 2002, 2006a). Mwanza is Tanzania's second largest city and home to a large

number of SMMEs in the wood products and furniture industries. Despite the difference in the firms interviewed and the locations of the research, a general comparison holds given the consistencies in the industry's organization throughout Tanzania and the similarities in the scale of the operations and clusters observed in both places. None of the SMME owners interviewed in 1999–2000 used mobile phones or computers, thus enabling a meaningful pre- and post-ICT comparison regarding the impact of new ICTs on activity constraints and the sociotechnical regime that governs the industry.

5   However, the size of the domestic market is inherently limited and this firm capturing market share may have prevented or displaced other domestic firms, so the "connection benefits" to the domestic economy arising from the use of new ICTs may be limited. If imports are being replaced, this does have substantial benefits for the domestic economy.

6   However, the effectiveness of these strategies varied. One firm in a small town in rural KwaZulu-Natal noted that while the staff had mobile phones, they often lost them or had them stolen and that numbers constantly changed, or they had them switched off. Consequently it was felt that this was not a form of communication that managers could rely upon. Another manager noted that often workers suffered from domestic disruption, and that this explained why many of them were absent and that "their problems are probably much bigger than my requirements of them".

7   The tour operator whose website is shown in the figure was not interviewed or included in the data analysis.

8   For example, one of the authors had to fill out a pdf form (received via email) with his credit card information put into it and then email this form back to the airline in order to purchase tickets to fly from Dar es Salaam to Zanzibar. The transaction took a number of email exchanges in order to get everything correct.

9   And one does not even need a formal website to maintain a web presence. One guest-house owner in South Africa noted that they were "not on the web, but were on the web". What they meant by that was that they did not have a website but that they were listed or mentioned on many other websites so that potential guests were able to find them.

Chapter Five
ICT Integration, Sociotechnical Regimes, and Global Production Networks

As detailed earlier, much has been written about the impacts of mobile phones, and other new ICTs on Africa (e.g., Donner, 2004, 2006; Obijiofor, 2009; Aker and Mbiti, 2010), with some claiming that they are having a transformative (i.e., immanent) effect on the continent's economies and societies (e.g., Okpaku, 2006; Smith *et al.*, 2011). Such transformations are thought to be occurring largely as a result of the region's improved connectivity with the international system; a development that advocates of the "New Economic Geography" (NEG) claim has been the primary obstacle to the continent's development in the post-colonial era (World Bank, 2009; Wilson, 2011). While international connection enabled by new ICTs may be taken as a prerequisite for certain forms of development, it is often taken as a synonym for it (e.g., Friedman, 2005), and with a few notable exceptions (e.g., Chew *et al.*, 2011) much of the literature does not explore the precise channels through which new ICTs might (immanently) contribute to structural diversification and upgrading of African economies towards (higher value-added) manufacturing or (tradable) services.

The remainder of the book addresses this issue by moving beyond firm-level indicators of ICT impact in order to determine whether the depth and forms of usage of new ICTs has enabled inter-firm and market integration and structural changes to markets, sociotechnical regimes, and the position of African SMMEs within and in relation to GPNs. In doing so our aim is

Africa's Information Revolution: Technical Regimes and Production Networks in South Africa and Tanzania, First Edition. James T. Murphy and Pádraig Carmody.
© 2015 John Wiley & Sons, Ltd. Published 2015 by John Wiley & Sons, Ltd.

to situate SMMEs geographically within the structural and relational contexts shaping their development, and to assess whether or not there are signs of progressive changes in the immanent conditions governing industrial and economic development in the region. More specifically, the goal is to assess whether ICTs are enabling new forms of industrial organization to emerge in these sectors: structural changes that might facilitate upgrading, increase the domestic and international competitiveness of African-owned enterprises, and improve the positionalities of these industries vis-a-vis GPNs such that greater value is captured locally, and in ways that contribute directly to social and industrial upgrading.

In this chapter, we examine the quality and depth of ICT absorption, focussing on whether and to what degree "thicker" forms of integration are occurring in industrial regimes, and the couplings linking our case study regions to GPNs. We do so by first assessing the type, value, and lifespan of the ICT-enabled information that is accessed, processed, and used by SMMEs. We then identify key supply and demand-side factors that are situated within, and generated by, wood product and tourism regimes and GPNs and which shape the depth and quality ICT absorption in these industries. Our findings detail how these factors contribute to the "thin" use or thintegration of ICTs, circumstances that limit their ability to contribute to a restructuring of sociotechnical regimes and the relationships between African firms and GPNs. In doing so we highlight how these challenges raise important general questions about the transformative potential of ICTs for African industries and economies.

Contextualizing ICT Integration and its Implications for Regimes and GPN Couplings

As described in Chapter 3, ICT integration within firms can be conceptualized along a spectrum from thin to thick based on the type, value, and lifespan of the information accessed, processed, and used for productive, innovative, or profit-making activities. For example, an SMME that has "thinly" informationalized its business activities may use ICTs primarily for voice or email communication to exchange discrete sets or bits of information that pertain to an immediate or short-term circumstance, problem, project, and/or customer inquiry. This kind of information typically has a short lifespan of utility (e.g., in relation to a single order or booking), is not stored digitally, and is not processed in a manner that can enable the business to track its performance, manage client relations, and/or develop new kinds of innovations or product ideas in response to market trends. In contrast, businesses that have become more "thickly" informationalized use ICTs to access and process information more intensively such that it can be fed back into performance evaluations, market trending activities, and the development of new products or process innovations.

When this kind of intensive information and communications management is taken up by many firms in a region, or at the global scale, the prospects for industrial transformation become more likely. As Zysman and Breznitz recently noted (2012: 132):

> The ICT revolution unleashed and has in turn been shaped by a constant revolution in social and market organisation. This constant experimentation, reshuffling, and the creation of new business models generate demand for new rules and new approaches to governance. There are two dramatic shifts in the story: the decomposition of production and the ICT-enabled transformation of services.

The decomposition of production entails the shift from vertical forms of integration to more geographically fragmented, horizontal, and/or decentralized webs or networks for exchange and supply-chain relations. Such a transformation can ideally enable SMMEs to identify strategically more profitable niches or specializations within production networks and to capture greater value through informationalized ties to domestic and international markets. Services can also be transformed through thick forms of ICT integration that lead to the development of information-intensive algorithms, decision-making rules, computing routines, and organizational structures that make firms more productive and which can transform the spatial organization of entire industries. As Zysman and Breznitz (2012: 135) further note:

> Business processes, from finance and accounting through customer support and customer relationship management, are altered when they can be treated as matters of information and data management. The algorithmic transformation of services permits routine and manual functions to be automated, which in itself enables a fundamental reorganisation of activities. It also permits the unbundling of the multitude of activities and tasks that constitute a service, the parallel to decomposition in manufacturing. Similar to production, these changes facilitate outsourcing and the easy relocation of activities.

When considered in relation to our case study industries of wood products and tourism, we view the possibility for a transition to thicker forms of ICT usage in these sectors to be influenced by supply-side and demand-side factors within firms, industrial regimes, sociotechnical landscapes, and the GPNs linked to African city-regions. Supply-side factors include intra-firm capabilities, ICT resources, capital availability, cultural factors, ICT infrastructure and service provisioning firms, educational and training institutions, and of course the supply of technologies themselves. In basic terms, thick forms of ICT integration require a certain level of these to be present in the regime context and/or in the "coupled" GPNs. Supply-side factors are an important consideration, but we view thick integration as primarily being a demand-driven process: one where information-processing capabilities are developed in direct response to the information requirements facing SMMEs

(Melville and Ramirez, 2008). Viewed from this perspective, the depth or extent of ICT integration is directly related to the complexity and speed of the processes through which production, marketing, service provision, and innovation are expected to occur in an industry and extant capabilities. In other words, context must be a central consideration.

For our purposes, context is manifest in the sociotechnical regimes and landscapes of our case study industries and countries, and the inward/outward GPNs that link African SMMEs and regimes to international actors. As Figure 3.2 highlights, regime contexts are relationally and terri-torially constituted and embedded within wider sociotechnical landscapes that influence the direction, pace, and scale of industrial and economic change. Inward (importing) and outward (exporting) GPNs may be linked to SMMEs situated in regimes, and the quality of these couplings – the degree to which they are organic, strategic, or structural in nature (MacKinnon, 2012) – determines in large part whether industrial and social upgrading is possible such that regions capture greater value. As we describe below, ICTs can contribute to firm, industry, and region-specific assets that shape the quality of these couplings particularly when thick forms of integration contribute to the right kinds of untraded interdependencies between regime and GPN actors. As Scott and Storper (2003: 587) noted:

> Regional economies are internally tied together through human and organiza-tional interdependencies – often untraded – that have a strong quasi-public goods character, meaning that they are the source of positive externalities that are more or less freely available to local firms but are the property of none.

Thick Integration in Wood Products and Tourism Regimes

In the wood products and furniture industries the information-processing capabilities of manufacturers have traditionally been relatively low given that product designs, customer demands, and raw material needs change slowly over time and within particular markets (Melville and Ramirez, 2008). In recent years, however, the industry's information-communication needs are changing in the context of the global information economy as supply chains become more fragmented, specialized, globalized, and governed through just-in-time and mass customization manufacturing strategies that rely increasingly on the use of ICTs (Apostolou et al., 1999; Lihra et al., 2008; Walcott, 2011). ICTs can also play a key role in enabling firms to implement cost-minimization strategies through the use of accounting software, increase the flexibility of their products through design software, and transition to e-commerce techniques for marketing and sales (Moodley, 2003; Quesada-Pineda, 2010). We view these kinds of innovations as indicators of "thicker" forms of ICT integration, ones that might enable firms to progressively reposition themselves in GPNs marked by intense competition and a shift towards the outsourcing of manufacturing jobs to places like China, Malaysia, and Indonesia (Kaplinsky *et al.*, 2002; Walcott, 2011).

Lead firms in GPNs who source wood products or furnishings from manufacturers in developing and emerging economies may play an important role in facilitating upgrading processes that engender thick forms of ICT integration. As Ivarsson and Alvstam (2010, 2011) demonstrate, IKEA has played a key role in helping Chinese and Southeast Asian furnishings manufacturers to upgrade their activities in a number of ways: accessing inputs and raw materials, production, factory organization, expansion, and management systems. The net result has been significant changes to the operational, adaptive, and innovative capabilities of many suppliers in the GPN. Some of these changes have involved IKEA-led investments in ICT-intensive forms of production and quality monitoring, computer numerically controlled (CNC) machinery, and the integration of suppliers into IKEA's electronic communication system or intranet. The latter is a particularly significant innovation for supplier firms, one that reflects what we envisage to be an example of "thick" ICT integration in the wood products sector.

> Through IKEA's Intranet, suppliers have a fast, updated and reliable access to information on orders, retail and warehousing stocks, product specifications and design, and on IKEA's long-term business plans, which significantly enhance production planning and delivery among the suppliers. Generally, their business communication with other customers only relies on basic e-mail correspondence. (Ivarsson and Alvstam, 2011: 742)

In contrast to wood products, tourism has always been a more communication- and information-intensive industry and one where new ICTs have played a significant role for the past decade or so, in particular. For most consumers, ICTs, and especially the internet, are essential for information-gathering (e.g., about destinations and prices) and are often used to conduct transactions (e.g., ticket purchases, accommodation booking) (UNCTAD, 2005; Buhalis and Law, 2008). ICTs enable tourists to create their own itineraries, and demand-driven forms of "mass customization" have become commonplace (Racherla *et al.*, 2008). The internet also provides a mechanism through which tourists can give feedback regarding the quality of a service experience, and websites such as TripAdvisor.com and LonelyPlanet.com are important peer-to-peer sources of information about attractions, hotels, and other destination-related services. On the supply side, ICTs can serve a critical role in helping destinations to manage the industry such that local firms can create and capture more value from markets. Internet-based destination management systems can be especially important in this regard, serving as key points of virtual contact between foreign tourists and local firms (UNCTAD, 2005). Through these web pages, consumers can gather information, obtain quotes, make bookings, provide feedback, and communicate directly with local SMMEs, thus reducing the need for intermediaries such as foreign tour operators. The effective use of such systems requires far more than the diffusion of mobile phones, computers, and the internet, as success depends on the ability to organize, integrate, and network SMMEs through common software, compatible hardware, effective algorithms, and a desire to collectively create and share knowledge about the destination and tourist services (Buhalis and Law, 2008; Racherla *et al.*, 2008).

Beyond extending, deepening, and speeding up the connections and flows of information between tourists, firms, and tourism destinations, thick integration is increasingly leading to "intelligent systems" (Gretzel, 2011) as a means for creating "digital business ecosystems" in destination locations (Bharadwaj *et al.*, 2013). Intelligent systems are able to evaluate conditions continuously in the environment (market), make real-time decisions in response to them, and to continuously learn how to adapt to emerging trends and contingencies (Gretzel, 2011).[1] For tourism destinations, intelligent systems can help to support a real and virtual interaction environment that facilitates information exchange, cooperative learning, and knowledge diffusion such that SMMEs can create and capture more value locally (Baggio and Del Chiappa, 2013). Informational capabilities such as these can be of great value to firms given the complexity, interdependency, and specificity of tourist decision- and subdecision-making processes, the mobility of tourists, and the multidimensional nature of tourist experiences (e.g., recreation, shopping, dining, touring). All told, "thicker" forms of ICT integration such as these hold the promise for industrial reorganization as firms use these technologies to manage customers, suppliers, workers, and intermediaries in a more direct, interactive, flexible, and real-time manner such that they are able to capture more value from global markets and, ideally, reposition Africa's tourist industry in GPNs.

As detailed in Chapter 4, there is little doubt that mobile phones, computers, and the internet are taking hold in the wood products and tourism industries in South Africa and Tanzania. But does the evidence demonstrate that "thicker" forms of ICT integration are taking place, and in ways that are transforming the structure, competitiveness, and viability of the sociotechnical regimes governing these sectors? Moreover, are the service provision and production demands placed on SMMEs by the global production networks, value chains, and consumer markets they serve increasingly more information intensive and sensitive, such that thicker forms of ICT integration are both necessary and profitable innovations? Our findings demonstrate that despite the ICT diffusion success story, thick integration remains elusive or non-existent for most firms/industries in our case studies, due in large part to the absence of significant "informational" demands placed on SMMEs by the sociotechnical regimes and global production networks within which they are embedded, in addition to a relative lack of capabilities and other supply-side constraints.

Thin or Thick Integration in Tanzania and South Africa?

In both of our case study industries and contexts the evidence demonstrates that thicker forms of ICT integration are largely absent within SMMEs with the exception, perhaps, of several firms in the tourism sector, particularly in South Africa. ICT-enabled transformation of sociotechnical regimes (e.g., from conventional forms of commerce to flexibly specialized e-businesses; from traditional tourism markets to digital business ecosystems) is not evident, although regimes and global production networks are being transformed in other ways, as we detail in chapters 6 and 7, as a result of the increasing penetration of imported manufactured goods into African markets and through (ICT-enabled) foreign intermediation into tourism markets. While these emerging trends reflect new forms of engagement between firms, industries, markets and the world economy, they are not leading to the kinds of organic or strategic couplings that can enable African SMMEs, workers, and regions to create, enhance, and capture greater value through globalization.

In Tanzania's wood products and tourism sectors, mobile phones are ubiquitous, smartphone use is on the rise, and computers and the internet are mixed in terms of their diffusion – common in most tourism SMMEs, but very rarely used in the wood products sector with the exception of larger and more formalized firms. While both sectors have seen firm-level benefits from the uptake of new ICTs, these are not significantly transforming business practices and/or the sociotechnical regimes governing these industries. Ties to GPNs are largely absent in the wood products industry, with the exception of the importers surveyed, while in tourism they are much more significant. However, in both cases, the couplings to GPNs are not inducing thicker forms of ICT integration, or industrial upgrading for that matter, as detailed in Chapter 6.

In the wood products industry, mobile phones are enhancing localized communication capabilities and the spatial organization/mobilization of SMMEs (e.g., their ability to separate retail and production activities), but they are not contributing to industry-wide changes to the structure of local markets, the quality and accessibility of outside sources of information (e.g., on technologies), and/or the abilities of SMMEs to access finance. Moreover, mobile voice communication does not substitute for the need to conduct much important business through face-to-face (F2F) interactions, especially where relationships have yet to be developed. Market structures are much the same as they were a decade ago (see Murphy, 2006a, 2007): hypercompetitive, with SMMEs operating with very thin profit margins, seasonally inconsistent demand, and domestic consumers who prioritize price over the quality and durability of furnishings. New, industry-relevant information continues to be accessed in the old ways – imitating the work of others, copying imported products, reading about or seeing new designs in furniture catalogues, through personal experiences and custom work with clientele, and by participating in F2F conversations with other SMME owners. Capital constraints continue to plague the sector, and only one or two of the firms sampled used m-banking, given the preference for hard-cash transactions.

Manufacturing technologies and production systems have changed little in the past decade, and computer numerically controlled (CNC) machinery is virtually absent. Couplings to GPNs are exclusively "inward" in nature, used by importers who have developed relationships with suppliers and manufacturers based in Asia. ICT use in these relationships is very basic – email and Skype communication for the most part – and business transactions are typically carried out through cash-for-goods exchanges and F2F meetings. While some SMMEs claim to have exported on a sporadic basis, sustained ties to outward GPNs are non-existent for the most part, and firms compete primarily in domestic markets where mobile phone voice/text communication is the primary use of ICTs. Even in the case of those SMMEs who have successfully sold to clients from foreign markets (e.g., Comoros, DRC), transactions were cash-for-goods exchanges arranged principally through F2F meetings in Dar. All told, there is little or no evidence of thick integration in Tanzania's wood products and furniture manufacturing industry.

In Zanzibar's tourism sector, computer and internet use is much more common, and most surveyed firms have websites and use email or Skype communication regularly. On the surface, SMME websites seem to be a significant development, but in practice they tend to be uninformative about prices, passive (e.g., they typically only provide an email request-for-information form), and similar in terms of design and the products offered. Consequently, most websites do little to distinguish one SMME from another and serve as secondary marketing strategies when compared with travel guidebooks, personal recommendations and references, and walk-in clientele. In addition to individual websites, several hotels advertise and sell accommodations through Expedia or other third-party websites, and some SMMEs market their services through social media and/or online chat rooms and other cyber-fora related to African travel. For many tour operators, direct email marketing to foreign tour operators is also used to drum up clients, although many observed that response rates to these emails were extremely low. Otherwise, new ICTs are, at best and in only a few cases, serving other needs such as information management, innovation development, accounting, and/or budgeting activities. In fact, and given

Zanzibar's inconsistent power supply, the vast majority of tour operators still use paper ledgers to organize their day-to-day activities. Like the wood products sector, ICT uptake in the tourism industry is primarily about basic communication improvements, albeit ones that facilitate both local and GPN-oriented forms of marketing and service coordination.

Many of the same trends are evident in South Africa as in Tanzania, but some of the specific implications are different, because of the higher level of ICT development in the country and its overall geoeconomic position. In the wood processing industry, ICTs have helped some firms to improve marketing capabilities, delivery times, time–space management, management of labor, and the sourcing of raw materials, inputs, and designs. However, they have had relatively limited applications in actual production and have thus not contributed substantially to a rise in manufacturing productivity (Carmody, 2011; Murphy *et al.*, 2014). Furthermore, while computers allow for improvements in production planning, accounting and communications, such as emailing of designs to subcontractors and CNC cutting, mobile and smartphones are more limited in their applications. Consequently, many firms in the wood products sector view new ICTs as ancillary rather than core technologies that can significantly increase profits or contribute to industrial restructuring and upgrading.

The evidence suggests that new ICTs have facilitated some innovation and greater value capture for some wood-product firms, mostly in local and regional markets, but not substantial forward and upward connection to GPNs, which might spur more widespread economic development and social upgrading. Rather, the findings show that many SMMEs are finding it increasingly difficult to upgrade their activities or enhance the value of their products through ties to GPNs, unless they already have extensive technological capabilities and/or well-established positions in high-end market niches or international markets. Moreover, ICTs are facilitating increased imports, enabling consumers to turn to foreign websites to purchase wood products, and helping to shift income overseas as manufacturers increasingly source raw materials from abroad. The net result is what one manufacturer described as a "cut-throat [domestic] market" and a significant decline in export opportunities as Asian (in particular) firms increasingly dominate global markets for wood products.

In the tourism sector, the internet, in particular, has helped many Cape Town SMMEs to more efficiently organize their booking and reservation systems, while being able to react much more flexibly to requests from potential clients. Many firms noted that it was very important to have their own website so that potential customers could look at the accommodations or tours online. The web's importance extended to the fact that tourism operators negotiate distanciated booking arrangements on a daily basis. Many guest houses have developed the capability to integrate an instant booking and confirmation tool directly into their own website, utilizing the

South African-designed software Nightsbridge. With this technology, poten-tial customers no longer need to send an email inquiry for reservation requests. That said, however, when it came to actually booking online, customers often preferred to use large booking reservation sites, such as Bookings.com or Expedia (foreign-owned corporations), because they trusted them, rather than releasing their financial data to unknown hotel operators.

In some cases the integration of local tourism SMMEs into GPNs and transnational circuits of accumulation is a relatively "thick" form of integration, whereas in other instances it is thin. As we detail in Chapter 7, however, even where substantial information management and processing takes place it is not clear that the benefits accrue to locally based firms proportionately. Thus, seemingly thicker forms of ICT integration may come with significant power asymmetries and extraversion as the benefits largely flow offshore to foreign firms, rather than to domestically-based ones. ICT integration has been an extremely important development for hoteliers, but many tour operators and so-called ground handlers still depend to a significant degree on personal networks and face-to-face interactions with "walk-in" clients. This is because tour operators often offer customized products and need more personal contact with either a client or a third-party intermediary (e.g., foreign tour operator) in order to market these effectively. In this context, building trusting, personal ties to tourists and foreign tour operators in GPNs requires more than simply a good internet connection, and business success often depends on the ability of its owner to travel to trade fairs and/or visit with intermediaries based in key markets. ICTs can help maintain these relationships once established, but their initiation normally requires much deeper and extensive forms of personal interaction or shared, successful business experiences (see also Christian, 2012).

All told, ICTs are having significant implications for the productivity of SMMEs in both industries and countries, but are playing a more important role in the development of the tourism sector. This is because computers and the internet have become core technologies in tourism, particularly with regard to marketing and administrative activities such as reservation management, while they remain somewhat ancillary or secondary to the production and sale of wood products. Cape Town's tourism sector seems to have benefited more significantly, although the value of ICTs remains limited in most cases to basic productivity improvements and enhanced mobilities, rather than intensive forms of information processing and knowledge creation. Also troubling, perhaps, is the observation that man-agers and owners in both sectors noted that mobile phones, in particular, have made it much easier and more efficient to manage staff on a real-time basis through phone calls to check on a worker's progress or to ask them to do new tasks. While these changes in labor force management capabilities may help to "lean" production or service delivery systems, important ques-tions remain unanswered regarding their cost in terms of worker's rights.

To summarize, evidence of thicker forms of ICT use and integration are hard to find in these sectors and places, as mobile phones, computers, and the internet are primarily used to facilitate discrete forms of communication that has value primarily in the context of a real-time or short-run transaction, order, or booking arrangement. While this *thintegration* can create efficiencies and enhance the spatial mobility of SMME owners in local markets, it cannot be expected to enable African firms and industries to dramatically improve their positionalities in GPNs or to compete more effectively with imported goods. Moreover, ICTs have not supplanted the need for face-to-face interactions to establish the trust necessary for businesspeople to participate in long-term exchange relations, particularly in instances where financial resources are highly constrained (wood products), or where reputation can be damaged through negative reviews that become available globally through the internet (tourism). Worse still, as we detail later on, ICTs have helped foreign-owned businesses and corporations more deeply penetrate African markets and to extract profits more easily through the offshoring (neo-intermediation) of transactions through websites such as Expedia and TripAdvisor. Simply stated, the balance sheet indicates that thick integration is not likely in the near term, and this can be explained by the supply- and demand-side factors influencing the depth and quality of ICT use among SMMEs and industries.

Thintegration and its Supply-Side Drivers

As demonstrated above, ICTs have contributed to significant communication improvements in firms, the enhanced visibility of African products and services in domestic and international markets, and to efficiency gains with respect to the everyday management of SMMEs. It is clear that ICTs are ubiquitous and vital tools for businesspeople, workers, and consumers, and that most cannot imagine doing business without mobile phones and, in many cases, computers and the internet as well. Moreover, and particularly in the tourism industry, new ICTs have enhanced the ability of SMMEs to reach out to clients and intermediaries in GPNs through websites, third-party booking systems, and more efficient communications via email, Skype, and so on. These gains have been due in part to the increased supply of mobile phones, internet connections, computers, and ancillary hardware and software components that have effectively reduced the cost of adoption. To complement these developments, a typical ICT4D proponent (e.g., Esselaar *et al.*, 2007) might argue for additional supply-side initiatives to decrease costs, increase ICT awareness and skills, upgrade internet and mobile telephony infrastructure, and improve the regulatory and institutional incentives for ICT diffusion. Through such programs and policies the supply of ICT capabilities and artefacts would increase, and this would ideally drive thicker forms of integration.

Table 5.1   Supply-side limitations on ICTs as reported by the sampled SMMEs

Supply-side issues	Wood products		Tourism	
	Dar es Salaam (n = 53)	Durban (n = 52)	Zanzibar (n = 47)	Cape Town (n = 51)
Costly, difficult to afford	32.1%	26.9%	31.9%	35.3%
Operational problems	7.5%	30.8%	57.4%	60.8%
ICT skills lacking	0.0%	1.9%	38.3%	0.0%
Market or govt. regulation issues	0.0%	38.5%	8.5%	7.8%
Unable to process credit cards	N/A	N/A	51.1%	N/A

As Table 5.1 indicates, several supply-side issues were identified as important limitations on the value of new ICTs for the SMMEs we sampled. In the wood products industry, more than 25% of businesspeople in both locations sampled found ICTs costly to use, while in Durban there were sometimes concerns expressed about their operation and the South African government's regulation of the telecommunications sector. The issue of cost was particularly significant for wood products SMMEs. One firm manager in Durban noted that many people would prioritize the landline when calling his office as they considered the mobile phone too expensive. Furthermore, several companies still used fax, although this was probably out of habit – a type of path dependence – rather than related to cost. Other companies cut costs through the use of a rerouting box with a subscriber identity module (SIM) card which allowed them to make calls from their landlines as if they were from a mobile phone, as calls from mobile-to-mobile are much cheaper than from landline to mobile. One manager using this technology estimated that this saved the company around R1500 (roughly US$200) a month. Another used a Premicell™ (http://pabxsolutions.co.za/html/premicells.html), which is a least-cost router for phone calls across networks: it finds the cheapest network to make the call. In Dar es Salaam, most SMME owners had acquired multiple pay-as-you-go SIM cards from different telecom providers as a means to reduce costs through the ability to make within-network calls. While these innovations reduced operating costs in firms, it is less clear as to whether they are having a significant impact on the overall profitability or performance of firms, given the hypercompetitive structure of markets and the consequently razor-thin profit margins. In a context where most firms use mobile phones, it may be imperative to have one to liaise with suppliers and customers, but they may still represent an additional squeeze on profits.

In tourism, similar supply-side issues were identified by SMMEs but with a greater frequency than in wood products (see Table 5.1). This is due in large part to, and is indicative of, the greater use of computers and the internet in Cape Town and Zanzibar. Particularly interesting are the high percentages of respondents in both places who complained of operational problems (nearly 60%) and the Zanzibar-specific issues related to a lack of ICT capabilities and fears associated with fraud, which discourage the use of credit-card payments. The reported operational problems covered a wide range of issues – from complaints about unreliable power supplies (Zanzibar), computer viruses (Zanzibar), and slow internet speed (Cape Town) – and were indicative of some of the kinks in the telecommunication systems servicing firms in both contexts. Beyond such concerns, Cape Town SMMEs were relatively well off in terms of their access to and use of ICT-driven marketing, sales, and service management programs (as detailed in Chapter 4) and reported few additional supply-side limitations. In contrast, Zanzibar firms often struggled to find competent individuals to service computers, design and manage webpages, and/or to provide insight into how best to leverage ICTs toward improved market access and intra-firm management. Moreover, their inability, and often unwillingness, to process credit-card payments has limited the capacity of Zanzibar SMMEs to secure clientele prior to their arrival in the archipelago. As a result, numerous business owners complained that they regularly lose clients once they arrive as street-level intermediaries divert them to alternative tour operators or lodging establishments.[2]

Supply-side challenges such as these characterize industrial regimes and are playing a significant role in shaping the nature, depth, and quality of ICT uptake in South Africa and Tanzania, and by extension the prospects for thicker forms of informationalization to emerge. Moreover, concerns about supply-side obstacles are a common focus of ICT4D scholars and practitioners who view their amelioration as a means to achieve imminent forms of ICT-driven development (Esselaar et al., 2007; Smith et al., 2011). General reductions in the cost of ICT consumption, broadband network expansion, and an increasing emphasis on "m-development" through the creation and diffusion of mobile applications to assist users with financial transactions, health management, civic participation, and so on, are viewed as key interventions able to create efficiencies and to signif-icantly improve the quality of livelihoods in Africa. Through the imple-mentation of ICT4D projects, along with complementary investments in other supply-side challenges (e.g., energy systems, education, health, civil society), individual and firm-specific capabilities can be enhanced such that mobile phones, computers, and the internet can realise their full potential. In other words, industrial regimes should be reconfigured in ways that increase ICT capabilities and create regional (informational) assets that attract the attention of buyers in GPNs.

What is clear from our study is that such an approach is, at best, a partial solution to the immanent (structural) challenges facing African firms and industries as the region becomes increasingly connected to the world economy. More specifically, a focus on e-business and immanent development raises important questions about the demand for thicker forms of ICT integration among African firms and industries. As Melville and Ramirez (2008) observe, the increasing informationalization of industries is largely a demand-driven process, a direct outcome of the extant relationships between buyers/consumers and the producers/service providers. Such demands can come from a shift to more flexible forms of production (e.g. just-in-time), through deeper integration into GPNs organized by leading retailers (e.g., IKEA), more complex or fragmented logistics or supply-chain management systems, and/or in response to the need to speed up innovation-development processes such that they are more closely aligned with real-time fluctuations in markets. When such demands are present, firms will be pulled deeper into informationalized forms of production, distribution, and service delivery and, ideally, be able to enhance the value of their products and services in domestic and international markets.

An added focus on demand-side considerations is also critical as it draws attention to the specific geographies and sociospatial relationships driving the development of industrial regimes and GPN couplings in Africa. Geographic factors include those embedded and place-specific practices, institutions, meanings, values, markets, and histories that constitute the sociotechnical regimes governing SMMEs and guiding the evolution of the tourism and wood products industries. Industrial regimes are key drivers of the demand for new ICTs and thicker forms of informationalization, yet they are often ignored or oversimplified in much of the ICT4D literature, which focuses largely on individuals and firms as the main scales of analysis. Moreover, a supply-side, ICT-specific emphasis undervalues the contingent and variegated ways in which new ICTs become embedded into existing regimes and what this technological absorption might mean with regard to immanent changes to the rules, practices, and meanings constituting the regime. In other words, the geographically situated regime generates particular demands for new ICTs in relation to pre-existing features, such as the structure of demand, consumer preferences, elasticity, rules, norms and conventions of production and service provisioning, which dictate the depth and specificity of the ICT integration needed for SMMEs to remain competitive in the markets they serve.

Globalized relationships also play a key role in shaping the demand for new ICTs primarily as they are manifest in the ties that firms and industries maintain to GPNs. The significance and quality of such couplings are shaped both by actors (e.g., consumers, SMME owners) and the assets situated in industry regimes, and by the buyers and sellers in GPNs. Crucial determinants of these relationships, and the power that ICTs can have in shaping them, come from what Gibbon and Ponte (2005) term the functional capacities and performance requirements or standards expected of suppliers by the buyers and consumers situated in relevant markets. Functional capacities account for the scale or size of production or service provisioning, the different roles (functions) that firms can play in a supply chain or GPN (e.g., production, design, quality control, and/or intermediation), and the degree to which firms deal directly with end users or consumers (i.e., marketing functions). Performance standards relate simply to the expectations built into exchange relationships such as those related to the quality, timeliness, standardization, flexibility, transparency, and/or ethicality of products and/or production and service-provisioning activities. GPNs generate demands for firm- and regime-specific capacities and performance standards (e.g., see Ivarsson and Alvstam, 2010, 2011), some of which can relate to communication and information processing capabilities. For example, once they are part of, or coupled to, a particular industrial regime, GPN actors can stimulate demand for ICT workers, skills, and investments in training programs by the state, labor movements, and other civil society actors.

Thintegration and its Demand-Side Drivers

The remainder of this chapter details the demand-side factors influencing the ways in which ICTs are, or are not, being integrated into the sociotechnical regimes and GPNs coupled to South Africa and Tanzania's wood products and tourism industries. The goal here is to demonstrate that the markets, regimes, and GPNs governing SMME activities are not "pulling" enterprises toward thicker forms of ICT integration. Such a demand will not be created *á là* Says Law – solely through an increased supply of ICT artefacts, skills, and infrastructure – but instead requires immanent (structural) transformations to regimes and production networks such that information shifts from a reactive to a proactive resource, and ICTs become complicit in the creation of knowledge that enhances the value of the products of SMMEs and the potential for African economies to capture greater value from global markets. In the absence of such transformations and shifts, thick integration, and, consequently, deeper forms of informational capitalism are unlikely to emerge from within African industries and economies, thus raising significant questions about the ICT4D project as it is currently organized.

Sociotechnical regimes and GPNs are characterized by relational configurations, heterogeneous actors, artefacts, and territorially embedded rules, norms, routines, and practices that play a central role in determining the kinds of ICT capabilities and technologies that are significant and demanded, or not, in an industrial sector. In this section we examine closely the industrial regimes in our case study industries and locations and the ways in which these are, and are not, articulated with inward and outward GPNs. In doing so, the goal is to assess the demand-side influences that are generated from both within regimes and through couplings between SMMEs and GPNs in wood products and tourism. The analysis shows that there is little demand for thick integration. Sociotechnical regimes are structured in ways that discourage the kinds of long-term innovations that more intensive forms of information processing and management can enable. Moreover, GPN couplings are largely structural in nature – based on extant (i.e., business-as-usual, extraverted) relationships between Africa and the world economy, and by-and-large not providing a means or incentives for upgrading in firms and regimes through more advanced forms of ICT absorption.

ICT Integration in Wood Products Regimes and GPN Couplings

In South Africa and Tanzania, the recent evolution of furniture and wood products manufacturing regimes and GPNs has made deeper forms of ICT integration often too costly and/or superfluous to the ability of SMMEs to compete in domestic or international markets. Instead, firms are being pushed either into highly marginal, survivalist forms of production and low-value markets, or into high-value, niche markets where handcrafted products are valued and demanded. In both cases, production remains largely labor-intensive in nature and many business owners are reluctant or unable to make capital investments that might increase the scale, consistency, and/or quality of manufacturing activities.

More specifically, wood product and furniture-making regimes are marked by several critical structural conditions that currently govern the demand for ICT-enabled forms of innovation and upgrading. The first relates to capital-availability constraints and/or the willingness of business owners to invest in production technologies able to increase shop-floor efficiencies through ICT-enabled forms of computer-aided design, flexible or just-in-time manufacturing strategies, high-speed production, electronic work-order management, benchmarking, and factory automation practices (e.g., see Drayse, 2011). As Bartel et al. (2007) demonstrated, when these kinds of technologies are linked up to other ICTs (especially computers and the internet), significant productivity improvements can occur at the plant level, manifest in an increased pace of production, greater responsiveness, and improved quality-control mechanisms. Moreover, the adoption of advanced technologies occurs in lock-step with a shift towards more information-intensive business practices that are often necessary for manufacturers in "mature" sectors to keep pace with the functional capacities and performance standards embedded in GPNs (Drayse, 2011).[3]

In South Africa and Tanzania, such investments are, in large part, not occurring given the hypercompetitive nature of domestic and international markets, the increasing penetration of imports, and the lack of finance available to industries such as wood products and furniture making. These regime conditions make it extremely difficult or unrealistic for many manufacturers to upgrade their machinery from manual to CNC systems such as those used by high-volume exporters in other world regions. In Dar es Salaam, there is a chronic lack of capital available for firms to make capital investments, and most SMME owners complained about the difficulties of maintaining a steady flow of income throughout the year due in part to the seasonality of markets and the competing demands on their income from family, among other things. Formal finance is also unavailable, as only one of the Dar SMME owners interviewed was accessing formal sector finance, and only one respondent mentioned that he was using mobile banking or phone-credit transfers for business transactions.

> My big problem is a lack of capital and I am unable to buy machines and can only make a little bit of extra [inventoried] furniture without having customers come first to leave an advance… I cannot get a loan from the bank as the conditions are too difficult. (Mwenge furniture manufacturer)

Despite substantial hype, mobile phones have done relatively little to change the structure of finance – particularly as it relates to the ability of SMMEs to access reasonably sized loans that can be used to upgrade facilities and machinery.

The Durban wood products and furniture regime has much more finance capital at its disposal, but given the market uncertainties at work and the fact that that country's industry is declining in global importance, business owners have been reluctant to make long-term capital investments (Lourens and Jonker, 2013). Chinese imports have impinged significantly on the growth of the domestic industry, and South Africa's export ranking (in furniture) fell from 36th to 51st place between 2001 and 2012 (Lourens and Jonker, 2013; Edwards and Jenkins, 2013; ITC, 2013). These trends have resulted in an estimated loss of nearly 1900 jobs (40.4% of total employment in the sector) between 2001–10 as the trade balance for furnishings shifted from a net surplus of $380m in 2004 to a deficit of $144m in 2011 (Edwards and Jenkins, 2013; South African Department of Trade and Industry, 2013). Given the circumstances, investments in advanced manufacturing technologies are a costly/risky endeavor, and even those firms in our survey using CAD programs and CNC machines do not think new ICTs can improve productivity given the labor-intensive nature of the production process. According to one interviewee, in terms of production the technology they relied upon was "engineering" rather than telecommunications. Not surprisingly, 60% of Durban SMME owners surveyed reported that ICTs had a limited ability to contribute to the development and everyday performance of their firms.

These findings have important implications in terms of the demands placed upon new ICTs, as it is labor that creates value for Tanzanian and South African manufacturers. Tanzanian manufacturers rely heavily on low-skilled labor and hand tools in the manufacture of wood products and furnishings, and ICTs have done little to transform the training and management practices of SMMEs. Training still occurs primarily through on-the-job apprenticeships or through vocational schools, and workers are managed in the same ways, albeit with easier communication thanks to mobile phones. Moreover, the organization or division of labor remains much as it was a decade ago, although new tasks have emerged in response to a shift from hardwood to lower-value medium-density fibreboard (MDF) products and upholstered sofas (e.g., painters and upholsterers play a much more significant role today). Beyond the expanded use of MDF, air compressors, and plastics for making, painting, and upholstering furniture, the technologies and materials used in production have changed little, and given the costs, lack of finance, domestic market expectations, and labor-intensive production systems, there is little demand for a deeper integration of ICTs into manufacturing practices.

In South Africa, labor-intensive manufacturing is also the norm, although workers are typically employed formally within SMMEs. Given their importance for the productivity and competitiveness of firms, manufacturers often strive to manage workers as carefully and intensively as possible in order to maximize profits. Like in Tanzania, the labor-intensity of furniture-manufacturing regimes has meant that thick forms of ICT integration are unlikely in the short run, although mobile phones have both threatened and strengthened the ability of businesspeople to control workers. On the one hand, some managers noted that there was a loss of productivity arising from factory staff being on their mobile phones during work hours for their personal affairs.[4] On the other hand, it is also clear that South African businesspeople are using ICTs as power resources, to discipline rather than displace labor. Several firms reported that mobile phones enabled them to monitor and track workers on a real-time basis, particularly those working outside of workshops. In the case of shop-floor employees, at least one SMME owner reported using cameras linked to computers, the internet, and smartphones for surveillance of employees on the shop floor: as the manager put it, to "keep an eye on the guys". According to this manager, information technology had changed the way in which manufacturing activity is organized, but not the speed at which it took place.[5]

ICT-enabled monitoring of workers reflects a situation where "liquefaction" (see Ritzer, 2011), a partial disembedding from place for capital, is occurring. In this instance, the manager could exercise authority at a distance through the multifunctionality of his mobile phone, through which he could view camera footage, and a "firming" of place for labor, as it was subject to remote discipline through these technologies.[6] ICTs do not have any independent causative power, as their impacts are determined by their uses, which are in turn imbricated in existing social structures. Stated another way, rather than leading to upgrading in firms, the demand for ICTs is premised on reproducing the unequal structure of South Africa's labor markets and manufacturing regimes, thus demonstrating how ICTs may facilitate the deepening of existing power inequalities in sociotechnical regimes and GPNs.

The lack of demand for greater ICT penetration is further indicated by the level of "communication saturation" experienced by business owners, particularly in South Africa. Several manufacturers complained that ICTs create an excessive demand for voice and text communications that made time management more difficult for SMME owners: indicative of the "productivity paradox" that is sometimes associated with new ICTs partic- ularly in circumstances where they are out-of-sync with managerial, techno- logical, and other firm-level capabilities (Brynjolfsson, 1993; Brynjolfsson and Hitt, 2000; Subramani, 2004; Krishnan *et al.*, 2007). One manager in Durban noted that his mobile phone was "a nightmare, it never stops"; another complained that ICTs meant he took work home and that his personal life was interrupted; a third believed that they did "way too much" email and internet (2–3 hours per day); and a fourth claimed that friends who had Blackberries™ were "more agitated, more stressed". Particularly stressful was the fact that customers expect "instant gratification" on requests for information, quotes, and so on, because of new ICTs. Some of the managers had developed strategies to deflect this saturation dynamic, such as switching off their mobile or keeping it in their desk drawer in work. Sentiments such these are indicative of two things: that the value of new ICTs as communication devices may have reached their limit in many firms; and that the demand for more intensive, real-time information is lacking in the current market environment, thus further limiting the prospects for thicker forms of integration.

One final, yet crucially significant, factor limiting the demand for thicker forms of integration stems from the absent, weak, and/or often declining relationships between SMMEs in South Africa and Tanzania and global production networks (GPNs). As evidenced with IKEA's ties to furnishing manufacturers in Asia (Ivarsson and Alvstam, 2010, 2011), couplings to outward GPNs could be significant drivers of ICT-related upgrading as foreign buyers often demand real-time updates of production schedules, inventories, and quality control and other information-intensive capabilities and performance standards. In both cases, however, these kinds of capability and performance demands are not being placed on our sampled firms, who primarily produce for the domestic market and thus remain decoupled or non-articulated with export-oriented GPNs. For those who do export some product, the depth of ICT use relates primarily to email use, websites, and, in one Durban case, advertising through Google Adwords. In Dar es Salaam, regularly exporting firms were nonexistent in the SMMEs surveyed, while in Durban the majority of exporting companies did so regionally, to eastern and southern Africa, with only a few firms exporting to the US, Europe, or other, non-African countries (e.g., Oman). Two of the companies exporting to the US produced low-volume, specialized and customized, rather than mass market, products. While the communication benefits of ICTs played an important role in facilitating the exporting process for these SMMEs, there was little evidence that international clients were demanding "thicker" informationalized production capabilities.

While outward GPN couplings are nonexistent or declining in significance, inward ties are increasingly having an impact on the structure and evolution of wood products and furnishing regimes in both countries. Importers are capturing a greater share of domestic markets, and the relationships of local firms with overseas manufacturers are typically coordinated through email, Skype, and mobile phone communications, with face-to-face interactions remaining important for cash exchanges and product inspections which often take place overseas at factories in (typically) Asia. Although these relationships often depend more critically on ICT use for basic communications, such inward couplings do little to foster a demand for thicker forms of ICT integration in importing SMMEs. Worse still, the increasing scale and scope of wood product imports is driving a trend toward hypercompetition and industrial downgrading in our case-study sociotechnical regimes, as we detail in Chapter 6.

For the vast majority of SMMEs in both contexts, the challenges associated with competing in international markets, especially against powerhouses like China, coupled with the existential threat posed by the significant expansion of imports into domestic markets, has forced firms to focus on more narrow, traditional market opportunities where they can develop strong, consistent, and reliable ties to clients and buyers. The evidence suggests that new ICTs have facilitated some innovation and greater value capture for some firms, mostly in local and regional markets, but not substantial forward and upward connections to GPNs, which would spur more widespread economic development and social upgrading. Moreover, there was little evidence of new ICTs contributing to industrial upgrading, which would facilitate greater access to export markets. ICT-intensive production capabilities mean little for one's competitiveness in these markets, as it is much more important to develop an excellent reputation with past customers, distributors, and suppliers. Doing so requires both positive experiences in prior transactions and the ability to build trusting ties to clients and other business partners. Such relationships demand strong, trusting ties, and this kind of trust building occurs primarily through shared experiences and face-to-face encounters (Murphy, 2006b).

For example, one Durban manager noted that while they received email enquiries from throughout Africa (e.g., Angola, Rwanda and Ghana), based on their website, they would make phone calls and then fly out to meet potential customers in person. In Dar es Salaam, the only kind of "exporting" activity observed was indirect as SMMEs sold furniture or wood products directly to individuals or importers based in foreign countries (especially the Comoros, DRC), who would then export it from Tanzania. In these cases, such transactions were sporadic and arranged almost exclusively through F2F interactions and cash-for-goods exchanges. Thus the importance of F2F (spatial proximity) in developing trust remains, even if new ICTs facilitated the initial contact and regular communications once relations were established. As SMME owners in Dar es Salaam noted:

> The mobile phone has changed business and you are able to have communication with customers and to bring them more regularly than in the past. The phone is important in that it reduces the time for communication... However, face-to-face communication is more important than the phone. (Magomeni furniture manufacturer)

> Once you are connected with someone the phone can be very important for communication if you have trust. (Magomeni furniture manufacturer)

To summarize, when considered in relation to the evolution of sociotechnical regimes and the GPNs coupled to them, it is clear that South Africa and Tanzania's wood products and furniture-manufacturing sectors are not being pulled towards the thicker forms of ICT integration that might facilitate a long-term process of upgrading, innovation, and urban–regional development. Moreover, where innovative niches are emerging, these relate primarily to higher-value, customized products, whose sale and development depend to a large degree on personal relationships that are best developed through F2F interactions, not ICT-mediated production and innovation-development strategies. While certain ICT capabilities may become more significant as niches develop – such as the use of computer-aided design and email communications – the small-scale, customized, and personalized nature of these markets means that ICTs will always play a supporting rather than a transformative role in their evolution. Other niches, such as those associated with information-intensive, larger-scale, mass customized, and/or flexibly manufactured products, are largely absent in both the South African and Tanzanian cases, thus further limiting the general demand for thicker forms of ICT use.

The reasons for this stem largely from sociotechnical landscapes that limit greatly the prospects for SMMEs to upgrade to more informationalized and capital-intensive forms of production: landscapes marked by a lack of finance, market volatility, liberalized imports that "crowd out" domestic manufacturers, and labor-intensive manufacturing systems. Further exacerbating the circumstances is the inability of firms to meet the functional capabilities and performance standards embedded in GPNs and international markets, and the lack of regional assets within Durban and Dar es Salaam that might enable or encourage strategic or organic couplings. Instead, most African SMMEs remain non-coupled with GPNs, or coupled to them in a "structural" manner such that significant forms of upgrading remain unlikely whilst these relationships facilitate the extraversion of value through ties to manufacturing centers in Asia. In short, the demand for thick integration is largely absent and unlikely to emerge even if supply-side limitations were addressed.

ICT Integration in Tourism Regimes and GPN Couplings

At first glance, the demand for thicker forms of ICT integration seems much more evident in South Africa and Tanzania's tourism industry, due in large part to the sector's growth in recent years, the rapid diffusion of new ICTs, the intrinsic reliance on GPN couplings for business, and the vital, sustained role that local SMMEs play in providing services. Mobile phones, computers, and the internet are ubiquitous technologies and nearly all of the business owners surveyed rely heavily on them for marketing, day-to-day management, and direct communications with clients. However, beyond passive (websites) and active (email, phone calls) forms of ICT-enabled communication, and in some cases online booking interfaces, Cape Town and Zanzibar SMMEs are, by and large, not experiencing and/or profiting from thicker forms of integration such as destination-management systems, ICT-enabled forms of knowledge sharing and cooperative learning, and/or an enhanced ability to use information control and access, to reposition themselves more positively in relation to foreign tour operators. The reasons for this stem largely from the structure of tourism sociotechnical regimes and GPNs. In both cases, informational and communication requirements, markets, and power relations constrain the demand for thicker integration, and effectively ensure and reproduce the power of traditionally dominant local firms, foreign investors, and international tour operators. Worse still, ICTs have enabled new transnational corporations (e.g., Expedia) to emerge in recent years, and these firms play an increasingly dominant role in governing the value chains and production networks associated with the global tourism industry.

Tourism sociotechnical regimes can benefit most significantly from ICT integration if it facilitates the emergence of destination management organizations (DMOs) that support SMMEs and promote social upgrading. While tourism development organizations in Cape Town and Zanzibar provide websites through which one can learn about the destination and identify tour operators, hotels, and other service and accommodation providers, these do not appear to be strengthening the ties between local SMMEs such that ICT-facilitated forms of cooperative learning, knowledge sharing, and innovation (what Baggio and Del Chiappa (2013) describe as an "intelligent digital business ecosystem") might emerge to strengthen the innovativeness, competitiveness, and resilience of local tourism regimes. More specifically, both contexts lack DMOs able to mediate effectively between international tourism markets and the diverse array of firm and non-firm specific stakeholders who directly and indirectly support the tourism industry. As d'Angella and Go (2009) noted, DMOs can serve a vital role as managers or "orchestrators" of the business networks in the tourism regime which store and use knowledge about tourists, firms, and international intermediaries in order to match local competencies with particular consumer and intermediary preferences. In doing so, the DMO can coordinate the actions of a diverse range of SMMEs, public officials, and other stakeholders in ways that improve industry performance in a more inclusive and distributive manner (Dwyer and Kim, 2003). As d'Angella and Go (2009: 431) noted:

> The DMO serves as a hub firm, or a facilitator, providing a map for destination tourism development. It can also function as a "controller", permitting firms to carry out certain activities, such as hosting congresses, leisure events and exhibitions... the main purpose of a DMO is to improve the development and management of tourism processes by enhancing coordination and collaboration between the stakeholders concerned at all levels.

ICTs can play a critical role in facilitating the knowledge-based marketing of destinations by supporting virtual networks that enable information sharing and the communication of "contextual data" through videos, images, and real-time face-to-screen conversations (Bruekel and Go, 2009). However, such outcomes require that collaborative and mutually beneficial relationships exist such that local firms are able and willing to contribute financial support, provide information, and hand over some control over bookings and promotion to the DMO, with the understanding that, in return, they will benefit from the economies of scale, coordination and planning capabilities, knowledge diffusion, and promotional activities that it can provide. More generally, and as is well documented in the tourism literature (e.g., Hall, 1999; Aas et al., 2005; Beritelli, 2011), collaboration and cooperation among stakeholders in a tourism destination are vital for the viability, quality, and sustainability of the industry as a broad-based economic development strategy. But cooperation is often complicated to achieve, given the diversity of actors – residents, tour guides, investors, developers, hoteliers, and so on – and the interpersonal and somewhat informal nature of the interactions between stakeholders. As Beritelli (2011: 623–4) noted:

> ...tourism destination communities distinguish themselves less by formal rules and norms of cooperation and more by autonomous key actors... where past individual experiences affect future behaviour more than the individual's

affiliation to his institution... Hence in order to increase cooperation or launch collective action, planners must pay attention to previously installed bonds of trust and understanding among actors.

If past experiences have created a climate of distrust (see Murphy, 2006b) between stakeholders in a tourism regime, key firm and non-firm actors may be excluded from income-generating opportunities, employment, and/ or decision-making processes as they relate to the development of destinations. Moreover, there will be little incentive or demand for collaborative initiatives between SMMEs that might drive a shift towards thicker forms of ICT integration.

The evidence from Cape Town and Zanzibar is clear that while there are inter-firm networks, tourism promotion agencies, and some collaboration among SMMEs, these relationships are rather limited in terms of who participates, the level of collaboration achieved, and their value-adding potential for the tourism sector as a whole. The reasons for this stem largely from the structure of these sociotechnical regimes, particularly the entrenched inequalities and conventions of distrust that exist between local service providers, governments, and residents. These embedded features effectively prevent the kind of collaboration, communication, and knowledge exchange that would warrant or demand thicker forms of ICT integration.

As major tourist destinations, both Zanzibar, and the Western Cape/Cape Town in particular, are tightly integrated into transnational circuits of capital and GPNs in the global tourism economy, although this of course varies from firm to firm. The global nature of the industry means that individual SMMEs must maintain global "pipelines" (see Bathelt *et al.*, 2004) or links to international tour operators, third-party booking systems, foreign markets, and past clients, but in these cases their maintenance is managed primarily by individual firms themselves. What is less apparent in both cases is whether, how, and to what extent firms interconnect locally to create a "buzz" in the industry that is able to facilitate cooperative learning, such as that which is supported by successful DMOs. Moreover, the couplings between tourism regimes and intermediaries/consumers in GPNs generally favor the latter, and thus have limited potential to enhance the value of the services the former provide and/or to stimulate social upgrading within these destinations (Christian, 2012).

In Cape Town, the tourism regime is characterized by rather limited networks linking SMMEs, poor leadership from state and industrial promotion actors, and racial segregation (a legacy of the apartheid era). Attempts at creating DMOs have not succeeded in providing an integrated platform where tourists can make direct bookings for accommodations and tours. Cape Town Routes, a first attempt, was by most accounts a failure, absorbed in 2012 by Wesgro, the Western Cape region's investment and trade promotion agency (http://wesgro.co.za/), in an attempt to merge business and leisure-travel marketing under one banner. Cape Town Tourism (http://www.capetown.travel/) took over the region's destination management responsibilities in 2008, but in 2012 the Cape Town city government took over the city's destination marketing through the establishment of a new directorate – the City of Cape Town Tourism, Events and Marketing Directorate – responsible for marketing of the city as a destination. This resulted in severe budget cuts to Cape Town Tourism (R10 million) that the city justified in order to finance the activities of the new directorate (MWeb, 2013). The conflict has left the destination marketing activities of the region and city in disarray, with many business owners disappointed by the lack of leadership from both Cape Town Tourism and the city's directorate. As the author of a well-known blog on tourism and hospitality issues in the Western Cape observed in September 2013:

> We have been particularly concerned to see how lip service has been paid to tourism marketing for Cape Town and the Western Cape, seasonality having become an increasingly serious problem, with almost no business in June and July… We have been outspoken about the lack of marketing for our region by Cape Town Tourism, Cape Town Routes Unlimited (now incorporated into Wesgro), and the City of Cape Town's new Tourism, Events, and Marketing Directorate, all of which have stood still and not done any significant marketing. (Whales Tales Blog, 2013)

The budget shortfall has also lead to problems in attracting major events to the region, and in October 2013 it was reported that the city "lost bids for more than 12 events in the past six months and two existing events have gone elsewhere because the city's limited bidding budget does not allow it to compete against international destinations with stronger currencies" (South African Tourism Update, 2013). All told, it is clear that attempts at creating public–private partnerships for the development of the Western Cape's tourism industry have been, at best, fragmented initiatives that are failing to create a shared sense of purpose and vision among firms, community members, and state agencies. As such, they are doing little to drive a demand for the kinds of knowledge-based networks where ICTs might play a critical role in facilitating innovation and industrial development.[7]

The second major factor driving the tourism regime's evolution stems from the structural legacy of apartheid and the fact that the overwhelming majority of SMMEs are owned and operated by white South Africans (Rogerson, 2004). Since 1996, the South African government has prioritized the development of "black" and other minority-owned firms, but progress toward a more racially diverse industry has been slow at best, with black-owned enterprises confined in large part to township tourism (Rogerson, 2008). For example, Booyens and Visser's (2010: 378) study of the Parys

Area (Free State Province) tourism industry is quite revealing, and it extends to our case study in Cape Town with the exception of township tours:

> It is clear that almost all of the tourism SMMEs were established enterprises owned by white entrepreneurs. Most of these white entrepreneurs did not have business partners from historically disadvantaged groups... The level of transformation in the Parys tourism system was therefore very low; only one black-owned township bed and breakfast was identified.

In response to this shortfall, South Africa's government and leaders in the industry developed the Tourism Black Economic Empowerment (BEE) Charter which calls for dramatic changes in the racial characteristics of business ownership, employment, skills, and so on, through the setting of milestones for the industry to achieve by 2014 (Tourism BEE Charter, n.d.). Beyond addressing the structural inequalities of the apartheid legacy, the Charter also views empowerment initiatives as a means of creating a "tourism culture" for all members of South African society.

Despite these efforts, the industry remains racially segregated: its leaders and promotional agencies unable to unite SMMEs under a common banner that might encourage them to deploy ICTs to create a more inclusive and distributive sector. A major reason for this stems in part from the levels of racially based or infused distrust between incumbent "white"-owned firms and the emerging group of "black"-owned tourism enterprises. As one guest house owner noted:

> Cape Town and the Western Cape [tourism industry] are still functioning because they are run by white people. The other provinces are run by black people, not that there is something wrong with that but it is the wrong black people. (Guest-house owner, Cape Town)

Beyond this, other concerns relate to the ways in which the BEE Charter is being implemented in order to diversify the leadership of Cape Town's tourism promotion agencies. As the "Whales Tales" blogger noted in a 2012 report on the Annual Meeting of Cape Town Tourism:

> This was not the only shock of the evening, which was preceded by the election of three new Board members, which according to the Cape Town Tourism constitution all had to be "Black" (defined as Black African, Coloured and Indian), it was explained by the election auditor Achmat Toefy. Nine nominations had been received for the three Board seats, and whilst the female quota of two has already been met by the incumbent Directors, there were no existing "black" Directors, and therefore members had to vote for 3 out of the 6 "black" nominees, despite excellent candidates such as "white" Guy Lundy, now at Future Insight Consulting. One wonders how many members refused to vote, or spoilt their ballot! (Whales Tales Blog, 2012)

A critical challenge lies not only in the structural power that white-owned firms have reproduced or "inherited" in the decades following the end of apartheid, but in the everyday practices and perceptions that reproduce inequalities and make tighter forms of collaboration seem a risky endeavor for those stakeholders having more to lose, perceived or otherwise (Beritelli and Laesser, 2011). All told, the tourism regime lacks a culture of collaboration and trust between many of the diverse range of actors who participate in it, thus depressing demand for a more deeply integrated, ICT-enabled destination management organization. Moreover, as Chapter 7 describes, rather than being densely interconnected locally, many tourism operators are integrated into ICT-enabled forms of extraversion, where foreign-owned websites serve as gatekeepers, surveillers, and rentiers in the African tourism industry.[8] These outside intermediaries exercise a great deal of power over Cape Town SMMEs, and exploit the opportunities created by the local industry's failure to create a more cooperative and collaborative environment that might induce the emergence of an informationalized DMO.

In Zanzibar, the structure of the sociotechnical regime and the GPNs feeding tourists into the local market are similarly segmented such that a demand for thicker forms of ICT integration is absent. Granted there are other, more conventional, supply-side obstacles at work here, such as Zanzibar's chronic infrastructure limitations, manifest most glaringly when the island went without grid-based electricity for three months from December 2009 to March 2010. Such supply-side limitations clearly limit the abilities of SMMEs to more thickly integrate ICTs into their activities, as evidenced by the continued reliance of most firms on paper ledgers for managing bookings and daily work schedules. But beyond these issues lie more significant structural challenges that will stifle collaboration and inclusiveness in the industry for years to come.

The major issue in this regard stems from the tension between foreign investors in the tourism industry and more traditional, locally based enterprises. In recent years, Zanzibar's tourism industry has grown significantly – from 125,000 arrivals in 2005 to nearly 170,000 in 2012[9] – and much of this growth has been driven by the increasing number of large-scale beach resorts that now populate the coasts of the islands (ZATI, 2013). These large firms are better connected to source markets for tourists (e.g., Italy) and are comfortable with credit-card payments in their home countries. In contrast, local firms have great difficulty building direct ties to source markets and operate primarily through cash-only business or, if absolutely necessary, take credit cards, but often only in person or if the booking is made through a third-party website such as Expedia. This means that local firms are at a significant disadvantage with respect to their ability to secure clients and guarantee tours or hotel rooms *a priori* (unless they use cash wire transfers – a system that costs money and with which many tourists, especially from North America, may be unfamiliar).

A number of structural and relational factors exacerbate these circumstances and discourage the emergence of a collective vision for the Zanzibar tourism regime: one that might prompt a demand for a more integrated or "joined up" destination management initiative. Major stakeholders – hoteliers, resort owners, tour operators, tour guides, travel agents, state and non-state agencies, communities, and local market intermediaries (some known as *papasi*) – are often at odds with one another, or unable or unwilling to collaborate in a mutually beneficial manner. The net result is a fragmented industry where trust is lacking and conflicts seem unlikely to be reconciled, given the lack of leadership and resources available at the state or municipal level.

Large hotels and tour operating businesses, often foreign-owned, maintain better ties to GPNs and have organized some of their marketing activities through the Zanzibar Association of Tourism Investors (ZATI, www.zati.org). ZATI membership is dominated by foreign hotel and other tourism interests, many of which are beachfront resorts that provide a wide range of services in-house. ZATI supports, primarily, foreign investors and is in large part seeking to promote the industry as a globally competitive sector able to meet the demands of high-volume, mid-to-high range tourists from Europe and other Western locations. As such, the ZATI membership is somewhat disconnected from indigenously owned SMMEs, namely tour operators and retail establishments, with some respondents stating that the organization was a "closed, ineffectual society... its members prone to gossip" or an "insular community". Within ZATI, interviewed members of the organization observed that business owners are reluctant to share information with each other and that there is tension between large-scale resort investors – particularly those catering to the Italian market – and firms striving to sustain the high-value, lower-volume market. As the owner of a boutique hotel observed:

> Many of the Italian investors – in particular – have been able to invest in huge resorts on the East and North coasts and there is so much overbuild right now – overbuild that is meant to cater to the worst kinds of tourists – the ones that do not appreciate the place as a cultural destination and who spend very little. (Hotel owner, Zanzibar)

In contrast, local tour operators and tour guides are represented by their own organizations – the Zanzibar Association of Tour Operators (ZATO) and Zanzibar Tour Guide Association (ZATOGA) – which work, for good reasons, at cross-purposes with ZATI. This is because ZATO and ZATOGA's interests are more locally focused and aimed primarily at protecting SMMEs from large-scale tourism ventures. By law, tour operators and those providing local transfers or excursions (e.g., to and from the airport) must be Zanzibar citizens such that greater value might be captured in the local economy. As the industry has expanded, however, hotels are increasingly working around this requirement either through informal subcontracts with local tour guides, through fake "partnerships" with local tour operators, and/or by simply providing the tourism service in-house. Moreover, internationally based, larger-scale tour operators (some are members of ZATI) are becoming a more common presence in the market, and this, coupled with the ability of tourists to book hotel rooms directly, has meant that local tour operators and low-budget hotels are in an increasingly disadvantageous position. Typical comments regarding this situation are as follows:

> There are two main problems in the industry. First, hotels are undercutting tour operators by organizing their own tours. This is partly caused through the fault of tourists themselves, as they would rather stay within the hotel itself rather than shop around for a tour operator. Second, outside agents are increasingly handling the entire tour themselves directly, rather than subcontracting with local tour operators. (Tour Operator, Zanzibar)

> Large tour operators (and hotels) are a powerful presence here, and most local agents are struggling because they lack their own contacts with outside agents... the large owners are more powerful than the locals and they have key ties to international agents who can bring the high volume business to the Island... The big hotels are dependent on the Italian tourists and if you have a good connection to [them] you are in a good business position. (Tour operator, Zanzibar)

Tour guides, represented by ZATOGA, generally side with tour operators, although it is clear that some guides benefit significantly through the informal subcontracting relationships they maintain directly with hotels. All told, most smaller tour operators, freelance tour guides, and budget hotels are at a significant disadvantage compared with boutique and expatriate-owned hotels and large-scale tour operators, unless they have developed individual ties to key intermediaries or clients locally and internationally. Not surprisingly, business owners guard these relationships very carefully in order that the benefits they create remain confined to her/his SMME.

Other stakeholders, namely local intermediaries and community members, are also at odds with actors in the industry, albeit for different reasons. Street-level intermediaries, known locally as "beach boys" or *papasi* (the Swahili world for tick), and other actors (e.g., hotel workers, waiters, bartenders) earn or complement their living by directing tourists – especially backpackers – to particular hotels, resorts, restaurants, shops, freelance tour guides, and tour operators, receiving a commission in return for the recommendation. Such actors are generally railed against by business owners, and one tour operator estimated that about 50% of tourists purchase some sort of service through these informal networks. In practice, however, such dislike is often somewhat superficial as *papasi* are tolerated and even supported by many business owners as a means to gain an advantage over the competition. As one Zanzibar tour operator noted: "It is very difficult to stay competitive unless you partake in corrupt activities such as pirating business away from hotels through papasi, etc." The presence of such intermediaries creates further tensions and distrust within the sector, while also supporting livelihoods. Eliminating the *papasi* from the streets has proven not to be possible, despite widespread support from organizations with sometimes diverse or divergent interests, like ZATI, ZATO, and ZATOGA.

With respect to tourism-affected communities in Stone Town and beach resort areas, tensions have been on the rise as evidenced by recent high-profile incidents involving tourists, tourism businesses, and Zanzibaris. The conflicts stem from a number of somewhat predictable tensions between local residents, migrant workers, and foreign tourists that have been exacerbated in recent years. A hotel owner described the drivers of one of these conflicts, identifying some of the complex cultural, economic, and political factors contributing to the tensions:

> ...[recently], on the East coast... locals got fed up with the hotels and shops in the area not creating any benefits for them – there the tourists tend to be Italians isolated from the rest of the community and the shops in the area were being set up by mainlanders who were not employing locals or creating other kinds of business opportunities. Only creating low-wage jobs. This, coupled with religious differences, alcohol consumption, and a desire among some local leaders (e.g., Imam) to reclaim these spaces for their own personal accumulation, led to a day or two of violence where these shops were burned and the mainland people effectively evicted... tensions [are] simmering just below the surface and these, coupled with political entrepreneurs, can create instabilities in the social fabric – particularly as it relates to the connections between migrants from the mainland and "genuine" Zanzibaris. (Hotel owner, Zanzibar)

More recently, there was a high-profile incident in Stone Town when two British volunteers had acid thrown in their faces by men travelling on a moped through the town's narrow streets (New York Times, 2013). While there may have been political motivations for this attack, occurrences such as these may also partly reflect the growing tension between the beneficiaries of the tourism trade and those local residents whose livelihoods are not improving as the industry grows.

In the absence of initiatives to benefit community stakeholders more directly through social upgrading, or to ameliorate the negative cultural, economic, and social impacts of the industry, tensions will remain high and the tourism regime will likely become more spatially and territorially segregated as isolated enclaves (e.g., large beach resorts) become a key strategy through which larger, foreign-owned firms may seek to manage the instability of the wider socioeconomic context. Resort owners typically maintain strong ties to international tour operators in GPNs based in key source countries (e.g., Italy), are able to coordinate day-long excursions directly on site, and have the infrastructure and staffing (e.g., security guards) to limit the interactions between *papasi* (beach boys) and guests. The net result is that it is these firms that are increasingly capturing greater value from tourists as the sociopolitical environment becomes more unstable: profits that are often channelled outside of Zanzibar.

As for the government's role in organizing Zanzibar's tourism industry, it has largely been unable to reconcile these competing interests, to improve the linkages between tourism firms and local suppliers, and/or to reduce corruption in the industry. When these circumstances are coupled with the rise of beach resort enclaves and direct flights from Europe to Zanzibar, the result has been a tremendous "leakage" of profits and capital out of the local economy (Anderson, 2013). This leakage occurs both through sourcing of foreign-produced inputs and legal and illicit profit repatriation. As one tour operator observed:

> If the government would do proper oversight it would lead to more revenue staying in Zanzibar. Right now much of the profit generated by the industry is slipping out through foreign investors… there is an evil circle of corruption which allows investors to leak out revenues, which decreases state revenue, which leads to more corruption. (Hotel owner, Zanzibar)

Clearly there are winners and losers associated with this cycle, and the state remains largely powerless to intervene in a manner that might both stem the corruption and bring diverse stakeholders together around a common vision for tourism's role in the Archipelago's long-term development. Indeed, to the extent that some state officials may be imbricated in illicit practices, they may have little incentive to reduce them. Moreover, the lack of resources in the state's budget has limited efforts at bridging the divides between winners and losers and/or developing novel marketing approaches that might encourage more innovative, ICT-enabled forms of collaboration and information sharing among SMMEs. Instead, the tourism commission has fallen back on more traditional means for marketing:

> …the limited destination marketing budget that does exist (primarily at the Commission and ZATI) is not being spent effectively – it is being used for print media instead of online promotion. The printing of endless quantities of brochures is especially maddening. (Tourism marketer, Zanzibar)

This approach has costs attached to it, both pecuniary and non-pecuniary.

To summarize, both Cape Town and Zanzibar's tourism regimes are characterized by a lack of incentives for, or histories of, strong collaboration among SMMEs, the government, and other stakeholders in the industry.

Connections to tourism GPNs are significant in both cases but these ties are not, particularly in the Zanzibar case, enabling substantially enhanced value capture locally, given that institutional and other mechanisms to encourage knowledge and other spillovers remain weak and unable to unify the sectors through a common "gaze" regarding how these destinations might develop such that the industry's economic benefits are distributed more widely. Moreover, and echoing Christian's (2012) recent findings regarding tourism GPNs in Kenya and Uganda, the most significant upgrading opportunities are available to large-scale tour operators, hoteliers, and those SMMEs able to interact directly (i.e., face-to-face) and build trust with buyers (e.g., tour operators) in foreign markets. As with the wood products industry, most GPN couplings can be characterized as "structural" in form, reproducing existing power asymmetries and inequalities rather than undermining or restructuring them. Given the travel and transaction costs involved, developing higher-value relationships is difficult for most SMMEs, who must instead try to differentiate their products based on successful experiences with clientele. All told, the net results are that regimes in general, and most SMMEs, lack a serious demand for thicker forms of ICT integration, such as those associated with destinations where the promotion of tourism has resulted in social upgrading. A progressive restructuring of the immanent conditions guiding the evolution of these tourism industries thus remains elusive, and ICT diffusion alone will not solve the structural problems at work in both cases.

Conclusion

This chapter assessed whether there are signs that thick forms of ICT integration are occurring in South Africa and Tanzania's wood products and tourism industries. While new ICTs have utility for firms and are widely used, their integration into SMME routines and practices has largely been "thin" and consequently has not contributed to industrial transformation or improvements to the quality of regime couplings to GPNs. The reasons for this stem primarily from the structural features of the markets, regimes, and global production networks associated with these economies and sectors, and less so with supply-side limitations on ICT diffusion such as those that are commonly emphasized in the ICT4D literature (e.g., ICT capabilities, infrastructures). SMMEs are embedded in markets, political economies, institutions, and social networks that effectively discourage firms/industries from taking on the costs of thick integration, given that they are unlikely to be rewarded for such actions in the short or medium term. As such, ICT-enabled forms of upgrading and value-capture remain unrealized and our case-study firms are forced to compete in either hypercompetitive, local, and mass-consumer markets, or higher-value niche markets marked by labor-intensive forms of product differentiation where success is determined in large part by the ability to develop strong interpersonal ties to clients and customers – the latter requiring F2F interactions in most cases. All told, thintegration is a logical and appropriate outcome given the sociotechnical regimes in which SMMEs are situated, and the demands of GPNs that are coupled to these, and ICTs alone will do little to immanently transform these conditions.

In a broader sense, the findings raise important concerns with regard to the ways in which we understand or frame questions of the role of ICTs in socioeconomic and industrial development. Rather than examine the diffusion and discrete uses of ICTs, our focus here was on the context for ICT adoption and absorption, understood conceptually as sociotechnical regimes and their couplings to GPNs. When such contexts, as demand-generating environments, are given an analytical center-stage, it is possible to understand more clearly where ICTs fit into the whole scheme of economic development, and where limits lie in terms of their transformative potential. In contrast, most ICT4D studies focus on the supply and use of ICT artefacts, thus avoiding thorny questions related to the institutional, market, and spatial contexts where firms operate. Our analysis reveals that in the absence of significant changes to the industrial regimes and global production networks governing activities in the wood products and tourism sectors in South Africa and Tanzania, the promise of ICT-enabled forms of industrial restructuring will remain absent, unable to emerge as the demand for thick forms of ICT integration remains latent.

Moving beyond this analysis, the next two chapters examine four processes and outcomes that mark the evolution of African industries in an age of informational capitalism. The first two are *downgrading* and *differentiation* – the effective loss of value-adding potential for African manufacturing and service providing firms, and one strategic response to this trend which seeks to reposition SMMEs in higher-end markets. The third and fourth processes are *neo-intermediation* and *ICT-enabled extraversion* – the rise of new forms of market intermediation by outsiders which have increasingly limited the access for African SMMEs to global markets, and which create new channels through which surplus value is extracted out of Africa. These processes further highlight the immanent challenges facing firms and industries, and raise important questions about the long-term implications of Africa's recent growth successes.

Notes

1   For example: "YourTour (www.yourtour.com) is an application that uses sophisticated algorithms to dynamically assemble tour packages. The mobile application for Urban Spoon (www.urbanspoon.com) is a context-aware system that also

integrates consumer reviews into its restaurant recommendations and makes the interaction process fun by allowing the user to shake the phone instead of pressing a button to initiate the recommendation process." (Gretzel, 2011: 760).

2   We detail some of these forms of intermediation in chapters 6 and 7.

3   Importantly, there are a wide variety of computer and ICT-enabled technologies, many of which are appropriately sized for smaller-scale businesses and able to be operated through low-cost computer programs. That said, there is a significant and positive association between firm size and the extent to which investments in such technologies are feasible (see Drayse, 2011).

4   One manager recounted a story of a driver who sent 380 texts on a company phone to his girlfriend in a month. In addition to the costs of sending these messages, the time spent sending them may also have reduced company productivity.

5   In a broader sense, the lack of trust between workers and management in South Africa relates to the highly exploitative labor regime in that country, as evidenced during the highly publicized mine shootings in Marikana in 2012.

6   Many of the companies in the survey in Durban noted that they did not use ICTs to recruit staff, but did this through referrals from existing staff members, who served as a reference for them. This was in case anything "went wrong"; the people were known to them and were thus more accountable in a context where some business owners "couldn't trust anyone".

7   Further evidence for the lack of demand is evident in the South African national tourism website (http://www.southafrica.net). It is vague and provides no direct booking opportunities or web links to particular businesses or regional tourism authorities.

8   For example, rather than provide a website where tourists can make direct bookings or be linked directly to the websites of service providers, Wesgro's Cape Town Tourism website instead maintains a TripAdvisor icon on its webpage through which visitors can link to Western Cape accommodations and attractions.

9   These statistics only account for arrivals by air; many tourists come to the islands via ferry from Dar es Salaam.

Chapter Six
Downgrading and Differentiation in African SMMEs

As was noted previously, there is now a substantial discourse about the notion that Africa is now "rising" or "emerging" onto the world economic stage (e.g., Mahajan, 2009; Robertson *et al.* 2012). This discourse is often based on statistics such as the fact that Africa now hosts several of the top ten fastest-growing economies in the world, or that it is, in some years, the fastest growing market for mobile phones. However, whether the continent is considered to be rising or not depends upon the metrics deployed, and the quality of that economic growth is often left unexamined. These are important lacunae; a proper conceptualization or assessment is required of whether or not the continent is truly "rising", such that poverty and inequality levels are decreasing and African industries and regions are creating, enhancing, and capturing more value through ties to domestic and international markets. New ICTs offer the promise for enhanced connectivities to global markets and GPNs, but are basic improvements in communications and thin forms of ICT integration creating a foundation upon which thicker forms of informationalization might emerge in the coming years?

As our findings demonstrate, the sociotechnical regimes and GPNs governing and coupling with SMMEs in South Africa and Tanzania's wood products and tourism sectors are not "pulling" our case-study firms and industries into deeper (empowering) forms of informationalization. While there are historical and place-specific reasons for these trends, as detailed in the previous chapter,

Africa's Information Revolution: Technical Regimes and Production Networks in South Africa and Tanzania, First Edition. James T. Murphy and Pádraig Carmody.
© 2015 John Wiley & Sons, Ltd. Published 2015 by John Wiley & Sons, Ltd.

there are also broader, structural factors at work stemming from decades of neoliberal reforms and the enhanced abilities of foreign firms (i.e., those with first-mover advantages) to coordinate and control GPNs. The net result has been an effective downgrading of the value of the products and services of many SMMEs as markets have become hypercompetitive, imports have penetrated increasingly, and new forms of intermediation are siphoning profits to non-local firms and foreign countries. New ICTs are doing little to reverse these trends as they are an outcome of the uneven competitive dynamics of the global economy, which are leading to a phenomenon of growth with often continued immiseration; a circumstance where economic growth does not coincide with social upgrading or improvements to the welfare of more vulnerable populations (Kaplinsky *et al.*, 2002; Carmody, 2013).

This chapter details the evidence for downgrading, describes its effect on the prospects for improved couplings between Africa and GPNs, and demonstrates the importance of situating ICT absorption within the multiscalar political–economic contexts where firms and entrepreneurs operate. Our focus here is on the wood products sector, given space constraints, and the fact that this sector more clearly demonstrates the trend toward industrial downgrading. There are similar trends in the tourism industry, particularly in Tanzania, but these are more effectively captured and understood through a focus on new forms of ICT-enabled (virtual) intermediation which are diverting value away from African SMMEs and into the pockets of outside firms, as we detail in the chapter that follows.[1] Despite the general finding that downgrading in the wood products sector is commonplace, we recognize the growth and success of some of the businesses we surveyed and highlight how such success stories typically hinge on the ability of SMMEs to differentiate and add value to their products through engagements with niche markets. In such markets, ICTs, capital-intensive forms of production, and globalized capabilities and performance standards mean relatively little as customization, face-to-face communication, and handcrafted, aesthetically pleasing products take priority. In these differentiated markets, ICTs matter for basic communication but the information requirements – more tacit and interpersonally generated – place significant constraints on the growth of SMMEs and do little to incentivize thicker forms of ICT integration. In short, upgrading in differentiated, niche markets can help a relatively small number of firms but it holds limited promise as a more widespread strategy to reposition African industries vis-à-vis the global economy.

Downgrading of African Industries: General Trends

Over the past decade, numerous scholars have documented in great detail the shifting positionalities of African farmers, fisher folk, and manufacturers within the global economy. A central objective of this research has been to determine whether economic globalization is enabling Africans to upgrade the value of their products and production systems such that more distributive forms of socioeconomic development might be sustained in the coming decades. Many of these studies focus on basic agricultural commodities (e.g., Fold, 2008; Amanor, 2009; Minten *et al.*, 2009; Raynolds and Ngcwancgu, 2010) and the influence that neoliberal economic policies, fair trade, certification and other labelling initiatives, and transnational FDI are having on the prospects for farmers. Other studies have focused on higher-value products such as wine (Ponte and Ewert, 2009), clothing (Gibbon, 2003), shoes (Meagher, 2010), cut flowers (Riisgard, 2009), and furniture (Kaplinsky *et al.*, 2002; Murphy, 2006a), assessing the ability of African firms to compete in export markets or outpace importers from Asia. Finally, but no less importantly, researchers have examined the wider implications of regional ties to global production networks, striving to understand the potential for these couplings to contribute to distributive development or social upgrading (Barrientos *et al.*, 2011; Christian, 2012; Goger *et al.*, 2014). A central concern in these works is not simply how African regions might get connected to GPNs or GVCs, but whether such couplings can lead to forms of value capture that alleviate poverty, enhance social services and infrastructures, and contribute to more skilled and empowered workers.

In general, the studies find that while some producers, such as the Madagascar farmers growing vegetables for French markets (e.g., Minten *et al.*, 2009), have achieved marginal improvements through their ties to international markets, most have struggled to upgrade their activities, increase the prices they receive for their products, and/or remain competitive with imports (Kaplinsky *et al.*, 2002; Murphy, 2007; Fold, 2008). Hypercompetition is the norm for many African SMMEs and smallholder producers, even in cases where fair-trade labelling and other social-standard initiatives have been implemented. Firms, farmers, governments, and workers remain largely unable to restructure value chains and production networks such that African economies are empowered more significantly with regard to international buyers and consumers (Riisgard, 2009; Raynolds and Ngcwancgu, 2010; Murphy, 2007; Meagher, 2010).[2] In some cases, such as South Africa's wine industry, a focus on lower-quality domestic markets and higher volume production may be a more remunerative strategy than striving to compete directly with imports or in export markets (Ponte and Ewert, 2009).

The immanent causes of this (continued) downgrading of African goods and services stems in part from the structure of the world economy and the manner in which the region has been integrated into global markets. Castells (1996) argued that the globe is increasingly divided into four different meta-regions: (1) high value producers, based on informational labor; (2) high volume producers, based on cost; (3) raw material suppliers; and (4) excluded regions. Africa has, in large part, straddled the last of these categories – benefitting significantly from the global resource boom yet remaining largely excluded, as a producer, from global markets for manufactured goods. Manufacturing has contributed a declining share to GDP across Africa, with the exception of East Africa, as competition from China, in particular, has effectively crowded indigenous firms out of domestic markets (UNCTAD, 2012). Export markets for African manufactures also remain largely inaccessible or increasingly untenable due to the intense competitive pressure facing firms.[3] As Kaplinsky *et al.* (2002: 1174) observed over a decade ago in the case of South Africa's manufacturing industries, firms are unable to meet the price points demanded by international buyers without significant devaluations to the country's currency, the rand:

> Our evidence suggests that South Africa is at the margin of coping with this growingly competitive world. It is an economy with a vigorous private sector and with a reservoir of relatively cheap skilled labor (especially in the skills which are in increasing demand to support the growth of intangibles in global value chains). If the evidence of the furniture, leather and clothing sectors is generalised, though, success in global product markets can only be sustained through a macroeconomic process of sustained currency depreciation. The larger the share of these traded goods sectors are in GDP (an increasing ratio as globalisation proceeds), the more likely is an outcome of immiserizing growth, as the international purchasing power of domestic income growth is eroded.

As we detail below, the circumstances have become increasingly more difficult in the past ten years as Asian imports have continued to flood markets and manufacturers have been forced to downgrade the value of their goods in domestic markets or to pursue competitive niches where economies of scale play a much less significant role.

Gibbon and Ponte's (2005) analysis highlights several underlying processes that are driving the downgrading of African commodities and manufactured goods. These include corporate financialization and shareholder valuation strategies, oligopolistic global markets, branding, contract manufacturing, supply-chain hierarchies, and the establishment of a new international trade regime organized by the World Trade Organization (WTO). In this context, a consumer product TNC's success hinges increasingly on its ability to create higher returns on capital expended (ROCE) that will translate directly into shareholder earnings and a higher price for the corporation's stock. ROCE can be increased in a variety of ways, by downsizing, creating economies of scope (e.g., focusing on areas where the firm can achieve market leadership), horizontal integration (e.g., through mergers, acquisitions, and alliances), branding, marketing, retailing, and consumer lending, and each of these strategies has geographic implications associated with it. What is important for our purposes is that these strategies aim to leverage brand and stock value in ways that enhance the power of TNCs as buyers of commodities and manufactured goods. The net result is that first- and second-tier, non-branded suppliers are often forced into externalized yet captive GPN or GVC relationships with lead firms should they hope to export to large-scale consumer markets based in core and emerging economies (Gereffi *et al.*, 2005). The value-adding possibilities at the "beginning" of these supply chains are highly limited and risky as buying firms externalize the risks of overproduction through outsourcing.

Further problematizing the circumstances facing African manufacturers has been the rise of what Gibbon and Ponte (2005) called a new international trade regime ruled by the World Trade Organization. The goal of the most powerful members of the WTO has been to "even" the playing field for global trade by eliminating specialized preferences for less-developed countries, dismantling international commodity agreements, and creating a dispute-settling mechanism for resolving conflicts between nations over trading practices.[4] In place of prior quota and other non-tariff barriers (NTBs) to trade have come multilateral and bilateral property rights agreements (e.g., TRIPs); trade related investment measures (TRIMs) which can override or supersede the taxation authority of individual countries; preferential trade, investment, and taxation treaties (e.g., the African Growth and Opportunity Act [AGOA] and double taxation treaties); and multilateral agreements on production standards, particularly those regarding public health concerns associated with food products and medicines. A central articulated objective of these initiatives has been to reduce the institutional divisions and economic distances between Southern producers and world markets such that comparative advantages can be more effectively realized and globalization can foster growth throughout regions like Africa.

While this new global landscape for trade and investment has created some opportunities for improved engagements between African industrial regimes and GPNs, particularly in primary commodity sectors, new entry barriers, value-adding challenges, uncertainties, and market volatilities have emerged to limit the potential for international trade to foster widespread development in the region. Farmers and manufacturers are generally faced with two scenarios with respect to participation in GPNs and international markets (Gibbon and Ponte, 2005).[5] The first is a situation, common in the clothing and coffee industries, where increases in entry barriers (e.g., scale economies, quality-control systems, logistics capabilities) have effectively closed off the possibility for African firms to become first-tier (higher value-adding) or even second-tier suppliers to GPNs. The second scenario, evident in the cocoa and cotton sectors, is one where the entry barriers associated with achieving first-tier supplier status remain too high for most African producers while global commodity prices have declined or remain highly volatile. In this case, technological changes, globalized performance standards, and increased capability requirements have reinforced the advantages of first-tier suppliers and global buyers whilst effectively eliminating the price premia that were formally associated with high-quality commodities such as Ghanaian cocoa or Egyptian cotton. The net result is a situation where most African producers and manufacturers remain marginalized (downgraded) within and/or decoupled from GPNs.

Beyond negative changes to the governance of GPNs, African farms and firms that strive to engage with international markets face significant risks in times of global crisis or recession. The financial crisis of 2008 demonstrated the vulnerability of African exporters to global shocks and the longer-lasting effects that a disruption to trade channels can have, given the region's dependence on foreign sources of finance to sustain trade (Berman and Martin, 2012). The deepened ties between commodity and financial circuits of capital have increased the volatility of commodity markets (e.g., coffee) thus raising further questions about how globalized trade might enable a sustained and consistent dynamic of upgrading in African firms, industrial regimes, and regions (Keane, 2012). Moreover, the most recent crisis shifted attention away from the prospects for African industries to upgrade and back to the region's *status quo* ante position as a low-cost source of the raw materials needed to re-establish and sustain economic growth and accumulation (Büscher, 2012). In the context of crisis and recession, trans-national capital, particularly in extractive industries, has exploited favorable institutional and FDI arrangements with African states and deployed "hedging" investment strategies in order to profitably manage the risks associated with global markets (Emel and Huber, 2008). In contrast, ordinary Africans bear the brunt of this risk as "bust" cycles lead to unemployment, instability, and recession, and the extractive sectors contribute little to the development of value-adding manufacturing or other industrial activities (Emel and Huber, 2008; Ayelazuno, 2014).

All told, the new international trade regime and geopolitical system are squeezing the GPNs that link international buyers to African suppliers and producers whilst simultaneously creating greater economic risk and uncertainty. The net result of these processes has been the emergence of extremely lean production networks and relatively thin forms of market integration into the global economy (Carmody, 2010). Given the fact that few of our sampled wood products firms and regimes are coupled to GPNs, these dynamics were less directly relevant to the practices of the surveyed SMMEs. However, the circumstances highlight the generally poor structural conditions – the sociotechnical landscape – facing African industrial regimes striving to integrate or articulate themselves into GPNs.

Beyond these conditions, there are a variety of other broad-scale mechanisms and processes that do affect SMMEs in South Africa and Tanzania's wood products and furniture sectors. Our discussion below first focuses on ways in which poverty, imports, and increased input costs are leading to downgrading in Tanzania's wood products and furniture sector.[6] We then describe how firms in both contexts, but particularly in South Africa, are striving to differentiate their products through competition in niche markets for customized wood products. As we demonstrate, ICTs are doing little to prevent or ameliorate the trend towards downgrading or to enable most SMMEs to significantly differentiate their products in higher-end markets. Instead, immanent conditions foster downgrading and raise significant questions about what ICT4D initiatives can do to transform them.

Downgrading in Dar es Salaam

We define downgrading as a decline in the value creation, enhancement, and capture opportunities available to SMMEs, industrial regimes, and regions in Africa. Beyond its significance for individual firms and industries, downgrading – especially through its value capture or social upgrading implications – can also have important implications for the general socio-economic and material development of regions. The generic drivers of downgrading were detailed in the prior section, and here we focus on those factors that are significant in our case study contexts but especially in Tanzania: (1) widespread and chronic poverty; (2) import liberalization; and (3) rising input costs, namely wood in these cases. These structural, market, and socioeconomic conditions are driving a significant downgrading of the products manufactured by most wood products SMMEs in South Africa and Tanzania, with the exception of those able to compete in high-value niche markets, most of which are domestically oriented. ICTs are doing little to stem downgrading, support social upgrading, and/or improve the ability of firms to compete in high-value "differentiated" markets domestically or internationally. In contrast, outside firms based in inward-oriented GPNs are able to leverage ICTs to increase the scope and scale of wood product imports, thus further exacerbating the downgrading trend as mainstream markets become flooded with low-value consumer goods and driven increasingly by ruthless, price-based competition. Given that their impacts are most pronounced in the firms that were sampled in Dar es Salaam, our empirical discussion draws principally on the Tanzania data.

A recent cover story in The Economist (2013b), titled "Towards the end of poverty", proclaimed that over a billion people might move out of poverty by 2030 provided global growth rates can be sustained. Despite this rosy scenario, it is clear that many Africans will remain mired in poverty well past that date, given that rates of consumption have barely increased over the past 20 years. The most recent data for Tanzania from the World Bank show that 68% of the population lived on less than US$1.25 a day in 2007 (World Bank, 2013b). A recent panel data survey also indicates that the number of Tanzanians living in poverty has increased in recent years, despite having one of the world's fastest growing economies, largely as a result of food price increases (Kimbute, 2012). For South Africa, the poverty headcount for 2006, using the national poverty line, was 23%. Consequently there are much larger markets in South Africa for many of the goods and services produced domestically, and poverty-driven down-grading is a more pressing reality within Tanzanian industry. This has also resulted in more differentiated outcomes in South Africa than in Tanzania, as discussed below.

In Tanzania, the implications of high poverty rates for manufacturing industries appear to be especially significant. Our evidence suggests that reduced consumer purchasing power constricts demand for higher-value products, reinforces a reliance on low-wage, labor-intensive forms of production, provides little incentive for firms to invest in new ICT and non-ICT-related technologies to increase productivity, and stifles demand for innovations that might align African SMMEs with the functional capacities and performance standards demanded of first- or second-tier suppliers in GPNs. In other words, high rates of poverty create unfavorable market conditions in industrial regimes: one that prevents even the more innovative SMMEs from being able to create, enhance, and capture more value through product and process innovations. As Wuyts (2001) observed in Tanzania, when such conditions are then combined with a rise in imported wage goods (i.e., everyday commodities purchased by labor), there is, in effect, a delinking of the primary commodity sector (especially agriculture) from the manufacturing sector. The end result is an economy where primary, unprocessed commodities are exported and domestic consumption is increasingly based on imported goods. Where SMME-based manufacturing does occur it is either unable to compete with imports in terms of quality or price and/or it is relegated to unfavorable, often informal, markets which provide subsistence but few prospects for upgrading (Lawrence, 2005; Nichter and Goldmark, 2009). Worse still, many Africans are turning to commercial rather than productive activities to sustain livelihoods, thus creating hypercompetitive markets for imported low-wage goods (e.g., see Lyons and Brown (2010) on the impacts of Chinese imports on urban markets in West Africa).

ICTs, but mobile phones especially, have improved the ability to communicate with customers and suppliers, but beyond facilitating imports they have not contributed to fundamental or positive changes in the structure of the wood products sociotechnical regime. Consumption patterns have changed as the design and quality preferences of domestic consumers have shifted away from traditional hardwoods and towards MDF-based furnishings and cushiony sofa sets; markets remain hypercompetitive, seasonally erratic, and organized primarily through face-to-face negotiations. Many of the SMME owners surveyed in the traditional market clusters of Keko and Magomeni complained about the increasing numbers of *fundi* (i.e., individual craftspeople) and the challenges they face in a hypercompetitive market environment.

In the past there were few *fundi*, now there are many many more today. (Kekofurniture manufacturer)

My business has been reduced significantly due to imports and the weak economy... Lots and lots of *fundi* are now competing against one another. Business has become difficult because customers do not have much and prices must be low. The customers are facing a difficult life situation. Incomes are low. (Magomeni furniture manufacturer)

Adding to the challenge has been a marked increase in face-to-face inter-mediation by on-the-street brokers (*madalali*) who are ever-present in the large furniture clusters (especially Keko and Magomeni) and who demand commissions from SMME owners in exchange for bringing customers to a shop (see Figure 6.1). An increasing number of individuals are choosing this kind of employment in response to the lack of alternative opportunities, and the presence of *madalali* is tolerated by many SMME owners given that any additional formal or informal sales help can ensure at least some income on a given day, even if it means a further reduction to an already low profit margin. Moreover, *madalali* can be difficult to avoid or deal with, and business owners need to be careful to treat them well since they can consis-tently redirect, at will, prospective clients to other SMMEs.

Figure 6.1   *Madalali* (street brokers) waiting outside a furniture shop in Keko ward, Dar es Salaam. Photo by James T. Murphy. Reprinted with permission from Pion Ltd., London, www.pion.co.uk and www.envplan.com

> We like to use *madalali* as they bring in customers for them and we may even act as *madalali* when we recommend a cushion maker to a customer who just purchased a couch [sofa] set… At first they were bad but now they are okay for business. (Magomeni furniture manufacturer)

> There are many many *madalali* here… The problem with them is that they can be tricky. You want to sell a *kabati* [cabinet] for Tshs 120,000. They tell you the customer will give only Tshs 90,000 and they tell the customer the price is Tshs 100,000. They are squeezing us. (Magomeni furniture manufacturer).

In response to these concerns, some SMMEs in Dar es Salaam's wood products and furniture manufacturing sector have migrated to newly developing areas of the city (e.g., Mwenge, Kawe, Tegeta, see Figure 4.1) in an attempt to avoid the congestion and *madalali* in traditional markets and to access higher-value clientele such as wealthy homeowners and property developers. However, this reorganization is limited by other regime factors such as the spatial distribution and quality of the electrical power system, the need for face-to-face meetings for transactions, and the horrendous road traffic in Dar es Salaam that can make it extremely difficult to go even short distances to deliver supplies or to meet with clients or suppliers. Because of these issues, the manufacturing and retail activities of most SMMEs continue to be co-located and concentrated in dense urban areas or sprawled along the sides of roads rather than being reorganized into formal retail shops and/or more permanent workshops in industrial or peri-urban areas.

> The environment we are working in is not very good and we need capital in order to have a show room [display area] inside in order to attract customers… our current premises are not good because the furniture sits outside, gets covered in dust, and is not very attractive to customers. (Magomeni furniture manufacturer)

This is true even in the case of more innovative SMMEs and/or those located in preferred locations close to high-end markets in Dar. As Figure 6.2 demonstrates, firms such as these need to remain close to major roads where the workshops and factories are visible to passers-by. The need for physical proximity and tight, direct control over everyday production activities effectively limits the contribution of new ICTs to more innovative regimes and the creation of competitive assets that can empower Tanzanian SMMEs in terms of imports.

Inward GPNs and Downgrading in Dar es Salaam

While Dar es Salaam's wood product regime remains almost entirely decoupled from outward (export-oriented) GPNs, inward (import-oriented) GPNs are playing an increasingly important role in meeting and driving consumer demands. Couplings to these GPNs are coordinated through Tanzanian and foreign-owned furniture importers who often maintain

Figure 6.2   Higher-end furniture-making operations in Dar es Salaam. Photos by James T. Murphy.

showrooms within the central business district or high-quality shopping malls where other luxury goods are for sale and where wealthier clientele can more easily park their automobiles. Compared with local manufacturers and retailers, these areas are quieter, cooler (often air-conditioned), and free from *madalali*. Importers were also found to rely more heavily on new ICTs to coordinate shipments, transfer money, review design options with clients, and arrange trips to exporting countries in order to inspect furnishings made by overseas manufacturers, although face-to-face communication remains essential for these businesspeople.

> If [the customer] cannot find what they want, we talk and talk and we get an idea… and we can download pictures to find what they want… Every day we receive over 30 emails from different [manufacturing] companies in China… they send us catalogues… so when the customer gives us an idea… we show him/her the catalogues and ask – "is this what you want?" (Central Dar es Salaam, furniture importer)

> She [the owner] goes to the sources… the factories or distributors in China, Indonesia, and Dubai… She travels at least three–four times a year… They send their catalogues before she's gone out… so she is able to pinpoint what it is she is going to buy when she gets there… She keeps in contact with the factories through emails and phone calls and to arrange visits… she has to do quality control in person… There is still a lot of one-to-one being done… face-to-face… literally touching to be sure that leather is leather… Whether you like it or not catalogues can give you a different picture." (Central Dar es Salaam, furniture importer)

The net result is that better-off importers are able to transcend low-value and hypercompetitive markets through ties to wealthy Tanzanian clients and relationships with foreign manufacturers that are maintained, in part, through the use of new ICTs. Developing these networks requires financial capital, trusting ties to high-value customers, interior design capabilities, and links to overseas manufacturers who can deliver quality products in a timely manner. Consequently new ICTs are helping to transform the sector, but not in the ways that their boosters envisage, through the integration of importing SMMEs into GPNs. The labor and capital-intensive activities undertaken by importers mean that the vast majority of furniture manufacturers in Dar es Salaam have little hope of overcoming the high entry barriers associated with those luxury market segments that might spur upgrading and innovations in quality and design. For most, the only alternative is to try and compete in markets where cutthroat price competition dominates and imports (from China especially) are taking up an increasingly significant share of mass consumer markets.

This latter circumstance reflects one aspect of the wider sociotechnical landscape within which Tanzanian and South African SMMEs and regimes are forced to contend: a neoliberal trade and investment environment that has opened wide the door for a flood of imported goods from Asia and the Middle East (e.g., Turkey or those transiting through Dubai). These conditions, when coupled with a very weak set of industrial development policies, promotion agencies, and supporting institutions, a chronic lack of investment capital for industries, and low levels of technological capabilities, effectively select for less innovative, low-quality, and non-exportable products made by survival-oriented SMME owners. Not surprisingly, there is also an increasing shift to commercial activities rather than production, as cheap imports are readily available and domestic consumers increasingly prefer Asian designs and the finish quality of MDF-type furnishings.

> Importing is much better given that the Tanzanian furniture makers cannot do the finishing that is needed to make their furniture sell for a higher price. If the furniture was better we would sell local furniture. (Kinondoni furniture importer)

All told, landscape and regime developments generated by the evolving structure of GPN couplings are making it even more difficult for most SMMEs to make a living. ICTs are simply not helping to change the nature, quality, and/or significance of these factors as drivers of the sociotechnical regime's (d)evolution.

The influence of Chinese imports on SMMEs has been significant in both countries, but especially so in Tanzania.[7] In Dar, furniture and wood products manufacturers had different perceptions of the impact of Chinese GPNs. A few felt as if China's presence and the flood of imports was "normal" competition. Many more expressed concern about the impact of Chinese competition as these products have become popular within Tanzanians due to the quality of the finishing work, the price, and the design style. While some noted that prices are higher for Chinese goods, the price differential is relatively small and it has made it difficult for many SMMEs to access marginally higher-end markets for furniture and building materials.

> The market has dropped because the Chinese are making cheap furniture that is pleasing to the eye even though the quality is very low – the furniture will break easily. The Chinese are using MDF [medium-density fibreboard] which is more expensive than hard woods but the finishing is better… The Chinese have changed the designs from being flat in the past, now the normal designs are ridged. (Magomeni furniture manufacturer)

> They are producing cheap doors [3 companies] here in Mikocheni [near Mwenge] in the industrial park. These are indoor MDF or pine "flash" doors [doors that don't get exposed to water, not used in the kitchen] that can be used in the interior of the household. These are very cheap doors and it is very hard to compete with the Chinese in this segment of the market… the market has gone down because of the Chinese. (Kawe furniture manufacturer)

Others felt that Chinese companies competed unfairly based on information failures. This respondent argued that customers in Tanzania did not understand the differences between soft woods, hardwoods, or MDF.

The Chinese now have 40–50% of the market in Tanzania. They are major competition but they do not have high quality furniture. Their furniture has a short life span... they are 100% spoiling the market... Getting people to understand quality is a huge problem. The Chinese succeed with soft woods and good finishing. (Keko furniture manufacturer)

Despite the concerns over quality, Tanzanian consumers have been drawn increasingly to Chinese furniture, and SMMEs in Dar es Salaam have been forced into direct competition with the style and design of these imports. Chinese-style furnishings are quite popular in Dar es Salaam and many SMMEs are imitating these styles in order to remain competitive.

If you use designs from the Chinese catalogue you can sell a lot. Tanzanians like the Chinese designs because they are different than the Tanzanian furniture. (Tegeta furniture manufacturer)

When coupled with the increased costs of hardwoods, this has resulted in a shift toward MDF-based and upholstered furnishings which require painting and upholstering labor in contrast to traditional wood-only designs. Figures 6.3 and 6.4 highlight the differences in traditional wood-only furnishings and the

(a)

Figure 6.3   Photos of (a) traditional couch set for sale in Tanzania (ca. 2000). Photos by James T. Murphy. Reprinted with permission from Pion Ltd, London, www.pion.co.uk and www.envplan.com

(b)

Figure 6.3   (*Continued*) (b) air compressor for MDF painting and sofa frames under construction (2010).

(c)

Figure 6.3   (*Continued*) (c) three *fundi* and their finished sofa (2010).

new, Chinese inspired designs. The shift in design is especially significant for micro-scale enterprises run by carpenters – firms that are already experiencing downgrading through poverty-driven hypercompetition and the increased presence of *madalali* in market places, and who now face the additional challenge of learning how to work with MDF and the costs associated with subcontracting tailors, painters, and upholsterers within their workshops.

The competition with imports has become quite intensive as Chinese and other (e.g., Turkish) firms set up wholesale operations in Dar es Salaam. Tanzanian consumers and retailers across a widening range of market segments are increasingly buying from wholesalers, particularly from Chinese firms who maintain close ties with manufacturing operations back home. As a representative of one of the largest Chinese wholesaler/ importers noted:

> The best [furniture] shops in Tanzania are Chinese because the prices are lower when you compare with other companies... because at times we do a survey... we see how other shops are doing, and at other shops you can even

Figure 6.4   A higher-end Dar es Salaam manufacturer/retailer in his showroom with his furnishings inspired by designs from Chinese imports. Photo by James T. Murphy. Reprinted with permission from Pion Ltd, London, www.pion.co.uk and www.envplan.com

stay there more than one hour and never see one customer… but at our shop, at Chinese shops, you can see that customers are coming in and going out every 15 minutes. (Central Dar es Salaam furniture importer)

This has become a lucrative business for the firm and one that relies on cash transactions and face-to-face meetings rather than ICT-determined forms of communication. In fact, one Tanzanian retailer interviewed discussed how he had recently visited China (through the support of an importer as described below) and placed an order for a container's worth of furnishings while also mentioning that he had no internet access or working email account. This SMME owner had abandoned production in favor of trade which required only "thin" forms of access to outside information, and meant that a computer and email were superfluous to the business' needs.

In contrast, a larger importing firm had production operations in Turkey and noted that they used mobile phones, fax and email intensively to communicate with their offices. In another case, a Chinese importer has developed a system through which Tanzanian furniture sellers are enabled to visit China in order to place orders directly from its parent company's factories. The importer relies significantly on ICTs to obtain visas for clients, communicate with factories, arrange visits, and keep customers informed about new furniture designs.

> The most important thing for us is the [internet] speed... because one of the managers is dealing with clearing and forwarding so she has to get everything very fast, no delays... we are also helping people go to China... [and] when we help ten of them... 4 or 5 we can catch as customers... because the moment that we sell to them in China we import the furniture [to Tanzania]... we are sending documents from China, booking hotels... everything should be done fast... it is like every month even twenty people can go to China. (Central Dar es Salaam furniture importer)

While couplings with inward GPNs are expanding and downgrading locally produced furnishings, exports of furnishings are almost non-existent in Tanzania.[8] A medium-sized firm in Dar es Salaam captured the sentiments about the challenges quite well:

> Exports – no, we stopped. We used [to] export quite a lot but then we found out that it was not really convenient because sometimes we couldn't meet the standards, and moneywise it was not really so good because when you sell in bulk they are asking for a discount... It was nice to say that we were exporting to the States and Europe, but not so good for your pockets. (Mwenge wood products manufacturer)

This firm had previously exported to the US, Europe and Kenya. Another SMME had previously exported flooring for a National Basketball Association (NBA) arena in Texas, amongst other projects. This was facilitated by an Indian-Tanzanian who had returned to Tanzania from the US and had become the firm's agent, showing the importance of F2F and personal communication for building trust in this instance. This firm had, however, stopped exporting as profit margins were too low and because the royalties on timber were increased by 300% in 2005 to reduce illegal logging. As its owner emphatically noted, "I will never go back into exporting from Tanzania".[9]

While furniture and value-added exports remain minimal, basic wood products, namely minimally processed timber such as logs and sawn wood, are leaving the country at unprecedented rates. The net result is that couplings to these outward GPNs add an additional squeeze on the value-creating possibilities for SMMEs as timber prices and wood-harvesting royalty fees have risen dramatically in the past decade. This is related to the high levels of demand for raw materials in international commodity markets in recent years, as the world economy finds itself in the midst of a "super-cycle" marked by a rise in commodity prices which is longer than usual. This has led to increased input prices and utility costs for firms in Africa (e.g., the cost of electricity has risen significantly in Tanzania; Balile, 2012). When coupled with other downgrading pressures, the commodity super-cycle is further marginalizing SMMEs who are by-and-large unable to purchase quantities of timber at lower cost, and/or pay increased royalty fees and prices in order to access the hardwoods that might give them a competitive advantage in high-value niche markets.

The increased demand for hardwoods in international markets is being driven in large part by Asian firms in GPNs, but particularly China (Barclay, 2007; Canby et al., 2008; Mayers, 2013). In 2008, Tanzania was ranked 9th of all African countries in exports of timber to China, and the overall volume and value of these exports has increased significantly since that time (Canby et al., 2008; ITC, 2013). As a result, SMMEs in Dar expressed concern about control by Chinese companies over timber supplies within the country:

> I admire the Chinese, in a way. They are so aggressive, hardworking. But in terms of business, they have made it very hard. …they have robbed this country, they have depleted this country in terms of trees… for a period of time even 90% of all the precious trees that were chopped in this country were smuggled abroad – they were going to China – I am not talking about cypress [lower value, soft wood], I am talking about mninga, mkongo [high-value hardwoods]… all these nice timbers… the prices [for hardwoods] are crazy… they shoot to the skies… this has happened in the past decade and the Chinese are smuggling all the timber. (Mwenge wood products manufacturer)

While most SMMEs purchase wood within Dar from locally based wholesale suppliers, those that purchase it directly from rural areas are sourcing increasingly from Mozambique where supplies are more plentiful and the woods less expensive. Whether this timber is sourced legally is another question, and one that we were unable to determine through our interviews. That said, it was noted by several respondents that corruption along the wood supply chain in Tanzania is rampant and is particularly vexing for SMME owners who try to secure lower cost and higher quality wood directly from rural areas.

> It should take about ten days to get the wood from the rural areas but it can take up to twenty due to issues with police and government officials… you need a forest certificate from the Maliasili [Department of Natural Resources] and corruption is a big problem with the police. (Kawe furniture manufacturer)

To summarize, SMMEs in Tanzania's wood products and manufacturing sectors have experienced significant pressure to downgrade their products as the markets available to most firms have become hypercompetitive, flooded with imports, and focused on new styles of products (e.g., upholstered, MDF-based furnishings) that are not in sync with the long-established capabilities of wood workers in the city. As a result, SMMEs have fewer value-creating opportunities, while value enhancement (i.e., upgrading) has been stifled by the need to "follow" or imitate the work of importers who are able to out-compete Tanzanian firms on the basis of cost and, in many cases, quality (perceived or otherwise). The rules and practices governing the wood products regime are changing, but in ways that lead to downgrading rather than innovation and more empowered links between SMMEs and domestic and international markets. With supply chains for timber increasingly squeezed by the overseas demand for sawn lumber and hardwood logs, it has become extremely difficult for SMMEs to generate and sustain the kinds of profit margins that might enable greater value capture as manifest in capital investments in machinery, show rooms, and improved manufacturing facilities. Moreover, the potential for outward-oriented couplings to GPNs (i.e., an export-led industry) is null in Tanzania at this stage and on the decline in South Africa.[10] As such, many business owners are turning to commercial trade in imported goods from GPN actors based in Asia, given the risks, hassles, complexities, and transaction costs associated with manufacturing activities. New ICTs, particularly mobile phones, are used by every SMME owner, but the communication benefits they provide mean little compared with the drivers of downgrading – immanent forces that call into question prospects for a truly dynamic and expansionary Tanzanian manufacturing sector any time soon.

Differentiation in Durban

The trend towards downgrading in South Africa and Tanzania's wood products industries means that there is little space for manoeuvring by SMMEs unless they have the capabilities, capital, and connections to establish and sustain ties to high-value niche markets.[11] In other words, rather than integrate into inward GPNs or compete directly with cheap imports, a better strategy for some SMMEs is to participate in alternative markets or regime niches that remain non-articulated with or decoupled from the markets affected by GPNs. While this was the case for a few of the Dar es Salaam manufacturers, such as the firm that produced ornate "Swahili" doors or the one that used salvaged wood from old dhows to make custom furnishings, many more of the Durban SMMEs surveyed had shifted their focus to producing customized furniture or interior designs for the domestic market. There are a variety of reasons for this, particularly the growing middle class in South Africa which can afford customized furniture, and the natural protection in this sector afforded by lead times, transport costs, and the desire of customers to be able to liaise directly with the producers. The globalization of competition in the furniture sector has led to economic introversion in the once heavily exporting South Africa sector, as firms focus more on the domestic market.[12]

In general, high-value differentiation is a strategy that relies upon the development of a respected reputation for quality, design, integrity, and service in a particular market segment. Our study identified firms competing in a number of narrower market segments such as kitchen design, workplace furnishings, pub interiors, custom artwork, high-end design, Zanzibari-style doors, and children's furniture aimed at "up-market" consumers in both Tanzania and South Africa. Figure 6.5 provides examples of differentiation strategies amongst the SMMEs surveyed in Durban. These markets can be quite lucrative for SMMEs, provided they have been able to establish themselves and created a word-of-mouth system of marketing through personal ties. Moreover, their owners often fear expansion given the costs and the potential to diminish the quality of their products and services.

I don't have a strategy for accessing the market. We work at full capacity already. Business comes to us... we are very well known, well established. Upper-class Black consumers are very quality conscious, and brand conscious. We are not a "brand" as such, but we are known everywhere. (Durban furniture manufacturer)

We could do more than we are doing if he had more staff... we decided to keep labour to an average level and hire extra staff from time-to-time... We don't advertise at all and have enough jobs. We work mainly through referrals and have built up confidence with 5 building contractors that keep us busy throughout the year. (Durban furniture manufacturer)

In contrast, another Durban company producing standardized products for the local market was shutting down as the furniture industry in South Africa was "dying". Differentiation can thus be seen as one of the only strategies remaining to counter the downgrading tendencies of mainstream GPN couplings and regime configurations.

Developing stable and high-value (differentiated/niche) market relations often requires intensive, personal interactions with clients, thus making ICTs relatively insignificant at the early stages of an SMME's development. The informational requirements for success are not easy to codify and depend to a large extent on the tacit capabilities of business owners to build trust with clients such that more spatially distanciated and ICT-enabled exchanges can emerge. Face-to-face interactions and a sense of small, personalized business dealings are crucial in this respect, thus favoring differentiation strategies that focus on domestic markets and spatial proximity.[13]

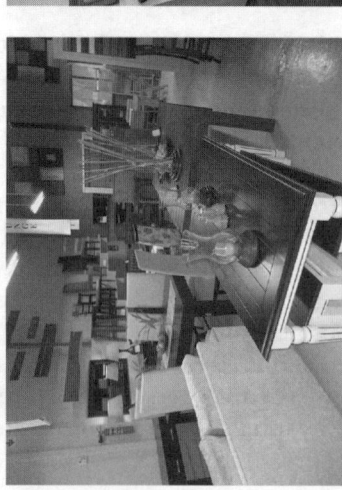

Figure 6.5 Market differentiation strategies evident amongst wood products and furniture manufacturers in Durban/KwaZulu-Natal. Photos by Ralph Borland.

We want to keep our business small so we can maintain quality and service and keep relationships with customers one-on-one. If someone walked in and wanted to export our product overseas we would be open to that, but are not pursuing it. Happy with being small and local, no time to look at business outside South Africa. (Durban furniture manufacturer)

We spend [much] time visiting potential clients… flying to Joburg, showing people photos of products, bringing them to our factory. Face-to-face work, flying there, people flying here. Final decision is made face to face, seeing the product in person. (Durban furniture manufacturer)

Given the success of these firms, and their available capital, ICTs such as computers are commonly used but their significance for differentiation strategies remains "thin" as they primarily facilitate communications with clients and basic searches on the internet for industry-specific information.

I need to be able to leave the factory more, meet new clients, it's a word of mouth industry… a value-added business. (Durban furniture manufacturer)

ICTs are thus far less relevant for value-enhancing processes, unable to initiate significantly or sustain the kinds of trusting ties and strong relationships that can facilitate upgrading and integration into high-value markets. Rather than talking about the geography of the information economy, it may be more important, in Africa in particular, to talk about the geography of the (dis)informationalized economy, where some firms are included and others excluded, and what the key components of success and failure are. In this case, those excluded are unable to access the more tacit forms of knowledge and innovation embodied in clients and which are not easily codified or communicated via voice and text. Moreover, the notion that ICTs can enable SMMEs to overcome information failures such as price distortions means little in a differentiated market.

Our customers are not price-oriented. I was recently asked to fit out a room for a customer, and before we've discussed the price, they've already agreed to buy, and I've gone out to measure the room. This is a factor of trust, that they know his prices are reasonable, but also of emphasis on quality. We first sold that customer couches 14 years ago. (Durban furniture manufacturer)

Price doesn't come into it… Price is always negotiable and people are prepared to pay for quality and service. They'd rather get something that will last than something cheap that will break in 6 months. (Durban furniture manufacturer)

All told, while the (understandably) thin uptake of ICTs has, in some ways, precluded the ability of African firms to achieve the productivity gains that might increase their competitiveness vis-à-vis low-value imports, it is clear that differentiated markets or niches remain somewhat immune to deeper forms of informationalization in the short run, dependent instead on more traditional forms of communication and information management.

While this immunity is welcome and promising for those SMMEs and regime actors able to benefit from the employment, profits, skills, and creativity generated in niches, differentiation is more than likely unable to generate wide-ranging developmental benefits for African regions. Social upgrading and value capture in some communities may be possible – such as artisanal or artistic cooperatives – but these will more than likely remain splintered or segregated from the poorest or neediest communities and market segments. As such, the challenge is two-fold. First, to develop initiatives and support mechanisms to enable the basic skills and creativity of differentiated SMMEs to percolate into sociotechnical regimes such that wider forms of industrial and social upgrading might be possible. Second, to stem the tidal wave of imports driven by inward GPNs that promote downgrading, whilst developing new couplings to outward GPNs where higher-quality niche commodities are valued.

Conclusion

This chapter moved beyond the ICT-specific discussion in order to interrogate the immanent (structural) forces driving the evolution of a South African and Tanzanian manufacturing industry. Emphasis was placed on two trends – downgrading and differentiation – driving the evolution of the sociotechnical regimes constituting the wood products and furniture making industries. Downgrading – a decrease in the value creating, enhancing, and capturing opportunities available to SMMEs and regimes – is greatly limiting the prospects for regions to create and enhance the value of their products, and is a direct outcome of chronic poverty, import liberalization policies, and the dramatically increased demand for raw materials (namely timber) in global markets. The result has been that mainstream manufacturing industries like wood products are on the run, unable to expand or create a competitive space for African SMMEs to generate a steady income unless they are able to differentiate their products significantly, access niche markets, and build close ties to a network of high-value clients. Such ties require capabilities and resources that are beyond the reach of most SMMEs, who are left to compete directly with cheap imports in hypercompetitive markets where innovation is less likely to be rewarded and where price determines quality.

Much of this recent transformation is being driven by inward GPNs and some FDI, particularly from China, which has become the global hegemon in the low-value wood products and furniture trade.[14] South African and

Tanzanian firms are finding it very difficult to compete directly with Chinese products, and it appears as if, beyond design emulation, such imports are doing little to stimulate domestic manufacturers or to create spillovers of technology and capabilities. Many firms are instead getting out of the "budget-line" industry (South Africa) or shifting into the commercial sale of imports from China (Tanzania) as it becomes apparent that head-to-head competition is a losing proposition. ICTs mean little in the context of these GPN dynamics, as they are largely ancillary communication aids that SMMEs need and use on a daily basis, but which cannot be expected to help reposition them in the global wood products sector. In contrast, those already empowered in GPNs – especially Chinese and other Asian firms – have been able to leverage improved communications and information access to enhance their competitive positions and penetrate more deeply into Africa's consumer markets. Thus extreme, ICT-facilitated, uneven development continues to characterize the industry as economies of scale, production and marketing capabilities and access to capital, amongst other factors, continue to play vitally important roles. This relates to the structure of power within GPNs and regimes, as more powerful actors find it generally easier to connect with those over whom they have authority or wish to sell to, rather than connecting forward along the value chain and marketing themselves and their products to more powerful actors, which also requires other, more highly developed, capabilities. Consequently the couplings that new ICTs are enabling are structural; not economically transformative but largely reproductive of extant (immanent) patterns of economic activity that have accompanied the neoliberal age in Africa.

Two final things that downgrading and differentiation patterns reveal are the power asymmetries in GPNs and the importance of marketing and social capabilities as a means to gain access to differentiated high-value markets. The first case was most clearly evident in South Africa where wholesale furniture producers were struggling to stay afloat through sales to domestic retail outlets. A respondent in Durban noted that, in terms of technology, the retail sector was "up-to-date" whereas the manufacturing sector was "in the Dark Ages". This is reflective of the power relations in GPNs, where the retailers, who are closest to the final customer, have more power. A respondent spoke of a prominent local retail chain who dictated the terms upon which manufacturers supplied them, such as having to store the stock themselves (Robbins, 2010). Rather than enable manufacturers to manoeuvre around these problematic conditionalities, ICTs may actually help to deepen power inequalities in GPNs. Actors with more power can more easily connect backwards to suppliers along the production chain and exercise authority downwards over workers (those with less power) using ICTs (see Chapters 4 and 5). In contrast, there was very little evidence of SMMEs being able, or even desiring, to connect forwards and/or upwards to international buyers in GPNs. In sum, while ICTs may now be a prerequisite for SMMEs to connect to large-scale markets or GPNs, they require many other production and marketing capabilities to be able to do this effectively, in addition to more conducive regime environments. In the absence of these, downgrading appears to be an inevitable outcome.

With respect to marketing and social capabilities, it is clear that successfully differentiated firms are quite skilled at establishing and managing the interpersonal relationships that create the "untraded inter-dependencies" vital for sustaining a position in high-value markets (Storper, 1997). Thus the challenge for SMME owners is to gain face-to-face access to higher-end customers and better suppliers who can help them to be more creative in relation to design trends and/or to increase the quality of their finished products. While there are significant opportunities for differentiation in South Africa, most Tanzanian firms face substantial obstacles to developing such relationships unless they become importers. For Tanzanian SMMEs who are relegated to Dar es Salaam's sprawling, noisy, and crowded market areas or manufacturing clusters, gaining access to higher-end clientele is highly unlikely as these consumers often prefer to purchase from more formal shops and importers, or on the basis of a personal recommendation about an SMME that was obtained from a friend or family member. ICTs mean relatively little in terms of gaining initial (F2F) access to such differentiated markets as class positionalities, communication skills, education status, race, spatial proximity, and/or ethnicity may play a significant role in enabling relational proximity, and hopefully trust to emerge. Such circumstances favor the larger/more formal (and often expatriate-owned) firms, and most SMME owners are limited to those markets where their material circumstances and socioeconomic and sociocultural positionalities are in line with those of lower-end clients.

Downgrading and differentiation are in essence outcomes of the structural conditions facing African manufacturers in the current age of neoliberal and informational capitalism. Imminent development strategies, those that seek to improve firm-specific capabilities incrementally through ICT diffusion, might help manufacturing SMMEs to tread water in an increasingly hostile regime environment, but ultimately they do little to challenge the structures, material conditions, and GPN couplings that reproduce it. Immanent changes to this environment are needed if African manufacturers are to reposition themselves in an informationalized and more deeply integrated global economy. When considering these issues, it is apparent that the "usual suspects" – human capital limitations, poor infrastructure, a neoliberal trade and investment environment, economic extraversion, and the absence of state-sponsored supporting institutions or industrial policy – are where the greatest challenges lie: issues whose rectification will require political struggles and labor- and capital-intensive interventions, rather than imminent and individuated ICT4D initiatives that reproduce rather than transform the structural environment.

Notes

1   In the case of tourism, downgrading is manifest in the loss of rents/profits that one would expect an SMME owner to obtain on the basis of her/his place-specific knowledge (e.g., when to go to places, how to get there, what to pay, etc.) through what we describe in Chapter 7 as "neo-intermediation". Such knowledge was traditionally held down in the destination, but now detailed information is available globally and free-of-charge through websites such as LonelyPlanet and TripAdvisor. The availability of this destination-specific knowledge has further empowered those firms (typically non-local) with the greatest access to higher-end clients in tourist-source regions, while making it more difficult for the SMMEs surveyed to carve out higher-value market niches. Instead, these firms increasingly serve a basic subcontracting role to foreign tour operators who can, from a distance, manage the day-to-day quality of their products quite effectively through the use of new ICTs. We detail the dynamics of neo-intermediation in Chapter 7.

2   For example, Meagher (2010) has shown how hypercompetition in a Nigerian shoe products cluster led producers to try to reduce input costs by using corn-flake packets to make insoles.

3   For example, major retailers such as Walmart, which has an annual turnover bigger than the entire economy of sub-Saharan Africa, engage in practices such as "cost-down pricing" (Stiglitz, 2006). This is where, in order to get a supplier contract, firms must commit to reduce prices on an annual basis, so that more of the profits accrue to Walmart.

4   In the case of the "Trade Court", Gibbon and Ponte (2005: 59) highlighted how the costs and capabilities required to pursue litigation or defend oneself within the WTO's dispute resolution mechanism puts less-developed countries at an extreme disadvantage: "Those who lack capacity to use the system therefore bring few cases, and when cases are brought against them, they tend to concede defeat before the case reaches a more costly stage of proceedings."

5   Much of this discussion is drawn from Gibbon and Ponte's (2005) book. Other empirical examples of problematic changes to the governance of value chains or GPNs linking Africa to the world economy can be found throughout the literature. For example, there are case studies on apparel (e.g., Palpacuer et al., 2005; Phelps et al., 2009), horticultural products (Friedberg, 2003; Ouma, 2010), palm oil (Fold, 2008), and cotton (Bassett, 2010).

6   Downgrading is most clearly evident in Tanzania, but there are also significant indicators that this is occurring in South Africa's wood products sector, particularly amongst SMMEs striving to compete in lower-value markets. For the purposes of clarity, our downgrading discussion focuses on the Dar es Salaam sample, and we highlight (through footnotes) similar trends in South Africa when relevant.

7   Several South African SMMEs (Durban furniture manufacturers) also com-
    plained about imports from China:

> Imports have affected us heavily, especially Chinese. They are cheap and
> low quality but the customer thinks it looks good and buys it. We try to
> match the price but it's difficult.

> The import market has been killing budget-line furniture... imported
> units (knockdown) come dirt cheap.

> Imports from China have knocked us pretty hard. We always end up
> cutting our prices, gets harder and harder to do so... We had a customer
> of 5 years who took a product of theirs, sent it to China and had it
> copied, then switched to these Chinese suppliers. No loyalty... Copyright
> is too expensive to enforce.

8   While South African timber products are not a major export commodity, exports
    of furnishings have been in steep decline (see Chapter 5), and most SMMEs in
    the wood products and furniture manufacturing industry are reluctant to begin
    significant export operations:

> We tried entering the export market before. I wrote to 30 UK department
> stores, offering to source "butler trays". ... Got a reply from only one,
> saying they were "too expensive". The KwaZulu-Natal Furniture Cluster
> took part in an export trip to Hungary and Russia, but no one there
> really wants to import product... and many would try and sell them back
> to you. [There is] fear that [importers] will copy our [South African]
> designs. I've heard "horror stories" of containers shipped out and then
> sent back to South Africa because importers "changed their minds".
> (Durban furniture manufacturer)

9   A buoyant domestic market for home and building construction meant that
    this firm had as much work as it wanted – "the construction industry in
    Tanzania is growing at 14% a year you know." Given the need to develop floor
    plans and other designs, this firm was relatively advanced in terms of its ICT
    usage, using computer-aided design (CAD), for example. Despite being a
    relatively technically advanced firm, the management had chosen to focus on
    the (growing) domestic market for the reasons outlined earlier.

10 In South Africa many firms in the survey noted that they could not compete on
    price with China. Intense international price competition has meant that export
    margins have been under pressure. By way of example, UK sterling prices of
    bunk beds that two South African manufacturers received fell by a third bet-
    ween 1996 and 1999/2000 (Morris and Dunne, 2004).

11 Differentiation strategies are also common in the tourism sectors of South
    Africa and Zanzibar, and numerous tour operators and hoteliers noted their
    desire to cater principally to high net worth individuals or particular markets
    (e.g., by country of origin or spending capacity). The major difference with the

wood products sector is two-fold. First, given that tourism is an inherently international market, SMMEs need to develop strategies for accessing and capturing international clients rather than domestic ones. Second, the tourism industry in Africa also has a large lower-end segment (e.g., backpackers) where local SMMEs often have a comparative advantage and one that can enable significant levels of value creation. The wider point is that differentiation in tourism can be both "high" and "low" and both strategies can lead to success stories for SMMEs. In contrast, the differentiation we document in the wood products sector is about higher-value markets only.

12   This is not entirely the case, but our sample was consistent with regard to the behavior of SMMEs in Durban's wood products sector, particularly for those firms utilizing a differentiation-based strategy. A few firms tried to develop export markets for high-value products, but very few, if any, rely principally on exports for their revenue. Those that have a significant exposure to international markets face the added vulnerability of shocks and recessions in the markets they serve, as noted by one business owner in Durban whose exports to the US plummeted after the 2008 financial crisis. Thus international interconnection, even in terms of markets, can sometimes have adverse consequences.

13   Our research did reveal one case where a long-distance relationship was established in the absence of an initial face-to-face meeting. This particular South African company exported products for hotels and casinos in Las Vegas, and a US-based distributor had found their website. The initial contact was made by email and then they started shipping containers of furnishings to the US, relying on payments via wire transfer. The trading partners only met after a year when the firm owner-manager went to Las Vegas. The fact that the distributor in the US trusted them was very important, as the Durban firm asked for full payment before they would ship. This level of trust may relate to the domestic context in the US where there are high levels of contract compliance. Either way, this business represented only a small percentage of the South African firm's revenue, dropping from 10% to 2% in the wake of the 2008 financial crisis.

14   For example, South Africa's 2011 exports of furniture, other than for bedrooms, were 0.38% those of China (263 times less), which controls approximately 30% of the global supply of furnishings (ITC, 2012).

Chapter Seven
Emerging Regime and GPN Configurations: Neo-intermediation and ICT-enabled Extraversion (with Bjoern Surborg)

Some of the purported benefits of new ICTs for economic development in the Global South are supposed to be achieved through disintermediation. Disintermediation occurs when "middle (wo)men" are cut out of value chains, and producers and consumers of products and services are more directly linked through their transactions. According to the accountancy firm KPMG (n.d.):

> Disintermediation, the process of taking the retailer out of the chain between the producer and the consumer, makes sense from a rational perspective. It shortens the value chain, reducing time and /or costs. Dell is one of the most prominent and successful examples of disintermediation in recent years.

In neoclassical economics, market failures such as exploitation often result from asymmetric information and bargaining power. Where agents have "full" information and markets are competitive (i.e., there are multiple buyers and sellers, so no one agent has market power) then exploitation is not meant to be possible (World Bank, 1981). Disintermediation is meant to help promote better or fuller information for farmers, manufacturers, workers, and service providers about the true value of their labor or products, and consequently to facilitate social and industrial upgrading.

Africa's Information Revolution: Technical Regimes and Production Networks in South Africa and Tanzania, First Edition. James T. Murphy and Pádraig Carmody.
© 2015 John Wiley & Sons, Ltd. Published 2015 by John Wiley & Sons, Ltd.

Most of the literature on the market information provision role and dis-intermediation facilitated by new ICTs is largely confined to agriculture and fisheries, which are characterized by more "linear" value chains (Jensen, 2007: Aker and Mbiti, 2010). This is undoubtedly important in certain contexts and is important given that the majority of Africa's population continue to derive at least part of their livelihoods from agriculture. According to the World Bank (2013c), agriculture accounts for 65% of Africa's labor force and a third of the continent's GDP. Different types of ICTs may be used for different purposes when marketing crops or other products or services. For example, there are now a number of mobile phone applications that convey information about current market prices to farmers, thereby enhancing their bargaining power with traders.[1]

The neoliberal vision for development holds that it is national, rather than transnational, merchant capital which exploits Africa's rural poor (Bates, 1981), and new mobile phone-based market linkage and information systems (MLISs), in particular, are meant to help level the playing field. Specifically, market linkage and information systems attempt to circumvent the problem of asymmetrical information that has limited the ability of African farmers to get the "best" prices for their commodities. MLISs can do this through the direct provision of information to farmers about prices, for example, or seek to connect producers to buyers to whom they would otherwise not have access. MLISs are also often thought to enable disinter-mediation within GPNs, thereby allowing a greater share of the market price to be retained by the direct producers, consequently reducing poverty.[2]

Prominent examples of these systems in an African context include Esoko in Ghana, which allows farmers to receive information about crop prices via text message, and ShopAfrica53, which accepts orders, for craft goods for example, via the internet and communicates this to (often) small producers via mobile phone text message. However, while such systems and businesses may reduce transaction costs and increase small producer incomes, this can be done without necessarily expanding markets or encouraging structural transformation of economies on to higher, more diversified growth paths. Furthermore, heightened competition, facilitated by new ICTs, may benefit large producers who can take advantage of economies of scale.[3] These services also represent a type of intermediation rather than disintermediation, and they may lead to virtual or seemingly placeless power forms of power asymmetries, as we detail below.

Research on the contribution of, and limitations on, ICTs to/for agricultural, fishery, and other basic commodity markets has provided insights regarding the potential for thicker forms of integration and informationalization in rural areas of Africa. However, rapid urbanization on the continent means that employment in other economic sectors will become increasingly important. Some service industries, for example, have the potential to benefit greatly from new ICTs, given the more intensive, real-time communication and information management needs that mark these activities. Our case studies of tourism in Cape Town and the Western Cape region (South Africa) and Zanzibar (as detailed in chapters 4 and 5) sought to determine whether ICTs were helping to reconfigure these industries and empower SMMEs. The findings demonstrated that, although mobile phones, computers, and the internet were being used intensively by most firms, there were few signs of the kinds of thick integration that might help to immanently transform the sociotechnical regimes and GPN couplings linking tourism SMMEs to international markets. This chapter details another significant finding, with a focus on the tourism industry: the emergence of ICT-enabled forms of inter-mediation – neo-intermediation[4] – which are reconfiguring the relations between customers, traditional intermediaries (e.g., tour operators), service providers, and destinations, and creating ICT-enabled forms of extraversion by firms and individuals outside Africa.[5]

Neo-intermediation and Reconfigured GPNs in the Tourism Industry

Tourism is an important and growing sector for many African economies. Globally, travel services account for approximately a third of service exports, whereas in Africa they account for more than half of the total (Wiig, 2003). However, the retention of revenue from tourism is as low as 30% for developing countries around the world as a result of import and factor income leakage through profit repatriation (Wiig, 2003). In this environment, tourism SMMEs strive and struggle to create, expand, retain and capture income in the context of the wider tourism system. Disintermediation, building more direct, personal ties to clients at a distance, is one of the ways firms may seek to do this, since it is here where new ICTs (especially the internet, websites, and email/Skype communication) can play a key role in reconfiguring tourism GPNs such that SMMEs might create and capture greater value for/from foreign markets.

As highlighted above, the discussion of disintermediation in both the media and academic literature is often celebratory; however, intermediaries in goods and service markets may perform a variety of valuable functions. At a basic level, intermediaries allow people to access products or services they want at particular times and places (Alderson, 1958). They allow for the "discrepancy of assortments" to be rectified – that is, they reconcile the mismatch between mass production by producers and individuated demand by consumers (Stern and El-Ansary, 1988). They also facilitate searching by producers and customers by structuring information and routinizing transactions, thereby potentially decreasing distribution costs (Stern and El-Ansary, 1988; Wynne et al., 2001). Financial intermediaries such as banks also serve vital functions in aggregating and allocating capital, while (generally) reducing risk for depositors by loan screening. Intermediation, then, may serve important functions rather than simply being a form of "dead weight loss" to the economic system, as is sometimes implied in the literature.

In increasingly information-rich environments, customers need ways to sort, refine and process information which are reliable and do not lead to information overload. Also with often huge increases in the supply of touristic services, with the number of hotel rooms rising from 4000 to 13,000 from 1990 to 2010 in Cape Town, for example, tourists need ways to organize or sort information about potential accommodation (Rogerson, 2013).[6] Word-of-mouth recommendations and websites provide the primary mechanism through which this is achieved. Thus, in contrast to many writings on the topic of disintermediation, informationalization may create greater demand for intermediation.

The need of tourists for accurate information about the range, quality, diversity, and price of services has significant implications for the contributions that new ICTs can make to upgrading and performance in SMMEs. In Zanzibar and Cape Town, the promise of ICT-driven forms of disintermediation is largely latent as many firms rely on personal networks developed through face-to-face relationships, shared experiences, and third-party referrals (weak ties) to establish links to clients in international markets. Moreover, many firms are now subject to new forms of intermediation such as a reliance on "virtual travel agents" and third-party booking systems. These virtual travel agents and tour operators, as we detail below, often have substantial economies of scale and network economies which result, ironically perhaps, in market concentration rather than disintermediation and more "perfect" forms of competition.

Intermediaries have always been and remain crucial to the success of tourism SMMEs, and are established and maintained in different ways (e.g., see Christian, 2012). The tourism businesses we sampled reported both using agents (or other partners) that they have met in person at some point as well as those that they had never met and would only communicate with electronically. Beyond ICT-enabled forms of intermediation in GPNs, spatially proximate actors often remain significant in determining how effective an SMME is in accessing tourists. The degree to which face-to-face communication is still important depends to some extent on the business owner's personal choice, rather than technological capabilities.

For example, tour operators, restaurateurs, and other local service providers benefit significantly from the development of strong ties to other firms who might provide referrals for their services when guests inquire about excursions, dining options, and so on. This is common in the case of specialized tours and experiences, such as scuba diving tours or township tours. In such cases, an SMME's success depends significantly on the maintenance and establishment of a dense inter-firm network within the destination: relationships where ICTs mean little to their initial establishment. These ties are also significant in that they serve as conduits for the flow of information about SMMEs that are vital for the development of reputational capital both at home and abroad. ICTs can play a significant role in "globalizing" such reputations through third-party referrals to international clients, who may inquire about activities and accommodations not provided by the firms involved in a particular transaction.[7] Reputational impacts can, of course, be a better or worse circumstance for an SMME, and it highlights the limited power that businesspeople may have in trying to manage their reputations vis-à-vis the competition and especially powerful gatekeepers (e.g., tourism promotion offices) who may have established strong opinions about the firm.

In Zanzibar, in particular, other forms of spatially proximate informal intermediation also remain important, manifest in the continued role that street brokers and "beach boys" – *papasi* – play in enabling or facilitating market access for SMMEs, especially hoteliers, restaurateurs, and tour operators.[8] Hotel employees, taxi drivers, and others who interact directly with tourists also take part in such practices, and like the *papasi* they receive small commissions from business owners in exchange for directing clients to their goods or services. The most visible of these intermediaries – *papasi* – are also the most problematic with regard to the Zanzibari tourism market, with many SMME owners and public officials complaining about their presence and harassment of tourists and business owners. One hotel operator in Zanzibar noted that the *papasi* were a constant problem for them as they would redirect clients away. To try to overcome this they would meet clients at the port and bring them directly to the hotel after they disembarked.

As is the case with Dar es Salaam's *madalali,* there has been a significant increase in the number of *papasi* even as new ICTs become more commonplace. The continued rise and presence of *papasi* can be linked to wider factors that have created a large pool of underemployed labor in Zanzibar despite the growth of the tourism industry – manifest especially in the lack of labor training available to locals who desire employment, the rise of inward migration to the islands by mainland Tanzanians and other East Africans seeking employment, and the stated preference for hiring non-locals by many SMMEs that are owned and operated by outsiders. Other respondents noted that it was tourists, especially "backpackers", trying to save a few dollars on guiding services that were fueling the demand for *papasi,* even if policy-makers and other tourism operators characterized them as "pirates". Finally, some linked the activities of *papasi* to the Archipelago's growing heroin trafficking and addiction problem, viewing the increasing number of street brokers as one outcome of the problem.[9] All told, *papasi* and other informal, spatially proximate intermediaries remain significant in the Zanzibari tourism industry, and it is unlikely, given the structural and market demand conditions driving their presence, that ICTs can enable many SMMEs to avoid them.

Street-level intermediaries remain a significant presence, but their impact on the industry and the prospects for SMMEs pales in comparison to new, ICT-enabled forms of neo-intermediation within tourism GPNs. For most firms the web is of vital importance to their business, even if it means they are imbricated in unequal, transnational mercantilist networks organized by multinational corporations such as Expedia, TripAdvisor, and Orbitz. These are very profitable enterprises that depend heavily on new ICTs and which control significant portions of the buyer-driven value chains that organize tourism activities around the globe.[10] Despite their growing importance, the nature of tourist-to-internet-to-African SMME communications and relationships often obfuscates the ability of foreign TNCs to concentrate power through accumulation and to serve as centers of calculation in the global tourism industry.

This is not meant to suggest that web-based intermediation is inevitably a negative circumstance for tourists and SMMEs. In fact, and as numerous business owners noted, it has created new channels for accessing clients, particularly through third-party and SMME operated websites. Moreover, the internet allows firms to (virtually) operate 24 hours, 7 days a week, thus ameliorating labor and time-zone difference challenges. All told, most tourism business owners in South Africa, and many Zanzibari firms, particularly hoteliers, rely extensively on web-based forms of intermediation. One South African guest-house owner noted that 90–95% of their business was from third-party websites, with the remaining 5–10% generated through more traditional travel agents. Another SMME owner mentioned that his guest house is listed on 20 different third-party websites which link directly into his booking system. More commonly, Cape Town business owners strive to be listed or reviewed on 5–10 websites:

> We started with booking.com in November 2011, and are working with Expedia at the moment. All together we want to have 8 or 9 portals and booking also possible on our own website directly with credit card payment. (Guesthouse owner, Cape Town)

In Zanzibar, hotel owners are turning increasingly to websites like Expedia and Hotels.com, although the penetration of these firms into local markets is limited primarily to higher-end, larger-scale, and foreign-owned enterprises. For at least one firm, the almost complete commitment of rooms to third-party websites has meant that there is little need to have an independent website:

> Most of our clients come from bookings on Expedia and Hotels.com. ... Through Expedia, people book directly, they pay and then they arrive with a serial number that we confirm. With only 10 rooms, it does not pay to have a website... our market is from everywhere and we get good ratings online. But

we are so small that we don't need a website (the information pages on bookings websites are enough). (Zanzibar hotel owner)

In South Africa, according to one manager in the former tourism promotion agency Cape Town Routes, "Tourists are becoming more informed and
cleverer – doing their own bookings rather than via tour operators".
However, these bookings are often not disintermediated, realized instead
through new intermediaries in GPNs such as booking websites. In Zanzibar
and Cape Town, tourists can book and pay for almost all of their costs
through foreign tour operators or third-party website owners who are now
better able, through the use of the internet and mobile phones, to manage
the real-time quality of the tourism experience in the context of an outsourcing or subcontracting arrangement.

For most respondents, particularly in South Africa, the benefits of third-
party, web-based forms of intermediation are viewed as significant, as are
the potential costs of not being listed or visible on these websites. However,
several respondents also noted the excessive commissions, impersonal interactions, and transaction costs associated with bookings through websites
such as Expedia.

> Viatour.com is a good solution, but they take 25% commission plus an annual
> fee. Webtickets (http://www.webtickets.co.za) is complicated to work with and
> the back engine is very labor intensive. Tried Computickets as well… but if there
> is a change, we have to go through the computickets bureaucracy. We would
> have given them R10,000 for marketing [approx. US$1,000], but it required a
> 2 year contract. Computickets also requires people to pick up tickets at a store
> and stand in line again and this is very inconvenient. (Cape Town tour operator)

> You can only debit Expedia on the day of check-in. Others send the money
> once they take the booking. You can't negotiate with Expedia. You do what
> you are told to do. (Cape Town guest house owner)

> I have problems with Expedia's "ground handler" here in East Africa (based
> in Arusha) as they are sometimes slow in paying their monthly bills… I don't
> like Expedia… it is sold in a very impersonal way. It is not sold with any
> sophistication. There is no contact between the hotel and the client before
> arrival, and there is a restrictive contract system. (Zanzibar hotel owner)

Other respondents noted that if you wished to have a higher ranking on
booking.com and thereby attract greater customer interest, it was possible
to pay a higher commission level. This represents a form of "ratcheting",
where small businesses are put in competition with each other to pay
higher levels of commission to the intermediary, facilitated by the "magnet"
effect of these market dominant websites. Ultimately, these pricing and
commission-charging practices subtract a substantial level of overhead

from the value which could arguably be captured by African SMMEs in profit. Moreover, the fact that commissions are captured by a foreign rather than a domestically owned company results in losses of multiplier and subsequent linkage effects within destination regions and industrial regimes.

The practice of charging high commission rates and ratcheting them up is nothing new, as traditional travel agents and tour operators have done so for years.[11] One respondent in Zanzibar recounted how a travel agent had charged tourists substantially more (€400) than the hotel "rack rate"[12] and that as a result they were inevitably disappointed with the hotel. Another noted that they wanted to avoid working with tour operators because they demanded many rooms at peak season, but provided little or no business during the off season. Beyond the similarities, however, internet-based forms of intermediation pose a much greater threat to the concentration of market power in the hands of a few firms, given both the global reach of these websites and the arms-length nature of website transactions. Those who wish to be listed have little room for negotiation about commissions and prices, but the alternative, delisting or non-listing, is viewed by many as a far worse circumstance. As such, SMMEs, particularly in South Africa, are compelled to market their services via these websites, given the need to fill guest houses, hotels, and excursions by any means necessary such that the business remains profitable. This neo-intermediation, rather than disintermediation, then creates new forms of virtual or seemingly placeless power, which may be more difficult to contest than those associated with other older forms of intermediation. Moreover, it facilitates a dynamic of concentration and accumulation within new kinds of lead firms (e.g., Expedia) and (typically) core regions, thus reconfiguring GPNs in ways that limit the prospects for organic or strategic couplings to Africa's tourism regimes. Instead, structural couplings are the norm and social upgrading remains elusive.

As Ghosh (1998) argued, the internet is a "natural" concentrating medium and a restricted number of firms ("magnets") will control channels for booking particular services. As noted earlier, this concentration of virtual capital seems to have come to pass, at least to some extent. According to one source, 57% of hotel reservations are now made on the internet (Statistics Brain, 2013), with brand websites operated by hotel chains, for example, accounting for the bulk of that, at approximately 65%, and merchant websites accounting for the balance. Whereas branded websites such as marriott.com have substantial "magnet" power, the lack of brands and recognition for SMME hotels and tour operators means they are often reliant on merchant websites, such as TripAdvisor and Expedia.com. Disintermediation of people and re-intermediation by foreign-owned websites can create unemployment, in addition to channelling income overseas that would have been spent domestically otherwise, even if it is captured by domestic intermediaries, resulting in a loss of associated multiplier and linkage effects (Murphy *et al.*, 2014). Consequently ICTs can contribute to exacerbated forms of uneven development, a circumstance that is particularly visible in Zanzibar.

Neo-intermediation and the Reconfiguration of Zanzibar's GPN Couplings

Ongoing changes to Zanzibar's tourism industry reflect the ways in which more concentrated forms of market power and neo-intermediation are threatening the prospects for SMMEs to take advantage of the sector's growth and increasing ties to GPNs. Concentration and neo-intermediation are being driven by new forms of web-based intermediation and the growing power of large hotel interests in the archipelago's tourism regime, as we described in Chapter 5. As a result, the more globally connected and capital-rich businesses, particularly those linked to the Zanzibar Association of Tourism Investors (ZATI), are better able to take advantage of the market access opportunities made possible through new ICTs and liberalized markets in Tanzania. When coupled with the industry's expansion and FDI into large-scale beach resorts, SMMEs, but especially tour operators, are increasingly forced to rely on commission-extracting intermediaries (e.g., Expedia, foreign tour operators) or to serve as (lower-end) subcontractors for more powerful firms based locally and outside Zanzibar.

Figures 7.1 to 7.4 show how value is created and distributed within and in relation to Zanzibar's tourism market, highlighting both current, idealized, evolving, and (potentially) dystopian scenarios that accompany the rise of internet-based forms of neo-intermediation. These diagrams are not a complete picture of the connectivities between all actors in the tourism sociotechnical regime but rather a schematic of the direct and varied links between consumers, local and non-local firms, and other intermediaries who operate in Zanzibar's tourism market. As such, their intention is to give a sense of the complex and evolving GPNs that link intermediaries to one another in the regime and to (partially) describe the different ways in which couplings are achieved.

Figure 7.1 charts the most common forms of intermediation today, those linking a typical tourist to accommodations, retail consumption, excursions, and transportation services within Zanzibar. Each "box" in the figure represents a node in the GPN where value is created and captured, either through the provision of services, information, and/or commissions. Outside of Zanzibar, foreign-produced guidebooks (GIP) and websites (WIP) commonly offer a first form of interaction with the destination, often followed by exchanges with travel agents (NLTA) and/or tour operators (NLTO).[13] Significant sums can be captured by these intermediaries through the

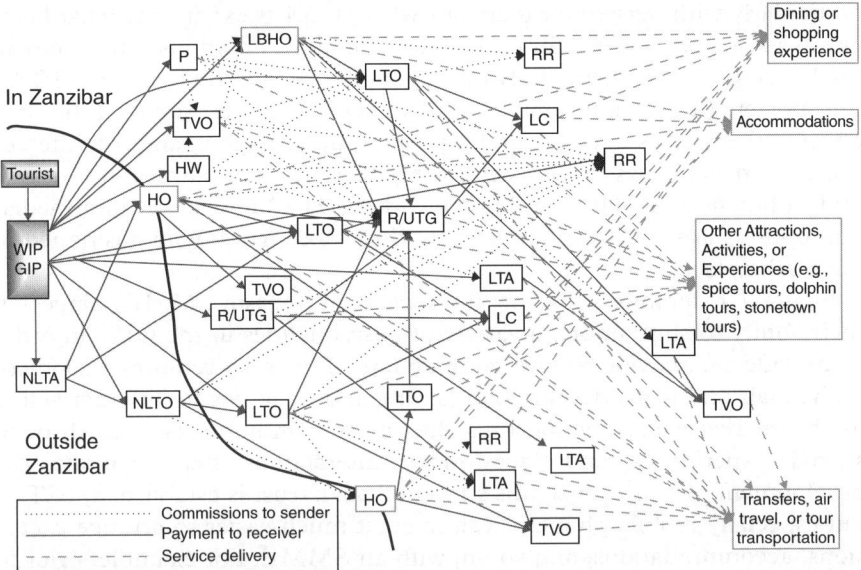

Figure 7.1 Common intermediation relationships in Zanzibar's tourism industry circa 2011. Note: Hotels may be owned by foreign investors and are thus depicted on the "boundary" between "in Zanzibar" and "outside Zanzibar". Abbreviations: WIP, website intermediation possible; GIP, guidebook intermediation possible; NLTO, non-local tour operator; NLTA, non-local travel agent; HO, hotelier; LTO, local tour operator; LBHO, low-budget hotelier; LTA, local travel agent; R/UTG, registered/unregistered (freelance) tour guide; HW, hotel worker; P, *papasi*; TVO, transporter/vehicle owner/taxi driver; LC, local communities; RR, retailers and restaurants.

commissions concomitant with pre-travel bookings. Mainstream hotels (HO), often foreign-owned (hence their location on the boundary of the within and outside Zanzibar zone in Figures 7.1–7.4), also serve as key points of coordination for many tourists: booked through third-party websites, by non-local tour operators or travel agents, or through direct communication with hoteliers. As we detail below, the positionalities of these intermediating actors/websites/guidebooks in the GPN empowers them significantly with regard to local SMMEs based solely in Zanzibar.

Within Zanzibar, the possible pathways through which tourists receive services are complicated by the diverse range of intermediaries competing to receive commissions or provide services to tourists. These include both local tour operators (LTO), low-budget hoteliers (LBHO), local travel agents (LTA), tour guides (R/UTG), and transporters (TVO) as well as the most informal intermediaries, represented here by *papasi* (P) and those hotel workers (HW) who may direct guests to the services of particular tour operators or other service providers in exchange for a small commission. Moreover, local communities (LC) also intervene in value-adding activities, particularly with regard to excursions where tourists experience what life is like in a Zanzibari village, for example. As Figure 7.1 demonstrates, tourism market actors – but particularly tour operators (LTO), travel agents (LTA), transporters (TVO), and tour guides (R/UTG) – are best served if they can position themselves to create and capture value through a range of different transaction pathways. Other actors, *papasi* (P), communities (LC), low-budget hoteliers (LBHO), and hotel workers (HW) have fewer intermediation options available to them and are thus more marginally positioned in the marketplace.

Figure 7.1 demonstrates how the success of tourism SMMEs hinges on their ability to shift among a variety of positionalities in the GPN in order to provide services or receive commissions. Doing so requires that these individuals and firms develop both strong and weak ties to different actors in the marketplace, relationships that most commonly emerge through shared experiences and face-to-face interactions that facilitate the development of trust. Once this strong or weak trust is established, ICTs – but especially mobile phones – can make it much easier to arrange excursions, accommodations, and so on, with an SMME. For example, prior to an interview with one tour operator in Zanzibar, we waited in the office while the business owner scrolled through his phone to find the right independent tour guide able to escort a couple who were interested in learning about the bird species in Jozani forest, a common day excursion from Stone Town. The first person he called was unavailable but the second guide in his address book was free, and after a brief negotiation over the phone, said guide arrived within 15 minutes and the tour was able to begin. These kinds of intermediation transactions occur every day, thus making it essential for SMME owners to develop wide-ranging networks through which value-adding activities – big or small – can be realized such that they maintain a steady income flow.

All of this said, however, such forms of intermediation are typically low-value exchanges that can have high transaction costs as tourists and exchange partners often negotiate aggressively with another. In contrast, those that book tours and accommodations directly from the outside – through third-party websites, non-local tour operators, overseas travel agents, and hotels having online booking capabilities – are far less able or likely to haggle over rates and are willing to pre-book excursions from a distance. These firms, in turn, then negotiate with local, Zanzibari SMMEs, often tour operators and transporters, and sometimes local communities, to subcontract excursions, airport transfers, meals, and experiences. The intense competition between local SMMEs for this business means that outside buyers and hotels have significant power to set prices and terms for subcontracting relationships. Moreover, the relationships between hotel owners and non-local tour operators and Zanzibari SMMEs are often well established and exclusive, meaning that firms not connected with these kinds of GPN actors may be left to only low-budget tourists and/or walk-in clientele. As one travel agent observed:

> If you cannot build a long-standing and trusting relationship with an international agent, it is very difficult for you to have a stable and consistent income. It is, however, very difficult to break in with a new agent and luck, or bad luck for someone else [in terms of the quality of their service], is needed in order for an international tour agent to break her/his ties with a Zanzibari agent. In essence, the market is currently saturated for these kinds of relationships and I instead work primarily with local hotel owners and the government to acquire business. (Zanzibar travel agent)

In this context, new ICTs mean relatively little in the absence of pre-established ties between firms, most of which emerge through successful, shared experiences.

> Some guy in Arusha can send a beautiful email, have a professional website, and appear to be a high quality tour operator... but can you trust someone simply based on that? One needs to physically visit a potential business partner. You have to double-check. (Zanzibar tour operator)

Despite the limitations, the promise for new ICTs is that, when coupled with successful shared experiences that facilitate trust-building, they might enable Zanzibari SMMEs to develop more direct, disintermediated ties to international markets. Figure 7.2 depicts what this idealized scenario might look like: a situation where intermediation relationships remain but where non-local travel agents and tour operators disappear entirely from the GPN. Also included in this scenario is the elimination of *papasi* and hotel-worker intermediation activities, something that most SMME owners, hoteliers, and public officials argue is necessary for the industry to improve its quality. If such disintermediation was possible, value creation and capture possibilities within Zanzibar would be enhanced significantly such that the regime might become more viable as an employment generator and livelihood strategy – assuming a destination management organization (DMO) and the institutional environment were supportive of initiatives to reduce poverty, improve public infrastructure, and facilitate industrial and social upgrading.

As was highlighted in Chapter 5, however, the Zanzibari tourism sociotechnical regime appears to be shifting toward a configuration wherein more, not less, value is "leaking" outside of Zanzibar through new kinds of couplings to GPNs. Through these reconfigurations, foreign tour operators, third-party websites, and large hotel interests are capturing more value through intermediation and/or the direct provisioning of excursions, transfers, retail, and dining experiences. The implications of these changes to the regime's GPN couplings are significant, as highlighted in Figure 7.3:

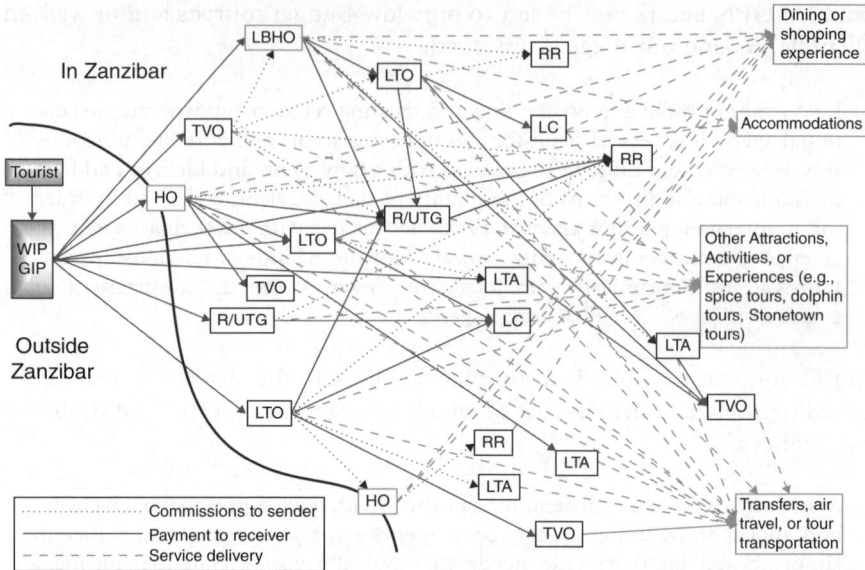

Figure 7.2 The potential for disintermediation to restructure market relationships in Zanzibar's tourism industry. Abbreviations: WIP, website intermediation possible; GIP, guidebook intermediation possible; NLTO, non-local tour operator; NLTA, non-local travel agent; HO, hotelier; LTO, local tour operator; LBHO, low-budget hotelier; LTA, local travel agent; R/UTG, registered/unregistered (freelance) tour guide; HW, hotel worker; P, *papasi*; TVO, transporter/vehicle owner/taxi driver; LC, local communities; RR, retailers and restaurants.

manifest in fewer opportunities for value creation and capture by Zanzibari SMMEs. Because hoteliers are still required to, or choose to, subcontract local tour operators, travel agents, freelance tour guides, and transporters for services such as tours, ticketing and transportation services, these actors remain part of the GPN. However, their positionality is continually eroding as hotels are providing such services in-house through the establishment of local "partnerships" with firms over which they can maintain tight control.

> Hotels are taking business from us and trying to undercut us by going directly to foreign agents… after we have negotiated and planned a tour, a hotel might approach the international agent with which we are working and attempt to cut us out of the equation… Hotels [also] occasionally avoid the Zanzibari laws preventing them from entering the tour operating business by using bribes, but the usual course of action is to establish a local partner as a tour company that is all but nominally part of the hotel. (Zanzibar tour operator)

These tactics ensure that many local SMMEs, especially tour operators, remain marginalized with respect to their value-adding possibilities.

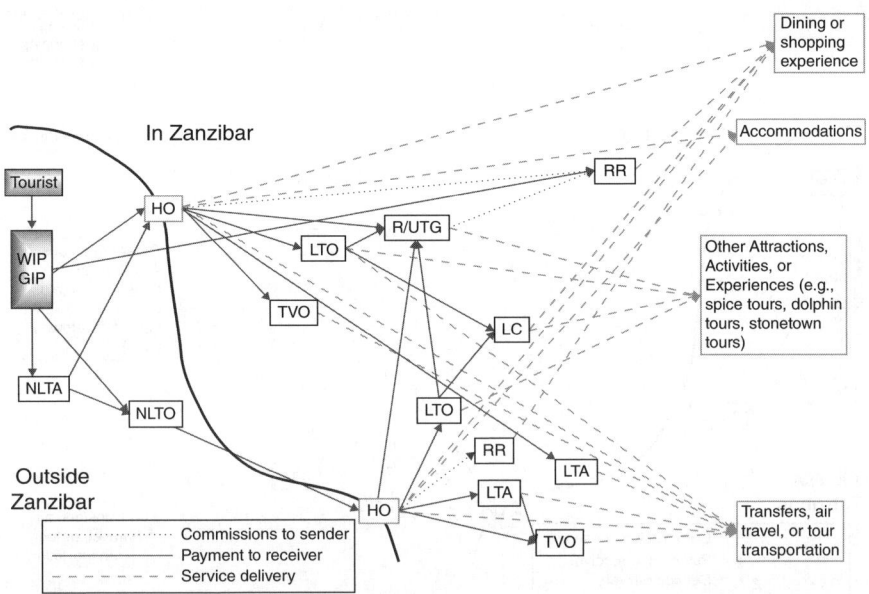

Figure 7.3   The shift in power toward third-party websites and hotels in Zanzibar's tourism industry. Abbreviations: WIP, website intermediation possible; GIP, guidebook intermediation possible; NLTO, non-local tour operator; NLTA, non-local travel agent; HO, hotelier; LTO, local tour operator; LTA, local travel agent; TVO, transporter/vehicle owner/taxi driver; LC, local communities; RR, retailers and restaurants.

As the power of outside intermediaries and large hotel interests increases in the Zanzibari tourism industry, there is fear that market power is becoming concentrated in the hands of a few hotel and tour operator interests. Figure 7.4 demonstrates what this "dystopic" scenario might look like with regard to the mainstream, medium and high-value tourism market (i.e., not "backpacker" or low-budget tourism). Hotels, non-local tour operators, and those who control third-party booking websites will have increasing control over the value web and many SMMEs and individual intermediaries may face a highly limited range of possibilities through which they can secure a livelihood. Moreover, Zanzibar itself will not achieve the kinds of organic or strategic couplings to GPNs that might enable the regime to enhance and capture more value locally. Instead, existing and evolving couplings are more structural in nature – reflecting historical patterns of extraversion as outside firms in core economies extract the surplus value created by tourists' "consumption" of the destination's amenities.

To summarize, the findings from Zanzibar and Cape Town reveal the limitations on new ICTs as technologies to allow African SMMEs and industrial regimes to establish and sustain more direct and higher-value couplings to GPNs. While some are benefiting from more direct/strong

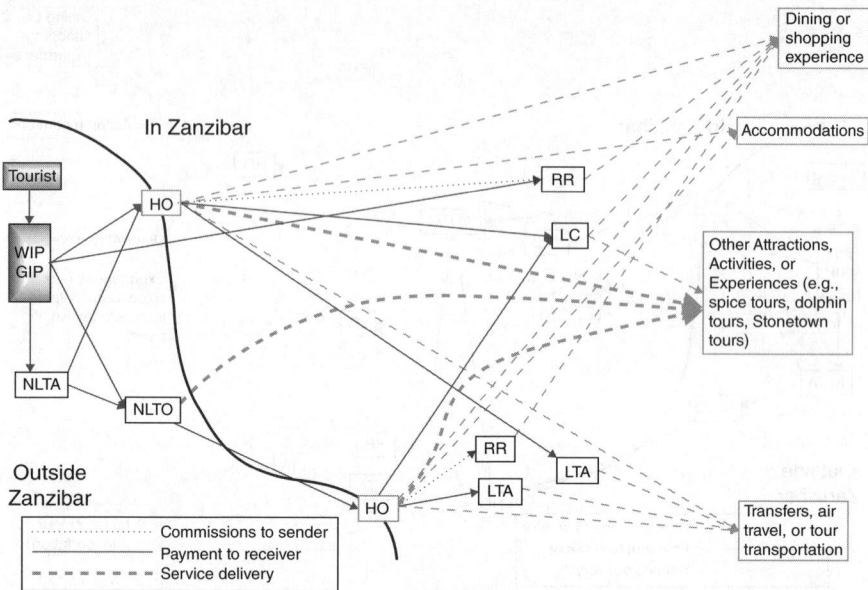

Figure 7.4   Dystopian disintermediation in Zanzibar's tourism industry. Abbreviations: WIP, website intermediation possible; GIP, guidebook intermediation possible; NLTO, non-local tour operator; NLTA, non-local travel agent; HO, hotelier; LTO, local tour operator; LTA, local travel agent; LC, local communities; RR, retailers and restaurants.

links to tourists, foreign tour operators, and others outside the region, particularly those SMMEs who have initiated or established trusting relationships through successful shared experiences, third-party referrals, and/or face-to-face interactions, still ICTs play, at best, an ancillary role. For most firms, new forms of intermediation – neo-intermediation – prevent them from capturing greater amounts of value from tourists, despite dramatic improvements in communications capabilities as a result of the internet and mobile phone technologies. This is in large part due to the lack of trust that tourists have in (often) distanciated African SMMEs and the power of outside intermediaries in GPNs to concentrate and control access to vital information about destinations and accommodations (see also Christian, 2012). Beyond being key nodes of capital accumulation, these actors and websites also serve as centers of calculation for tourists: virtual locations where clients and agents valuate tourism commodities, and where booking algorithms determine the prices for services and marketing frames effectively brand destinations through symbolic images and other forms of representation. One website which plays a particularly important role in both image construction and booking is TripAdvisor, and it is worth examining its impact in some detail.

TripAdvisor: Center of Calculation and Site of Place Fetishization

TripAdvisor is increasingly becoming a global standard of reference for travellers, who seek a quick evaluation of the quality of a service. TripAdvisor is the world's largest travel site and has established itself as a leading intermediary in tourism GPNs. It offers advice and reviews from previous travellers with links to booking tools. The site has more than 200 million unique monthly visitors, and over 100 million reviews and opinions, and operates in 30 countries worldwide (from TripAdvisor.com). In both Zanzibar and the Cape Town, TripAdvisor is viewed by many as an important source for clients, particularly for hotel, bed and breakfast, hostel, and guest house owners.[14]

As one guest-house owner in South Africa expressed it – "One of the biggest drivers in the tourism sector now is TripAdvisor" – and this was echoed by many other respondents in both tourism case study locations, one of whom said it was like a "bible" for their business partners. In the South African tourism survey, 51% of firms stated they have a presence on TripAdvisor (67% for accommodation and 43% for tour providers). Of these 26 firms on TripAdvisor, 14 (53%) believe it has a positive effect on their business, while 10 (38%) had a negative opinion of its impact on their business. Consequently TripAdvisor reviews play an increasingly important role, not just in marketing, but even in the restructuring of space.

Many respondents expressed reservations about the fact that anyone, not necessarily guests, can make postings on TripAdvisor, in contrast to some other websites where you have to have been a guest to post. Moreover, some noted that one negative review can set an SMME's ranking back quite a bit:

> I know some Cape Town operators have PR [public relations] companies who produce for them [on TripAdvisor]. It is very clear what they are doing and it is so false. (Cape Town tour operator)

> You love it so long as it is good. And I have just now got the most dreadful, it was not a dreadful review, it was actually a very unjust review, and I mean I am writing back. But I mean, I have just gone from number 8 to number 18 on TripAdvisor on the basis of that. [...] There is nothing I can do about it, now I just got to wait for other nice reviews and hope that I go up the scale again. (Cape Town guest-house owner)

Another respondent noted that it was difficult to keep pace with the reviews even though they could be highly significant for revenue generation. As this respondent further noted "as one drops below five [ranking on the website], people do not look at that business anymore". For firms such as these, TripAdvisor was a "continual battle" but one with significant consequences as evidenced by another respondent who noted that their TripAdvisor ranking had dropped so far that they had to sell the business and start a new one.

In terms of the restructuring of space, a hotel operator in Zanzibar noted that a tourist had posted a TripAdvisor review which complained about people wandering in and out of the lobby area and restaurant of the hotel. This resulted in the hotel hiring a security guard to keep locals out. New ICTs have also resulted in other forms of restructuring within the wider context of tourism regimes. For example, in South Africa new ICTs are implicated in the reproduction of segregation, poor containment and labor control as closed-circuit TVs monitor the downtown of Cape Town from which street children are banned (Samara, 2011).

Other respondents expressed opinions about the lack of sophistication and nuance that comes with website-based reviews. One noted that "TripAdvisor is everything I hate about talk shows", implying that opinions should not be given unmediated expression. Others expressed reservations about the "faceless" and impersonal nature of communications with TripAdvisor and other booking websites. According to another respondent this detracted from the customized and personalized nature of service delivery in the industry, although this was contradicted by another interviewee who argued that you could not compete just on price anymore, but had to compete on "everything", including quality service.

Websites like TripAdvisor can also serve to reinforce the concentration of visitors at particular touristic attractions and sites. Table 7.1 shows what an analysis of TripAdvisor reviews and recommendations revealed in relation to Cape Town. TripAdvisor, then, may not just concentrate attention and bookings on particular hotels or guest houses, but also particular touristic attractions. The Victoria and Alfred Waterfront, which is now owned by Dubai World, is South Africa's most visited tourist attraction, receiving about 22 million visitors a year. Arguably there is a cycle of cumulative causation at play here, as the most visited tourist attractions receive the most reviews, although Langa township did achieve 18% of the number of reviews of Table Mountain. This township is perceived to be one of the safer ones and has a tourist information center through which walking tours are available.

Table 7.1   TripAdvisor reviews of Cape Town attractions (as at 15 February 2012)

Type of attraction	Attraction	Number of reviews	Visitor photos	Attraction rank (of 111)
Urban nature	Table Mountain	724	664	1
Urban lifestyle	Victoria & Alfred Waterfront	426	196	13
Urban poverty, apartheid history	Khayelitsha Township	6	1	59
	Langa Township	128	39	5

While the internet is often held to be a democratizing force, it may paradoxically also lead to certain voices being elevated above others and a concentration of opinion. This includes both the "collective" opinions that consumers encounter on websites like TripAdvisor or Amazon.com, but also certain individuals who are frequent contributors to discussion boards and/or product reviews. For example, certain "destination experts" have a disproportionate impact in creating and disseminating knowledge that is communicated through websites like TripAdvisor. For example, one of Zanzibar's "experts" is Karl Gingrich of Findlay, Ohio, who has posted over 11,000 times on TripAdvisor – http://www.tripadvisor.com/members-forums/Karl_Gingrich (last accessed 3 December 2013). Karl, who has travelled to Tanzania many times, is an "expert" on a wide variety of Zanzibar and Tanzania specific places and topics, including: the climate, exchange rates, airport taxes, Tanzania vs. Kenya, visas, crime, accommodations, vaccinations, cocktail bars, women's safety, airlines, buses, and safari companies. Moreover, he is easy to contact directly should you have a question and will receive a "reviewer badge" if he writes one more review of a tourism service. For South Africa there are people like "BwanaDave" (http://www.tripadvisor.com/members forums/bwanadave, last accessed 3 December 2013) who serve as information gatekeepers, confidently responding to a diverse range of queries from prospective and current travellers of all kinds.[15]

Consequently power over information in the GPN may be concentrated in individuals who are sometimes far removed from the everyday circumstances. They achieve this status by taking the time to post opinions and through the creation of (virtual) forms of "relational proximity" to tourists – based on language, nationality, appearance, confidence, and writing style – that imbue their perspectives with an air of trustworthiness that many travellers to Africa seek before making booking arrangements. TripAdvisor thus serves as what Jeacle and Carter (2011) term a calculative regime that engenders trust among its users while simultaneously enrolling them in a tourism GPN that may increasingly work to the disadvantage of SMMEs in Zanzibar and Cape Town. This again reveals one of the paradoxes of the web. While there is a proliferation of information, access to and absorption of particular types of information may be highly concentrated. This may result in essentializing imaginaries and centers of calculation which may recursively produce space: in this case destinations governed increasingly by third-party websites, foreign investors, and information gatekeepers able to guide tourists to favored nodes of accumulation.

Finally, beyond their calculative, intermediative, and governing power, SMME and third-party websites such as TripAdvisor also serve as sites where representations of destinations are created and reproduced. In a world in which information is ubiquitous (for some) web-based representations may contain aspects of both fetishization and defetishization. Following Büscher (2013), and as is depicted in Figure 7.5 in images from

Figure 7.5 "Exotic" Africa as depicted through an SMME's website. Reprinted with permission of Ma Betty's Cultural Village, http://www.mabettys.co.za/ (last accessed 5 June 2014).

the website of an SMME, fetishization of "primitive" and "exotic" cultures is part of the tourist experience in South Africa and Zanzibar. However, as Figure 7.6 demonstrates, defetishization is also at play as consumer-tourists (in South Africa) know that commodities such as gold or diamonds are often produced under highly exploitative labor conditions. In the case of Zanzibar, defetishization can be seen in the "slave-trade tours" that openly acknowledge the archipelago's historical significance in the promulgation of slavery. Rather than exploiting idealized fetishizations of life in Africa, such imaginaries can make tourism commodities more valuable in the minds of some consumers.

Moments of fetishization and defetishization are also evident in TripAdvisor fora on travels to Africa where discussions include basic tips about currency, transport, crime, and so on, and commentators make suggestions about ways to combine both comfort, scenery, and cultural experiences. These conversations often drift back and forth from romanticized accounts about getting away from it all, to "defetished" concerns about health and safety. As this commentator (Songbird8 from Monrovia,

(a)   (b)

Figure 7.6   The defetishization of (a) diamond mining in South Africa, and (b) the slave trade in Zanzibar. (a) Photo by P. Carmody; (b) photo by James T. Murphy.

California) stated in forum posts on her/his safari to Tanzania (http://www. tripadvisor.com/ShowTopic-g293747-i9226-k4827444-Access_2_ Tanzania-Tanzania.html#36014994, last accessed 3 December 2013):

> The next morning Ray took us to visit a local Iraku (sp?) village where we were given a tour by his friend Paulo. This was an amazing experience for we spoiled westerners. Our teenage sons got to see a way of life they have no awareness of. We talked with Paulo's adopted mother in her tiny hand-made brick house while she cooked over her small wood fire. We watched the local villagers making these bricks from clay they dig out by hand and then fire in kilns actually made of the stacked dried bricks. Lastly we were served tea made over a small fire in a tiny one room "restaurant". Now whenever I smell wood smoke I think of Africa… The tent camp was another new experience for our family. Who knew you can actually shower in so little water? Also to be able to actually see stars without the interference of ambient lighting was incredible… We actually heard lions in the distance at night after we'd gone to bed.

In a response that follows she/he then defetishizes the village experience by reminding readers that African travel is precarious with regard to a family's health and well-being; best not to get too close to the reality of village life.

> Up to the time we visited the village we'd been extra careful about food and water (the stories you hear about getting sick made us all very cautious). Our 13 year old son was especially concerned having had a Global Health class last year in school – the teacher had done much too good a job teaching them about all the potential hazards of 3rd world countries. As we sat down in the little restaurant and began talking with the proprietress I realized she was making us tea! I wasn't concerned about the tea itself as it was boiled, but I'd

seen her rinsing the cups in a bucket of water under the table before filling them. Well, there was no way to say no to the tea without being rude, so we all took a deep breath and drank the tea. I'm happy to say there were no unwanted repercussions for any of us though I did find out recently that our 13 year old just pretended to drink his. Proud of him for having the presence of mind to fake drinking the tea so as not to offend!

All told, websites such as TripAdvisor serve to create and reinforce certain imaginaries – intermediating or shaping perceptions of places and sometimes capturing value through the process. Thus the representations of place and transactional intermediation are linked through review and booking websites – a concrete (or perhaps virtual) representation of the informational economy. This feeds in to what we argue is a new mode of capital accumulation facilitated by powerful GPN actors (TNCs) able to deploy the internet as a tool for information control and management. This is not a purely "virtual economy" but one dynamically and recursively linked to "offline realities" (Graham and Zook, 2011).

Conclusion: Neo-intermediation and ICT-enabled Extraversion

This chapter has demonstrated that the promise of ICTs as tools to enable tourism SMMEs and regimes in South Africa and Tanzania to disintermediate and capture greater value from international markets remains limited or largely unfulfilled despite the successful diffusion of computers and internet. In Zanzibar, old forms of spatially proximate intermediation (e.g., *papasi*, ties to other businesspeople) remain crucial for SMMEs to position themselves effectively in the GPN, as foreign tourism and hotelier interests increase their power to control the market in part through their ability to intermediate and control the highest value-adding opportunities. In South Africa, SMMEs are arguably faring better but most remain highly dependent upon multiple third-party websites in order to sustain sufficient access to key markets. This dependence has created new costs for firms, primarily through the need to provide commissions, and new vulnerabilities as SMMEs are subjected to web-based reviews and rankings of their services that can shift their positionalities in GPNs quite significantly.

Our results have shown that, in contrast to simplistic accounts of disintermediation that are often propounded in the mainstream literature, intermediation is on the rise or being reconfigured into new forms. There are a variety of reasons for this. In some instances it is to do with labor supply push: in Zanzibar, for example, where high levels of unemployment mean that workers in informal markets intermediate themselves between consumers and tourism producers. While tourists may find this somewhat irritating at times, these intermediaries do have local knowledge and provide a service in the regime.

In this case face-to-face contact is important, given tourists' lack of familiarity with the local environs, which may create a certain dependency/insecurity. In other instances neo-intermediation is driven by the law of value, as firms replace sales representatives with advertising through web-based mechanisms, for example. In other cases "economies of time" mean that tourists prefer to book "directly" through websites rather than send emails. What all of these examples demonstrate is the importance of information in mediating market exchange, in addition to time and trust.

In the South African case, new ICT usage and infrastructure has facilitated the growth of the tourism regime. This has brought employment benefits and linkage and multiplier effects. However, the growth of tourism has also been facilitated by a cheap labor economy, a legacy of apartheid (Samara, 2011). The dominance of foreign-owned websites and the value which they capture is also a cause for concern, as this replicates previous patterns of economic extraversion by offshoring or extracting social surplus, thereby potentially reducing domestic investment (in other sectors). Consequently companies in core countries of the global economy exert increasing dominance in the GPN, even if indirectly.

All told, new ICTs have facilitated the rise of new calculative regimes in the tourism industry where capital accumulation is being concentrated through neo-intermediation and web-driven leakages to firms outside Africa (Jeacle and Carter, 2011). The "magnet" or concentrating functions that large foreign-owned websites may serve enable them to create new forms of virtual power and to profit from these. Moreover, these websites create oligoptica (Latour, 2005), where a "global gaze" is concentrated on particular hotels, for example, mediated through websites. In doing so, ICTs also help to reproduce and create fetishized and defetishized imaginaries of Africa: representations that facilitate the accumulation process but which do little to contribute to immanent changes in the region's couplings to GPNs.

Considered more broadly, this type of e-business facilitates a new mode of capital accumulation that involves more obviously place-based processes in combination with "virtual" ones. In an increasingly service-driven global economy, one where the distinction between tradable and non-tradable services is partially and unevenly breaking down as a result of this hybrid mode of capital accumulation, this has important implications for international development. An example of this blurring is the purchase of hotel rooms through international websites, a service which must still be consumed at the point of production but can be bought and traded internationally. Transnational web-based corporations increasingly capture value through this new mode of accumulation and have, through thick forms of ICT integration, greatly enhanced their positionalities in tourism GPNs. As detailed above, this has uneven consequences for tourism SMMEs, regimes, and consumers.

The fact that virtual accumulation through an offshore website is based on actual service delivery and experiences taking place in destinations (reality) has given rise to what we term *ICT-enabled extraversion*, a process that in some ways replicates previous, structural GPN-regime couplings as foreign websites and travel companies often capture many of the gains which would otherwise accumulate locally, in addition to those derived from advertising. However, touristic SMMEs often find it difficult not to list on foreign-owned websites, given their dominant market positions. Ultimately, ICTs are providing (imminent) communication, information, and market access benefits, but doing little to (immanently) restructure the GPNs for tourism that determine, in large part, the value creation, enhancement, and capture opportunities available to African firms and destination regions.

Notes

1   However, it would appear to be the internet that offers the greatest potential for shortening the relational distance between producers and consumers, described later, while also acting as a potential channel of re- or neo-intermediation.
2   Many discussions about intermediation also assume that African farmers and fisher folk act as *homo economicus*. However intermediation in agriculture and fisheries is sometimes not just a strictly economic transaction. For example, on the shores of Lake Victoria in Kenya there is an elaborate "*jaboya* system" where women traders provide sex in order to be able to access fish from fishermen. The resultant sexual network (Epstein, 2008) has resulted in very high rates of HIV prevalence in the area, of over 26%. Mobile phones are imbricated in this system (Camlin *et al.*, 2013). In agriculture and fisheries, then, the story of and evidence for disintermediation is more complex than is often thought.
3   We are grateful to Dorothea Kleine for this point.
4   We are grateful to Richard Heeks for this point.
5   As was highlighted in Chapter 6, intermediation is a significant concern in the wood products industry, particularly in Dar es Salaam where street-level actors (*madalali*) and more formal businesspeople (e.g., Chinese wholesale furniture importers) populate nodes in value chains and production networks. ICT-enabled neo-intermediation is also occurring in South Africa's wood products sector, as consumers can use intermediaries such as Nevada Furniture (http://www.nevadafurniture.co.za/) should they want to purchase and import foreign-made furnishings from companies like Ikea. Our focus here is on new forms of intermediation in the tourism industry, a service sector where "disintermediation" is expected to occur as a result of improved communications and where the industry-scale ramifications of neo-intermediation are more clearly evident.
6   For a discussion of urban tourism in South Africa, see Rogerson and Visser (2011).
7   For example, an international traveler may book a room at a hotel and inquire – prior to arrival – about a good tour operator who might provide an excursion to Table Mountain in Cape Town or a spice plantation in Zanzibar.
8   *Papasi* is the Kiswahili word for tick.
9   For information about Zanzibar's drug problem, see Mail and Guardian (2011) and Voice of America (2012).

10   In the past decade, tourism and travel services (including accommodation) were the single biggest product or service bought online (UNCTAD, 2002, cited in Wiig, 2003). For example, Expedia declared profits of almost US$200 million in the third quarter of 2012 (Levy, 2012).

11   For example, traditional tour operators in Namibia used to charge from 35–40% commission for accommodation and packages (Wiig, 2003).

12   The rack rate is the price that clients get charged when dealing directly with the hotel, and is often substantially more than going through booking websites, for example.

13   Foreign-produced guidebooks have traditionally played and continue to play a key role in helping tourists to organize their travel experiences. These include such publications as the *Rough Guide* series, *Lonely Planet*, and other, non-English guides such as the French *Routard* and German *Baedeker* series. Importantly, many of these guidebook publishers now operate websites by the same name where tourists can access information that is displayed passively on webpages or in a more direct/active fashion through posing questions on bulletin boards and traveler forums (e.g., LonelyPlanet.com's "Thorntree" forum – http://www.lonelyplanet.com/thorntree/index.jspa).

14   Given lower levels of income, infrastructural development and payment restrictions, the web is arguably somewhat less important in Tanzania as a form of intermediation. One tour operator in Zanzibar noted that "due to our needs, we have seen a great need for online marketing… but one can't totally abandon face to face business models either". That said, it is likely, given the growth in Zanzibar's tourism industry, that third-party websites like TripAdvisor will become much more significant in the coming years.

15   On the Lonely Planet website there are also people like "Stefo" (Germany) and "Orion Mike" (Australia) who participate in many of the conversations related to Zanzibar, e.g., http://www.lonelyplanet.com/thorntree/thread.jspa?thread ID=2362137 (last accessed 4 December 2013).

Chapter Eight
Conclusion

This book began by examining critically the meta-discourse that has accompanied the rapid diffusion of new information and communications technologies throughout the world, focussing specifically on the ICT4D discourse and its purported implications for economic development in Africa. We noted an overt technocentrism in much of the extant literature, which serves to obscure the concrete developmental impacts of new ICTs. Our central argument was that the mainstream ICT4D discourse generally overstates the role that mobile phones, computers, the internet can play in transformative forms of socioeconomic and industrial change in Africa. The major reason for this stems from the framing of ICTs as imminent drivers of development – instrumental, intentional, and individuated – rather than situating them, and development processes more generally, within the context of the immanent conditions of global capitalism. These are manifest principally in a world economy organized by core and emerging geopolitical powers and transnational corporations, promoting a market-led, private-sector vision of economic globalization that has largely exacerbated the unequal ties between Africa and the world system. By focussing on the imminent project of development, mainstream ICT4D practitioners and promoters often fail to consider the influence that longstanding market, political, and institutional structures and power relations will have on the nature and quality of ICT integration within the Global South. In other

Africa's Information Revolution: Technical Regimes and Production Networks in South Africa and Tanzania, First Edition. James T. Murphy and Pádraig Carmody.
© 2015 John Wiley & Sons, Ltd. Published 2015 by John Wiley & Sons, Ltd.

words, the emergence of a "global information economy" since the 1990s has/will not, in and of itself, transform the contradictions, unevenness, and exploitation inherent in contemporary political–economic processes.

Regardless of these concerns, some would still argue that ICTs leave open the possibility for progressive changes to the immanent conditions of capitalism globally and within developing regions. Our study has sought to critically interrogate and disrupt this discourse by undertaking a systematic analysis of the way in which new ICTs have been absorbed into firm-specific routines and practices, and consequently whether and how they have reconfigured sociotechnical regimes and production networks in South African and Tanzania. Rather than searching for these changes in relation to specific imminent development initiatives (e.g., a UNIDO program to promote computerized logistics), as is commonly the case in the ICT4D literature, we instead focused on the role that ICTs are playing in typical SMMEs in order to understand whether the regime and GPN conditions structuring economic activities in the region are changing in the wake of Africa's ICT revolution. If (positive) ICT-enabled immanent changes have occurred, or are occurring, these would be evident in the greater levels of innovativeness, competitiveness, and performance in enterprises, the rise of e-businesses, beneficial structural improvements to the regimes governing the evolution and development of industries, and enhanced (strategic or organic) couplings between regimes and GPNs that might enable greater value capture or social upgrading within African regions.

As Figure 8.1 summarizes, we found that the multi-scalar impacts of new ICTs on our case study firms, industrial regimes, and GPN–regime couplings have been dialectical, facilitating both change and continuity across different dimensions. Our analysis reveals that although ICTs increase the efficiency of communications and reduce some transaction costs for SMMEs, the capability gains associated with their use are generally offset by pressure on profit margins resulting from market liberalization policies, the stagnation of mass consumer markets, and industrial regimes unable to keep pace with the quality and productivity of foreign importers. Rather than facilitating the creation of regional assets that might support organic or strategic forms of coupling to GPNs, our case studies show how ICTs have limited impacts on the immanent conditions that are strengthening and/or reproducing the Africa's uneven "structural" ties to the world economy.

Within SMMEs, there have been some noteworthy (imminent) impacts accompanying ICT adoption. Informational and transactional resources were enhanced, albeit in ways that were limited with respect to the ability of firms to upgrade and capture more value from domestic or international markets. Strategic resources have been generally improved in the tourism industries of both countries, manifest most clearly in enhanced, web-based marketing and reservation-management capabilities. In wood products,

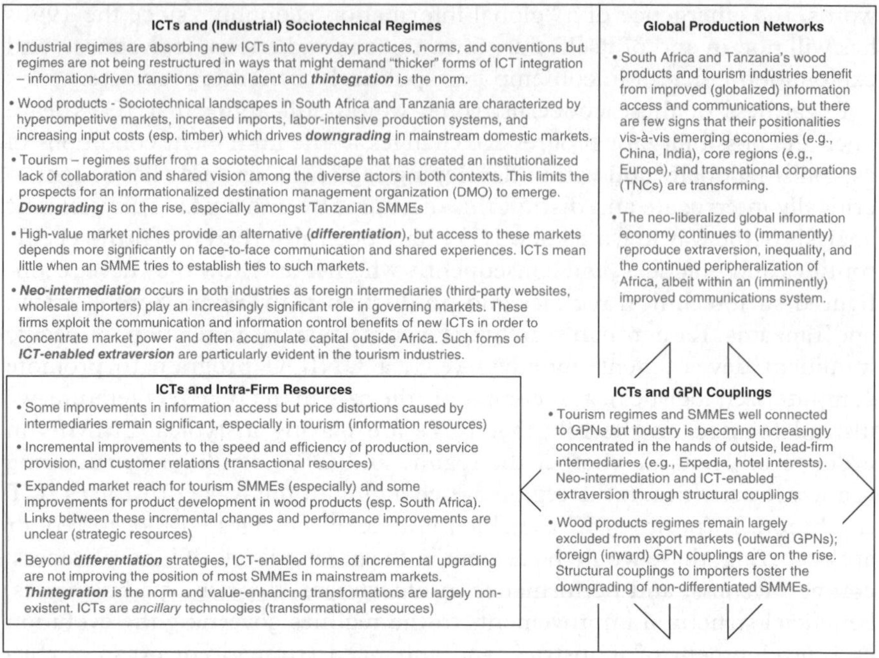

ICTs and (Industrial) Sociotechnical Regimes

- Industrial regimes are absorbing new ICTs into everyday practices, norms, and conventions but regimes are not being restructured in ways that might demand "thicker" forms of ICT integration – information-driven transitions remain latent and *thintegration* is the norm.

- Wood products - Sociotechnical landscapes in South Africa and Tanzania are characterized by hypercompetitive markets, increased imports, labor-intensive production systems, and increasing input costs (esp. timber) which drives *downgrading* in mainstream domestic markets.

- Tourism – regimes suffer from a sociotechnical landscape that has created an institutionalized lack of collaboration and shared vision among the diverse actors in both contexts. This limits the prospects for an informationalized destination management organization (DMO) to emerge. *Downgrading* is on the rise, especially amongst Tanzanian SMMEs.

- High-value market niches provide an alternative (*differentiation*), but access to these markets depends more significantly on face-to-face communication and shared experiences. ICTs mean little when an SMME tries to establish ties to such markets.

- *Neo-intermediation* occurs in both industries as foreign intermediaries (third-party websites, wholesale importers) play an increasingly significant role in governing markets. These firms exploit the communication and information control benefits of new ICTs in order to concentrate market power and often accumulate capital outside Africa. Such forms of *ICT-enabled extraversion* are particularly evident in the tourism industries.

Global Production Networks

- South Africa and Tanzania's wood products and tourism industries benefit from improved (globalized) information access and communications, but there are few signs that their positionalities vis-à-vis emerging economies (e.g., China, India), core regions (e.g., Europe), and transnational corporations (TNCs) are transforming.

- The neo-liberalized global information economy continues to (immanently) reproduce extraversion, inequality, and the continued peripheralization of Africa, albeit within an (imminently) improved communications system.

ICTs and Intra-Firm Resources

- Some improvements in information access but price distortions caused by intermediaries remain significant, especially in tourism (information resources)

- Incremental improvements to the speed and efficiency of production, service provision, and customer relations (transactional resources)

- Expanded market reach for tourism SMMEs (especially) and some improvements for product development in wood products (esp. South Africa). Links between these incremental changes and performance improvements are unclear (strategic resources)

- Beyond *differentiation* strategies, ICT-enabled forms of incremental upgrading are not improving the position of most SMMEs in mainstream markets. *Thintegration* is the norm and value-enhancing transformations are largely non-existent. ICTs are *ancillary* technologies (transformational resources)

ICTs and GPN Couplings

- Tourism regimes and SMMEs well connected to GPNs but industry is becoming increasingly concentrated in the hands of outside, lead-firm intermediaries (e.g., Expedia, hotel interests). Neo-intermediation and ICT-enabled extraversion through structural couplings

- Wood products regimes remain largely excluded from export markets (outward GPNs); foreign (inward) GPN couplings are on the rise. Structural couplings to importers foster the downgrading of non-differentiated SMMEs.

Figure 8.1   Summarizing the results in relation to the multi-scalar conceptual framework.

strategic resource enhancements were much less visible and significant with the exception of those firms using computers for product design and development, mainly observed in South Africa. These kinds of changes amount to incremental rather than radical innovations, and for the vast majority of firms ICTs have not contributed to the development of transformational resources that might reposition SMMEs more profitably and sustainably within domestic markets and GPNs. Those firms that have been able to reposition themselves have done so primarily through differentiation strategies that succeed largely on the basis of face-to-face interactions and shared experiences, which help to build trust and establish a firm's reputation. All told, our intra-firm (imminent) findings reveal that while ICTs are useful and valued technologies that have been thinly integrated into SMMEs, they remain ancillary to the core functioning and performance of enterprises: unable to transform firms and industrial regimes such that they might significantly upgrade the value of their products and services in domestic markets and GPNs.

When viewed from a typical ICT4D perspective, the problem of thintegration would be characterized as an (imminent) supply-side challenge that could best be resolved through improvements to ICT-related infrastructures, markets, regulations, knowledge, and skills. While we accept that there are supply-side factors at work here, our analysis revealed more significant, immanent features of the industrial regimes, socioeconomic conditions, institutions, and GPNs that govern the activities of SMMEs and effectively limit the demand for thicker forms of ICT integration in South Africa and Tanzania. In the wood products sector, Asian imports, chronic poverty, labor-intensive manufacturing systems, and rising input costs have created hypercompetitive consumer markets and led to an effective downgrading of locally produced merchandise, except in cases where SMMEs can differentiate their products and compete in high-value niche markets. Under these conditions, there is little demand or incentive for informationalized technological upgrading given the costs and the stiff competition from imports. Moreover, manufacturing powerhouses such as China increasingly dominate GPNs and African markets, thus limiting the possibilities for export-led endogenous industrial development strategies, even in South Africa. The net result is that the couplings between GPNs and South Africa and Tanzania's wood products regimes are based primarily on importation and reselling activities, rather than production. This circumstance bodes poorly for the long-term prospects for this industry to capture greater value and generate more employment through economic globalization.

On the surface, tourism SMMEs seem to be in a much better position to experience immanent transformations through ICT integration, given the already globalized nature of the industry and the prospects for ICTs to enable more direct communications and exchanges with distanciated customers. As we detailed, ICTs are contributing significantly to strategic and other resources within firms, but the promise of disintermediation remains unrealized for many as new kinds of foreign, internet-enabled intermediaries have emerged (e.g., TripAdvisor) to concentrate market power, control information about destinations, and achieve significant levels of capital accumulation outside Africa. This constitutes what we describe as a form of ICT-enabled extraversion, a circumstance where web pages act as virtual, seemingly placeless sites, but which enable capital to be accumulated and concentrated in real places, most typically outside of Africa.

In order to reverse this trend toward extraversion through neo-intermediation, tourism regimes in Cape Town and Zanzibar will need to develop more effective and unified destination-management organizations (DMOs) able to promote a shared vision, facilitate information-sharing among SMMEs, and ensure that greater amounts of value from tourism are held down within these destinations. The longstanding histories of institutionalized inequality (e.g., apartheid, colonialism) that mark the sociotechnical landscapes in both locations, and the recent impacts that the liberalization of FDI has had on the structure of tourism markets, particularly in Zanzibar, have created fragmented regimes unable to unite the diverse groups of actors under the banner of a shared understanding regarding the sector's vision, needs, and resources. In this context, collaboration is lacking, conflicts are continual, and there is little chance that an informationalized DMO might emerge to challenge the power of new intermediaries. Once again, the immanent conditions of capitalist reproduction in both contexts preclude the prospects for thicker ICT integration and the structural transformation of the tourism industry.

Although our study finds that there are significant immanent limitations on ICT4D strategies, this is not to say that ICTs are not important, vital, and/or powerful technologies that are changing the ways in which business and production activities are carried out. In fact, the evidence is clear that mobile phones, computers, and/or the internet are often "must-have" technologies in the wood products and tourism industries in both countries. Uptake has thus been rapid and fairly uniform within the case-study contexts, and many business owners cannot imagine being able to do what they do without new ICTs. That said, and as detailed throughout the book, the structure of the domestic and international markets accessible to most SMMEs in South Africa and Tanzania, coupled with the continued onslaught of neoliberal trade and investment policies, effectively limits the potential of ICTs as leveling or upgrading technologies. All told, our analysis reveals that while there are some success stories among the SMMEs sampled, the results also show the ways in which ICT diffusion is implicated in the downgrading of African firms and the creation of new patterns of uneven development in the region. For example, in both the tourism and wood products sectors, social upgrading remains elusive in most situations and ICTs have helped foreign capital to reach deeper into African markets through FDI and imports. As such, the economic impacts of ICTs may be transformative through their continued facilitation of the continent's economic extraversion.[1]

While it is clear that some of these findings are specific to our chosen industries and case-study locations, we believe that the trends are generalizable beyond these specific contexts. With respect to the wood products case, its relevance stems from the longstanding structure of Africa's commodity exports and imports to and from the global economy. On the export side, sub-Saharan Africa's recent growth "renaissance" is being driven overwhelmingly by the expansion of the region's petroleum and mineral trade. Between 2000–2012, sub-Saharan Africa's total export trade increased from US$94 billion to $455 billion (United Nations, 2013). Approximately 75% of exports in 2012 were crude (unprocessed) raw materials, metals, minerals, and petroleum products, while manufactured, non-agricultural commodities paled in comparison. In stark contrast, and as we have demonstrated, imports of manufactured goods, particularly from Asia, have increased manifold as emerging economies such as China and India have flooded the sub-continent with low-cost consumer goods. Although the region's overall trade balance remains positive, only 10 out of 44 countries had a positive balance at some point between 2010 and 2012 – all of these being significant exporters of minerals and/petroleum products (Angola, Chad, Cote d'Ivoire, DRC, Equatorial Guinea, Gabon, Nigeria, Sudan) (United Nations, 2013). The experiences of SMMEs in the wood products sectors of South Africa and Tanzania reflect the general trend toward growth in natural-resource, extractive industries, and consumer demands for wage goods that are being concomitantly and increasingly met through imports (especially from China). Such trends are evident even in South Africa, once a significant exporter of many manufacturing goods, yet now very much in decline in the wake of the onslaught of Asian imports. All told, we are confident that the experiences of our manufacturers and their industrial regimes reflect those of many African and other developing region contexts.

With regard to tourism also, our evidence confirms many trends evident in the sector's GPNs, with our case studies highlighting, in particular, the impact of neo-intermediation and ICT-enabled extraversion. Cape Town and Zanzibar are two of the more established destinations for tourists in the sub-Saharan region, with South Africa and Tanzania being leading and growing destinations. As such, the impacts of ICTs on SMMEs and regimes in these contexts serve as highly relevant and transferable experiences with respect to both the challenge of achieving thicker forms of ICT integration and the growing inequalities between globalized, leading actors in tourism GPNs (e.g., Expedia) and local SMMEs based in "Southern" destinations. As Christian (2012) observed in Kenya and Uganda, we too documented how the dynamic of concentration (through neo-intermediation and extraversion) and fragmentation (through differentiation) in the sector is being fuelled in part by differences in the ICT capabilities of SMMEs compared with intermediaries like TripAdvisor. The power of such third-party websites undoubtedly can be observed not only in other African destinations but throughout the global travel and tourism industry.

Major Trends: Deepening Dependence in an Informationalized Global Economy

The study identified a number of ICT-facilitated trends in the industries under study, particularly thintegration, downgrading, differentiation, neo-intermediation, and ICT-enabled extraversion. While there have been many benefits to the introduction of new ICTs, their cumulative impact has been to deepen the continent's dependence and extraversion. This is not to do with any "independent" causative power that new ICTs might have, but rather the way in which they have been absorbed into existing (immanent) structures through their deployment by different social actors imbued with different power capabilities. Although this book did not deal with some of these issues, there are several specific channels through which new ICTs have reinforced dependence and extraversion, including:

- Increased technological dependence as Africa becomes dependent on imported ICTs and lacks the manufacturing capabilities needed to produce their own.
- Facilitation of imports and FDI into African economies which result in leakages of capital outside the region.
- ICT-enabled extraversion through web-based forms of information control and centralization which facilitate capital accumulation by transnational corporations and others based outside Africa.
- The dumping of e-waste and second-hand ICTs into African markets from core and emerging economies (not detailed here).
- The increased demand and valuation of minerals (e.g., coltan) needed in the production of ICT artefacts: a trend that further reifies comparative advantages in extractive industries historically linked to the dynamics of extraversion (not detailed here).

This is not to deny the manifold benefits which new ICTs may bring, but to place their adoption in the contexts where, for example, they have further heightened price and quality competition in product and service markets, often to the advantage of those with the most highly developed capabilities, social networks and access to capital. However, it may also be true that in some sectors new ICTs have helped to expand the "size of the pie" rather than just resulting in zero-sum competition. In tourism, in particular, the emergence of the web may have substantially contributed to disturbing, disrupting and hopefully doing away with long-term misperceptions about Africa as a supposedly "Dark Continent". The relatively rapid growth of numbers of tourist arrivals to Africa would suggest that this might be the case.

Some of the trends that we have identified are not exclusive to Africa or the Global South. For example, French and Leyshon (2004) identified the tendency towards reintermediation in the financial services industry in the developed world previously through websites. In doing so they demonstrated how this has led to a deepening of uneven development within financial services, and an intensification of the location of core activities within a few international financial (or calculation) centres (French and Leyshon, 2004: 285). What makes the experience of Africa distinctive, however, is the particular spatiality of this re- or neo-intermediation, as it is often foreign-owned firms who are now able to extract proportions of place and other forms of rent in ways that they were not able to previously. This combination of deepening extraversion and rising tourist numbers might be classified as a form of informationalized "dependent development" (Evans, 1979). Thus rather than new ICTs "ending geography" (O'Brien, 1992), they are instead reconfiguring it, and in certain ways reinforcing extant trends of "adverse differential incorporation" (Bush, 2007). This adverse incorporation is now partially achieved through a web of internet-based interactions and transactions, where the core of these systems remains located in developed countries.

Is Africa "Rising" Through Informationalization?

Writing in the early 1980s, the agricultural economist Alain de Janvry (1981) developed his ideas about the political economy of development using the concepts of articulation and disarticulation. His central idea was that economic underdevelopment resulted from social and sectoral disarticulation, which were linked. Whereas in developed countries there was a developed capital goods sector which provides inputs to, and demand for, the consumer goods sector (sectoral articulation) and the working class had mass purchasing power to buy the products of industry (social articulation), this was not the case in the underdeveloped world. There he identified two types of disarticulated economies – export-oriented and import-substituting. In export-oriented disarticulated economies, primary products are exported for external consumption, with wages being kept low to facilitate this dynamic (see also Wuyts, 2001). As a result, the domestic economy lacks propulsive dynamism. In import-substituting disarticulated economies, highly skewed income distributions mean that manufacturing is oriented towards serving the needs of the elite and fails to propel wider structural transformation.

Since de Janvry's seminal book was written, globalization has changed this configuration somewhat, even as the core–periphery structure of the global economy has remained substantially intact (Grasland and Van Hamme, 2010). Partly facilitated by new ICTs and liberal global capital and trade regimes, new GPNs have emerged (Coe et al., 2004). This in turn has created new patterns of "network trade", where final products contain components manufactured in many different countries (Broadman, 2007). For some, these new forms of spatial articulation have resulted in the world becoming "flat", as new ICTs allow information processing and other activities to take place, potentially, virtually anywhere in the world (Friedman, 2005). Regional development tends to exhibit a long-lived path dependence (Neffke et al., 2011), however, and others have noted an accentuation of uneven global development (Jomo and Baudot, 2007). Sub-Saharan Africa (SSA), in particular, continues to receive relatively little inward foreign direct investment in manufacturing and services, and around three-quarters of what the sub-continent exports is unprocessed primary commodities (Bond, 2006). Thus, for the most part, SSA can be characterized as a region constituted by export-oriented disarticulated economies. Are ICTs fundamentally changing this through the facilitation of new kinds of GPN-regime couplings that might support industrial and social upgrading?

The answer to this question would appear to be no at this stage, as there is little evidence of structural diversification in Africa's exports in our case study contexts. In fact the reverse seems to be happening, as evidenced both by our findings regarding thintegration, downgrading, and ICT-enabled extraversion, and the statistics on the structure of African economies. For the 39 African countries for which data is available, the proportion of exports accounted for by agricultural products, fuel and minerals from the continent actually rose from 69.4% in 2000 to 71.3% in 2009, and there was a roughly corresponding drop in the proportion of total exports accounted for by manufactures (calculated from World Trade Organization, 2011). From 1990 to 2008, manufacturing as a proportion of GDP in Africa fell from 15% to 10% (UNCTAD, 2012). Some have argued that, as a result of increased resource dependence in exports, there has actually been a technological downgrading of African economies (Economist Intelligence Unit, 2002), despite the much vaunted "mobile phone revolution".[2] This neocolonial trade structure reproduces, rather than substantially reducing, poverty (Carmody, 2011). Thus, as our analysis details, the potentiality of international information flows facilitated by new ICTs has not resulted in substantial structural change to African economies as they remain disarticulated and export-oriented.

As noted in Chapter 1, one of the main tropes in relation to the continent is that Africa is now rising and emerging onto the world economic stage. One element or axis of this discourse relates to the impacts of new ICTs on the continent's development. The assumption is that the continent is "catching up" with the levels of development of other world regions – that is, that the predictions of modernization theory are being realized. However, the results of our study question that. There are multiple paths to modernity (Chabal and Daloz, 1999) and the particular path being followed across Africa will not, it appears, lead it to the types and levels of development of Europe or North America. This raises key questions about who benefits from the celebratory "rising" discourse, and how mainstream ICT4D initiatives are implicated in the reproduction of these immanent conditions.

Rethinking ICT4D Initiatives and Ideology

According to proponents of the new economic geography (NEG), such as the World Bank, Africa is underdeveloped because it is distant from markets in Europe, North America, and East Asia (World Bank, 2009). In this imaginary, new ICTs may serve as a primary means through which to transcend geography and allow full and fruitful participation in the global economy. However, this framing neglects the different forms of social and economic interconnection that new information technologies facilitate and allow. These external and internal forms of connection can be understood, heuristically, as spatial articulations (to the outside world) and social articulations (primarily within localities in Africa). New ICTs theoretically make both spatial and social articulation easier to achieve; however, the impact of these articulations are not necessarily positive.

Within our case study SMMEs, industrial regimes and regions, new ICTs are used for both kinds of articulation but with mixed results. Spatial articulations appear to be, on the surface at least, enhanced through the relative ease of communications to outside firms, customers, and/or intermediaries. In reality, however, the spatial articulations concomitant with these communications are either non-existent for the most part (in the case of wood products SMMEs) or complicit in new forms of market concentration, extraversion, and offshore accumulation (tourism SMMEs). Export-ready manufacturing industries do not seem to be emerging in response to improved communications, whilst service sectors like tourism are being undermined through new configurations of actors in GPNs.

Where ICTs are having a more significant impact in Africa stems from their support for social articulations within industries and communities. This is not always positive, since ICTs can be used, as in the case of South Africa's wood products industry, to reproduce repressive working conditions through the surveillance of labor, arguably a form of social "downgrading" as it enforces a stricter work regime. In other cases, however, ICTs support communications in localized networks of businesspeople whilst improving the pace and responsiveness of production and service provisioning activities. Such communications can also improve the scale and scope of information dissemination within industrial communities and consumer markets, thus creating the kind of "buzz" needed to support learning and innovation. As Bathelt *et al.* (2004: 38) stated:

> ...[local] buzz consists of specific information and continuous updates of this information, intended and unanticipated learning processes in organised and accidental meetings, the application of the same interpretative schemes and mutual understanding of new knowledge and technologies, as well as shared cultural traditions and habits within a particular technology field, which stimulate the establishment of conventions and other institutional arrangements.

An enhanced ability to create local buzz is an important ICT-driven development, but one which has failed to result in industrial transformation due to the inability of industrial regimes to create the kinds of regional assets needed to enhance, strategically or organically, the spatial articulations between African firms and GPNs. Those articulations or couplings are largely structural in nature, based on old patterns of extraversion, and unable to channel the knowledge and capital needed to reposition African industries vis-à-vis the global economy. Such couplings will not emerge or be enhanced merely by (imminent) supply-side improvements to ICT markets, infrastructures, and skills within Africa, as they require immanent changes to the structural features of the current phase of economic globalization. Consequently, even though ICTs are meant to be the quintessential technologies of globalization, they (particularly mobile phones) are used primarily in Africa for localized and often social purposes.

While the social implications of ICTs are arguably disruptive and transformational (Avergerou, 2010), their mere diffusion is not resulting in the creation of a knowledge economy in Africa. Instead, our findings indicate that sub-Saharan Africa is becoming an informationalized agrarian and resource-extractive economic region produced through economic extraversion as ICTs are absorbed into unchanged (immanent) structures governing the region's couplings to GPNs (Abrahamsen and Williams, 2011). These inequitable structural couplings provide, at best, limited prospects for social upgrading, and (re)produce poverty as already marginalized individuals, communities, and regions are inserted into them.

Again, this is not necessarily exclusive to the continent. Other studies have revealed the fallacies of trying to construct a Silicon Valley in other world regions, and the heavy involvement of the US state, through procurement, in establishing that technopole (Sokol, 2013). In the case of sub-Saharan Africa, the region's problematic articulation into the global information economy is driven by corporate interests largely outside of the continent. As Power (2011) notes:

> ...whilst some foreign partners (China included) have actively sought to encourage this focus on high-technology solutions, modernism and the hardware of development due to vested interests – Chinese companies stand to make a lot of money from helping the government to deliver on such a "vision".

A major consequence of the fact that the "information revolution" in Africa is largely externally driven is that imminent forms of development have been promoted over immanent strategies that might result in structural transformation.

Ironically, perhaps, while much of the ICT4D literature is neoliberal in inspiration, it is arguably only when neoliberalism is transcended that real development in Africa will be possible in earnest (Soludo *et al.*, 2004). Further problematizing the ICT4D discourse is its reproduction of the modernization paradigm, which sees development occurring as a result of processes of contagious diffusion from richer to poorer parts of the world. This techno-liberal boosterism, where there is conflation of information technology with free markets and liberal democracy, does little to address the fundamental structural problems of African economies. While World Bank researchers argue that Africa is now being propelled into cutting edge transnational production networks (Broadman, 2007), there is scant evidence of this happening on a substantial scale from the macro trade statistics or our micro-level analysis (Carmody, 2010). Africa remains technologically dependent across a range of sectors, including ICTs, and whilst new ICTs have imminent benefits, they ultimately do little to raise national measures of productivity or facilitate economic diversification.

In short, the ICT4D literature suffers from an intellectual disarticulation between the spread of ICTs and their supposed impacts. Africa is incorporated into the global technological revolution primarily in a dependent manner, as an importer rather than producer of technology. The main benefit of ICTs in Africa is thus the greater access to information and communication they allow. However, to expect ICTs to enable significant development in places is to overload their real-world impacts. Other (immanent) structures of economic production and flows of trade and investment are much more important in achieving that, and these are fundamentally determined by power relations. Mainstream ICT4D proponents, practitioners, and policy-makers would do well to decenter the technologies themselves and to focus instead on these structural features: asking critical questions about what ICTs might really contribute with regard to their reconfiguration. We would argue that in many cases the answer is little or nothing, and that a much greater emphasis on the immanent drivers of the "D" in ICT4D would better serve the interests of SMMEs as well as those of the poor, vulnerable, and marginalized in regions like Africa.

And what about the impacts of ICTs on capabilities and resources that might improve livelihood strategies and reduce poverty? Although our focus was on firms and industries, several inferences can be made with regard to this question. The first is that ICTs are necessary for most SMMEs to maintain a presence in domestic markets and to function in a basic manner if they hope to be competitive. More generally, they have become integrated into the everyday lives and livelihood activities of most Africans, particularly in urban areas, and thus serve an important role in maintaining and managing personal business, family, and friendship networks. This is significant but not transformational in the sense of reducing vulnerabilities and chronic poverty in South Africa and Tanzania. Moreover, ICTs place an added burden on the fiscal resources that individual and households draw from, thus raising concerns about what needs may go unmet in order to pay for mobile phone and internet services.

The second implication is that micro-scale and small enterprises seem to be those least able to upgrade their activities or reduce the vulnerability of their livelihood strategies through improved communications and information access. These circumstances are most apparent in Dar es Salaam and Zanzibar where hypercompetition, rising input costs, and neo-intermediation are reducing the demand and value of the products and services produced by the smallest enterprises. Having a mobile phone, an email address and website may be necessary for many SMMEs to enter wood product and tourism markets, but there are no clear links between this uptake and improvements to livelihood security. In other words, social upgrading remains elusive despite the widespread diffusion of ICTs across the gamut of socioeconomic classes.

The third implication is that ICTs enable business owners to place workers under closer scrutiny and surveillance on a day-to-day basis. In contexts where regulatory protections for labor may go largely unenforced or lack significant teeth, the notion that productivity might be monitored more closely raises important questions about fairness and justice for those workers who may face extraordinary constraints on their livelihoods. For example, workers who have significant family care needs (e.g., single mothers), health issues (e.g., HIV-AIDS), and/or other circumstances which occasionally limit their abilities to perform certain tasks or be on the job may face added pressures, as mobile phones and other ICT-enabled surveillance systems monitor their real-time performance (e.g., see Ellway, 2013). Without effective institutional protections, such individuals, as well as workers more generally, may lose their jobs and productivity expectations may increase substantially, particularly in contexts where markets are hyper-competitive and highly cost-sensitive.

A fourth and final implication is that ICTs alone will do relatively little, without other imminent and immanent changes, to empower those living in poverty or having vulnerable livelihoods. As Sen (2001) noted, successful development in a market society requires a combination of tactics and strategies aimed at building individual and community-scale capabilities, reforming property and land rights, providing entitlements that meet basic needs, and creating mechanisms that enable those most marginalized in society to take advantage of economic opportunities (e.g., through credit provisioning schemes). ICT access alone will not lead to development unless their diffusion is concomitant with the provision of other kinds of support and entitlements, many of which have little or no direct connection to ICTs (Alampay, 2006). Importantly, however, entitlements are not cost-free as they require a productively immanent economic structure to generate the resources to pay for them. Moreover, industrial upgrading and economic diversification require more than access to entitlements, as they depend on an active government strategy to build competitive advantage and deepen markets in the manufacturing and services sectors in particular (Rodrik, 2008). Communication efficiencies and the reduction of information asymmetries alone cannot substitute for that.

Evolving Economic Geographies of the Global South: Sociotechnical Regimes and GPNs

Beyond its significance for policy-makers and practitioners in the ICT4D community, the book also has a few implications for future scholarship, particularly in economic and development geography. From a conceptual perspective, our approach drew on literatures from organization and management studies (resource-based views of firms), sociotechnical transition theory, and global production networks, in order to capture the multi-scalar characteristics, drivers, and implications of industrial change in contemporary Africa. By doing so we were able to develop an in-depth, integrative, and multidimensional perspective that revealed the complex and sometimes paradoxical roles that ICTs are (or are not) playing in the evolution of our case study industries and economies. Our conceptual approach also enabled us to achieve a rigorous comparative analysis of two industries and two countries. The take-away point of all this is that integrative, multi-scalar analyses can be achieved without falling back into the realm of "thick description" and amethodological approaches. This is important given the tendencies of many economic geography studies which highlight exceptions and difference rather than developing transferable, yet mutable, approaches to the study of the contemporary variegations of neoliberal capitalism. In doing so, such studies can provide the basis for a more rigorous, substantive, and sustained (heterodox) challenge to the orthodoxies of neoclassical economics and the "new" economic geography. As Peck (2012: 126) notes:

> The promise of probing, comparative research designs here is that they entail a decisive explanatory step beyond the identification of alternative, divergent, idiosyncratic economies, moving on to position these relationally, relative to their others. This way, they become more than free-floating cases, implicitly imagined as exceptions, or spots on an otherwise barely charted landscape. Instead, they would hold the potential of generating new explanatory transects across that landscape, evoking conceptually specified and empirically documented registers of meaningful economic geographical difference.

In more specific terms, we found that viewing SMMEs as repositories of capabilities/resources and industries as sociotechnical regimes coupled to GPNs was productive and enlightening. Particularly useful was the emphasis on the regime scale, and economic and development geographers could benefit from a critical engagement with sociotechnical transitions theory, given its ability to conceptually account for the role of institutional features, path dependencies, relationalities, practices, diverse actors, and multi-scalar dynamics as drivers of development. When linked to both a GPN framework at the global scale, and a grounded micro-scale emphasis on the resources and capabilities in/of firms, the sociotechnical regime approach provides a means for situating these multi-scalar dynamics within a common framework that allows for a systemic explication of the drivers, directions, and implications of industrial change. Moreover, this approach enabled us to account for both agentic processes and the structural features of regimes and sociotechnical landscapes that immanently reproduce particular forms of capitalist development in Africa. The wider point of all this is that geographers can benefit from the use of meso-level concepts such as a sociotechnical regime in order to achieve the kind of "explanatory [comparative] transects" that Peck (2012) envisioned.

Finally, but no less significantly, the study was an explicitly "hybrid" one in the sense that we melded ideas from economic and development geography into a single analysis that focused on the everyday activities of Africans rather than those of actors outside the region. In doing so, our broader objective was to further an emerging research agenda on economic geographies of the Global South (see Murphy, 2008; Vira and James, 2011) and to suggest that development geography and development studies would benefit from more research that focuses in-depth on the economic and industrial processes that are complicit in underdevelopment, the reproduction of poverty, environmental degradation, and other development challenges. In shifting the analytical center towards the economic-industrial side of development problems, rather than implicitly assuming that a somewhat monolithic set of economic institutions functions similarly everywhere, it may be possible to identify and specify more clearly the critical, context-specific blockages that limit livelihood possibilities in cities, communities, and regions throughout the Global South.

This is crucial given the immanent nature of underdevelopment and the fact that it is largely driven and reproduced by complex, multi-scalar, and often contested assemblages (what we characterize here as capabilities, regimes, landscapes, and GPN couplings) of heterogeneous power relations, actors, materials, technologies, and institutions (McFarlane, 2009). We know far too little about how these assemblages are constituted in developing regions, what happens when attempts are made to integrate them with "globalized" assemblages such as those associated with neoliberalism, how and why particular assemblages mutate and reorganize in new and sometimes unexpected ways, and whether a critical unpacking of their constitution might reveal points of potential resistance and reconfiguration that can improve material conditions and livelihood possibilities. There is much work to be done, and we hope our intervention contributes to a critical, pluralized conversation both within and beyond the ICT4D and geography communities.

Notes

1   We are grateful to Jonathon Rigg for this point.
2   Increasing resource intensity in the export structure has been driven by both demand for Africa's natural resources, and competitive displacement pressures on manufacturing arising from competition with Chinese products in particular (Kaplinsky, 2008).

References

Aas, C., Ladkin, A. and Fletcher, J. (2005) Stakeholder collaboration and heritage management, *Annals of Tourism Research* 32(1): 28–48.

Abraham, R. (2007) Mobile phones and economic development: evidence from the fishing industry in India, *Information Technologies and International Development* 4(1): 5–17.

Abrahamsen, R. and Williams, M.C. (2011) *Security Beyond the State: Private Security in International Politics.* Cambridge: Cambridge University Press.

Acedo, F.J., Barroso, C. and Galan, J.L. (2006) The resource based theory: dissemination and main trends, *Strategic Management Journal* 27(7): 621–36.

African Brains (2011) Kenya: IT incubation centre iHub grows ten-fold in first year. Available at http://africanbrains.net/2011/04/12/kenya-it-incubation-centre-ihub-grows-ten-fold-in-first-year/ [accessed 31 December 2013].

Africa Partnership Forum (2008) *ICT in Africa: Boosting Economic Growth and Poverty Reduction.* Report prepared in the 10th Meeting of the Africa Partnership Forum in Tokyo on 7–8 April 2008 by Gerster Consulting under a mandate from the Africa Partnership Forum Support Unit. Available at http://www.africapartnershipforum. org/meetingdocuments/40314752.pdf [accessed 31 December 2012].

Agnew, J. (2012) *Territorial Politics after the Financial Crisis,* Plenary presentation at the Regional Studies Association Winter Conference 2012. Available at http://www. regionalstudies.org/uploads/conferences/presentations/winter-conference-2012/ plenaries/john-agnew.pdf [accessed 31 December 2013].

Aker, J.C. (2010) Information from markets near and far: mobile phones and agricultural markets in Niger, *American Economic Journal: Applied Economics* 2(3): 46–59.

Aker, J.C. and Mbiti, I. (2010) Mobile phones and economic development in Africa, *Journal of Economic Perspectives* 24(3): 207–32.

Aker, J.C., Collier, P. and Vincente, P. (2011) *Is Information Power? Using Cell Phones during an Election in Mozambique.* Mimeo.

Africa's Information Revolution: Technical Regimes and Production Networks in South Africa and Tanzania, First Edition. James T. Murphy and Pádraig Carmody.

Alampay, E. (2006) Beyond access to ICTs: measuring capabilities in the information society, *International Journal of Education and Development using Information and Communication Technology* 2(3): 4–22.

Alden, C. (2003) Let them eat cyberspace: Africa, the G8 and the digital divide, *Millenium: Journal of International Studies* 32(3): 457–76.

Alderson, W. (1958) Factors governing the development of marketing channels, in *Marketing Channels for Manufactured Products* (ed. R.M. Clewett). Homewood, IL: Richard Irwin: 5–34.

Allen, S. and Chandrashekar, A. (2000) Outsourcing services: the contract is just the beginning, *Business Horizons* 43(2): 25–34.

Amanor, K.S. (2009) Global food chains, African smallholders and World Bank governance, *Journal of Agrarian Change* 9(2): 247–62.

Amin, A. and Cohendet, P. (2004) *Architectures of Knowledge: Firms, Capabilities, and Communities*. Oxford: Oxford University Press.

Amit, R. and Zott, C. (2001) Value creation in e-business, *Strategic Management Journal* 22(6–7): 493–520.

Anderson, W. (2013) Leakages in the tourism systems: case of Zanzibar, *Tourism Review* 68(1): 62–76.

Anwar, M.A., Carmody, P., Surborg, B. and Corcoran, A. (2013) The diffusion and impacts of information and communication technology on tourism in the Western Cape, South Africa, *Urban Forum*, October. Netherlands: Springer, DOI: 10.1007/s12132-013-9210-4.

Apostolou, D., Sakkas, N. and Mentzas, G. (1999) Knowledge networking in supply chains: a case study in the wood furniture sector, *Information, Knowledge and Systems Management* 1: 267–81.

Appadurai, A. (1996) *Modernity at Large: Cultural Dimensions of Globalisation*. Minneapolis: University of Minnesota Press.

Asche, H. (2011) *Domestic policy implications of Chinese economic engagement in Africa*. Background Paper for the *African Economic Outlook 2011*. Paris: OECD Development Centre.

Asche, H. and Fleischer, M. (2011) Modernizing Rwanda: Information and communication technologies as driver for economic growth? Electronic University of Leipzig Chapters on Africa (e-ULPA) No. 2. Available at http://www.uni-leipzig.de/~afrika/index.php?option=com_content&task=view&id=287&Itemid=87 [accessed 11 July 2013].

Avergerou, C. (2010) Discourses on ICT and development, *Information Technologies and International Development* 6(3): 1–18.

Ayelazuno, J. (2014) Oil wealth and the well-being of the subaltern classes in Sub-Saharan Africa: a critical analysis of the resource curse in Ghana, *Resources Policy* 40: 66–73.

Ayonka, J. (2010) *The Politics of Ideology in Information and Communication Technologies for Development: An African Case Study*. Unpublished Masters thesis, Lund University, Sweden.

Baggio, R. and Del Chiappa, G. (2013) Tourism destinations as digital business eco-systems, in *Information and Communication Technologies in Tourism 2013* (eds L. Cantoni and Z. Xiang). Proceedings of the International Conference in Innsbruck, Austria, January 22–25, 2013, Berlin: Springer: 183–94.

Bailard, C.S. (2009) Mobile phone diffusion and corruption in Africa, *Political Communication* 26(3): 333–53.

Bain, P. and Taylor, P. (2000) Entrapped by the 'electronic panopticon'? Worker resistance in the call centre, *New Technology Work and Employment* 15(1): 2–18.

Bair, J. and Werner, M. (2011) The place of disarticulations: global commodity production in La Laguna, Mexico, *Environment and Planning A* 43(5): 998–1015.

Balile, D. (2012) Electricity prices hamper Tanzania economy, *Sabahi Online*, available at http://sabahionline.com/en_GB/articles/hoa/articles/features/2012/03/06/feature-01 [accessed 31 December 2013].

Barclay, E. (2007) China spurring illegal timber trade in Tanzania, *National Geographic News*, available at http://news.nationalgeographic.com/news/2007/12/071221-tanzania-logging.html [accessed 16 December 2013].

Barnes, T. and Sheppard, E. (2010) 'Nothing includes everything': Towards engaged pluralism in Anglophone economic geography, *Progress in Human Geography* 34: 193–214.

Barnett, M.N. (2011) *Empire of Humanity: A History of Humanitarianism*. Ithaca, NY: Cornell University Press.

Barney, J. (1991) Firm resources and sustained competitive advantage, *Journal of Management* 17(1): 99–120.

Barney, J., Wright, M. and Ketchen, J. (2001) The resource-based view of the firm: Ten years after 1991, *Journal of Management* 27(6): 625–41.

Barrientos, S., Gereffi, G. and Rossi, A. (2011) Economic and social upgrading in global production networks: a new paradigm for a changing world, *International Labour Review* 150(3–4): 319–40.

Bartel, A., Ichniowski, C. and Shaw, K. (2007) How does information technology affect productivity? Plant-level comparisons of product innovation, process improvement, and worker skills, *Quarterly Journal of Economics* 122(4): 1721–58.

Barua, A., Konana, P., Whinston, A.B. and Yin, F. (2004) An empirical investigation of net-enabled business value, *MIS Quarterly* 28(4): 585–620.

Bassett, T.J. (2010) Slim pickings: Fairtrade cotton in West Africa, *Geoforum* 41(1): 44–55.

Bates, R.H. (1981) *Markets and States in Tropical Africa: The Political Basis of Agricultural Policies*. Berkeley: University of California Press.

Bathelt, H. and Turi P. (2011) Local, global and virtual buzz: the importance of face-to-face contact in economic interaction and the possibilities to go beyond, *Geoforum* 42: 520–29.

Bathelt, H., Malmberg, A. and Maskell, P. (2004) Clusters and knowledge: local buzz, global pipelines and the process of knowledge creation, *Progress in Human Geography* 28(1): 31–56.

Bayart, J.-F. (2000) Africa in the world: a history of extraversion, *African Affairs* 99: 217–67.

Benkler, Y. (2006) *The Wealth of Networks: How Social Production Transforms Markets and Freedom*. New Haven, CT: Yale University Press.

Benner, C. (2006) South Africa on-call: Information Technology and labour restructuring in South African call centres, *Regional Studies* 40(2): 1025–40.

Beritelli, P. (2011) Cooperation among prominent actors in a tourist destination, *Annals of Tourism Research* 38(2): 607–29.

Beritelli, P. and Laesser, C. (2011) Power dimensions and influence reputation in tourist destinations: empirical evidence from a network of actors and stakeholders. *Tourism Management* 32(6): 1299–1309.

Berkhout, F., Smith, A. and Stirling, A. (2004) Socio-technological regimes and transition contexts, in *System Innovation and the Transition to Sustainability: Theory, Evidence and Policy* (eds B. Elzen, F. Geels and K. Green). Cheltenham: Edward Elgar: 48–75.

Berman, N. and Martin, P. (2012) The vulnerability of sub-Saharan Africa to financial crises: the case of trade, *IMF Economic Review* 60(3): 329–64.

Best, M.H. (1990) *The New Competition: Institutions of Industrial Restructuring.* Cambridge, MA: Harvard University Press.

Bhagwati, J. (2004) *In Defense of Globalisation.* New York: Oxford University Press.

Bharadwaj, A.S. (2000) A resource-based perspective on information technology capability and firm performance: an empirical investigation, *MIS Quarterly* 24(1): 169–96.

Bharadwaj, A., El Sawy, O.A., Pavlou, P.A. and Venkatraman, N. (2013) Digital business strategy: toward a next generation of insights, *MIS Quarterly* 37(2): 471–82.

Bhavnani, A., Chiu, R.W., Janakiram, S. and Silarszky, P. (2008) *Role of mobile phones in sustainable rural poverty reduction.* Report from the ICT Policy Division, Global Information and Communications Department (GICT), Washington: World Bank. Available at http://siteresources.worldbank.org/EXTINFORMATIONANDCOM MUNICATIONANDTECHNOLOGIES/Resources/The_Role_of_Mobile_ Phones_in_Sustainable_Rural_Poverty_Reduction_June_2008.pdf [accessed 24 May 2013].

Bijker, W.E., Hughes, T.P. and Pinch, T.J. (eds) (1987) *The Social Construction of Technological Systems: New Directions in the Sociology and History of Technology.* Cambridge, MA: MIT Press.

Bimber, B. (1990) Karl Marx and the three faces of technological determinism, *Social Studies of Science* 20(2): 333–51.

Binns, T. and Nel, E. (2002) Tourism as a local development strategy, *Geographical Journal* 168: 235–47.

Birdsall, W.F. (1996) *The Internet and the ideology of information technology,* INET96 Proceedings 96, available at http://www.isoc.org/inet96/proceedings/e3/e3_2.htm [accessed 31 December 2013].

Bond, P. (2006) *Looting Africa: The Economics of Exploitation.* London: Zed.

Booyens, I. and Visser, G. (2010) Tourism SMME development on the urban fringe: the case of Parys, South Africa, *Urban Forum* 21(4): 367–85.

Boschma, R.A. and Lambooy, J.G. (1999) Evolutionary economics and economic geography, *Journal of Evolutionary Economics* 9(4): 411–29.

Bratton, M. (2013) Citizens and cell phones in Africa, *African Affairs* 112(447): 304–19.

Breukel, A. and Go, F.M. (2009) Knowledge-based network participation in destination and event marketing: a hospitality scenario analysis perspective, *Tourism Management*, 30(2): 184–93.

Bridge, G. (2002) Grounding globalisation: the prospects and perils of linking economic processes of globalisation to environmental outcomes, *Economic Geography* 78(3): 361–86.

Broadman, H.G. (2007) *Africa's Silk Road: China and India's new economic frontier.* Washington, DC: World Bank.

Brynjolfsson, E. (1993) The productivity paradox of information technology, *Communications of the ACM* 36(12): 66–77.

Brynjolfsson, E. and Hitt, L.M. (2000) Beyond computation: information technology, organizational transformation and business performance, *Journal of Economic Perspectives* 14(4): 23–48.

Buhalis, D. and Law, R. (2008) Progress in information technology and tourism management: twenty years on and ten years after the internet – the state of eTourism research, *Progress in Tourism Management* 29: 609–23.

Burawoy, M. (2000) *Global Ethnography: Forces, Connections, and Imaginations in a Postmodern World.* Berkeley: University of California Press.

Burke, R. (2012) Google pays just 0.14% tax in seven years, *Irish Independent*, 9 December.

Burrell, J. (2010) Evaluating shared access: social equality and the circulation of mobile phones in rural Uganda, *Journal of Computer-Mediated Communication* 15(2): 230–50.

Büscher, B. (2010) Derivative nature: interrogating the value of conservation in 'boundless Southern Africa', *Third World Quarterly* 31(2): 259–76.

Büscher, B. (2012) The political economy of Africa's natural resources and the 'Great Financial Crisis', *Tijdschrift Voor Economische En Sociale Geografie* 103(2): 136–49.

Büscher, B. (2013) *Transforming the Frontier. Peace Parks and the Politics of Neoliberal Conservation in Southern Africa.* Durham, NC: Duke University Press.

Bush, R. (2007) *Poverty and Neoliberalism: Persistence and Reproduction in The Global South.* London: Pluto.

Camlin, C.S., Kwena, Z.A. and Dworkin, S.L. (2013) Jaboya vs. Jakambi: status, negotiation, and HIV risks among female migrants in the 'Sex for Fish' economy in Nyanza Province, Kenya, *AIDS Education and Prevention* 25(3): 216–31.

Canby, K., Hewitt, J., Bailey, L., *et al.* (2008) *Forest Products Trade Between China and Africa: An Analysis of Imports & Exports.* Forest Trends and Global Timber, available at http://www.forest-trends.org/publication_details.php?publicationID=515 [accessed 13 November 2013].

Cape Town Partnership (2011) Case study 3.2: World Design Capital 2014: MXit, available at http://www.capetown.gov.za/en/DesignCapital/Documents/BIDBOOK_CS_3_2_Queation_43.pdf [accessed 31 December 2013].

Carmeli, A. and Tishler, A. (2004) Resources, capabilities, and the performance of industrial firms: A multivariate analysis, *Managerial and Decision Economics* 25 (6–7): 299–315.

Carmody, P. (2007) *Neoliberalism, Civil Society and Security in Africa.* New York: Palgrave MacMillan.

Carmody, P. (2010) *Globalisation in Africa: Recolonisation or Renaissance?* Boulder, CO: Lynne Rienner.

Carmody, P. (2011) *The New Scramble for Africa.* Cambridge: Polity.

Carmody, P. (2012) The informationalization of poverty in Africa? Mobile phones and economic structure, *Information Technologies and International Development* 8(3): 1–17.

Carmody, P. (2013) *The Rise of the BRICS in Africa: The Geopolitics of South-South Relations*. London: Zed.

Castells, M. (1996) *The Rise of the Network Society: The Information Age: Economy, Society, and Culture Volume I*. Malden, MA: Blackwell.

Castells, M. (1998) *End of Millennium: The Information Age: Economy, Society, and Culture Volume III*. Malden, MA: Blackwell.

Castells, M. (1999) *Information Technology, Globalisation and Social Development*, UNRISD Discussion Paper No. 114. Geneva: United Nations Research Institute for Social Development.

Castells, M. (2003) The networked society, in *The Global Transformations Reader: An Introduction to the Globalisation Debate* (eds D. Held and A.G. McGrew). Oxford: Polity.

Castells, M. (2005) The network society: from knowledge to policy, in *The Network Society: From Knowledge to Policy* (eds M. Castells and G. Cardoso). Washington, DC: Johns Hopkins Center for Transatlantic Relations: 3–21.

Castells, M. (2011) A network theory of power, *International Journal of Communication* 5: 773–87.

Chabal, P. and Daloz, J.-P. (1999) *Africa Works: Disorder as Political Instrument*. Oxford: International African Institute in association with James Currey.

Chan, J. and Pun, N. (2010) Suicide as protest for the new generation of Chinese migrant workers: Foxconn, global capital, and the state, *The Asia-Pacific Journal: Japan Focus*. Available at http://japanfocus.org/-jenny-chan/3408 [accessed 16 September 2013].

Chang, H.-J. (2008) The Third World industrial revolution in historical perspective, in *Issues in Economic Development and Globalisation: Essays in Honour of Ajit Singh* (eds P. Arestis and J. Eatwell). London: Palgrave Macmillan: 8–27.

Chéneau-Loquay, A. (2009) The impact of the mobile phone sector on development: mixed results? *Private Sector and Development: Proparco's Magazine* 4 (November): 17–21.

Chew, H., Levy, M. and Ilavarasan, V. (2011) The limited impact of ICTs on micro-enterprise growth: a study of businesses owned by women in urban India, *Information Technologies and International Development* 7(4): 1–16.

Chowdhury, S.K. (2006) Investments in ICT-capital and economic performance of small and medium scale enterprises in East Africa, *Journal of International Development* 18(4): 533–52.

Christian, M. (2012) Economic and social up(down)grading in tourism global production networks: findings from Kenya and Uganda, *Capturing the gains* Working Paper 11, available at http://www.capturingthegains.org/publications/workingpapers/wp_201211.htm [accessed 12 March 2014].

Clark, D. (2006) *The Capability Approach: Its Development, Critiques and Recent Advances*. Global Poverty Research Group Working Paper Series, GPRG-WPS-032, available at http://economics.ouls.ox.ac.uk/14051/1/gprg-wps-032.pdf [accessed 31 December 2013].

Coe, N.M., Dicken, P. and Hess, M. (2008) Global production networks: realizing the potential, *Journal of Economic Geography* 8(3): 271–95.

Coe, N.M., Hess, M., Yeung, H.W., *et al.* (2004) 'Globalizing' regional development: a global production networks perspective, *Transactions of the Institute of British Geographers* 29(4): 468–84.

Coe, N.M. and Hess, M. (2013) Global production networks, labour and development, *Geoforum* 44: 4–9.

Cole, S. (1986) The global impact of information technology, *World Development* 14(10): 1277–92.

Collier, P. (2007) *The Bottom Billion*. Oxford: Oxford University Press.

Cooke, P. (2012) Twilight of the gods, in *Re-Framing Regional Development: Evolution, Innovation and Transition* (ed. P. Cooke). New York: Routledge: 234–55.

Corbett, S. (2008) Can the cellphone help end global poverty, *The New York Times* 13 April.

Couclelis, H. (2009) Rethinking time geography in the information age, *Environment and Planning A* 41(7): 1556–75.

Couldry, N. (2004) The digital divide, in *Web. Studies*, 2nd edn (eds D. Gauntlett and R. Horsley). London: Arnold: 185–94.

Cowen, M.P. and Shenton, R.W. (1996) *Doctrines of Development*. London: Routledge.

Cox, K. (2008) Globalisation, uneven development and capital: reflections on reading Thomas Friedman's *The World is Flat*, *Cambridge Journal of Regions, Economy and Society* 1(3): 389–410.

Crang, M., Crosbie, T. and Graham, S. (2006) Variable geometries of connection: urban digital divides and the uses of information technology, *Urban Studies* 43(13): 2551–70.

Crouch, G.I. and Ritchie, B. (1999) 'Tourism, competitiveness, and societal prosperity', *Journal of Business Research* 44(3): 137–52.

d'Angella, F. and Go, F.M. (2009) Tale of two cities: collaborative tourism marketing: towards a theory of destination stakeholder assessment, *Tourism Management* 30(3): 429–40.

Datta, D., Ejakait, A. and Odak, M. (2008) Mobile phone-based cash transfers: lessons from the Kenya emergency response, *Humanitarian Exchange Magazine* 40(October). Available at http://www.odihpn.org/humanitarian-exchange-magazine/issue-40/mobile-phone-based-cash-transfers-lessons-from-the-kenya-emergency-response [accessed 25 August 2013].

Dean, J. (2012) The limits to communication, *Guernica: A Magazine of Art and Politics* 1 October, available at http://www.guernicamag.com/features/the-limits-of-communication/ [accessed 31 December 2013].

Dean, W. and Evans, J.R. (1994) *Total Quality Management, Organization and Strategy*. St Paul, MN: West Publishing Company.

Debbage, K.G. and Daniels, P. (1998) The tourist industry and economic geography: missed opportunities, in *The Economic Geography of the Tourist Industry* (eds D. Ionnides and K.G. Debbage). London: Routledge: 17–30.

Dedrick, J., Kraemer, K.L. and Linden, G. (2009) Who profits from innovation in global value chains? A study of the iPod and notebook PCs, *Industrial and Corporate Change* 19(1): 81–116.

Dedrick, J., Kraemer, K.L. and Linden, G. (2010) *The distribution of value in the mobile phone supply chain*, Working Paper, Personal Computing Industry Center, University of California, Irvine.

de Janvry, A. (1981) *The Agrarian Question and Reformism in Latin America*. Berkeley: University of California Press.

de Janvry, A. and Garramón, C. (1977) Laws of motion of capital in the center–periphery structure, *Review of Radical Political Economics* 9(2): 29–38.

de Luna Martinez, J. (2007) Financial services: dealing with limited and unequal access, in *Services, Trade and Development: The Experience of Zambia* (eds A. Mattoo and L. Payton), Basingstoke and New York: Palgrave Macmillan with the World Bank: 155–90.

De Silva, H. and Ratnadiwakara, D. (2009) Using ICT to reduce transaction costs in agriculture through better communication: a case study from Sri Lanka, available at http://lirneasia.net/wp-content/uploads/2008/11/transactioncosts.pdf [accessed 31 December 2013].

Dicken, P. (1998) *Global Shift: Transforming the World Economy*, 3rd edn. London: Paul Chapman Publishing Ltd.

Dicken, P. (2004) Geographers and 'globalization': (yet) another missed boat?, *Transactions of the Institute of British Geographers* 29(1): 5–26.

Diga, K. (2007a) *Mobile phones and poverty reduction: IDRC Field Study*. Available at http://www.slideshare.net/kdiga/mobile-cell-phone-poverty-reduction-in-africa [accessed 22 July].

Diga, K. (2007b) *Mobile cell phones and poverty reduction: Technology spending patterns and poverty level change among households in Uganda*. Unpublished Masters thesis, University of Kwa-Zulu Natal.

Digital Opportunities Task (DOT) Force (2001) *Digital opportunities for all: meeting the challenge*. Report of the Digital Opportunity Task Force, Group of Eight.

Donner, J. (2004) Microentrepreneurs and mobiles: an exploration of the uses of mobile phones by small business owners in Rwanda, *Information Technologies and International Development* 2(1): 1–21.

Donner, J. (2006) The use of mobile phones by microentrepreneurs in Kigali, Rwanda: changes to social and business networks, *Information Technologies and International Development* 3(2): 3–19.

Dosi, G. (1982) Technological paradigms and technological trajectories: a suggested interpretation of the determinants and directions of technical change, *Research Policy* 11: 147–62.

Drayse, M.H. (2011) Globalization and innovation in a mature industry: furniture manufacturing in Canada, *Regional Studies* 45(3): 299–318.

Duffy, R. (2007) Gemstone mining in Madagascar: Transnational networks, criminalisation and global integration, *Journal of Modern African Studies* 45(2): 185–206.

Duncombe, R. (2006) Using the livelihoods framework to analyze ICT applications for poverty reduction through microenterprise, *Information Technologies and International Development* 3(3): 81–100.

Dunn, E., Sebstad, J., Batzdorff, L. and Parsons, H. (2006) Lessons learned on MSE upgrading in value chains: a synthesis paper, *AMAP BDS Knowledge and Practice microREPORT #71*, Washington: United States Agency for International Development.

Dwyer, L. and Kim, C. (2003) Destination competitiveness: determinants and indicators, *Current Issues in Tourism* 6(5): 369–414.

Economist Intelligence Unit (2002) *Business Africa*, 2: 1–15.

Edwards, L. and Jenkins, R. (2013) *The impact of Chinese import penetration on the South African manufacturing sector*. Working Paper Series No. 102, South Africa Labour and Development Research Unit, University of Cape Town.

Egyedi, T.M., Mehos, D.C. and Vree, W.G. (2009) *New Perspectives on Inverse Infrastructures*, paper presented at the second international conference on 'Developing 21st century infrastructure networks'. Chennai, India, 10 December, IEEE.

Ellram, L.M., Tate, W.L. and Billington, C. (2004) Understanding and managing the services supply chain, *Journal of Supply Chain Management* 40(4): 17–32.

Ellway, B.P. (2013) Making it personal in a call centre: electronic peer surveillance, *New Technology, Work and Employment* 28(1): 37–50.

Emel, J. and Huber, M.T. (2008) A risky business: mining, rent and the neoliberalization of 'risk', *Geoforum* 39(3): 1393–1407.

Emerging-Market.org (2007) *Zanzibar Tourism Sector Profile*. Available at http://www.emerging-market.org/tanzania/tanzania-tourism-and-travel/zanzibar-tourism-sector-profile/ [accessed 15 January 2008].

Epstein, H. (2008) *The Invisible Cure: Africa, the West and the Fight Against AIDS*. London: Penguin.

Esselaar, S., Stork, C., Ndiwalana, A. and Deen-Swarray, M. (2007) ICT usage and its impact on profitability of SMEs in 13 African countries, *Information Technologies and International Development* 4(1): 87–100.

eTransform Africa (2012) *The Transformational Use of Information and Communication Technologies in Africa*. Washington, DC: World Bank and African Development Bank.

Etzo, S. and Collender, C. (2010) The mobile phone 'revolution' in Africa: rhetoric or reality? *African Affairs* 109(437): 659–68.

Evans, P.B. (1979) *Dependent Development: The Alliance of Multinational, State, and Local Capital in Brazil*. Princeton: Princeton University Press.

Fan, P. (2011) Innovation, globalization, and catch-up of latecomers: cases of Chinese telecom firms, *Environment and Planning A* 43: 830–49.

Florida, R. and Kenney, M. (1994) The globalization of Japanese R&D: the economic geography of Japanese R&D investment in the United States, *Economic Geography* 70(4): 344–69.

Fold, N. (2008) Transnational sourcing practices in Ghana's perennial crop sectors, *Journal of Agrarian Change* 8(1): 94–122.

Forbes (2011) *India's Richest*, 26 October. Available at http://www.forbes.com/lists/2011/77/india-billionaires-11_Sunil-Mittal_EM57.html [accessed 1 January 2014].

Forbes (2013) *An Overview: Why Microsoft's Worth $42*, 9 January. Available at http://www.forbes.com/sites/greatspeculations/2013/01/09/an-overview-why-microsofts-worth-42/ [accessed 30 December 2013].

Forestier, E., Grace, J. and Kenny, C. (2002) Can information and communication technologies be pro-poor?, *Telecommunications Policy* 26(11): 623–46.

Freeman, C. (1991) Innovation, changes of techno-economic paradigm and biological analogies in economics, *Revue Economique* 42(2): 211–31.

Freeman, C. (1994) The economics of technical change, *Cambridge Journal of Economics* 18(5): 463–514.

Freeman, C. (1995) The 'National System of Innovation' in historical perspective, *Cambridge Journal of Economics* 19(1): 5–24.

Freeman, C. (2001) A hard landing for the 'New Economy'? Information technology and the United States national system of innovation, *Structural Change and Economic Dynamics* 12: 115–39.

Freeman, C. and Perez, C. (1988) Structural crises of adjustment, in *Technical Change and Economic Theory* (eds G. Dosi, C. Freeman, R. Nelson, *et al.*). London: Frances Pinter: 38–66.

Freeman, C. and Soete, L. (1997) *The Economics of Industrial Innovation*, 3rd edn. London: Pinter.

Freidberg, S. (2003) Cleaning up down South: supermarkets, ethical trade and African horticulture, *Social and Cultural Geography* 4(1): 27–43.

French, S. and Leyshon, A. (2004) The new, new financial system? Towards a conceptualisation of financial reintermediation, *Review of International Political Economy* 11(2): 263–88.

Friedman, T.L. (2000) *The Lexus and the Olive Tree*. New York: Anchor Books.

Friedman, T.L. (2005) *The World is Flat: A Brief History of the Twenty-First Century*. New York: Farrar, Straus and Giroux.

Fuchs, C. (2010) Labor in informational capitalism and on the internet, *Information Society* 26(3): 179–96.

Fuchs, C. and Horak, E. (2008) Africa and the digital divide, *Telematics and Informatics* 25: 99–116.

Galbreath, J. (2005) Which resources matter the most to firm success? An exploratory study of resource-based theory, *Technovation* 25(9): 979–87.

Gates, B. (2008) How to fix capitalism, *Time* 31 July: 23–9.

Gebre-Egziabher, T. (2007) Impacts of Chinese imports and coping strategies of local producers: the case of small-scale footwear enterprises in Ethiopia, *Journal of Modern African Studies* 45: 647–79.

Geels, F.W. (2002) Technological transitions as evolutionary reconfiguration processes: a multi-level perspective and a case-study, *Research Policy* 31(8–9): 1257–74.

Geels, F.W. (2004a) From sectoral systems of innovation to socio-technical systems: insights about dynamics and change from sociology and institutional theory, *Research Policy* 33: 897–920.

Geels, F.W. (2004b) Understanding system innovations: a critical literature review and a conceptual synthesis, in *System Innovation and the Transition to Sustainability: Theory, Evidence and Policy* (eds B. Elzen, F. Geels and K. Green). Cheltenham: Edward Elgar: 19–47.

Geels, F.W. and Kemp, R. (2006) Transitions, transformations, and reproduction: dynamics in socio-technical systems, in *Flexibility and Stability in the Innovating Economy* (eds M. McKelvey and M. Holmen). Oxford: Oxford University Press: 227–56.

Geels, F.W. and Schot, J. (2007) Typology of sociotechnical transition pathways, *Research Policy* 36(3): 399–417.

Gereffi, G. (1999) International trade and industrial upgrading in the apparel commodity chain, *Journal of International Economics* 48(1): 37–70.

Gereffi, G., Humphrey, J. and Sturgeon, T. (2005) The governance of global value chains, *Review of International Political Economy* 12(1): 78–104.

Ghosh, R.A. (1998) Cooking pot markets: an economic model for the trade in free goods and services on the Internet, *First Monday*, 3(2), available at http://firstmonday.org/ojs/index.php/fm/article/view/580/501 [accessed 1 January 2014].

Gibbon, P. (2003) The African growth and opportunity act and the global commodity chain for clothing, *World Development* 31(11): 1809–27.

Gibbon, P. and Ponte, S. (2005) *Trading Down: Africa, Value Chains, and the Global Economy*. Philadelphia: Temple University Press.

Giddens, A. (1984) *The Constitution of Society*. Oxford: Oxford University Press.

Gillwald, A. and Stork, C. (2008) *Towards evidence-based ICT policy and regulation: ICT access and usage in Africa*, Research ICT Africa Vol. 1, Policy Paper 2. Johannesburg: Research ICT Africa. Available at http://www.researchictafrica.net/publications/ Towards_Evidence-based_ICT_Policy_and_Regulation_-_Volume_1/RIA%20 Policy%20Paper%20Vol%201%20Paper%201%20-%20Household%20 Survey%20Methodology%20and%20Fieldwork%202008.pdf [accessed 1 January 2014].

Giuliani, E., Pietrobelli, C. and Rabellotti, R. (2005) Upgrading in global value chains: lessons from Latin American clusters, *World Development* 33(4): 549–73.

Goedhuys, M. (2007) Learning, product innovation, and firm heterogeneity in developing countries: evidence from Tanzania, *Industrial and Corporate Change* 16(2): 269–92.

Goger, A., Hull, A., Barrientos, S., *et al.* (2014) *Capturing the gains in Africa: making the most of global value chain participation*. Background paper prepared on behalf of the Organisation for Economic Cooperation and Development, Duke University, Center on Globalization, Governance, and Competitiveness. Available at http:// www.cggc.duke.edu/pdfs/Duke_CGGC_2014_Capturing_the_Gains_in_Africa. pdf [accessed 12 March 2014].

Goldstein, A., Pinaud, N., Reisen, H. and Chen, X. (2006) *The Rise of China and India: What's in it for Africa?* Paris: OECD Development Centre.

Graham, M. (2010) Justifying virtual presence in the Thai silk industry: links between data and discourse, *Information Technologies and International Development* 6(4): 57–70.

Graham, M. (2011) Time machines and virtual portals: the spatialities of the digital divide, *Progress in Development Studies* 11(3): 211–27.

Graham, M. and Mann, L. (2013) Imagining a Silicon Savannah? Technological and conceptual connectivity in Kenya's BPO and software development sectors', *The Electronic Journal of Information Systems in Developing Countries*, 56. Available at https://www.ejisdc.org/ojs2/index.php/ejisdc/article/view/1107 [accessed 1 January 2014].

Graham, M. and Zook, M. (2011) Visualizing global cyberscapes: mapping user generated placemarks, *Journal of Urban Technology* 18(1): 115–32.

Graham, S. (1998) The end of geography or the explosion of place? Conceptualizing space, place and information technology, *Progress in Human Geography* 22(2): 165–85.

Graham, S. and Marvin, S. (2001) *Splintering Urbanism: Networked Infrastructures, Technological Mobilities and the Urban Condition*. London and New York: Routledge.

Grasland, C. and Van Hamme, G. (2010) La relocalisation des activités industri-elles: une approche centre-périphérie des dynamiques mondiale et européenne, *L'Espace géographique* 39(1): 1–19.

Green, D. (2008) *From Poverty to Power: How Active Citizens and Effective States can Change the World*. Oxford: Oxfam International.

Gregor, S., Martin, M., Fernandez, W., et al. (2006) The transformational dimension in the realization of business value from information technology, *Journal of Strategic Information Systems* 15(3): 249–70.

Gregory, D. (2013) Tahrir: politics, publics and performances of space, *Middle East Critique* 22(3): 235–46.

Gretzel, U. (2011) Intelligent systems in tourism: a social science perspective, *Annals of Tourism Research* 38(3): 757–79.

GSMA (Global Systems Mobile Association) (2011) *Africa Mobile Observatory 2011: Driving Economic and Social Development through Mobile Services*. Available at http://www.gsma.com/publicpolicy/wp-content/uploads/2012/04/africamobileobservatory2011-1.pdf [accessed 1 January 2014].

Hackett, R. (2012) "Devil bustin' satellites." How media liberalization in Africa generates religious intolerance and conflict, in *Displacing the State: Religion and Conflict in Neoliberal Africa* (eds J. Smith and R. Hackett). South Bend, IN: University of Notre Dame Press: 163–208.

Hahn, H.P. and Kibora, L. (2008) The domestication of the mobile phone: oral society and new ICT in Burkina Faso, *Journal of Modern African Studies* 46(1): 87–109.

Hall, C.M. (1999) Rethinking collaboration and partnership: a public policy per-spective, *Journal of Sustainable Tourism* 7(3–4): 274–89.

Hardt, M. and Negri, A. (2000) *Empire*. Cambridge, MA: Harvard University Press.

Hart, S.L. (2005) Innovation, creative destruction and sustainability, *Research Technology Management* 48(5): 21–7.

Hart, S.L. and Christensen, C.M. (2002) The great leap: driving innovation from the base of the pyramid, *MIT Sloan Management Review* 44(1): 51–6.

Hart-Landsberg, M. (2013) *Capitalist Globalization: Consequences, Resistance and Alternatives*. New York: Monthly Review Press.

Harvey, D. (1999) *The Limits to Capital*. London: Verso.

Harvey, D. (2013) Keynote address for the 45th Conference of Irish Geographers, National University of Ireland, Galway, 17 May. Available at http://davidharvey.org/2013/06/video-45th-conference-of-irish-geographers-keynote/ [accessed 9 September 2014].

Hecht, G. (2012) *Being Nuclear: Africans and the Global Uranium Trade*. Cambridge, MA: MIT Press.

Heeks, R. (2002a) Information systems and developing countries: failure, success, and local improvisations, *Information Society* 18(2): 101–12.

Heeks, R. (2002b) I-Development not e-Development: Special Issue on ICTs and development, *Journal of International Development* 14: 1–11.

Heeks, R. (2007) Introduction: Theorising ICT4D research, *Information Technologies and International Development* 3: 1–4.

Heeks, R. (2008) ICT4D 2.0: the next phase of applying ICT for international development, *Computer* 41(6): 26–33.

Held, D., Goldblatt, D. and Perraton, J. (1999) *Global Transformations: Politics, Economics, Culture*. Cambridge: Polity.

Henderson, J., Dicken, P., Hess, M., *et al.* (2002) Global production networks and the analysis of economic development, *Review of International Political Economy* 9(3): 436–64.

Hess, M. (2004) 'Spatial' relationships? Towards a reconceptualization of embeddedness, *Progress in Human Geography* 28(2): 165–86.

Hickey, S. and Mohan, G. (2005) Relocating participation within a radical politics of development, *Development and Change* 36(2): 237–62.

Hill, M. (2007) Confronting power through policy: On the creation and spread of liberating knowledge, *Journal of Human Development* 8(2): 259–82.

Horner, R. (2014) Strategic decoupling, recoupling and global production networks: India's pharmaceutical industry, *Journal of Economic Geography* in press.

Hughes, A., Wrigley, N. and Buttle, M. (2008) Global production networks, ethical campaigning, and the embeddedness of responsible governance, *Journal of Economic Geography* 8(3): 345–67.

Humphrey, J. and Schmitz, H. (2000) *Governance and Upgrading: Linking Industrial Cluster and Global Value Chain Research*. IDS Working Paper 120. Brighton: Institute of Development Studies, University of Sussex.

Humphrey, J. and Schmitz, H. (2002) How does insertion in global value chains affect upgrading in industrial clusters? *Regional Studies* 36(9): 1017–27.

Huuhtanen, M. (2012) Nokia cuts 10,000 jobs, *BusinessWeek*, 24 June 2012. Available at http://www.businessweek.com/ap/2012-06/D9VD2DNG1.htm [accessed 15 November 2013].

Ibrahim, M. (2011) African leaders must harness potential of the young, Mo Ibrahim Foundation. Available at http://www.moibrahimfoundation.org/en/opinion/about-mo-ibrahim-foundation/the-opinion/mo-ibrahim-african-leaders-must-harness-potential-of-the-young.html [accessed 15 June 2013].

ILO (International Labour Organization) (2008) M-Pesa International Money Transfer Service, Safaricom. Available at http://www.ilo.org/dyn/migpractice/migmain.showPractice?p_lang=en&p_practice_id=70 [accessed 1 January 2014].

Imai, K. and Shiu, J. (2007) *A Divergent Path of Industrial Upgrading: Emergence and Evolution of the Mobile Handset Industry in China*. IDE Discussion Paper 125.2007.10, Institute of Developing Economies-JETRO. Available at http://ir.ide.go.jp/dspace/bitstream/2344/640/3/ARRIDE_Discussion_No.125_imai.pdf [accessed 13 October 2013].

infoDev/ World Bank (2013) *infoDev's 2013–2015 Work Program*. Washington: World Bank. Available at http://www.infodev.org/infodev-files/resource/InfodevDocuments_1200.pdf [accessed 15 September 2013].

International Organization for Standardisation (ISO) (2009) *The ISO Survey 2008*. Geneva: International Organization for Standardisation.

ITC (International Trade Centre) (2008) *International Trade Statistics*, available at http://www.intracen.org/tradstat/ [accessed 21 July 2008].

ITC (International Trade Centre) (2012) *International Trade Statistics*, available at http://www.intracen.org/tradstat/ [accessed 20 October 2012].

ITC (International Trade Centre) (2013) *International Trade Statistics*, available at http://www.intracen.org/tradstat/ [accessed 19 August 2013].

ITU (International Telecommunication Union) (1999) *Challenges to the Network: Internet for Development*. Geneva: ITU.

ITU (International Telecommunication Union) (2006) *World Information Society Report*. Geneva: ITU. Available at http://www.itu.int/osg/spu/publications/world informationsociety/2006/report.html [accessed 12 December 2013].

ITU (International Telecommunication Union) (2012) *Measuring the Information Society*. Geneva: ITU. Available at http://www.itu.int/ITU-D/ict/publications/idi/ [accessed 19 August 2013].

ITU (International Telecommunication Union) (2013) *ICT Facts and Figures: The World in 2013*. Geneva: ITU. Available at http://www.itu.int/en/ITU-D/Statistics/ Documents/facts/ICTFactsFigures2013-e.pdf [accessed 1 January 2014].

Ivarsson, I. and Alvstam, C.G. (2010) Supplier upgrading in the home-furnishing value chain: an empirical study of IKEA's sourcing in China and South East Asia, *World Development* 38(11): 1575–87.

Ivarsson, I. and Alvstam, C.G. (2011) Upgrading in global value-chains: a case study of technology-learning among IKEA-suppliers in China and Southeast Asia, *Journal of Economic Geography* 11(4): 731–52.

Jaglin, S. (2008) Differentiated networked services in Cape Town: echoes of splintering urbanism? *Geoforum* 39: 1897–1906.

James, J. (2011) Are changes in the digital divide consistent with global equality or inequality? *The Information Society* 27: 121–8.

James, J. (2014) Product use and welfare: the case of mobile phones in Africa, *Telematics and Informatics* 31: 356–63.

Jeacle, I. and Carter, C. (2011) In TripAdvisor we trust: rankings, calculative regimes and abstract systems, *Accounting, Organizations and Society* 36(4): 293–309.

Jensen, R. (2007) The digital provide: information (technology), market performance, and welfare in the South Indian fisheries sector, *Quarterly Journal of Economics* 122(3): 879–924.

Jessop, B. (2002) *The Future of the Capitalist State*. Cambridge: Polity.

Jidema, N. (2011) Huawei's $100 Android phone emerges as Kenya's best seller, *The Next Web*, available at http://thenextweb.com/africa/2011/06/24/huaweis-100-android-phone-emerges-as-kenyas-best-seller/ [accessed 2 January 2014].

Jomo, K.S. and Baudot, J. (eds) (2007) *Flat World, Big Gaps: Economic Liberalization, Globalization, Poverty and Inequality*. Hyderabad: Orient Longman.

Jones, A. and Murphy, J.T. (2011) Theorizing practice in economic geography: foundations, challenges, and possibilities, *Progress in Human Geography* 35(3): 366–92.

Judd, D. (2006) Commentary: tracing the commodity chain of global tourism, *Tourism Geographies* 8(4): 323.

Juma, C. (2001) Global governance of technology: meeting the needs of developing countries, *International Journal of Technology Management* 22(7–8): 629–55.

Kabanda, S. (2011) 'E-Commerce Institutionalization is not for us': SMEs perception of E-Commerce in Tanzania, *African Journal of Information Systems* 3(1): 1–16.

Kaplinsky, R. (2008) What does the rise of China do for industrialisation in Sub-Saharan Africa? *Review of African Political Economy* 35(115): 7–22.

Kaplinsky, R. and Manning, C. (1998) Concentration, competition policy and the role of small and medium-sized enterprises in South Africa's industrial development, *Journal of Development Studies* 35(1): 139–61.

Kaplinsky, R. and Readman, J. (2000) *Globalization and Upgrading: What Can (and Cannot) be Learned from International Trade Statistics in the Wood Furniture Sector?* Brighton: University of Brighton and Institute of Development Studies, University of Sussex.

Kaplinsky, R., Morris, M. and Readman, J. (2002) The globalization of product markets and immiserizing growth: lessons from the South African furniture industry, *World Development* 30(7): 1159–77.

Kaplinsky, R., Memdovic, O., Morris, M. and Readman, J. (2003) *The Global Wood Furniture Value Chain: What Prospects for Upgrading by Developing Countries: The Case of South Africa.* Vienna: United Nations Industrial Development Organization (UNIDO).

Karim, L. (2011) *Microfinance and its Discontents: Women in Debt in Bangladesh.* Minneapolis: University of Minnesota Press.

Keane, J.A. (2012) The governance of global value chains and the effects of the global financial crisis transmitted to producers in Africa and Asia, *Journal of Development Studies* 48(6): 783–97.

Kelsall, T. (2013) *Business, Politics and the State in Africa: Challenging the Orthodoxies of Growth and Transformation.* London: Zed.

Kemp, R. and Rotmans, J. (2005) The management of the co-evolution of technical, environmental and social systems, in *Towards Environmental Innovation Systems* (eds M. Weber and J. Hemmelskamp), Berlin: Springer: 33–55.

Kemp, R., Schot, J. and Hoogma, R. (1998) Regime shifts to sustainability through processes of niche formation. The approach of strategic niche management, *Technology Analysis and Strategic Management* 10(2): 175–95.

Kenny, C.J. (2000) Expanding Internet access to the rural poor in Africa, *Information Technology for Development* 9(1): 25–31.

Kimbute, J. (2012) Economic and welfare trends in Tanzania since 2008: poverty still rising, inequality stagnates, educated youth biggest unemployed group, *Business Times*, 19 October 2012. Available at http://www.businesstimes.co.tz/index.php?option=com_content&view=article&id=2128:economic-and-welfare-trends-in-tanzania-since-2008-poverty-still-rising-inequality-stagnates-educated-youth-biggest-unemployed-group&catid=1:latest-news&Itemid=57 [accessed 9 September 2014].

Kleine, D. (2013) *Technologies of Choice? ICTs, Development, and the Capabilities Approach.* Cambridge, MA: MIT Press.

Kleine, D. and Unwin, T. (2009) Technological revolution, evolution and new dependencies: What's new about ICT4D? *Third World Quarterly* 30(5): 1045–67.

Knox-Hayes, J. (2013) The spatial and temporal dynamics of value in financialization: Analysis of the infrastructure of carbon markets, *Geoforum* 50: 117–28.

Kottemann, J. and Boyer-Wright, K. (2009) Human resource development, domains of information technology use and levels of economic prosperity, *Information Technology for Development* 15(1): 32–42.

KPMG (n.d). 'Mediation or Disintermediation?' Is that the question for retail banking?, *KPMG Perspectives*, available at https://www.kpmg.com/global/en/issuesandinsights/articlespublications/perspectives/pages/mediation-or-disintermediation.aspx [accessed 1 January 2014].

Krishnan, M.S., Rai, A. and Zmud, R. (2007) The digitally enabled extended enterprise in a global economy, *Information Systems Research* 18(3): 233–6.

Krugman, P. (ed.) (1995) *Development, Geography and Economic Theory*. Cambridge, MA: MIT Press.

Labrooy, M. (2013) Africa's smartphone revolution, *E-learning Africa News*. Available at http://www.elearning-africa.com/eLA_Newsportal/africas-smartphone-revolution/ [accessed 2 November 2013].

Lambooy, J.G. (2002) Knowledge and urban economic development: an evolutionary perspective, *Urban Studies* 39(5–6): 1019–35.

Latour, B. (1987) *Science in Action*. Cambridge, MA: Harvard University Press.

Latour, B. (2005) *Reassembling the Social: An Introduction to Actor–Network Theory*. Oxford: Oxford University Press.

Lawhon, M. and Murphy, J.T. (2012) Socio-technical regimes and sustainability transitions: insights from political ecology, *Progress in Human Geography* 36(3): 354–78.

Lawrence, P. (2005) Explaining Sub-Saharan Africa's manufacturing performance, *Development and Change* 36(6): 1121–41.

Leonard, D.K. and Strauss, S. (2003) *Africa's Stalled Development: International Causes and Cures*. Boulder, CO: Lynne Rienner.

Lepawsky, J. and McNabb, C. (2010) Mapping international flows of electronic waste, *Canadian Geographer* 54(2): 177–95.

Levy, A. (2012) Expedia Jumps After Third-Quarter Profit Tops Estimates, *Bloomberg Business News*. Available at http://www.bloomberg.com/news/2012-10-25/expedia-jumps-after-third-quarter-profit-tops-estimates.html [accessed 31 December 2013].

Lihra, T., Buehlmann, U. and Beauregard, R. (2008) Mass customization of wood furniture as a competitive strategy, *International Journal of Mass Customization* 2 (3–4): 200–215.

Linden, G., Kraemer, K.L. and Dedrick, J. (2009) Who captures value in a global innovation network? The case of Apple's iPod, *Communications of the ACM* 52(3): 140–44.

Line, T., Jain, J. and Lyons, G. (2011) The role of ICTs in everyday mobile lives, *Journal of Transport Geography* 19: 1490–99.

Lines, T. (2008) *Making Poverty: A History*. London: Zed.

Lourens, A.S. and Jonker, J.A. (2013) An integrated approach for developing a technology strategy framework for small- to medium-sized furniture manufacturers to improve competitiveness, *South African Journal of Industrial Engineering* 24(1): 50–67.

Lyons, M. and Brown, A. (2010) Has mercantilism reduced urban poverty in SSA? Perception of boom, bust, and the China-Africa trade in Lomé and Bamako, *World Development* 38(5): 771–82.

MacKinnon, D. (2012) Beyond strategic coupling: reassessing the firm-region nexus in global production networks, *Journal of Economic Geography* 12(1): 227–45.

Mahajan, V. (2009) *Africa Rising: How 900 million African Consumers Offer More Than You Think*. Upper Saddle River, NJ: Wharton School Publishers.

Mail and Guardian (2011) Hidden addiction in Zanzibar, 31 January. Available at http://mg.co.za/article/2011-01-31-hidden-addiction-in-zanzibar [accessed 16 December 2013].

Markard, J., Raven, R. and Truffer, B. (2012) Sustainability transitions: an emerging field of research and its prospects, *Research Policy* 41(6): 955–67.

Marx, K. (1887 [1967]) *Capital: A Critique of Political Economy: Vol. I: The Process of Capitalist Production*. New York: International Publishers.

Mascarenhas, O. (2010) Broadening the agenda for ICTs for poverty reduction: PICTURE-Africa, *Information Technologies & International Development*, 6(SE): 37–44.

Mata, F.J., Fuerst, W.L. and Barney, J.B. (1995) Information technology and sustained competitive advantage: a resource-based analysis, *MIS Quarterly* 19(4): 487–504.

Mattsson, J., Sundbo, J. and Fussing-Jensen, C. (2005) Innovation systems in tourism: The roles of attractors and scene-takers, *Industry and Innovation* 12(3): 357–81.

Mayers, J. (2013) China in Africa's forests, International Institute for Environment and Development, 20 March, available at http://www.iied.org/china-africa-forests [accessed 1 January 2014].

Mbelle, A.V.Y. (2005) *Productivity Performance in Developing Countries. Country Case Studies: Tanzania*. Vienna: United Nations Industrial Development Organization.

McFarlane, C. (2009) Translocal assemblages: space, power and social movements, *Geoforum* 40(4): 561–7.

McGrath, S. (2013) Fuelling global production networks with 'slave labour'?: Migrant sugar cane workers in the Brazilian ethanol GPN, *Geoforum* 44: 32–43.

McGreal, C. (2007) Mbeki criticised for praising 'racist' Sarkozy, *The Guardian*, 26 August, available at http://www.theguardian.com/world/2007/aug/27/southafrica.france [accessed 1 January 2014].

Meadowcroft, J. (2005) Environmental political economy, technological transitions and the state, *New Political Economy* 10(4): 479–98.

Meagher, K. (1995) Crisis, informalization and the urban informal sector in sub-Saharan Africa, *Development and Change* 26(2): 259–84.

Meagher, K. (2007) Manufacturing disorder: liberalization, informal enterprise and economic 'ungovernance' in African small firm clusters, *Development and Change* 38(3): 473–503.

Meagher, K. (2010) *Identity Economics: Social Networks & the Informal Economy in Nigeria*. Oxford: James Currey.

Melville, N. and Ramirez, R. (2008) Information technology innovation diffusion: an information requirements paradigm, *Information Systems Journal* 18: 247–73.

Melville, N., Kraemer, K. and Gurbaxani, V. (2004) Review: Information technology and organizational performance: An integrative model of IT business value, *MIS Quarterly* 28(2): 283–322.

Mhone, G. (1982) *The Political Economy of a Dual Labour Market in Africa*. East Brunswick: Fairleigh Dickinson/Associated University Press.

Miller, D. (2014) Rebounding Mac, plummeting iPod highlight winning Apple quarter. Available at http://www.macworld.com/article/2091741/apple-revenues-up-but-profits-flat-in-first-quarter.html [accessed 3 September 2014].

Mills, G, and Herbst, J. (2012) *Africa's Third Liberation: The New Search for Prosperity and Jobs*. London: Penguin.

Minten, B., Randrianarison, L. and Swinnen, J.F. (2009) Global retail chains and poor farmers: Evidence from Madagascar, *World Development* 37(11): 1728–41.

Molina, A. (2003) The digital divide: The need for a global e-inclusion movement, *Technology Analysis and Strategic Management* 15(1): 137–52.

Molla, A. and Licker, P. (2005) Maturation stage of eCommerce in developing countries: a survey of South African companies, *Information Technologies and International Development* 2(1): 89–98.

Molony, T. (2007) 'I don't trust the phone; it always lies': Trust and information and communication technologies in Tanzanian micro- and small enterprises, *Information Technologies and International Development* 3(4): 67–83.

Molony, T. (2008) Running out of credit: the limitations of mobile telephony in a Tanzanian agricultural marketing system, *Journal of Modern African Studies* 46(4): 637–58.

Moodley, S. (2003) E-Commerce and export markets: small furniture producers in South Africa, *Journal of Small Business Management* 41(3): 317–24.

Morris, M. and Dunne, N. (2004) Driving environmental certification: its impact on the furniture and timber products value chain in South Africa, *Geoforum* 35(2): 251–66.

MTN (2009) *2008 Annual Report*. MTN. Available at https://www.mtn.com/Investors/Financials/Pages/annualreports.aspx [accessed 1 January 2014].

Muchie, M., Gammeltoft, P. and Lundvall, B. (2003) *Putting Africa First: The Making of African Innovation Systems*. Aalborg, Denmark: Aalborg University Press.

Murphy, J.T. (2002) Networks, trust, and innovation in Tanzania's manufacturing sector, *World Development* 30(4): 591–619.

Murphy, J.T. (2006a) The sociospatial dynamics of creativity and production in Tanzanian industry: urban furniture manufacturers in a liberalizing economy, *Environment and Planning A* 38(10): 1863–82.

Murphy, J.T. (2006b) Building trust in economic space, *Progress in Human Geography* 30(4): 427–50.

Murphy, J.T. (2007) The challenge of upgrading in African industries: socio-spatial factors and the urban environment in Mwanza, Tanzania, *World Development* 35(10): 1754–78.

Murphy, J.T. (2008) Economic geographies of the Global South: missed opportunities and promising intersections with development studies, *Geography Compass* 2(3): 851–73.

Murphy, J.T. (2012) Global production networks, relational proximity, and the sociospatial dynamics of market internationalization in Bolivia's wood products sector, *Annals of the Association of American Geographers* 102(1): 208–233.

Murphy, J.T. (2013) Transforming small, medium, and micro-scale enterprises? Information-communication technologies (ICTs) and industrial change in Tanzania, *Environment and Planning A* 45(7): 1753–72.

Murphy, J.T. and Schindler, S. (2011) Globalizing development in Bolivia? Alternative networks and value-capture challenges in the wood products industry, *Journal of Economic Geography* 11(1): 61–85.

Murphy, J.T., Carmody, P. and Surborg, B. (2014) Industrial transformation or business as usual? Information-communication technologies and Africa's place in the global information economy, *Review of African Political Economy* 41(140): 264–83.

Muto, M. and Yamano, T. (2009) The impact of mobile phone coverage expansion on market participation: panel data evidence from Uganda, *World Development* 37(12): 1887–96.

Muwanguzi, S. and Musambira, G. (2009) The transformation of East Africa's economy using mobile money transfer services: a comparative analysis of Kenya and Uganda's experience, *Journal of Creative Communications* 4: 131–46.

MWeb (2013) Cape Town Tourism's funding uncertainty, available at http://www.mweb.co.za/Entrepreneur/ViewArticle/tabid/3162/Article/4410/cape-town-tourisms-funding-uncertainty.aspx [accessed 16 December 2013].

Mwesige, P.G. (2004) Cyber elites: A survey of internet café users in Uganda, *Telematics and Informatics* 21: 83–101.

Myers, G. (2013) From expected to unexpected comparisons: changing the flows of ideas about cities in a postcolonial urban world, *Singapore Journal of Tropical Geography* 34: 1–15.

Naude, W. (2009) Geography, transport and Africa's proximity gap, *Journal of Transport Geography* 17(1): 1–9.

Neffke, F., Henning, M. and Boschma, R. (2011) How do regions diversify over time? Industry relatedness and the development of new growth paths in regions, *Economic Geography* 87(3): 237–65.

Nelson, E.G. and de Bruijn, E.J. (2005) The voluntary formalization of enterprises in a developing economy: the case of Tanzania, *Journal of International Development* 17(4): 575–93.

Nelson, R.R. (1993) *National Innovation Systems: A Comparative Analysis*. University of Illinois at Urbana-Champaign's Academy for Entrepreneurial Leadership Historical Research Reference in Entrepreneurship.

Nelson, R.R. and Winter, S.G. (1982) *An Evolutionary Theory of Economic Change*. Cambridge, MA: Belknap Press of Harvard University Press.

Nest, M.W. (2011) *Coltan*. Cambridge: Polity.

Nest, M.W. and Grignon, F. (2006) *The Democratic Republic of Congo: Economic Dimensions of War and Peace*. Boulder, CO: Lynne Rienner.

New York Times (2013) Questions follow acid attack on British women in Zanzibar, 14 August. Available at http://www.nytimes.com/2013/08/14/world/europe/in-zanzibar-two-smiling-men-douse-young-british-women-with-acid.html [accessed 16 December 2013].

Nichter, S. and Goldmark, L. (2009) Small firm growth in developing countries, *World Development* 37(9): 1453–64.

Noman, A., Botchwey, K., Stein, H. and Stiglitz, J. (2012) *Good Growth and Governance in Africa: Rethinking Development Strategies*. The Initiative for Policy Dialogue Series. Oxford: Oxford University Press.

Nye, D. (2006) *Technology Matters: Questions to Live With*. Cambridge, MA: MIT Press.

Obijiofor, L. (2009) Mapping theoretical and practical issues in the relationship between ICTs and Africa's socioeconomic development, *Telematics and Informatics* 26(1): 32–43.

O'Brien, R. (1992) *Global Financial Integration: The End of Geography*. London: Pinter.

OECD (Organization for Economic Cooperation and Development) (2009) *Factbook 2009*. Geneva: OECD.

Okpaku, J.O. (2006) Leapfrogging into the information economy: harnessing information and communications technologies in Botswana, Mauritania and Tanzania, in *Attacking Africa's Poverty: Experience From the Ground* (eds L. Fox and R. Liebenthal). Washington: World Bank: 149–75.

Osumare, H. (2012) *The Hiplife in Ghana: West African Indigenization of Hip-Hop.* Basingstoke and New York: Palgrave Macmillan.

Ouma, S. (2010) Global standards, local realities: private agrifood governance and the restructuring of the Kenyan horticulture industry, *Economic Geography* 86(2): 197–222.

Overa, R. (2006) Networks, distance, and trust: telecommunications Development and changing trading practices in Ghana, *World Development* 34(7): 1301–15.

Oyedemi, T.D. (2012) Digital inequalities and implications for social inequalities: a study of internet penetration amongst university students in South Africa, *Telematics and Informatics* 29: 302–13.

Oyelaran-Oyeyinka, B. (2007) Learning in local systems and global links: The Otigba computer hardware cluster in Nigeria, in *Industrial Clusters and Innovation Systems in Africa: Institutions, Markets and Policy* (eds B. Oyelaran-Oyeyinka and D. McCormick). Tokyo, New York and Paris: United Nations University Press: 100–131.

Oyelaran-Oyeyinka, B. and Lal, K. (2006) Learning new technologies by small and medium enterprises in developing countries, *Technovation* 26(2): 220–31.

Oyen, E. (2004) Poverty production: a different approach to poverty understanding, in *Advances in Sociological Knowledge: Over Half a Century* (ed. N. Genov). Wiesbaden: VS Verlag für Sozialwissenschaften: 299–315.

Palpacuer, F., Gibbon, P. and Thomsen, L. (2005) New challenges for developing country suppliers in global clothing chains: a comparative European perspective, *World Development* 33(3): 409–30.

Park, J. and Roome, N. (2002) *The Ecology of the New Economy: Sustainable Transformation of Global Information, Communications and Electronics Industries.* Sheffield: Greenleaf.

Park, S.G. (1997) 'Disarticulations' in the Information Society: barriers to the universal access to information highways in developing countries, *International Information and Library Review* 29: 189–99.

Peck, J. (2012) Economic geography: island life, *Dialogues in Human Geography* 2(2): 113–33.

Peet, R. (2007) *Geography of Power: Making Global Economic Policy.* London: Zed.

Peiffer, C. and Englebert, P. (2012) Extraversion, vulnerability, to donors, and political liberalization in Africa, *African Affairs* 111(444): 355–78.

Pejout, N. (2010) Africa and the 'second new economy', in *The Political Economy of Africa* (ed. V. Padayachee). London: Routledge: 232–44.

Perry, M. (1999) *Small Firms and Network Economies.* London: Routledge.

Phelps, N.A., Stillwell, J.C. and Wanjiru, R. (2009) Broken chain? AGOA and foreign direct investment in the Kenyan clothing industry, *World Development* 37(2): 314–25.

Ponte, S. and Ewert, J. (2009) Which way is 'up' in upgrading? Trajectories of change in the value chain for South African wine, *World Development* 37(12): 1637–50.

Power, M. (2011) Angola 2025: The future of the 'World's Richest Poor Country', *Antipode* 44(3): 993–1014.

Prahalad, C.K. (2004) *The Fortune at the Bottom of the Pyramid: Eradicating Poverty Through Profits*. Philadelphia: Wharton School Publishing.

Prahalad, C.K. and Hart, S.L. (2002) The Fortune at the Bottom of the Pyramid, *Strategy + Business* 26 (First Quarter): 2–14.

Puri, J., Mechael, P., Cosmaciuc, R., *et al.* (2010) *A Study of the Connectivity in Millennium Villages in Africa*. Paper presented at ICTD Conference, 15th December, Royal Holloway, University of London. Available at http://www. gg.rhul.ac.uk/ict4d/ictd2010/papers/ICTD2010%20Puri%20et%20al.pdf [accessed 1 January 2014].

Putnam, R.D. (2000) *Bowling Alone: The Collapse and Revival of American Community*. New York: Simon & Schuster.

Quesada-Pineda, H. (2010) *The ABCs of Cost Allocation in the Wood Products Industry: Applications in the Furniture Industry*. Publication 420-147, Virginia Cooperative Extension, Virginia Tech University, Blacksburg, VA. Available at http://pubs.ext. vt.edu/420/420-147/420-147.html [accessed 1 January 2014].

Qureshi, S. (2007) Information technology innovations for development, *Information Technology for Development* 13(23): 311–13.

Racherla, P., Hu, C. and Hyun, M.Y. (2008) Exploring the role of innovative technologies in building a knowledge-based destination, *Current Issues in Tourism* 11(5): 407–28.

Radelet, S.C. (2010) *Emerging Africa: How 17 Countries are Leading the Way*. Washington, DC: Center for Global Development.

Rai, A., Patnayakuni, R., and Patnayakuni, N. (2006) Firm performance impacts of digitally enabled supply chain integration capabilities, *MIS Quarterly* 30(2): 225–46.

Raiti, G. (2007) The lost sheep of ICT4D research, *Information Technologies & International Development* 3(4): 1–7.

Raynolds, L.T. and Ngcwangu, S.U. (2010) Fair trade Rooibos tea: connecting South African producers and American consumer markets, *Geoforum* 41(1): 74–83.

Research ICT Africa (2006) *Towards an e-Index: SME E-access and Usage Across 14 African Countries*. Johannesburg: Research ICT Africa. Available at http://www. researchictafrica.net/publications/Research_ICT_Africa_e-Index_Series/ SME%20e-Access%20and%20Usage%20in%2014%20African%20Countries. pdf [accessed 1 January 2014].

Rettie, R. (2008) Mobile phones and network capital: facilitating connections, *Mobilities* 3(3): 291–311.

Riisgaard, L. (2009) Global value chains, labour organization and private social standards: lessons from East African cut flower industries, *World Development* 37(2): 326–40.

Ritzer, G. (2011) *Globalization: The Essentials*. Chichester: Wiley-Blackwell.

Robbins, G. (2010) Beyond local economic development? Exploring municipality-supported job creation in a South African city, *Development Southern Africa* 27(4): 531–46.

Robertson, C., Mhango, Y. and Moran, M. (2012) *The Fastest Billion: The Story Behind Africa's Economic Revolution*. London: Renaissance Capital.

Rodney, W. (1972) *How Europe Underdeveloped Africa*. Nairobi: East African Educational Publishers.

Rodrik, D. (2008) Understanding South Africa's economic puzzles, *Economics of Transition* 16(4): 769–97.

Rogers, E.M. (1962) *Diffusion of Innovations*. New York: The Free Press.

Rogerson, C.M. (2004) Transforming the South African tourism industry: the emerging black-owned bed and breakfast economy, *Geojournal* 60(3): 273–81.

Rogerson, C.M. (2008) Shared growth in urban tourism: evidence from Soweto, South Africa, *Urban Forum* 19(4): 395–411.

Rogerson, C.M. (2013) The economic geography of South Africa's hotel industry 1990–2010, *Urban Forum* 24(3): 425–46.

Rogerson, C.M. and Visser, G. (2011) African tourism geographies: existing paths and new directions, *Tijdschrift Voor Economische En Sociale Geografie* 102(3): 251–9.

Rotberg, R. (2013) *Africa Emerges: Consummate Challenges, Abundant Opportunities*. Cambridge: Polity.

Rotberg, R. and Aker, J. (2013) Mobile phones: uplifting weak and failed states, *Washington Quarterly* 36(1): 111–25.

Roy, A. (2010) *Poverty Capital: Microfinance and the Making of Development*. London: Routledge.

Russill, C. (2008) Sublimity and solutions: problematization in ICT for development perspectives, *Communication and Critical/Cultural Studies* 5(4): 383–403.

Ruttan, V. (2001) *Technology, Growth, and Development*. New York: Oxford University Press.

Sachs, J. (2005) *The End of Poverty: How we can Make it Happen in our Lifetime*. London: Penguin.

Sachs, J. (2008) *Commonwealth: Economics for a Crowded Planet*. London: Penguin.

Sáinz, J.P.P. (2003) Globalization, upgrading, and small enterprises: a view from Central America, *Competition and Change* 7(4): 205–21.

SAITIS (South African Information Technology Industry Strategy Project) (2002) *ICT Diffusion and ICT Applications in Usage Sectors*. Johannesburg: SAITIS.

Sala-i-Martin, X. and Pinkovskiy, M. (2010) *African Poverty is Falling… Much Faster than You Think!* National Bureau of Economic Research Working Paper No. 15775, available at http://www.nber.org/papers/w15775 [accessed 1 January 2014].

Samara, T.R. (2011) *Cape Town after Apartheid: Crime and Governance in the Divided City*. Minneapolis: University of Minnesota Press.

Santhanam, R. and Hartono, E. (2003) Issues in linking information technology capability to firm performance, *MIS Quarterly* 27(1): 125–53.

Santos, M. (1979) *The Shared Space: The Two Circuits of the Urban Economy in Underdeveloped Countries*. London: Methuen.

Schmidt, C. (2006) Unfair trade: E-waste in Africa, *Environmental Health Perspectives* 114(4): 232–5.

Schumpeter, J.A. (1939) *Business Cycles: A Theoretical, Historical, and Statistical Analysis of the Capitalist Process: Volume I*. New York: McGraw-Hill.

Schwanen, T. and Kwan, M.P. (2008) The Internet, mobile phone and space-time constraints, *Geoforum* 39(3) 1362–77.

Schwanen, T., Kwan, M.P. and Ren, F. (2008) How fixed is fixed? Gendered rigidity of space-time constraints and geographies of everyday activities, *Geoforum* 39(6): 2109–21.

Scott, A.J. (2006) The changing global geography of low-technology, labor-intensive industry: clothing, footwear, and furniture, *World Development* 34(9): 1517–36.

Scott, A.J. and Storper, M. (2003) Regions, globalization, development, *Regional Studies* 37: 579–93.

Seers, D. (1963) The limitations of the special case, *Oxford Bulletin of Economics and Statistics*, 25(2): 77–98.

Selwyn, B. (2013) Social upgrading and labour in global production networks: a critique and an alternative conception, *Competition & Change* 17(1): 75–90.

Sen, A. (1999) *Development as Freedom*. New York: Knopf.

Sen, A. (2001) Economic development and capability expansion in historical perspective, *Pacific Economic Review* 6(2): 179–91.

Shadbolt, P. (2009) Where Africa goes to buy its mobile phones, *Financial Times, 31* January. Available at http://www.ft.com/intl/cms/s/0/4609e212-eb64-11dd-bb6e-0000779fd2ac.html#axzz2ozAeiSIJ [accessed 30 December 2013].

Shove, E. (2004) Sustainability, system innovation and the laundry, in *System Innovation and the Transition to Sustainability: Theory, Evidence and Policy* (eds B. Elzen, F. Geels, and K. Green). Cheltenham: Edward Elgar: 76-94.

Sife, A.S., Kiondo, E. and Lyimo-Macha, J.G. (2010) Contribution of mobile phones to rural livelihoods and poverty reduction in Morogoro region, Tanzania, *Electronic Journal of Information Systems in Developing Countries* 42(3): 1–15.

Sizemore, C. (2012) Africa: the last investment frontier, *Forbes* 8 August, available at http://www.forbes.com/sites/moneybuilder/2012/08/08/africa-the-last-investment-frontier/ [accessed 1 January 2014].

Sklair, L. (2001) *The Transnational Capitalist Class*. Malden, MA: Blackwell.

Skuse, A. and Cousins, T. (2007) Managing distance: rural poverty and the promise of communication in post-Apartheid South Africa, *Journal of Asian and African Studies* 42(2): 185–207.

Slater, D. and Kwami, J. (2005) *Embeddedness and Escape: Internet and Mobile Use as Poverty Reduction Strategies in Ghana*. Working Paper 4, Information Society Research Group (ISRG), UK. Available at http://r4d.dfid.gov.uk/PDF/Outputs/Mis_SPC/R8232-ISRGWP4.pdf [accessed 1 January 2014].

Smith, A. and Raven, R. (2012) What is protective space? Reconsidering niches in transitions to sustainability, *Research Policy* 41(6): 1025–36.

Smith, A., Stirling, A. and Berkhout, F. (2005) The governance of sustainable socio-technical transitions, *Research Policy* 34(10): 1491–1510.

Smith, A., Voss, J-P. and Grin, J. (2010) Innovation studies and sustainability transitions: the allure of the multi-level perspective and its challenges, *Research Policy* 39: 435–48.

Smith, A., Pickles, J., Buček, M., *et al.* (2014) The political economy of global production networks: regional industrial change and differential upgrading in the East European clothing industry, *Journal of Economic Geography* in press.

Smith, D.M. (2009) Africa calling: mobile phone usage sees record rise after huge investment, *The Guardian* 22 October. Available at http://www.guardian.co.uk/technology/2009/oct/22/africa-mobile-phones-usage-rise [accessed 1 January 2014].

Smith, M., Spence, R. and Rashid, A. (2011) Mobile phones and expanding human capabilities, *Information Technologies and International Development* 7(3): 77–88.

Sokol, M. (2013) Silicon Valley in Eastern Slovakia? Neoliberalism, post-Socialism and the knowledge economy, *Europe-Asia Studies* 65(7): 1324–43.

Soludo, C., Ogbu, O.M. and Chang, H. (2004). *The Politics of Trade and Industrial Policy in Africa: Forced Consensus?* Trenton, NJ: Africa World Press.

Souter, D., Scott, N., Garforth, C., *et al.* (2005) *The Economic Impact of Telecommunications on Rural Livelihoods and Poverty Reduction: A Study of Rural Communities in India (Gujarat), Mozambique and Tanzania.* Commonwealth Telecommunications Organisation report for the UK Department for International Development. Available at http://www.telafrica.org/R8347/files/pdfs/FinalReport. pdf [accessed 1 January 2014].

South African Department of Trade and Industry (2013) Trade statistics, available at http://tradestats.thedti.gov.za/ReportFolders/reportFolders.aspx?sCS_referer=&sCS_ ChosenLang=en [accessed 11 November 2013].

South African Tourism Update (2013) 'Cape Town battles to compete internationally' 15 October. Available at http://www.tourismupdate.co.za/NewsDetails.aspx? newsId=70208 [accessed 16 December 2013].

South Africa Tourism (2012) *2011 Annual Tourism Report.* Available at http://www. tourism.gov.za/AboutNDT/Publications/Tourism_AnnReport_2011_12.pdf [accessed 19 August 2013].

Sparke, M. (2013) *Introducing Globalization: The Ties that Bind.* London: Wiley-Blackwell.

Statistics Brain (2013) Internet travel hotel booking statistics, available at http:// www.statisticbrain.com/internet-travel-hotel-booking-statistics/ [accessed 1 January 2014].

Steinmueller, W.E. (2001) ICTs and the possibilities for leapfrogging by developing countries, *International Labor Review* 140(2): 193–210.

Sterling, B. (2009) *The Caryatids.* New York: Del Rey.

Stern, L.W. and El-Ansary, A.I. (1988) *Marketing Channels*, 3rd edn. Englewood Cliffs, NJ: Prentice Hall.

Stiglitz, J.E. (1999) The World Bank at the millennium, *Economic Journal* 109(459): F577–97.

Stiglitz, J.E. (2006) *Making Globalization Work.* London: Allen Lane.

Stiglitz, J.E. (2010) Comments made at workshop at University of Manchester, 'Beyond the BRICs: Emerging powers and global poverty reduction', 28 June.

Stiglitz, J.E. and Weiss, A. (1981) Credit rationing in markets with imperfect information, *American Economic Review* 71(3): 393–410.

Stork, C., Calandro, E. and Gamage, R. (2013) The future of broadband in Africa, *Info* 16(1): 76–93.

Storper, M. (1997) *The Regional World: Territorial Development in a Global Economy.* New York: Guilford Press.

Subramani, M. (2004) How do suppliers benefit from information technology use in supply chain relationships? *MIS Quarterly: Management Information Systems* 28(1): 45–73.

Subramanian, H. and Overby, E. (2013) *An empirical analysis of spatial arbitrage: Examining arbitrageur behavior and the effect of electronic commerce.* Workshop presentation at the University of Minnesota, Information and Decision Sciences Department, 25 October. Available at http://misrc.umn.edu/workshops/2013/fall/ Overby.pdf

Sundbo, J. (2001) *The Strategic Management of Innovation*. Cheltenham: Edward Elgar.

Tanzania Communications Regulatory Authority (TCRA) (2010a) *Status of Telecom Market: March 2009 Report*. Dar es Salaam: Government of Tanzania.

Tanzania Communications Regulatory Authority (TCRA) (2010b) *Quarterly Telecommunications Statistics: June 2010 Report*. Dar es Salaam: Government of Tanzania.

Taylor, I. (2014) *The BRICS and "Africa Rising": Diversifying Dependency?* Oxford: James Currey.

Taylor, P.J. and Flint, C. (2000) *Political Geography: World-system, Nation-State and Locality*. 4th edn. London: Longman.

Teklehaimanot, A., McCord, G.C. and Sachs, J. (2007) Scaling up malaria control in Africa: an economic and epidemiological assessment, *American Journal of Tropical Medicine and Hygiene* 77(6): 138–44.

The Economist (2000) The hopeless continent, 13 May.

The Economist (2013a) Africa rising: a hopeful continent, 2 March.

The Economist (2013b) Towards the end of poverty, 1–7 June.

Thompson, M. and Walsham, G. (2010) ICT research in Africa: need for a strategic developmental focus, *Information Technology for Development* 16(2): 112–27.

Thrift, N.J. (2005) *Knowing Capitalism*. London: Sage.

Thrift, N.J. (2011) Lifeworld Inc. – and what to do about it, *Environment and Planning D* 29(1): 5–26.

Timamy, M.H.K. (2007) *The Political Economy of Technological Underdevelopment in Africa: Renaissance Prospects, Global Tyranny, and Organized Spoilation*. Lagos: CBAAC.

Tippins, M.J. and Sohi, R.H. (2003) IT competency and firm performance: is organizational learning a missing link? *Strategic Management Journal* 24(8): 745–61.

Tourism BEE Charter (n.d.) *Black Economic Empowerment Charter for the South Africa Tourism Industry*, available at http://www.tourismbeecharter.co.za/ [accessed 16 December 2013].

Ty, P.H., Heeks, R. and Chuong, H.V. (2012) Integrating digital and human data sources for environmental planning and climate change adaptation: from research to practice in central Vietnam, in *Linking Research to Practice: Strengthening ICT for Development Research Capacity in Asia* (eds A. Chib and R. Harris). Singapore: Institute for Southeast Asian Studies (ISEAS): 132–46.

UNCTAD (United Nations Conference on Trade and Development) (2002) *E-commerce and Development Report 2002*. Geneva: United Nations.

UNCTAD (United Nations Conference on Trade and Development) (2005) *Information Economy Report 2005*. Geneva: United Nations.

UNCTAD (United Nations Conference on Trade and Development) (2010) *Economic Development in Africa: Report 2010: South–South Cooperation: Africa and the New Forms of Development Partnership*. Geneva: United Nations.

UNCTAD (United Nations Conference on Trade and Development) (2012) *Economic Development in Africa: Report 2012: Structural Transformation and Sustainable Development in Africa*. Geneva: United Nations.

UNDP (United Nations Development Program) (2013) *2013 Human Development Report: Rise of the South: Human Progress in a Diverse World*. New York: UNDP.

United Nations (2013) *2012 International Trade Statistics Yearbook*. Available at http://comtrade.un.org/pb/ [accessed 18 April 2014].

United Nations Comtrade Database (2011) Commodity trade database. Available at http://comtrade.un.org/db/ [accessed 17 August 2012].

United Republic of Tanzania (2003) *National Information and Communication Technologies Policy*. Dar es Salaam: United Republic of Tanzania.

United Republic of Tanzania (2007) *The Economic Survey 2006*. Dar es Salaam: United Republic of Tanzania.

Unwin, T. (2009) Introduction, in *ICT4D: Information and Communication Technology for Development* (ed. T. Unwin). Cambridge: Cambridge University Press: 1–3.

van Amerom, M. and Büscher, B. (2005) Peace parks in southern Africa: bringers of an African renaissance? *Journal of Modern African Studies* 43(2): 159–82.

van Deursen, A. and van Dijk, J. (2010) Internet skills and the digital divide, *new media & society* 13(6): 893–911.

Vira, B. and James, A. (2011) Researching hybrid 'economic'/'development' geographies in practice: methodological reflections from a collaborative project on India's New Service Economy, *Progress in Human Geography* 35(5): 627–51.

Voice of America (2012) Zanzibar falls victim to the international heroin trade, 4 March. Available at http://www.voanews.com/content/zanzibar-falls-victim-to-the-international-heroin-trade-141414703/181120.html [accessed 16 December 2013].

W3Techs (2013) Content language survey, 30 December. Available at http://w3techs.com/technologies/overview/content_language/all [accessed 30 December].

Wade, R.H. (2002) Bridging the digital divide: new route to development or new form of dependency? *Global Governance* 8(4): 443–66.

Walcott, S. (2011) The furniture foothills and the spatial fix: globalization in the furniture industry, *Southeastern Geographer* 51(1): 6–30.

Wasserman, H. (2011) Mobile phones, popular media, and everyday African democracy: transmissions and transgressions, *Popular Communication: The International Journal of Media and Culture* 9(2): 146–58.

Wesolowski, A., Eagle, N., Noor, A.M., *et al.* (2012) Heterogeneous mobile phone ownership and usage patterns in Kenya, *PLoS ONE* 7(4). Available at http://www.plosone.org/article/info%3Adoi%2F10.1371%2Fjournal.pone.0035319 [accessed 23 April 2014].

Whales Tales Blog (2012) Cape Town Tourism loses destination marketing role, vote of no confidence by City of Cape Town! (first impressions), 19 October. Available at http://www.whalecottage.com/blog/cape-town/cape-town-tourism-loses-destination-marketing-role-vote-of-no-confidence-by-city-of-cape-town-first-impressions/ [accessed 16 December 2013].

Whales Tales Blog (2013) Five years of blogging looking forward, 30 September. Available at http://www.whalecottage.com/blog/cape-town/five-years-of-blogging-looking-back-looking-forward/ [accessed 16 December 2013].

Whittaker, D., Zhu, T., Sturgeon, T., *et al.* (2010) Compressed development, *Studies in Comparative International Development* 45(4): 439–67.

Wiig, A. (2003) Developing countries and the tourist industry in the internet age: the case of Namibia, *Forum for Development Studies* 1: 59–87.

Wilson, G. (2007) Beyond the dichotomies in technology for development, *Geography Compass* 1(2): 119–35.

Wilson, J. (2011) Colonising space: the New Economic Geography in theory and practice, *New Political Economy* 16(3): 373–97.

Wilson, J. (2014) The shock of the real: the neoliberal neurosis in the life and times of Jeffrey Sachs, *Antipode* 46(1): 301–21.

World Bank (1981) *Accelerated Development in Sub-Saharan Africa: An Agenda for Action.* Washington, DC: World Bank.

World Bank (1998) *South Africa: Cape Peninsula Biodiversity Conservation Project.* Global Environmental Facility. Washington, DC: World Bank.

World Bank (2004) *World Development Indicators.* Washington, DC: World Bank.

World Bank (2009) *World Development Report 2009: Reshaping Economic Geography.* Washington, DC: World Bank.

World Bank (2010) *Transformation Ready: The Strategic Application of Information and Communication Technologies in Africa.* Washington, DC: World Bank.

World Bank (2011) *World Bank Information and Communication Technologies Sector Strategy.* Washington, DC: World Bank.

World Bank (2012a) *2012 Information and Communications for Development Report: Maximizing Mobile.* Washington, DC: World Bank.

World Bank (2012b) *Growing Innovation: infoDev Annual Report 2010–2011.* Washington, DC: Information for Development Program, World Bank.

World Bank (2013a) *African Development Indicators.* Washington, DC: World Bank.

World Bank (2013b) World Data Bank. Available at http://databank.worldbank.org/data/home.aspx [accessed 19 August 2013].

World Bank (2013c) *Fact Sheet: The World Bank and Agriculture in Africa.* Washington, DC: World Bank.

World Bank (2014) http://data.worldbank.org/indicator/IT.CEL.SETS.P2 [accessed 13 May 2014].

World Tourism Organization (2007) *Tourism Market Trends 2006.* Madrid: World Tourism Organization.

World Tourism Organization (2013a) *Yearbook of Tourism Statistics 2007–2011.* Madrid: World Tourism Organization. Available at http://resources.metapress.com/pdf-preview.axd?code=j5q3th986t8mwjhp&size=largest [accessed 19 August 2013].

World Tourism Organization (2013b) *World Tourism Barometer.* Madrid: World Tourism Organization. Available at https://s3-eu-west-.amazonaws.com/storageapi/sites/all/files/pdf/international_tourism_by_region.pdf [accessed 19 August 2013].

World Trade Organization (2011) Statistics database. Available at http://www.wto.org [accessed 17 August 2012].

WTTC (World Travel and Tourism Council) (2006) *South Africa: Travel and Tourism: Climbing to New Heights.* London: World Travel and Tourism Council.

Wuyts, M. (2001) Informal economy, wage goods and accumulation under structural adjustment theoretical reflections based on the Tanzanian experience, *Cambridge Journal of Economics* 25(3): 417–38.

Wynne, C., Berthon, P., Pitt, L., *et al.* (2001) The impact of the Internet on the distribution value chain: the case of the South African tourism industry, *International Marketing Review* 18(4): 420–31.

Ya'u, Y.Z. (2004) The new imperialism and Africa in the global electronic village, *Review of African Political Economy* 31(99): 11–29.

Ya'u, Y.Z. (2005) Globalisation, ICTs and the new imperialism: perspectives on Africa in the global electronic village, *Africa Development* 30(1–2): 98–124.

Yeung, H.W. (2005) Rethinking relational economic geography, *Transactions of the Institute of British Geographers* 30(1): 37–51.

Yeung, H.W., Liu, W. and Dicken, P. (2006) Transnational corporations and network effects of a local manufacturing cluster in mobile telecommunications in China, *World Development* 34(3): 520–40.

Yilmaz, Y. and Bititci, U. (2006) Performance measurement in the value chain: manufacturing v. tourism, *International Journal of Productivity and Performance Management* 55(5): 371–89.

Zanzibar Association of Tourism Investors (ZATI) (2013) New tourism arrival figures for Zanzibar – 2012, available at http://198.136.54.91/~wwwzati/new-tourism-arrival-figures-for-zanzibar-2012/ [accessed 31 December 2013].

Žižek, S. (1989) *The Sublime Object of Ideology*. London: Verso.

Zysman, J. and Breznitz, D. (2012) Double bind: governing the economy in an ICT era, *Governance*, 25(1): 129–50.

Index

Note: page numbers in *italics* refer to figures; page numbers in **bold** refer to tables.

Africa's Information Revolution: Technical Regimes and Production Networks in South Africa and Tanzania, First Edition. James T. Murphy and Pádraig Carmody.
© 2015 John Wiley & Sons, Ltd. Published 2015 by John Wiley & Sons, Ltd.